The First Directorate

The First Directorate

OLEG KALUGIN

Former Chief of Counterintelligence and Major General, KGB

My 32 Years
in Intelligence and Espionage
Against the West

with Fen Montaigne

St. Martin's Press   New York

DESIGN BY JUDITH A. STAGNITTO

Library of Congress Cataloging-in-Publication Data

Kalugin, Oleg, 1934–
    The First Directorate / Oleg Kalugin with Fen Montaigne.
      p.   cm.
    "A Thomas Dunne book."
    ISBN 0–312–11426–5
    1. Kalugin, Oleg, 1934–   . 2. Espionage, Soviet. 3. Spies—
Soviet Union—Biography.   4. Soviet Union. Komitet
gosudarstvennoĭ bezopasnosti.   I. Montaigne, Fen.   II. Title.
III. Title: 1st Directorate.
DK275.K34A3   1994
327.12'092—dc20
[B]   94-12912
                                        CIP

First Edition: September 1994

10 9 8 7 6 5 4 3 2 1

Contents

The First Directorate

Prologue

I n the summer of 1959, I found myself in New York City, having just completed a year's course of study at Columbia Journalism School. For a twenty-four-year-old Soviet kid, it had been a dream year, capped by a three-week trip across America. My presence in the United States at the height of the Cold War had generated a lot of interest: *The New York Times* even wrote a profile of me. Headlined "A Popular Russian," the Man-in-the-News piece described me as "a real personality kid." It went on to say that I was the son of a Leningrad city clerk and was chosen for the Fulbright student exchange by my professors at Leningrad University and by "Soviet educational authorities." I had to chuckle, of course. It was all a lie.

The Soviet educational establishment had not sent me to America for a year. The KGB had. I was not, as the article described, a bright young Soviet journalist. I was a green KGB officer, the son not of a city bureaucrat but of a man who also had worked for the Soviet secret police. And in August 1959, I was on the verge of plunging into my first espionage case—a tangled affair that would spectacularly launch my career in the spy game, but would later return to haunt me, eventually leading to my falling out with the KGB.

That August, just a few weeks before my return to the USSR, Soviet officials asked me to work as a host at an exhibit of Soviet achievements in technology and culture. I was happy to do it, in part for the money, but also because I was a true believer in Communism and the Soviet cause. It was the peak of Premier Nikita

Khrushchev's liberalization of Soviet society. Our military might was growing, our sciences were roaring ahead. Just two years before, we had launched the first satellite, *Sputnik*—an event that convinced us and the world that we were closing fast on Khrushchev's oft-stated goal: "We will catch and overtake America!"

The exhibit at the Columbus Circle Coliseum on 59th Street featured luxurious Soviet limousines, the latest furs, fashionable footwear, and row upon row of radios, tape recorders, and cameras. I knew the show was something of a Potemkin village, but I overlooked that and figured it would demonstrate to America what the Soviet Union—just fourteen years after the war that had devastated our country—was capable of doing. I was assigned to the cultural section where, surrounded by books and paintings, I was to expound on the glories of Socialist Realism. One of my first customers was a famous one: Vice President Richard Nixon. He came on opening day, and somehow wandered into my section alone—a jowly, glum-looking man who was not particularly friendly. Once I overcame my confusion at seeing this celebrity, I buttonholed him and began my spiel. Soon, however, I was elbowed aside by a phalanx of aides, bodyguards, and Soviet officials.

I spent several weeks preaching the Soviet gospel to an at-times hostile American public, and by the end I was worn out and hoarse. One hot, muggy evening in late August, I shuffled out of the exhibition hall and began making my way up Broadway, heading for my apartment. It was about seven o'clock, and I was barely two blocks from the Coliseum when a bespectacled, gray-haired man, accompanied by an attractive Chinese woman, approached me.

"We saw you at the exhibition," said the man. "May we talk to you?"

With those words began my fateful relationship with the spy the KGB soon came to call "Cook."

Cook spoke to me in English, but I immediately recognized his accent as that of a Russian. Though I was exhausted and hardly wanted to be embroiled in another debate, I answered in Russian that I could talk with them. And when this tall stranger, who introduced himself as Anatoly, began to speak, my interest was piqued. After complimenting me on my English, he criticized me for not being staunch enough in my defense of Communism.

"Don't you feel the Soviet Union is going astray, trying to emulate America?" Anatoly asked, as the three of us stood on the Manhattan sidewalk in the summer twilight. "Your country is a great one. It has its own path. Socialism should be free from all this bourgeois stuff."

It was a rarity, of course, to hear someone in America criticizing Soviet Communism for not being sufficiently orthodox. Nevertheless, I was not interested in listening to his political philosophy, so I decided to steer the conversation in a different direction.

"What do you do?" I asked.

"I work for Thiokol," Anatoly responded, referring to the giant chemical company.

"Really?" I said. "And what's your line of work?"

"I am a rocket engineer," he replied.

My fatigue disappeared immediately.

"Why should we stand here talking on the street?" I said. "Let's go to a cafeteria."

We drank coffee and ate pastry at a cafeteria on 63rd Street, and I tried to appear nonchalant as I questioned Anatoly and his wife. He told me he was from a peasant family in the Kuban region of southern Russia; after working as a translator for the German Army, he had retreated with Nazi forces and eventually emigrated to America. He studied to be a chemical engineer and landed a job at Thiokol.

His wife, the daughter of the vice-president of the Chinese Academy of Sciences, was a Maoist who had succeeded in convincing her husband of the righteousness of the Communist cause. She had persuaded him that it was repulsive to work for a company so closely tied to the military-industrial complex. My hopes began to rise steadily, and then Anatoly dropped this piece of news: Thiokol was involved in the production of solid rocket fuel, and he was working on the project.

I could barely contain myself as I got their phone number and suggested offhandedly that we meet again. We parted, and the next morning I skipped work at the exhibit and went immediately to see Fyodor Kudashkin, our KGB contact at the Soviet U.N. Mission in New York. He was clearly interested, and instructed me to meet with Anatoly again, warning me that it might be an FBI set-up.

As few days later I met Cook in another cafeteria—again accompanied by his wife, Selena. After several minutes of small talk, Anatoly said he was prepared to bring me documents showing how Thiokol was producing solid rocket fuel.

My report set off a furor at our KGB-infested U.N. office. Kudashkin and my higher-ups at the Committee for State Security sent an urgent, ciphered cable to Moscow, seeking clearance to hold the meeting and take the documents. Moscow gave its approval, for the Thiokol secrets could be a tremendous boost in our competition with the United States to build better military and space rockets. The only caveat from KGB headquarters was that I be accompanied by a more senior KGB officer with diplomatic immunity; if Anatoly was an FBI plant, the senior agent would take the fall and face nothing worse than expulsion. When Moscow cabled its okay for our meeting with the Thiokol scientist, headquarters also gave him the codename "Cook."

We met Cook several days later near Columbia University. With my KGB colleague at the wheel, we drove to Cook's home in the suburbs of northern New Jersey. My stomach was churning. My young career in the KGB was about to take a remarkable turn for the better, or else we were driving into an FBI trap that could create an international incident and doom my chances of working effectively overseas in the future.

When we arrived at the tiny, nondescript house, Selena was busy preparing a Chinese dinner. We sat in the living room with Cook, sipping cocktails. The scientist stood up and walked into another room, and the senior agent and I exchanged an anxious, hopeful glance. Cook returned with a triumphant look, clutching a handful of packages. He opened one envelope and passed the contents to me: it was a detailed description of the technology of the fuel and its components, as well as a CIA document analyzing the state of the USSR's chemical industry. Then he pulled out his *pièce de résistance*—a test tube containing a black jelly. It was a sample of the United States' top-secret solid rocket fuel.

I fingered the test tube. My fellow officer and I sat there in silence, holding our breath as we half expected a squad of FBI agents to burst through the door. But no one came. We moved to Selena's table and ate her delicious Chinese food. We made small talk. But I wanted nothing so much as to flee that house with our booty. I was an ambitious young officer, and I knew the test tube and documents I held in my hands were an extraordinary coup for someone just starting out in the KGB.

The next day, word came down from the KGB's technical staff in New York that the papers and the fuel were a great find. Moscow showed immense interest in the Thiokol scientist and, after one more meeting, I handed over my catch to higher KGB officials in New York. I received a commendation; as I returned to Moscow that August of 1959, I never expected to see Cook again.

Twenty years later, however, I would, this time in Moscow. And when we crossed paths again, Cook, the man who so auspiciously launched my career in the KGB, would set in motion its undoing. But I am getting ahead of myself.

Within months of leaving New York that summer, I returned to the United States and began my career in earnest. Over the next twenty years, I found myself at the very heart of the Cold War spy game. I ran agents out of New York. In Washington, I oversaw the work of the American spy John Walker. My officers even tried to bug the U.S. Congress. At age forty, I became the youngest general in the postwar history of the KGB, and for ten years matched wits with the CIA around the world.

As deputy chief and then chief of the KGB's Foreign Counter-intelligence Directorate, I was immersed in the world of espionage, a job that was at times exhilarating, at times depressing, and often messy. My unit ran moles deep inside French and Italian Intelligence and tried to recruit CIA agents from Beirut to Helsinki. We played a key role in rehabilitating the famed British spy, Kim Philby, who had been tossed aside by my predecessors and was living a dejected, drunken life in Moscow. We also had a hand, unfortunately, in the assassination of the Bulgarian dissident Georgi Markov. Foreign Counterintelligence even had to step in when we learned that an Asian country was preparing to blackmail a top Soviet Military Intelligence man. The material to be used against him? Proof that his wife was having sex with the family dog.

I served for ten years at the KGB's headquarters buildings in Moscow, and worked closely with the men who ran the world's largest secret police organization. I came to deeply respect Yuri Andropov, the hard-nosed chairman who would go on to briefly lead the Soviet Union. And I worked intimately with—and grew to loathe—Vladimir Kryuchkov, who took over the KGB when I left Moscow and played a decisive role in the failed coup of August 1991. I saw firsthand how the buffoons from the Communist Party politicized the KGB and blindly did the bidding of Soviet leader Leonid Brezhnev.

Some of my colleagues predicted I would one day become chief of Soviet Intelligence, perhaps even head of the KGB. Indeed, until 1979 my career seemed unstoppable. But then, as I attempted to come to the aid of the man who had been my first intelligence asset—Cook—I ran headlong into the system I had served so faithfully. In 1980, I was sent into high-level bureaucratic exile in Leningrad, where for seven years I saw at close range the rot of the Brezhnev era. In 1990, thoroughly disenchanted with the agency and the system to which I had devoted my life, I went public and became the highest-ranking KGB officer ever to expose the inner workings of the organization and still remain in the Soviet Union.

This book, then, is the story of the journey of a warrior in the Cold War. On one level it is a story of espionage, as seen through the eyes of a man who battled the United States and the West even as his nation's empire was—with 20/20 hindsight—in its death throes. But this is more than a spy story. It is the story of one man who, like so many of his compatriots, started off with a deep, even fanatical, belief in his country and its Communist cause. When I headed to New York as a young man of twenty-four, I was confident we were not far from the "shining future" that our leaders from Lenin to Khrushchev had promised us. That blind faith carried me forward for years, helping me to overlook the 1956 Soviet invasion of Hungary, the 1968 occupation of Czechoslovakia, the growing isolation and senility of our leaders. I myself spread a string of lies and disinformation to further our cause in the Cold War.

Like most of my countrymen, I thought our system could be fixed. And then I collided with the KGB itself, and realized that what we had built was rotten beyond salvation. The road to my conversion was unique. Yet tens of millions of other Soviets reached the same point by a different route. Like Boris Yeltsin and countless other Soviets, I became a radical critic of the system which had nurtured me and brought me success. That may be difficult for many readers to understand.

But then they have not lived my life . . .

ONE

A Stalinist Boyhood

I never saw myself as a renegade, and even now, as I mull over the reasons for my split with the KGB, I ask myself half-seriously: Was my grandmother to blame? It was she who, unbeknownst to my parents, spirited me away to a Russian Orthodox Church shortly after my birth and had me secretly baptized. In 1934, just as Stalin's repressions were gaining steam, that was a heretical and dangerous act. And though I am not a religious man, I sometimes like to think it was my mother's mother who sowed the seeds of the rebel who would emerge a half century later.

At the time of my birth, September 6, 1934, my father was a guard at Leningrad's secret police headquarters. When he found out that my *babushka* had had me baptized, he was angry and scared. My mother would later laugh when she told that story, but at the time my father thought it a careless and stupid move. After all, his job was to stand in front of the secret police's imposing, concrete Big House on Liteiny Prospect, guarding the headquarters and the adjacent jail. The Big House, completed in 1933, occupied a square block, and its basement and courtyard were the scene of the execution of countless victims of Stalin's purges. Later, my father would tell me how he used to stand guard outside and listen to the screams of those being tortured and murdered by Stalin's goons in the Big House.

My father, Daniil, was born in 1905, the son of peasants from the Oryol region of central Russia. He survived the chaos and famine of the Russian Revolution and the ensuing civil war and was drafted into the Red Army in the early 1920s. After his discharge, he had no desire to return to the countryside, so he moved instead to Leningrad. There, in the cradle of the Bolshevik Revolution, this poorly educated man—dark-haired, handsome, and with a trace of Tatar blood—found work as a guard for the secret police, then known as the NKVD.

My mother, a quiet, blue-eyed Russian named Klavdia, came from a line of skilled factory workers who had been in St. Petersburg for more than a century. She was working at a weaving factory when she met my father in 1932, and fell in love with the sharply dressed policeman with the slicked-back black hair. I was born two years later and—in Soviet terms—definitely under a bad sign. Just three months after my birth, the renowned Leningrad Communist boss Sergei Kirov was gunned down at the city Party headquarters at Smolny. It's now known that Stalin ordered Kirov's assassination, but at the time the Soviet leader blamed the killing on a far-reaching plot and used it to usher in a wave of purges in which millions would die. My father took me, aged three months, to Kirov's funeral at the Tavrichesky Palace. Though I know it must be impossible to remember, I feel I can vividly recall—no doubt from my parents' later accounts—the scene that cold, overcast December day. A huge crowd of mourners, dressed in black, stood outside the palace, listening to a funeral march. Because of his NKVD connections, my father managed to get close to Kirov's coffin, which rested on a bier strewn with flowers. These scenes took place, but I cannot explain how it is they seem vivid to me. Under such grim circumstances did my life begin, in the midst of a wave of terror that would ultimately claim the lives of 20 to 40 million of my countrymen.

I was seven when the Nazis invaded the Soviet Union on June 22, 1941, and to this day I recall my first glimpse of the war. On a sultry afternoon in late June, I was at a Young Pioneer camp on a lake near Leningrad, hunting maybugs with a pretty girl. The far side of the lake was rocked by explosions from Nazi bombers, and the flustered nurses caring for us shooed us back to our dormitories. A week later, my mother and I boarded a train for Yaroslavl, where we transferred to a ship that ferried us down the Volga River to Gorky. There, anchored in port, we came under heavy bombardment. Snuggling close to my mother, I looked through the porthole and followed the floodlights sliding across the dark sky as explosions rang in my ears. Our ship made a safe dash out of the harbor; later we were told that another vessel with hundreds of evacuees, most of them children, was sunk by a direct hit.

We traveled by train to the Siberian city of Omsk, where my mother and I—I was an only child—waited out the war. Because we were the family of an NKVD policeman, we lived in relative comfort and had enough to eat. In the winter, I would don skates and grab the bumpers of passing trucks, howling with delight as they pulled me through the icy streets of the village. In the spring, we floated down the Ishim River on ice floes. When summer came, we fished and picked berries and mushrooms in the forested taiga. And all the while, I followed the progress of the war with maniacal zeal, listening every night to the news crackling out of our black radio set and devouring the newspapers that would occasionally make it to our remote village. I marked on a map the cities that had been taken by the Red Army, and one of the first books I ever owned was entitled *Behind Enemy Lines*. With a picture of Stalin on the first page, the book told of the glorious exploits of Soviet guerrillas. I still have it in my library.

In the spring of 1944, with the 900-day Siege of Leningrad ended and Nazi troops in retreat, my mother and I began a two-week rail trip from Siberia back to our native city. We returned to find Leningrad in ruins and most of my mother's family dead after the siege, which had killed an estimated 1 million people. The city seemed deserted, the streets littered with tank traps and populated by emaciated figures who moved slowly to and fro. Many buildings were in ruins—the golden spires of the Admiralty and the Mikhailovsky Castle were almost the sole reminders of the city's past glory. Not far from our old apartment, a German bomb had taken off the facade of a six-story building, and on the top floor a grand piano stood in full view. My father survived the siege only because he had been guarding the Party elite at Smolny and was able to obtain enough food. But virtually all of my mother's family perished: her mother, father, and youngest brother all died of starvation in 1942, and her three older brothers were killed at the front. Only her sister survived. Such devastating losses were common in a country in which 27 million people perished in the war.

After the war, Leningraders worked furiously to rebuild, but the reminders of the conflict were everywhere. One hot summer day, outside the Leningrad Writer's House, I saw a man on his hands and knees drinking from a puddle. Stunned, I approached the stranger—his face gaunt and covered in stubble, his clothes in tatters—and asked him if I could help. He raised his head and, tears streaming down his face, explained in broken Russian that he was a German prisoner of war trying to make his way home. I handed him an apple, and rushed home in a state of confusion.

Mostly, however, I saw our victory in the Great Patriotic War—as Soviets called it—as the ultimate proof that our Communist system was the best in the world. Again and again, Stalin's propagandists told us that only the Soviet Union was able to stop the Nazi menace, and such knowledge convinced me and my compatriots that our nation was unvanquishable. I would realize, in later years, that one of the pillars on which the Soviet Union rested was the myth that our country only prevailed in the war because of its Communist ardor and discipline. Party leaders wrapped themselves in the mantle of the war, and for decades—in a vain attempt to shore up the crumbling Communist edifice—they played upon the enormous sacrifices the people made from 1941 to 1945.

Our old apartment had been destroyed, so we moved into a communal apartment in the former palace of the noble Obolensky family. The cramped, cozy squalor of Soviet communal apartments barely diminished the grandeur of this historic building. A wide marble staircase, flanked by powerful statues of Atlas and a massive gilded mirror, led to our apartment on the third floor. Six families of the proletariat had moved into what used to be three large halls for receiving guests, sharing a kitchen and a bathroom. Our room had stucco oak leaves on its impossibly high ceilings, wood paneling, walls covered in scarlet silk, and a fireplace of hand-painted tiles. Each of the six families had its own table in the enormous communal kitchen; squabbles were inevitable, of course, and my mother tired of such close quarters. But this communal life had its pleasures. I fondly recall the father of the family who lived on the other side of a flimsy partition from us. He served in the Northern Fleet, and during his rare visits home he would grab his guitar and we would hear his deep, baritone voice late into the night. Another neighbor, a wounded war veteran, bought me books and fed my voracious appetite for literature. Yet another member of the communal apartment, who worked in a fish store, would occasionally bring us black caviar.

As I moved into my teenage years, at the peak of the Stalin personality cult in the late 1940s, I became more and more indoctrinated into Communism. At fourteen, I joined the Young Communist League, the *Komsomol,* and eventually went on to become head of the organization at my school. Like most of my peers, I devoured the works of Arkady Gaidar, who produced a series of what might best be described as Communist *Hardy Boy* books. They were superpatriotic tales filled with young characters constantly doing courageous and noble deeds for the good of the Motherland. It was Gaidar's books that first planted the seed in my mind of becoming a KGB officer. One work, *The Military Secret,* featured a boy who died protecting secret information from the enemies of Communism. Another, *The Fate of the Drummer,* recounted how a boy discovered a gang of spies and was shot by them. In a bizarre twist of history, it was Arkady Gaidar's grandson—Yegor Gaidar—who a half century later would deliver the *coup de grâce* to Communism by masterminding Boris Yeltsin's radical market reforms.

The following summer, I attended a camp for children of secret police workers. There, I met with university students attending the Security Ministry's Higher School. They were confident and fun-loving, and sang songs in English and Russian to the younger campers. I wanted to be like these dashing officer-trainees, and a career in the Intelligence Service beckoned.

One incident, which took place during a summer visit to southern Ukraine, showed the extent to which I had been inculcated with a zealous belief in Communism. We were staying with friends in a village, enjoying the abundance of southern fruits and vegetables. Some of the village kids mentioned that the local doctor was taking money on the side from patients. I was outraged, and considered it my duty to protect the people of the village against corruption, bribe taking, and this doctor's instinct for private ownership.

"You hicks!" I told the village teenagers. "Don't you know what the doctor is doing is against the law. It's anti-Soviet!"

I marched over to the doctor's cottage and began violently shaking a pear tree in the front yard. A fat woman flew out the front door, cursing and trying to cuff me. I fled, thinking I had roused the doctor's wife or sister. But the village kids told me the fat woman *was* the doctor, and I returned the next morning for a showdown. I began shaking the pear tree again, and when she emerged in a rage, I lectured her with all the righteous indignation of a true *Komsomol* leader. At first she refuted my allegations, but after a few minutes she relented and began to apologize for what she had done, blaming it on poverty and village tradition. I felt as if I had scored a victory for the Communist cause.

In my seventeenth year, two events occurred that were to shape my life: I fell in love with my future wife, Ludmilla, and I decided to join the secret police and become an intelligence agent. The

KGB—then known as the Ministry of State Security—seemed like the logical place for a person with my academic abilities, language skills, and fervent desire to fight class enemies, capitalist parasites, and social injustice. My English, already proficient after years of reading English-language classics and listening to the BBC, was good enough to get me into the diplomatic service. But that seemed too tame, too civilian, and I chose instead to join the security forces.

My father strongly objected. By 1950, he knew only too well—from the screams he heard as a jail guard to the countless Communist Party bosses he saw disappear during his days at Smolny—what was really going on in our country. He told me furtively about what he had seen and heard in the security forces, but rather than repulsing me, his stories made the life of a secret policeman seem even more intriguing. After all, wasn't the KGB on the front line of the battle against capitalism and world imperialism? The thought of dying for one's country and the Socialist ideal stirred my blood. His talk of the screaming prisoners didn't sound nice, but I thought to myself, "What else can you expect in a bitter struggle with our enemies?"

After passing four entrance exams with high marks, I enrolled in the Security Ministry's Institute of Foreign Languages in Leningrad—one of two schools in the country designed to train KGB officers. The other, the Higher KGB School, was in Moscow. In the spring of 1952, shortly before I entered the Institute of Foreign Languages, I spoke at my high school graduation, proudly proclaiming that I intended to undergo training for service in the Security Ministry—an admission that my father, sitting in the audience, thought foolish and dangerous.

"I am convinced that there will be enough work in my lifetime cleaning out the scum that poisons the existence of the world's first Socialist state," I told the audience.

We had all been taught that true Communism was at hand, and that when the shining future was attained there would be no need for armies or security services or secret police.

"I may wind up 'the Last of the Mohicans' when the suppression apparatus becomes redundant along with other governmental structures," I continued, "but I have resolved to embark upon this path and—once I do so—to follow it to the end."

The audience applauded enthusiastically. And so, with the cheers of my classmates ringing in my ears, I marched—confidently and blindly—into the arms of the KGB.

TWQ

Initiation

Walking for the first time into the high-walled compound of the Institute of Foreign Languages, I knew I was entering a mysterious world, off limits to all but a few of my countrymen. For the next four years in Leningrad and for two more at the KGB's Advanced School in Moscow, I would undergo a course of study that was part boot camp, part university education, part spy school—all with the aim of turning myself into a first-rate intelligence agent. I would polish my English and German and tackle Arabic, as well. I would be given my first code name. I would learn how to detect and evade surveillance, how to conceal a microdot of photographed documents, how to cultivate intelligence assets, how to use a gun. I would get a glimpse of the inner workings of the Communist state to which I had sworn allegiance. And, for the first time, I would experience the faintest twinges of doubt about the system I had worshipped.

It was a good thing I entered the Institute brimming with Communist fervor and youthful vigor, for the first few months there were trying. The Institute building, which before the Revolution had housed Czarist military cadets, was located in the center of Leningrad. The inner courtyard was sealed off from the outside world by a high wall on one side and by buildings on the others. Our barracks were Spartan, affording a view of streetcar tracks and little else. And, in the first year, the place was not so much a language institute as it was a military academy. We slept in large, open barracks, twenty to a room, and woke up at 7:00 A.M. to run and do calisthenics. Before breakfast, KGB officers inspected us and our uniforms for the slightest defect, and an unpolished buckle or un-shaven chin could lead to the loss of our cherished Sunday leave. I was not yet engaged to Ludmilla, the trim, round-faced Russian beauty I had fallen in love with. I would sit in the barracks and torture myself by wondering if she would meet another boy, or by remembering that time we sat at a park along the Neva River, when I discovered a small hole in her tight-fitting dress and stared, spell-bound, at her stocking-covered thigh.

There were one hundred students in our class, and the largest group was studying German; most of those graduates would later go to work in East Germany, which was swarming at the time with KGB officers. Twenty of my classmates and I were in the English Department, and others were studying French, Japanese, Chinese, and Persian. I apparently was the only member of my class who had come to the Institute straight from high school, the others having served in the army or worked at factories, in mines, or on collective farms. Many of my fellow students were none too bright; nearly three fourths of the class would not make the grade into foreign intelligence and would wind up in the Soviet Union instead, engaged in a usually vain—and often absurd—search for spies. The Institute even had a quota for "representatives of the working class." One of them, a former Siberian miner named Nikolai Chaplygin, was a dimwitted man with a huge head, a flattened nose, and boorish manners. He would later inform on me when I went AWOL for a day to visit Ludmilla.

In March 1953, six months into my studies at the Institute, an event occurred that shook the country to its foundations: Stalin died. The Soviet leader was paralyzed by a stroke on March 2, and over the next several days much of the country sat by the radio awaiting word on his condition. It is difficult for people of other ages and other countries to imagine how a nation might have worshipped such a monster, but the truth is that most of us—those who had not felt the lash of his repression—did. We saw him as a man who led the country through the war, who turned a backward nation into a su-perpower, who built up our economy so that there was employment and housing and enough food for all. His propaganda machine was all-powerful; I still remember reading two books—*Conspiracy Against Russia* and *Conspiracy Against Peace*—which portrayed the mass trials of the 1930s not as brutal show trials, but as valiant efforts to root out anti-Soviet agents. I revered Stalin. And so for four days in March we waited anxiously for news of our leader. I slept next to the radio the night of March 5–6, and just before dawn an announcer read out a bulletin saying Stalin had died. I choked back tears, buried my head in the pillow, and lay awake until reveille.

The country came to a standstill. Classes were suspended at the Institute, and when I called my mother, she said, "Our father is dead." On the day before Stalin's funeral she told me, "It's not only our father who's died, but also God, who kept us all under His wing."

I kept a diary of those days, and an excerpt gives a sense of the blind devotion we had for the Soviet dictator.

"Our loss is huge, of course, but sometimes it seems that it's all nonsense," I wrote on the day of Stalin's funeral.

> Stalin isn't dead. He cannot die. His physical death is just a formality, but one that needn't deprive people of their faith in the future. The fact that Stalin is still alive will be proven by our country's every new success, both domestically and internationally. Any good initiative in our country should now be called a Stalinist one. The entire generation which was born in his era will live with his name. . . . Days like these make each person critically reassess the things he or she has been doing in life. I, for one, must work harder in all directions without wasting time on idle chatter.

A week after Stalin's death, one of the Institute's administrators, a Lieutenant Sozinov, summoned me to his office. He was a kind, almost fatherly figure, and as I went to meet him I wracked my brain to figure out what I might have done wrong. As we made small talk at the beginning of our conversation, it hit me: Somebody must have told the administration I was listening to the BBC and other shortwave radio broadcasts in English. Before he brought it up, I blurted out that I had been tuning into the stations to improve my vocabulary and accent.

"What else do you listen to besides the British broadcasts?" Sozinov asked, looking me straight in the eye.

"Well, I listen to music, too," I replied.

"What kind of music?"

"Western music," I said.

"What kind?"

"Jazz," I said. "Sometimes classical."

"What do you read?"

"Textbooks," I replied, growing increasingly uneasy. "Western fiction and books on intelligence."

"Why are you only interested in the West?" Sozinov asked.

"Because I expect to be an intelligence agent in the West," I answered, "and an intelligence agent has to know everything about his future theater of war."

Sozinov finally let me go, apparently satisfied with my openness. I didn't walk away from our talk lamenting that I lived in a totalitarian system. I merely told myself that the next time I listened to short-wave radio broadcasts, I would have to be more discreet.

Still, not long after Stalin's death the iron grip the security services had on the country began to loosen, ever so slightly. And for those of us training to go into the Ministry of State Security, the revelations that began to trickle out about our future employer were disconcerting. A month after Stalin's demise, the Ministry of State Security announced that the vaunted secret police had tortured a group of Jewish doctors and falsely accused them of plotting to murder senior government officials. Some high-ranking secret police officers were arrested for their role in the so-called "Doctors' Plot," which had touched off a wave of anti-Semitism in the country. Shortly afterward, Stalin's secret police chief—Lavrenti P. Beria—was arrested and executed for allegedly being an agent of Western intelligence services. Much later, details would emerge about Beria's abominable cruelty, including his fondness for picking up young boys and girls off the street and raping, torturing, and killing them. Just the "Doctors' Plot" revelations and Beria's arrest were enough, however, to send me into a paroxysm of doubt about my beloved Ministry of State Security, and I briefly considered joining the Foreign Ministry or the central bureaucracy of the Communist Party. But the disclosures about the Ministry of State Security soon stopped, and our leaders in Moscow and the Institute's administrators assured us that the bad apples had been removed from our service.

My fellow students and I, in a taste of what was to come under the Khrushchev "thaw," began openly to discuss the problems and inequities in Soviet society—something we would never dared to have done under Stalin. One classmate, who had served in the navy in the Soviet Far East, had earlier talked only of the haunting beauty of the remote Kamchatka Peninsula and the native tribes that lived there. After Stalin's death, he described in detail the abject poverty of the peninsula—the leaky, tar-paper shacks, the meager diet of fish and bread, the rampant corruption of the local Communist Party bosses. Even under Stalin, I thought to myself, people lived like cattle. It was the beginning of a long process of awakening—a process that would drag on for decades because I and many fellow Soviets blamed our misfortunes on the aberrations of leaders such as Stalin or Brezhnev, all the while failing to see that the system itself was the problem.

In the fall of my second year at the Institute, our instructors began the long-awaited intelligence courses. We learned about the Bolsheviks' first secret police organization—the *Cheka*—and were still spoon-fed the pronouncements of Stalin. "The *Cheka* is the punitive organ of Soviet power," Stalin said in one of our readings. "It punishes mostly spies, conspirators, terrorists, bandits, speculators, counterfeiters. It is something like a political court-martial, set up to safeguard the revolution from the assaults of the counter-revolutionary bourgeoisie and their agents."

Our instructors were uniformed officers of the Leningrad Security Ministry, and I realize now that many of them must have had a hand in sending thousands of people to their deaths during the 1930s and 1940s. They stood before us and praised the kangaroo courts and mass repressions as a manifestation of revolutionary vigilance, and we hung on their every word. They also spent hours hammering into us the notion that the most important intelligence tool was the use of informers and moles; we even read a detailed nineteenth-century account by Czar Nicholas II's Counterintelligence chief on how to cultivate such intelligence assets. With all the talk of agents and double agents, my young eyes started to open up to reality as I realized that people often were not what they seemed to be.

By the end of my second year, my love for Ludmilla came to rule my life—and nearly got me thrown out of the Institute. One Saturday in May, my parents went out of town and I wrangled a leave of several hours. Ludmilla and I walked through the shady Summer Garden and along the embankment of the Neva River. As night fell, we snuck into my parents' apartment. Passions flared, and Ludmilla burst into tears when I told her I had to be back at midnight. She refused to let me go. Finally, I persuaded her to wait in the apartment and promised I would be back in a few hours.

There was one problem: I had no Sunday pass. I slept fitfully until 5:00 A.M., when my best friend at the Institute and I hatched an escape plan. We crept to a classroom that faced the street, and tied one end of a rope to my waist and another to a desk. I eased out the fourth-floor window and began to rapel down as my friend, Yuri, guided the rope. I was almost to the ground when the rope became caught on something. I was suspended one floor from the street, my legs flailing about, when a duty officer from a neighboring military academy appeared. He watched me in silence.

"Doing some mountain climbing," I said. "It's part of the curriculum."

Just then I remembered I had tucked a knife in my belt. I cut the rope and dropped to the pavement with a thud, then moved nonchalantly toward the Institute's gate. When I was out of sight of the officer, I dashed for the streetcar. Shortly after sunrise I was back in Ludmilla's arms.

The next day I tried to sneak into the Institute with a group that was returning to barracks after its morning calisthenics. I had just about made it when one of the officers pulled me aside and asked for my pass. The Siberian miner, Chaplygin, was standing a few yards away, smirking. He let it be known that he was the one who had snitched on me after he noticed I was absent Sunday night. I was hauled on the carpet and threatened with dismissal, and am sure that only my father's connections with the Security Ministry and my good performance at the Institute kept me from being expelled.

That September, Ludmilla and I were married. The celebration took place in my family's communal apartment, where forty-five guests drank forty bottles of vodka; I got drunk for the first time in my life as I downed tumbler after tumbler of vodka during the toasts. It was a glorious day, and the world seemed full of possibilities. Our first daughter, Svetlana, was born nine months later.

In 1955, my third year at the Institute, our instructors began to give us some on-the-job training. I was taken to the International Sailors' Club at the Leningrad port, a place where foreign and Soviet seamen congregated. It was—as was everything in the country that involved foreigners—crawling with KGB agents. The first time my instructor, Captain Borisenko, and I walked into the club, he pointed to a pretty blond hostess and said, "She's one of ours." We walked to the bar, and the bartender bowed obsequiously. "This one is ours, too," Borisenko said under his breath.

My superiors gave me the chance to get involved in the recruitment of an informer at the port, an engineer. His file was surprisingly thick, testimony to the efficiency of our totalitarian state and the long arm of the KGB. Leafing through it, I found a background check on the port engineer, an employment questionnaire, official references and reports on him from fellow colleagues and KGB stooles. It was clear he would make an excellent informer. He was a loyal Communist Party member, an author of several inventions, and even played on the port's basketball team.

One night, when the engineer was on duty, we drove down to speak with him. My instructor did the talking, asking the man about the atmosphere in the port, the mood of the workers, examples of shoddy performance or poor management, and any suspicions he had about foreign sailors with whom he had come in contact. We ended the conversation by telling the engineer it was his patriotic duty to secretly inform the KGB about any wrongdoing or suspicious activity at the port. The engineer said he would do it gladly, with one caveat: His wife was jealous of his time and he had to be careful about coming home late. My instructor and the engineer discussed possible meeting places, and the KGB officer gave the new recruit his first assignment—to submit profiles of his close co-workers and contacts.

Shortly afterward, I accompanied another senior officer to a meeting with a longtime KGB agent and informer, who was the chief of records at the port. We met her at a Leningrad apartment that served as a KGB safe house. The apartment was occupied by a former KGB surveillance agent, who had set the table with a half-liter of vodka, a bottle of red wine, salmon, red caviar, and a host of other delicacies that were exceedingly hard to come by. After a glass of vodka, the informer—an attractive middle-aged woman—began talking non-stop about management problems at the port, wrongdoing of senior Communist Party members, and the shady relationship of an acquaintance of hers, a store worker, with the port management. It soon became clear that the KGB was digging up dirt on a high-ranking port boss so he could be brought before regional Party officials and fired. It also became clear to me that our society was packed, top to bottom, with people informing on one another. As a future KGB officer, I thought this would certainly make our work easier. Yet, at the same time, it made me increasingly wary of the people around me: it was difficult to know who to trust.

I spent another week at the Investigations Department of the KGB, witnessing interrogations, confrontations of suspected criminals, and routine investigations. Then I was given a task that brought me face to face with the reality of Stalin's terror—an assignment which has stuck with me until this day. My superiors handed me a few dozen case files of people convicted and shot by the Stalin regime in the 1930s. Khrushchev's famous speech denouncing Stalin and his crimes was only a few months away, and it's clear now that the KGB was preparing itself—and its young workers—for the flood of revelations to come.

Passing me the files, an officer said that my job was to inspect the case records and see if any procedural mistakes had been made during the investigation and trial of these several dozen people. My conclusions would serve as the basis for possibly reinvestigating and posthumously exonerating the convicted. As I took the thin folders, I was apprehensive that I would have no idea how to judge whether the people had been properly convicted. My fears were groundless, however, for it was clear from the record that virtually all the cases were a sham. There was no testimony from witnesses, no cross-examination, no physical evidence—indeed, there was no proof at all. The yellowing files contained only the prosecution's summations, the verdicts handed down by the notorious *troika* kangaroo courts—made up of a regional Communist Party secretary, a prosecutor, and a KGB boss—interrogation transcripts, confessions, and the sentences. In most instances it was death.

I remember two cases in particular. In one, the secret police picked up a man by mistake. When the officers realized their error, they shot the man anyway. At the peak of Stalin's terror in the mid-1930s, secret police bosses throughout the Soviet Union were working furiously to meet—and usually exceed—quotas on the number of "enemies of the people" who had to be rounded up and shot. Nearly all the arrested were innocent, of course, but this man seemed to me particularly unfortunate. On the back of his death sentence, the following words were scribbled: "The convicted man was improperly identified. After he was apprehended on the street and brought into jail, where he was subjected to physical methods of interrogation, it turned out that the detainee had been brought in mistakenly. Put on the planned execution list on orders from the leadership."

Another case involved alleged sabotage by some collective farm workers and local officials. Before the war, Soviet trade representatives purchased a large herd of purebred swine overseas. Some of these pigs made their way to the Leningrad region, where authorities at a collective farm failed to unload them and feed them on time. Several hundred pigs died, and a dozen officials from the rural region and the collective farm were accused of sabotage and shot. Later, it became clear that such crimes were commonplace. But for a twenty-one-year-old aspiring secret agent, who only months earlier had viewed Stalin as a god, reading these records had a profoundly disturbing effect. Nevertheless, I would soon rationalize these terrible cases as the excesses of one despot—excesses that I was convinced the new Soviet leadership under Khrushchev was correcting.

Any doubts I had about the true brutality of Stalin's regime were erased in February 1956, when Khrushchev gave his famous speech at the Twentieth Communist Party Congress denouncing the Soviet dictator. The speech, which laid bare the cruelty of the Stalin era, was not officially published in the Soviet Union until Gorbachev arrived on the scene decades later. But word of the scathing attack on Stalin quickly leaked out, and within a few days a Party official at the Institute read us excerpts of Khrushchev's address. The speech set off heated debates among students and instructors at the school, but it did not kill our faith in the system. We figured that, had Lenin lived and a maniac like Stalin not seized power, things would have been far different, and we were determined to make our Communist system human again. Khrushchev's speech and his ensuing efforts to reform Soviet society indelibly marked my generation, which included men like Gorbachev and Yeltsin. Known as the "Generation of the Sixties," because of the era when we began to move into positions of power, my contemporaries and I balanced a strong belief in Communism with the painful realization of the enormous blunders and cruelty that had characterized our state. Our faith in Communism was so strong that Gorbachev, even after being ousted in the failed coup of August 1991, would return to Moscow still proclaiming his belief in the "Socialist choice."

In June 1956, I graduated with honors from the Institute of Foreign Languages and was chosen—along with just five other classmates—to head to Moscow for advanced training in intelligence. It was a wrenching experience leaving my hometown, my wife, my baby daughter. My father was proud of me, but otherwise had become embittered over his shoddy treatment by the KGB: Khrushchev, attempting to rein in the secret police, had cut salaries, pensions, and benefits, and my father was living on a measly 78 rubles a month. He took to referring to Stalin as "that mustachioed gypsy" and called Khrushchev a "village smartie." Were it not for his old KGB buddies, who hired him to do part-time surveillance work of foreigners at Leningrad's Astoria Hotel and at a campground near the city, he would have lived out his years in poverty.

I arrived in Moscow on a sunny August morning after the overnight train ride from Leningrad. In the courtyard of the KGB Advanced School, I noisily greeted my old friends with whom I had graduated six weeks before. Soon, several dozen young KGB officers boarded buses that drove us through the grime and chaos of Moscow. The capital was in the midst of a postwar construction boom; we passed dozens of factories belching smoke and innumerable half-finished housing projects. Before long we were bumping through the Russian countryside, where peasant women—kerchiefs wrapped around their heads—tended tiny gardens behind their worn, wooden cottages. About 15 miles out of the city, the bus turned off the main road and a formidable-looking green gate swung open. We found ourselves in a bucolic, blessedly quiet spot. Fir and pine trees swayed softly in the summer breeze and the air was redolent with resin. Neatly painted two-story houses were connected by tarmac paths. There was a large cafeteria with a wide choice of dishes and a library with dozens of foreign newspapers. It was the country campus of the KGB's higher spy school, and it looked like heaven.

Things moved quickly from the start. Our class supervisor, a grizzled captain named Vizgin, called us in one by one. I was given the code name "Oleg Kedrov," and was told that from now on no one was to use my real name. Even though I was proficient in English and German, Vizgin suggested I specialize in Arabic. I was dismayed, but nevertheless dove into my studies and painfully began to try to master this alien, guttural language. By the end of my two-year stint at the Advanced School I could communicate fairly well in Arabic, though I never was called upon to use it. The one time it came in remotely handy was years later in Beirut, where I saw a pretty young Egyptian woman in a bar and recited—word for word—a proclamation of love I had seen in an Egyptian film. The woman smiled and told me her price was $10. I declined.

Other students were studying Hindu, Farsi, Japanese, Urdu, Turkish, and a host of other languages, all in preparation for being dispatched around the globe to do battle with America and its capitalist allies. We studied diplomatic protocol, etiquette, economics, the international workers' movement, and Marxism, reading such alluring works as *A Critique of Modern Bourgeois Philosophical and Sociological Theories.* What eventually came in handy, however, were the intensive courses on intelligence and surveillance work. We spent hours discussing how to cultivate spies and moles, coming up with scores of reasons why someone might want to—or be forced to—cooperate with the KGB: blackmail after an illicit sexual encounter, greed, displeasure with a country or its army or intelligence services, ideological causes. Instructors spelled out case histories and solicited our views on how best to recruit potential intelligence assets.

We also underwent intensive technical training. KGB specialists showed us how to set up radio transmitters, how to use and detect bugging devices, how to make microfilm and conceal it in household items. We learned the basics of coding and cryptology. We received special instruction on how to find our bearings when dropped into unknown territory. We were taught how to conceal film and other objects. We spent days in central Moscow tailing experienced KGB officers and being tailed by them. I got to the point where I could spot a tail with relative ease and pass a package to a fellow agent without my tail noticing it.

In October 1956, Soviet troops invaded Hungary to crush the uprising there, but the propaganda within the Soviet Union was so strong that neither I nor my colleagues ever doubted that what we were doing there was right. Our lecturers had a field day with the Hungarian rebellion, portraying it as a struggle between the old and the new, as the death throes of the bourgeois order. It was a counterrevolution, pure and simple, our instructors said. And they wasted no time pointing out that the Hungarians were strong supporters of the Nazis. Senior officers showed us photographs and footage of partisans brutally executing Hungarian secret police officers who had defended the Communist Party headquarters in Budapest. I listened to the BBC's account of the uprising, but dismissed it as Western propaganda. I was twenty-two and a shining example of *Homo sovieticus*—Soviet man. No one could persuade me that my government had done anything monstrous.

In 1957, I proudly became a member of the Communist Party. Early the following year, with our two-year course at the Advanced Intelligence School drawing to a close, our administrators and people from the KGB personnel office began placing future graduates in new jobs. Rumors abounded that several of us would be chosen to spend our lives as "illegals," which would entail changing our identity and moving to a Western country with a new passport to take up a new life. At first I was intrigued by this prospect, but when the reality set in—a life apart from Ludmilla and our daughter, Sveta I realized I wanted nothing to do with it. Luckily, my supervisors informed me I would be joining the KGB's Oriental Department and moving soon to Cairo.

Suddenly, however, my life took an unexpected turn. One of the Advanced School's top administrators called me into his office and said, "We suggest you take a trip in a different direction. You've been noticed by the American Department. They're picking out young people to take a graduate course in the United States. What do you think?"

I couldn't believe my luck. "Of course I agree!" I blurted out.

Over the next several days, I daydreamed constantly about America—the skyscrapers of New York and Chicago, the cowboys of the West, the endless stream of shiny cars. And then, in August 1958, I was summoned by the personnel office, and for the first time in my life set foot in the KGB's imposing yellow stone headquarters in central Moscow. Known as Lubyanka, for the name of the pre-Revolutionary street on which it was located, the massive nine-story building was the symbol of the might of the KGB. Outside stood the statue of the KGB's founder, Felix Dzerzhinsky, for whom the square in front of the headquarters was named. Inside the building, which housed an insurance company under Czar Nicholas II, were the offices of the KGB chairman and his top deputies. In the basement was a labyrinth of cells and torture chambers in which scores of prisoners perished during the Stalin years. I was unaware of what lay underground as I walked into Lubyanka, and was immediately overcome with a sense of awe and elation at my first glimpse of the KGB's inner sanctum. It was one of the great moments of my life as I stepped into the headquarters, all marble and granite. The wooden parquet floors were buffed to a rich, golden brown; the long red runners were spotless; the elevators ran smoothly, the canteen was stocked with the best foods. Entering Lubyanka, I felt as if I had arrived at the seat of power in the country.

The KGB chairman at the time, Ivan Alexandrovich Serov, was a holdover from the Stalin era. He was a brutal man, who had forcibly deported tens of thousands of people from their native Caucasus Mountain region and had participated in the suppression of independence movements in the Baltic states and Eastern Europe. Most recently, he had cruelly put down the 1956 revolt in Hungary. He was on his way out, and the KGB was looking for a new generation of bright young officers, untainted by the crimes of the Stalin era. I was to be one of the new guard.

Already, with the revelations of what had taken place during the

Stalin years, the KGB's reputation had been tarnished. Khrushchev was trying to bring the agency to heel—cutting pay, perks, and pensions. By the time I officially joined the KGB that summer, the organization was still feared, but it did not inspire the terror or respect it had under Stalin. I recall riding in a taxi that summer with several fellow officers. The driver was insufferably rude, and one of my colleagues flashed his KGB identification card to frighten the brazen cabby.

"Who cares?" the cab driver said as he looked at the ID. "You are no longer our masters."

He was wrong, of course. We would remain one of the pillars of Soviet rule for another three decades.

I spoke to the people in the personnel department, then went to see the head of the KGB's North America Department, Alexander Feklisov. He would later become KGB station chief in Washington, and play a key role as a go-between in the 1962 Cuban missile crisis. When I met him, he laid out the purpose of my one-year visit to New York, which would be made under the auspices of a Fulbright Foundation student exchange.

"Just lay the foundation for future work," Feklisov told me. "But don't overstep the line. Now that you've been picked to go to America, make it your business to learn more about the country. Buy yourself good maps. Improve your English. Find out about their way of life. Communicate with people and make as many friends as possible."

I needed a cover story for my student exchange, and Feklisov and others suggested I pose as a graduate of the Philology Department of Leningrad University; it was this ruse that eventually would be swallowed by *The New York Times* and others in the United States. I traveled to Leningrad to cook up a past, and spent a month at the university, talking to students and professors, familiarizing myself with the campus and picking a topic for my non-existent senior thesis. After several weeks, I "graduated" from Leningrad University and became the proud holder of degree number 981064, dutifully signed by one Professor Alexandrov, member of the USSR Academy of Sciences.

Back in Moscow, as I prepared for my trip to America, I was given the rank of senior lieutenant and awarded a salary of 300 rubles—a decent sum in those days. I lived in the Peking Hotel, a model of Stalinist Gothic architecture, and was assigned a desk in Lubyanka in a dark, high-ceilinged room. Sharing the office with me was a jaunty, easygoing KGB officer, Vadim Kosolapov, just returned from a two-year tour at the U.N. Secretariat in New York. Kosolapov had the self-assured air of someone who had just tasted the forbidden fruit of capitalist life and gotten away with it, and he tutored me in the ways of bourgeois America. It sounded great, though I knew we were in the process of building a more just and noble society. I even had time to look through KGB files to see if there might be some fallow agents we could reactivate in the United States. I found one, an American journalist who had worked for the KGB and then been expelled from the USSR in June 1941 for reporting (correctly) about Hitler's imminent attack on the Soviet Union. His file showed he was still alive in the United States, working for a newsmagazine, and I suggested to our office in New York that we try to persuade him to work for us again. Our agents approached him, but were rebuffed.

By early September, our group of Fulbright exchange "students" was ready to go to America. Our visit was the first by young Soviets since the end of World War II—a sign that, though the Cold War was raging, the United States and the Soviet Union were taking small steps toward rapprochement. Of the eighteen Soviets in our group, half were officers of the KGB or Soviet Military Intelligence, known as GRU; the other half could be counted on to cooperate with us. There were four students assigned to Columbia University. One was from GRU. Two of us were from the KGB. And the fourth was from the Central Committee of the Communist Party. His name was Alexander Yakovlev, and he would go on to forge a close relationship with Mikhail Gorbachev and become one of the architects of *perestroika*. When our group first met that September at the headquarters of the Communist Youth League (*Komsomol*), Yakovlev struck me and my KGB colleagues as provincial and not terribly bright. He had fought in World War II, receiving a serious wound that left him with a limp for the rest of his life. After the war, Yakovlev taught high school history in the northern Russian city of Yaroslavl, then became regional secretary of the Communist Party. He moved to Moscow to train as a bureaucrat and ideologue at the Central Committee—the nerve center of the Communist Party. In time, my respect for Yakovlev would grow. But in 1958, no one would have dared predict that he would later team up with Gorbachev and Eduard Shevardnadze to begin the revolution that would ultimately topple Soviet Communism.

Komsomol leader Sergei Romanovsky—a sleek, self-confident

bureaucrat—received us in his spacious office and proceeded to bore us with a platitude-filled pep talk about holding high the banner of Communism and the value of developing international contacts. When he finished his little speech, this leader of Soviet youth flashed a self-satisfied smile and waited for applause or a rousing endorsement of his talk. Instead, there was silence.

"Is that all clear?" he asked, a note of irritation creeping into his voice.

A few people quietly muttered in the affirmative.

"And how is your knowledge of English?" he asked, now clearly annoyed.

Again he was met with silence, as no one wanted to brag about his language skills.

Finally, one of us responded, "Well, I suppose we can manage to string a few words together."

That did it. Sick of our insubordination, Romanovsky exploded, "What do you mean, 'a few words'! Didn't you study the language in depth, complete special courses in ministry institutions? As far as I can see, your group is not up to coping with a complex political undertaking. I will send a recommendation to the Central Committee that you all be kept here!"

We sat there in stunned silence before being ushered out. For a week, our trip to America seemed to hang in the balance. Then one day we were told it was back on, and we began making last-minute preparations. Later, we found out it was Yakovlev who had saved our skins by calling the Central Committee and reassuring the Party that Romanovsky had overreacted and that our group was more than prepared for America.

Ludmilla came to Moscow from Leningrad on the eve of my departure and we said farewell. Then, on an overcast day in late September, we boarded a TU-104—a bomber refitted as a passenger plane—for the flight to Copenhagen. There is nothing quite like the sensation of that first flight abroad, as the ancient plane gathers speed and, groaning and shuddering, lifts off the ground and pokes through the clouds to the bright blue sky above. I was ecstatic—until I felt the plane banking sharply, and heard the stewardess announcing that we were returning to Moscow because of bad weather over Copenhagen. We spent an anxious night in the Soviet capital, then took off again the next day, landing in Denmark at dusk. As we walked through the airport, I was to experience a feeling I would have countless times on future trips abroad: the shock of leaving the gray, monochrome world of the Soviet Union and landing in a place virtually exploding with colors and sights. We spent a few hours in the Danish capital, overwhelmed by the almost clinical cleanliness, the beautiful shop windows, the sea of lights.

That night we took off on our fourteen-hour SAS flight to America. For much of the trip our eyes were glued to the windows, and we wondered aloud whether the lights below were those of Ireland or Iceland. We were too excited to do more than doze, and the following morning, as the sun began to burn off a light fog, we realized we were over America. I could see below me the landscape of our arch enemy—thousands of tiny suburban houses, endless freeways and brightly colored automobiles. We touched down smoothly at Idlewild Airport, stepped off the plane, and soon were greeted by a smiling Immigration officer.

"Welcome to the United States," he said, as our group of spies, Intelligence officers, and Communist Party bureaucrats happily arrived in the land of the free.

THREE

America

y instructions from Fyodor Kudashkin, the head of KGB Counterintelligence in New York, were clear: Stay out of trouble, act like an ordinary student, and don't try to recruit anyone. It was not a tough assignment, and I dove into it with enthusiasm.

After all, I was twenty-four and had been turned loose in New York City with the princely sum of $250 a month in Fulbright spending money. I was living for free in Columbia's John Jay Hall, taking a few journalism courses and being encouraged by the school newspaper—and the KGB—to sniff around New York and get acquainted with American life.

For the first few weeks, I walked ceaselessly around Manhattan, overwhelmed by its power and beauty and bustle. The Soviet capital—which then looked more like an enormous village than a world-class city—had no building taller than the thirty-story spire of Moscow State University. To such unsophisticated eyes as mine, the Empire State Building and Manhattan's other skyscrapers seemed like magnificent, otherworldly creations. I had, of course, read up on New York and knew vaguely what to expect. (I had, in fact, read so much and seen so many films that on our ride in from Idlewild Airport I kept pointing out landmarks, prompting our American host to remark suspiciously, "Mr. Kalugin, you seem to be quite familiar with America.") But no amount of reading could prepare me for the reality of New York City, with its stark contrasts of wealth and poverty. We in the Soviet Union had been deluged with propaganda about America's ghettos, its unemployed, its enormous racial problems. As I walked through Harlem, the Bowery, the Bronx, and other poor areas of the city, however, I was stunned that such a wealthy society could do so little to eradicate such pervasive poverty. My first year in New York actually strengthened my faith in Communism: I believed that although we were far poorer than the United States, we at least tried to offer all our citizens a decent level of education, housing, and health care. Odd as it looks now, it seemed clear to me then that the United States didn't have the Soviet Union's vitality. Our achievements in science and the triumphs of our space program convinced me we would overcome our relative poverty and our Stalinist past and—by the end of the century—become a far better place to live than America.

At Columbia, I was constantly surrounded by students who peppered me with questions about the Soviet Union and delivered lectures as to why America was superior to the USSR. It was autumn 1958, and Boris Pasternak was being condemned by Soviet authorities for his allegedly anti-Socialist novel *Doctor Zhivago,* which had just been awarded the Nobel Prize for Literature. I lamely defended the regime, though I never said it publicly, I believed the persecution of Pasternak was wrong. I also was bombarded with other questions: Why was my country enslaving the nations of Eastern Europe? Why wouldn't our government let artists paint what they wanted and let people say what they pleased? I defended our system as best I could, arguing that the process of building a Communist state was an arduous one, fraught with dangers and inevitably accompanied by mistakes. I had to walk a fine line between not sounding like a brainwashed propagandist, while also still broadly defending the actions of my government.

Several young American students frequently hung out in our rooms or spoke with us after classes. They asked us questions about our backgrounds and about life in the USSR, and soon it became clear that their interest was more than just passing curiosity. I and my Soviet colleagues became convinced that the young Americans were FBI agents assigned to keep an eye on us and determine whether we were from the KGB or might be interested in defecting. Other students would jokingly call us KGB agents, and I would deflect these comments with a lighthearted remark. Otherwise, we felt free to go about our business, and I rarely, if ever, noticed I was being followed as I roamed New York City.

I visited scores of neighborhoods and all the major museums. I saw ball games and went to the Metropolitan Opera. I rode buses and subways for hours, and saw more than one hundred films. I went to a strip club in Greenwich Village, shelling out $40 for a drink with one of the dancers. I even won election to the Columbia University Student Council, undoubtedly becoming the first KGB officer—and, I imagine, the last—to serve on that body.

All the while, I bounced around the city writing articles for the Columbia University newspaper. Once, when the Bolshoi Ballet came to town, I set off with a photographer to interview the dancers. The guards at the main entrance to the Metropolitan Opera House denied us access to the rehearsal, so we decided to sneak in the back door. After making our way down a darkened passageway, we suddenly came to the stage area, where we photographed the famed dancers—including Galina Ulanova—as they practiced. I introduced myself as a Soviet student and tried to talk to the dancers, but they reacted with hostility and suspicion. Soon, two policemen showed up and tossed us out. The next day, fearing I had created an incident, I went to see my KGB supervisor, Kudashkin, at the U.N. Mission and told him what had happened. He smiled, and showed me a detailed report on the incident that already had been submitted by one of the Bolshoi *prima ballerinas,* a KGB informer. The soloist had accused me of being an American provocateur who had tried to pass himself off as a Soviet citizen. I, too, was amused by the incident: Was there any organization we didn't control?

As the school year drew to a close in the spring of 1959, Fidel Castro—who had just overthrown the Batista regime but had not yet become an implacable Communist enemy of the United States—came to Columbia and spoke on the campus' main square. His fiery speech describing the overthrow of Cuba's tyrannical regime was received enthusiastically by the students, and as I stood in the crowd I was moved almost to tears by his revolutionary fervor. Around the time of the speech, *The New York Times* published its profile of me. It ran with a picture, and after it appeared I felt like a celebrity as strangers stopped me in the street and wished me well. Several publishers called, asking me to write my life story, and a university in Philadelphia even offered me a position as a graduate assistant.

When school ended, my three Soviet colleagues from Columbia and I set off on a three-week trip—sponsored by a university consortium—around the United States, visiting Philadelphia and Chicago, parts of Wisconsin and Iowa, New Orleans and Washington, D.C. We were treated to an intimate view of the American heartland, which was then riding the boom years of the late 1950s. It was a land of Cadillacs and Chevrolets, of Zenith and Motorola TV consoles, of the latest refrigerators and dishwashers and toasters, of drive-ins and jukeboxes and countless miles of gorgeous roads. The supermarkets were packed with a dizzying description of goods, and everywhere the people seemed friendly and guileless. I was a guest for several days on a farm in Iowa, where the hospitable but laconic owners woke me at 6:00 A.M., fed me a hearty breakfast, and spent the next twelve hours instructing me in the intricacies of driving a tractor and sowing corn.

That trip—and all my time in America—gave me a brief twinge of doubt about our Communist system. The freedom I experienced to poke around America, to engage people in discussions on any topic—all of it contrasted sharply with the mood in my country, where such a friendly, open attitude often was met with a stiff rebuke or a door slammed in one's face. As the years went by and I would return to the USSR from operations abroad, I increasingly experienced the sense that I was slipping behind some gloomy Communist curtain. In 1958, I knew our life was grimmer, but just figured we had a longer way to go than the more fortunate people of America.

When I returned to New York, I went to work as a host at the Soviet exhibit and plunged into the Cook affair. Soon, however, it was time to return to the Soviet Union. Alexander Yakovlev, who had become our unofficial leader, had occasion to sum up our year abroad to the American press. He had remained aloof from the American scene—Yakovlev held a doctrinaire, deeply skeptical view of capitalism and his war wounds made it impossible for him to bound around the city as I did—but it was clear that he, too, had been impressed by what he had seen. When a reporter asked him about our student exchange, Yakovlev responded like a diplomat: "This was a brilliant example of international cooperation . . . I did not have sufficient time to appreciate the beauty of the local girls, because I spent all my time over my books, but one thing I can now say with certainty: The American and Soviet people can live in peace. Before coming here, I had my doubts about this."

By September 1959, I was back in Russia, working for the KGB's First Chief Directorate—Foreign Intelligence. My New York trip had been an undoubted success, particularly my work with Cook, and senior officers assured me my KGB career was off to a fine start. I was happy to be reunited with Ludmilla and my four-year-old daughter, and moved back into Lubyanka awaiting my next assignment. Almost immediately my superiors asked me to take a trip in connection with the Cook case: His sister, Louisa, lived in the southern Russian region of Krasnodar, and now that Cook was working with us, the KGB wanted to make sure she didn't write him and arouse the suspicion of the FBI. I was dispatched to inform Cook's sister that he was doing well in America and that any communication with him must go through our hands.

Early one morning I arrived in the sister's village and quickly found her cottage. Introducing myself as a Soviet student just returned from America, I told her I had met Anatoly—Cook—in New York.

"You can be proud of him," I said, referring to a brother she hadn't seen in fifteen years. "He is a real Soviet patriot, but, as you can imagine, this makes life difficult for him in America. He has to conceal his political views in order to keep his job. So it would be better if you didn't send any letters directly to him through the mail. I'll give you an address you can use in Moscow, and your letters will be personally delivered to him."

The middle-aged woman burst into tears.

"I thought at first you must be from the KGB," she sobbed. "For the past fifteen years they have hounded us to death. They even phone at night, saying, 'Why don't you contact your brother and get information for us? Have you forgotten what you promised?' They send anonymous, threatening letters. At work our family is branded as traitors—they claim Anatoly is a spy. It's absolute hell!"

Anger welled up in me, and I felt ashamed to be a part of the agency that had harassed this family for years over the emigration of one of its members.

"These people are from the Stalinist past," I assured her. "Forget about them. I've got friends at the KGB. They're completely different people and they'll make sure this sort of thing will stop."

Louisa composed herself and promised to send all future correspondence to her brother through Moscow. I said goodbye, and heard nothing from her until twenty-four years later, after Cook had fallen afoul of the KGB.

Not long after I returned to Moscow I was summoned by the personnel department and given some great news: I was being sent back to New York as a correspondent for Radio Moscow, and had to meet urgently with the chairman of the State Radio Broadcasting Committee. I was delighted to be heading back to America, and with an excellent cover: For the time being, I would be Radio Moscow's sole representative in the United States, at the ripe age of twenty-five.

The following morning I met with Sergei Kaftanov, the State

Radio chairman, in what amounted to a mere formality: If the KGB wanted to use Radio Moscow to place an officer in America, he could do little to stop it.

"Do you know anything about journalism?" the portly, dour Kaftanov asked me.

I told him I had just graduated from Columbia Journalism School, and that my studies had given me a solid grounding in English, journalism, and American life. He nodded portentously, and signed an order appointing me to his staff. I spent a half-year in the State Radio Committee's offices in Moscow, learning the operation and practicing my journalism skills. Among my young colleagues was Yevgeni Primakov, who years later—after the 1991 coup—would go on to become head of Russia's new Foreign Intelligence agency. In the winter of 1959–60, however, my co-workers thought I was just another cub reporter. It wasn't until six months later—when a rumor swept the huge, pink stone Radio Committee building that this rookie correspondent was being given the plum America assignment—that my colleagues realized I wasn't what I seemed to be, and that another government agency was behind my appointment.

I took up my new posting in New York in June 1960, joining an already large group of Soviet KGB officers posing as correspondents in America. In the days of the Cold War—indeed, up to the end of the Gorbachev era—about two thirds of Soviet foreign correspondents were connected with the KGB. The TASS news agency, Radio Moscow, the Novosti Press Agency, and *Izvestia* were especially heavily staffed by KGB officers. In fact, the only publication the KGB couldn't infiltrate and control was *Pravda,* the official organ of the Central Committee of the Communist Party. The correspondents from *Pravda* were untouchable, and KGB officers could only get information from *Pravda*'s staffers if we asked tactfully; otherwise, if we pushed *Pravda*'s people too hard, we could face a rebuke from the Party. But *Pravda*'s independence from the KGB was not a great loss, for we had more than enough resources. Even Soviet journalists who were not officially part of the KGB could be counted on to help us at any time. Vladimir Kryuchkov, who went on to head the KGB under Gorbachev and then to mastermind the August 1991 coup, liked to refer to these non-KGB correspondents as "our assistants." The FBI and CIA knew that most of the working Soviet journalists in America were spooks; I'm sure U.S. officials had little doubt what I was doing in their country.

Another transparent ruse in the espionage game was our so-called "U.N. Mission" in New York, which in fact was little more than a nest of KGB spies and intelligence officers. Originally located in a four-story brownstone building at 67 Park Avenue, and later moved to a Third Avenue high-rise, the mission was headquarters to about three hundred Soviets, more than a third of whom were KGB officers. The remaining Soviets were diplomats and support personnel attached to the United Nations. The KGB contingent occupied an entire floor of the brownstone and a large staff of technical specialists made sure that security was tight. Several rooms, including that of the KGB's New York station chief, were protected against electronic eavesdropping, and it was there that we held top-secret conversations. The technical staff also had installed so many jamming devices that even if one of our officers had become a double agent and entered the brownstone with a hidden microphone, there was no way he could have transmitted to the outside. We assumed that all our apartments and telephones were bugged, and acted accordingly.

When I first arrived in New York, the KGB station chief was a cultured and highly respected figure, Vladimir Barkovsky. Lean, athletic-looking, with piercing blue eyes and an energetic manner, Barkovsky inspired the New York staff with his boundless enthusiasm and shrewd assessment of our mission in America. Though he deserved to be made a general, he never rose to that rank because he didn't kowtow to Moscow or color his reports to suit his superiors at Lubyanka. I worked only briefly with Barkovsky, but nevertheless grew to have deep respect and affection for him. I remember sitting with him one day, discussing an intelligence matter, when he suddenly became quite still and turned his head in the direction of a radio playing softly in the corner of his office.

"That's from Blomdahl's *Aniara*," the KGB veteran said dreamily, leaning back in his chair. "Heavenly music."

Though I went by my real name at Radio Moscow, I was given the KGB code name "Felix," which the agency used in communications inside our New York station and in messages to Moscow. I was assigned to Political Intelligence—as opposed to Scientific and Technical Intelligence—which meant that my job was to seek out promising American and foreign recruits who could supply the KGB with classified or unclassified information about American foreign and domestic policy. In the United States as a whole, the main targets of KGB penetration were the White House, Congress, the State Department, the CIA, the FBI, the Pentagon, leading scientific research centers and think tanks, and major corporations. In New York, I was assigned to develop sources at the U.S. Mission to the United Nations, the United States Information Agency (USIA), and the American and foreign press corps.

Cook had given me an exhilarating—and misleading—first impression of the nature of my work. I expected to be developing such top-quality spies and sources at a steady clip, but the fact is that in five years in New York City I never again ran across an agent as good as Cook. I would develop lower-level agents and go to extraordinary lengths to cultivate sources and insert them into the American government, but neither I nor my colleagues had much luck. Indeed, the best agents the KGB ever had—I would see this firsthand as deputy chief of station in Washington—were the volunteers who walked into our embassy and literally dumped material in our laps. Most of these spies, such as the legendary John Walker, were not motivated by ideological reasons, but merely wanted money. In my thirty-four-year tenure with the KGB, the great spies who came to us because they believed in Communism, such as Kim Philby, dwindled steadily and finally disappeared altogether. At the same time, the number of KGB officers who grew disaffected with Soviet Communism and defected to the West rose sharply. The result was that the KGB was hit by a devastating double-whammy in which the number of good spies was shrinking while the number of defectors was soaring, all of which left us further and further behind the CIA.

Though I became involved with some secret operations in New York in my early years—and was the target of several FBI set-ups—my main function was to gather political intelligence from a variety of public sources. We also engaged in numerous "active measures," in which we spread disinformation and stirred up trouble in the black and Jewish communities, among others. And when Moscow wanted to hammer home its official line—as it did when accusations arose of Soviet involvement in the assassination of President John F. Kennedy—we in Political Intelligence were called upon to propagate the Soviet point of view.

At first, however, in that summer of 1960, I had to put on a convincing display that I really was a Radio Moscow correspondent, and that meant working long hours as a journalist while also trying to take my first steps in intelligence gathering. I worked out of a spacious apartment on Riverside Drive, where my wife doubled as bureau secretary. The KGB and Radio Moscow paid me a combined salary of $480 a month in the beginning, plus expenses. Inheriting a blue Chevrolet Bellair, an Ampex studio tape recorder, and a typewriter from the previous correspondent, I obtained accreditation from the United Nations and the New York City Police Department and began my work. I filed reports frequently from New York, usually by phone, and soon heard from the State Radio Committee that they liked my work. Of course, I had to put a pro-Soviet slant on the news; on one occasion I received a written rebuke when a report on America's reaction to the Franco dictatorship in Spain did not make the United States look sufficiently venal. In that same critique of my work, my superiors at Radio Moscow neatly summed up my job in New York.

"Our task is to expose the way of life in the capitalist world, and it is especially important to do so in relation to the United States," my editors wrote.

Not all my work, however, had an ideological slant. I particularly enjoyed one thirty-minute report I prepared, "An Evening in New York," in which I roamed the nightclubs, restaurants, and theaters on a Saturday night and put together a picture of how New Yorkers spent their free time. Soviet listeners liked the piece so much that Radio Moscow replayed it several times.

The biggest story I was to cover in my relatively brief career as a journalist was the arrival of Nikita Khrushchev in New York in Septmber 1960—a trip that would forever be remembered by one event: The moment when the Ukrainian peasant yanked off his shoe and pounded it on his desk at the United Nations General Assembly. A new Radio Moscow bureau chief—sent to free me up to begin work in earnest for the KGB—arrived shortly before Khrushchev. And so, on a warm September morning, I stood on the dock at a dingy New York pier and watched as the *Baltika* slid into berth. As a Radio Moscow correspondent, I would have no trouble getting close to Khrushchev. In any case, my status as a KGB officer assured access—my superiors had told me to stay close to the Soviet leader just in case something happened.

As soon as he came down the gangplank, a group of Soviet and American correspondents stuck microphones in Khrushchev's face and began firing questions at him. It was the first time I had seen a Soviet leader in the flesh and, standing just a few feet away, I took the measure of the man. He was not impressive. Short, fat, and cursed with a heavy, piglike face spotted with warts, Khrushchev was a rude, rough-hewn figure. To add insult to injury, he spoke

Russian like a peasant, stumbling over long words and placing stresses on the wrong syllables. All in all, I found him repulsive. But as I stood listening to him issue a now-forgotten greeting to the American people, I realized that this was the man who had turned Soviet society around following the nightmarish Stalin years. He represented the new generation of Russian politicians and seemed committed to genuine change. Unlike his predecessor, he also seemed close to the people, displaying the unpretentious charm of a Slavic peasant. Gazing upon this stocky little Ukrainian holding forth on American soil, I soon felt a sense of pride.

Khrushchev came to know my face, and later in his visit—as a crowd of American reporters pushed me aside and surrounded the Soviet leader—he waved a hand in my direction and said, "You—come closer! Stand beside me at all times and record everything I say. Otherwise the Americans will distort my words. These sharks will write all sorts of rubbish!"

My affection for him grew after that scene; to this day I still have some of the tapes from Khrushchev's New York visit.

On the day of his famous speech, I sat in the press balcony at the U.N. General Assembly and watched in shock as Khrushchev used his shoe as a debating prop. He was angry at an address delivered by British Prime Minister Harold Macmillan, and reacted the way he might have at a Communist Party meeting in Kiev. But this was New York, the whole world was watching, and I said to myself, "Jesus Christ, a man of his stature behaves like a peasant! This is not a bar somewhere in the Ukraine." It was an embarrassment to the Soviet Union, and such erratic behavior would eventually lead—four years later—to his abrupt removal from power.

I attended several receptions for the Soviet leader, dutifully recording his toasts and speeches. They were so peppered with Russian profanity, however, that I couldn't put them on the air. Khrushchev's KGB bodyguards had told me that he could hold his liquor, and that proved to be true. I can still see the vaunted Soviet leader and his hangers-on knocking back vodka and laughing uproariously at off-color jokes.

After Khrushchev's departure, it was time for me to step back from my radio work and get down to KGB business. I decided to contact several students I had known during my days at Columbia, two of whom were studying nuclear physics. We knew it was exceedingly difficult to develop senior, high-ranking officials or scientists as intelligence assets, so our plan was to attempt to recruit young Americans and plant them in government agencies or research institutes. Indeed, the famous Cambridge University spy ring involving Kim Philby had been just such an operation: Drawing in potential spies early, then reaping the benefits as they moved up the government ladder into classified positions.

I got in touch with a physics graduate student at Columbia named Nicholas, whom I remembered as holding extreme left-wing political views. He said he was happy to hear from me, and we agreed to meet near the campus. It turned out that he was working in a laboratory engaged in nuclear research, and I told Nicholas bluntly that the world's first Socialist state could not be allowed to lag behind the West in the race for scientific and military supremacy. It was his duty as a radical to help us out, I said, and he agreed. At our next meeting, he brought me some material about U.S. nuclear weapons research, but it turned out to be unclassified and of little value. When I expressed disappointment, he promised to bring me some classified material, and I anxiously awaited our next meeting. But Nicholas showed up empty-handed, saying not only had he had trouble smuggling out the material, but also he had discussed the matter with his parents—both of whom were Communists—and they had decided that what he was doing was too dangerous. Listening to his excuses, I grew increasingly exasperated and finally exploded.

"So this is what your radicalism is worth!" I told the twenty-five-year-old student. "You talk about peace and you really don't do anything to forward the cause. When it comes to issues of war or peace, the triumph of socialism or capitalism, there can only be one choice. But you talk about things that are way over your head. You're just a bullshit artist."

He listened silently, a look of shame spreading across his face. But he held his ground, and as he walked away I figured that would be the last I heard of Nicholas.

Several days later, however, as I was walking near my office on the Upper West Side, an older man stopped me, introduced himself as Nicholas's father, and asked to have a word with me. We drove to midtown Manhattan and had breakfast.

"I'm sorry about my son's behavior," he told me as we sat in a coffee shop. "But you have to understand his predicament. We had always believed in the emergence of a Socialist America. But now, toward the end of our lives, we realize this is impossible. Let Nicholas carry on his work in peace and we'll help you instead. I'll do everything I can for you and your country."

At first I was suspicious of Nicholas's father, but the look in his eyes—that of a 1930s fellow traveler who was determined to fan the remaining sparks of Communist spirit—convinced me he was genuine. We set a time for our next meeting, and agreed not to talk over the phone.

I returned to the U.N. Mission and told our station chief, Barkovsky, of the recruitment of Nicholas's father, a businessman. Barkovsky reprimanded me for breaking a basic KGB procedure forbidding officers to recruit agents without prior approval from Moscow. But I countered that it would have been foolish to have said no to a man who offered his services, adding that I was certain he was not an FBI plant. Barkovsky sent a cable to Moscow headquarters, which soon sent a return dispatch warning me never again to proceed with an unauthorized recruitment. But the coded cable from Lubyanka also ended with these words: "Allowing for the initiative and courage shown by Comrade Felix, I suggest he be promoted to the rank of senior case officer."

And so I was. Though Nicholas was of little value, his father turned out to be a good KGB asset, as we used him on numerous occasions to run messages and deliver materials to agents living outside the 25-mile city radius to which we were restricted. We rarely paid the man—once I gave him a clock as a token of our appreciation—and after I left New York, I never heard of him or his son again. I assume the father has passed away after doing his bit for the dying Communist cause. And the son—well, he is middle-aged and probably settled down with a family in the suburbs, our fleeting coak-and-dagger experience a bizarre, uncomfortable memory from the days of his radical youth.

I knew two other students who had expressed a willingness to help the Soviet Union. One, at our urging, had applied to work at the CIA. He was rejected, for reasons that were never clear to us. The second went on to the University of Chicago, where he studied nuclear physics and became involved in the anti-war movement. Under the guise of preparing material for Radio Moscow, I asked him for detailed reports on the radical student movement in America, and he obliged with a lengthy treatise on the subject. He fed us information on other matters, such as his physics work, and we paid him a small amount for his help. After I left New York in 1964, however, I lost touch with him and don't know whether he continued helping the KGB.

As the months passed, I worked hard at getting to know as many journalists, businessmen, and U.N. diplomats as I could. I was elected vice-president of the United Nations Correspondents' Association. In addition, I was assigned to work with several of the non-KGB Soviet journalists, who we paid to help us pull together information—largely unclassified—on the situation in the United States. Such a case arose after Kennedy was elected, when Moscow ordered us to compile everything we knew about the president. One colleague who often helped me, an Italian correspondent with Communist sympathies, was well plugged in to the American political scene and had gotten wind of Kennedy's compulsive womanizing. We filed a detailed cable on rumors of Kennedy's sex life, and word filtered back that Lubyanka was pleased with the report.

In the beginning, my superiors frequently reminded me that what I might pick up in the course of my reporting around New York could be as important as a package of classified documents. One such incident occurred when I went to hear a lecture at Columbia by Professor Zbigniew Brzezinski. He outlined in detail a plan for widened American involvement in the Vietnam War, just then getting under way. Knowing that Brzezinski was well respected and influenced American policymakers, I returned to our KGB station and informed my superiors of his lecture.

"This is tremendous!" said one of my supervisors. "We must cable it to Moscow immediately."

I filed a detailed report on Brzezinski's plan for American escalation in Vietnam. Several weeks later, when we received Moscow's monthly evaluation of our intelligence work, I learned that my cable had been relayed to the ruling Communist Party Politburo and discussed there.

"See, Oleg," said one of my commanding officers, "your open information wound up in the Politburo. Now you know how important it is to pick up things from well-placed, knowledgeable people, even if the stuff isn't classified."

In November 1960, following my superiors' advice to get to know as many influential Americans as possible, I struck up a friendship with Jay Rockefeller, scion of the Rockefeller family and future governor and senator from West Virginia. We met in a TV studio in New York, hit it off, and began to correspond. The young Rockefeller was then a student at Harvard, and in April 1961 he invited me to visit his family's vacation estate in Vermont. After receiving permission from the U.S. State Department to travel outside the New York area, I drove to Vermont. I never expected that this prominent young American would become one of our intelli-

gence operatives, but went instead because such high-level contacts could help me in my understanding of the United States. In addition, the KGB might one day want to use someone like Rockefeller as a conduit for information to U.S. leaders. I went, also,
because I liked Rockefeller, with whom I shared a certain youthful
idealism.

The Rockefeller *"dacha"* was not the grand estate I was expecting; indeed, it was a modest, wooden building (lacking central heat-
ing) set amidst the picturesque forests and lakes of Vermont. Jay
and a friend—Frank Kellogg, son of the former U.S. Secretary of
State—greeted me warmly, and we proceeded to spend the next few
days walking the ice-rimmed paths of the estate and sitting in front
of a crackling fireplace, all the while engaged in wide-ranging discussions of philosophy and U.S.-Soviet relations. I argued that the
world was inevitably moving toward socialism, collective property,
and a sort of blissful egalitarianism. The two Americans responded
that my vision was nice but unrealistic, and espoused the virtues of
America's rugged individualism.

"And what will happen to us, representatives of the ruling circles
and of 'bourgeois' society, in your new world?" Kellogg asked me.
"What awaits us—physical annihilation or isolation in special reed-
ucation camps?"

Being the good *Homo sovieticus* I was, I responded, "I assume
that those of you who are willing to accept the new order will join
the ranks of its active builders, and will come under the protection
of the state. There will be no more mass repressions."

We parted amicably, and I returned to New York and included
details of my visit in a cable to Moscow. The response came back,
"That's a good contact. Keep up the good work."

I stayed in touch with Jay Rockefeller for several more years,
writing him and occasionally talking on the phone. But in 1967,
after marrying the daughter of Senator Charles Percy and moving
into politics himself, Rockefeller stopped all communication with
me. I imagine that, by that time, the FBI had told him I was a
suspected KGB officer and advised him to sever our relations.

Back in New York, I continued meeting a wide variety of well-
known Americans as part of my cover work as a Radio Moscow
correspondent. Among them were Eleanor Roosevelt, Edward R.
Murrow, the actresses Shelley Winters and Natalie Wood, the artist
Rockwell Kent, and many others. Some of these celebrities traveled
in left-wing political circles and I would see them frequently; the

hope never died that one of them would one day be the source of good information, political or otherwise.

I also worked ceaselessly—and usually futilely—to cultivate moles and intelligence assets. Early on, I met a correspondent from the Australian Broadcasting Corporation, a young man of liberal political views who seemed to have close ties to officials from his country. I started getting friendly with him, but must have overplayed my hand. One day, we agreed to meet on an "urgent matter," but when I arrived at the rendezvous site I was met not by the correspondent, but by a hard-eyed man from the Australian Mission. I realized at once that he was a security officer.

"What do you want?" I asked him.

"I just wanted to have a look at you," the Australian said, giving me a knowing stare. "I have heard a lot about you from your friend the journalist."

It was clearly a warning for me to back off, and I did.

My KGB colleagues and I tried on numerous occasions to employ romance as a tool in recruiting agents. I became friendly with the secretary of the Ceylonese Ambassador to the United Nations, and through her got to know a woman who worked as an archivist at the Australian Mission. She had access to valuable classified information, and I began to court her—all in the line of duty, of course. But our budding "romance" came to an abrupt end when Australian security people warned her that she would be sent home if she so much as spoke to me again.

A while later, I went to a party and met a Canadian woman from Radio Free Europe—an agency then largely controlled by the CIA and consequently a major KGB target. We went to the theater and restaurants and strolled in the park like a pair of lovers. At Easter, she dragged me into church for midnight mass, and for the first time in my life I found myself surrounded by true religious believers. I enjoyed the sounds of the organ and the singing of the choir, but when the Canadian woman dropped to her knees to pray, I—an avowed atheist—was not about to follow suit. The collection plate was passed and I refused to make a donation, not out of stinginess, but because it would have been against my ideological convictions to do so.

Pretending I needed information for my news broadcasts, I asked her to bring me some papers from Radio Free Europe. She obliged, handing me some moderately helpful reports and internal documents from the station. But then this staunch Catholic somehow found out I was married and ruefully told me she could not have a relationship with a married man.

"Oleg, I like you so much, but I will never be able to meet with you again," she said.

No amount of entreaty on my part could change her mind, not even my assurances that all I wanted was a platonic friendship. I admired her for her convictions, and wrote it all off to experience. Had we gotten more deeply involved, my superiors had authorized me—and all my colleagues—to sleep with a woman if necessary. The KGB also told us that, should we get caught in the act by the FBI, under no circumstances were we to become flustered or contrite. If the FBI threatened to send black and white photos of a tryst to an agent's wife, the agent was told, in effect, to respond, "Oh, please send color prints. They're much prettier." I never actually had to hop in the sack with a potential asset; but at the same time I feigned romantic involvement and kissed a woman now and then. Ludmilla never knew, for I figured it was all in the line of duty and was not interfering with my love for my wife.

Nine times out of ten we got nowhere on the romantic front. One colleague did manage to romance a secretary from the British U.N. Mission and obtain some classified material from her. But mostly we struck out. I was frequently reminded of Mayakovsky's words about how poetry is like mining radium—you process thousands of words just to get a good line. And so we sifted through thousands of souls, just to find one good agent.

In 1961, a colleague and I went to a party given by some women from the staff of the United Nations Secretariat. We didn't arrive until midnight, and as we entered the apartment building I questioned the wisdom of showing up so late. My KGB colleague brushed aside my fears, saying the party would just be getting into full swing. We rode the elevator to the twentieth floor and knocked on the woman's door. We continued to knock, then heard a voice on the other side of the door calling the police. My friend and I scrambled down twenty flights of stairs. We had just about made a clean getaway when two New York policemen burst into the lobby, put our hands behind our backs, and began to search us. The police only let us go after the inhospitable hostess—whose party had long since ended—confirmed that she knew us. Just to be safe, we reported the incident to our station chief the next morning, but heard nothing more about it.

After I had been in New York a year or so, the FBI Counter-

Intelligence people must have been certain of two things: one, I was KGB; and, two, I was a womanizer. Soon my American counterparts were making heavy-handed attempts to compromise me by luring me into sexual encounters.

The first incident took place after I met a pretty woman at a reception hosted by the left-wing American publisher Carl Marzani. A fellow traveler and open admirer of the Communist system, Marzani published Socialist and leftist literature in the United States. He had close ties to the Soviet government and the KGB, which secretly gave him money to keep his publishing house afloat. KGB officers frequented his parties, and one night a colleague suggested I might find it useful to attend one of Marzani's receptions.

His apartment was filled with a motley assortment of Communists, liberals, and KGB spooks—all of them watched, undoubtedly, by FBI informers in attendance. Midway through the party, a comely blonde, who introduced herself as Ann, seemed to take an intense interest in me and my colleague, and as the evening drew to a close she invited us to her apartment for a drink. We accepted and went to her place, just a few blocks away.

We were suspicious from the start, but decided to play along. She seemed pushy and ill at ease, as if playing a role. Though she was undeniably attractive, she had the worn, cynical expression of a prostitute. And her apartment scarcely looked lived in. What also made me wary were pictures of her with some Washington politicians and top military officers. As we sat down and had a drink, she began rattling off the names of the influential people she knew in the nation's capital. We stayed at her place until 2:00 A.M., and at one point I found myself stifling a laugh. This was all too good to be true: a pretty American woman with top-flight Washington connections wanted to hop in bed with me. Did the FBI think I was really that stupid?

I decided not to call her again, feeling certain it was a set-up. Then, two weeks later, she telephoned me.

"I have something very important to discuss with you," she said. "Why don't you stop by tonight—say around nine o'clock?"

I agreed to come, but decided to show up at her place an hour and a half early, just to throw off any plans the FBI might have to frame me. At seven-thirty I knocked on her door and caught her by surprise. Flustered and obviously dismayed, she pulled herself together and offered me a drink. She left the living room and returned a minute later with a folder in her hand.

"These are classified documents showing the latest developments in plane construction, including blueprints for Douglas aircraft," she said, avoiding eye contact with me. "A friend of mine would like you to have them."

"My dear," I responded, leaning back in my chair, "I'm flattered that you've decided to give me these documents. But I have nothing to do with Douglas aircraft or the latest aviation designs. Don't bother showing me these papers—I wouldn't understand them. I'm a Radio Moscow correspondent. I have nothing to do with planes except when I fly them."

"But this is very valuable material—you'll never find anything like this in Moscow," she responded.

"I don't even have friends in aviation," I said. "But if you like I can put you in touch with the Soviet trade representative, if your friends at Douglas are interested in selling their aircraft to our country."

This idea didn't suit her. What she wanted was clear: I would take the documents, walk out, and be arrested by the FBI for espionage. I didn't even have a diplomatic passport during my tour of duty in New York, and was not about to fall for such a blatant sting operation.

We sat in silence for a while. Then she offered me another drink, which I declined. She began ummistakably coming on—moving closer and giving me sexy, suggestive looks. I looked at my watch. It was about eight-fifteen—forty-five minutes before our appointed meeting—and I decided it was time to go. I never saw her again.

Six months later, an FBI agent who had been feeding us information reported that this woman had set several traps for KGB agents in New York, myself included. This FBI man was an interesting case, an example of the bizarre forms of cooperation we sometimes received. His motivation for helping us was unclear: Was he angry at his bosses? Fed up with American life? One day he approached our new station chief, Boris Ivanov, on the street. The FBI agent was assigned to the team that followed Ivanov, and he must have known our chief was unwatched at the time. The American said he wanted to help us, and gave Ivanov some information about FBI activity against several Soviet citizens in New York City. At first, Ivanov was highly suspicious. But then, through personal meetings and the mail, the FBI agent sent other snippets of information about his agency's counter-intelligence work against the KGB. He proved to be reliable, and eventually tipped us off that one of my main recruits—a Greek who was attempting to woo female U.N. and U.S. government employees—was actually a double agent working for the FBI. Our mysterious federal source never asked for money.

Ivanov and the New York KGB station never lost its skepticism about this FBI mole. But a decade later, when I became head of the KGB's Foreign Counterintelligence operations, I had occasion to look through our files. His report on my meeting with the seductress who offered the Douglas blueprints was uncannily accurate. Indeed, as I sat in Moscow reading his case file, I became certain he was genuine. We had, however, lost touch with him in the late 1960s. In the early 1970s, I ordered our agents in New York to locate the man, and they did. He was retired and living in Queens. When we approached him he said he had no desire to resume contact with us.

"I gave you guys all I knew," he told our officers. We let the matter drop. To this day, I still don't know what prompted this FBI man to risk jail and the ruination of his career by channeling information to the KGB.

Not long after my encounter with the attractive blonde, I attended a reception of the United States Information Agency in New York. There I met another beauty, a striking redhead, who introduced herself as a former Miss Pennsylvania. She most decidedly did not look like a hooker, but I became suspicious of her immediately. Miss Pennsylvania—or whoever she was—also came on strongly and was quite seductive. She didn't fit in with the intellectual crowd at the reception, and I asked her what she was doing there.

"I live nearby," she responded.

She acknowledged she had a husband, saying only that he was a very rich man who was "doing something for the U.S. government." We drank and talked a while, then agreed to meet later in the week.

I called her up and we wound up in a bar in midtown Manhattan. After a few drinks, she looked me straight in the eye and said, "I'd like to go with you someplace."

I acted taken aback, and asked where she had in mind.

"I know a nice motel in New Jersey," she said.

I remembered reading that it was illegal in America to take a woman across state lines with the explicit purpose of having sex with her. So I told her, "Why go that far? We could find a place nearer home. There are plenty of hotels here."

We talked a while before I finally excused myself and went home. I had little doubt that this, too, was an attempt to catch me in an embarrassing situation that would later be used to blackmail or expel me. After all, we in the KGB did it all the time.

One of my most ambitious—and dismally unsuccessful—efforts to mix sex and espionage involved a Greek-American agent we referred to as "Pompei." Unfortunately, Pompei turned out to be a double agent, and my involvement with him would come back to haunt me later. It was my shenanigans with Pompei that eventually prompted the FBI, leaking information through columnist Jack Anderson, to publicly identify me in the late 1960s as a KGB officer. By then I was deputy chief of station in Washington, and the disclosure that I was with the KGB killed any chances I had of rising to station chief in the American capital.

I first heard of Pompei, whose name was John Makris, in 1963, when Moscow cabled me and said that a Greek-American who had been working for us in New York had dropped out of sight. My assignment was to find him and see what he might be able to do for us. I went at the appointed time to the place where he was supposed to have prearranged monthly meetings with the KGB. Makris, as expected, didn't show. Then I went to his old apartment, where the landlady gave me the address of a Greek restaurant he frequented.

"What should I tell him?" the owner asked me.

"Tell him that his friend from the United Nations is looking for him," I replied.

When I came back a week later, the owner gave me Makris's new address. I went there, and when the Greek opened the door I gave him a codeword, to which he responded properly. I instructed him to show up the last Thursday of the month, at noon, at Brentano's bookstore, where he would be met by a KGB agent. The agent would ask him, "Do you know if they still carry any books by Mr. [Nikos] Kazantzakis?" To which Makris was to reply, "No," and suggest another Greek writer.

Makris showed up, and announced his willingness to work with us again. Despite his mediocre looks, he was apparently something of a Don Juan, and we decided to use him to recruit secretaries from the United Nations, the local FBI, and the State Department. Using $10,000 in KGB money, we set him up as head of a bogus travel agency, and turned him loose with a few hundred dollars a month in spending money to troll the bars around the United Nations.

He seemed to sleep with enough women, but nothing ever came of these relationships. Finally, he met a young teacher from Manhattan and persuaded her to take the tests for a low-level job at the State Department. She agreed, and we waited for some word of her progress.

As it turned out, the Greek had been working for the FBI. So, too, had the young woman. I didn't find that out until a few years later in Washington, and now I kick myself for not picking up strange signals from the start. I recall one occasion, in particular, that should have set off alarm bells. After we had set him up in the tourist business, Pompei announced he was going to Spain for a month. And almost as an afterthought, he said to me, "You must have a lot of illegals in Spain with whom you've lost touch. I could pass money to them if you want."

"Illegals" are agents working in foreign countries under deep cover, and they are prized intelligence assets. I thought it strange at the time that he would mention illegals in Spain, but figured that perhaps Makris wanted to be more useful to us than he had been so far. So I forgot about it—until our FBI mole later warned us about the Greek. In the meantime, I kept urging Makris on to greater conquests in love and espionage, realizing Moscow would not look favorably upon pouring so much money into an agent who was producing so little. But he never provided us with anything even remotely interesting.

During my five years in New York, the Cold War sputtered along, and my fellow agents and I inevitably experienced the fallout from major world events. In 1961, when East Germany erected the Berlin Wall, I did my best to spread the official Soviet line in New York. I thought the Wall was a bad idea, but maintained publicly it was a German—not a Soviet—creation designed to protect East Germany's shaky economy. After all, East Germany was a small country, I argued, and it would be ruined if many of its citizens were lured to the West by higher living standards.

Making the case for the Wall was not easy, but another event occurred in 1961 that was a propagandist's dream and made me proud as I have ever been to be a Soviet. On April 12, 1961, Soviet cosmonaut Yuri Gagarin became the first man in space, completing a brief orbit of the earth in his tiny capsule before landing in a field in southern Russia. His 108-minute flight shook the world, and showed that the Soviet Union had truly become the planet's other great superpower. At first, many Americans seemed pleased that a man finally had been launched into space. But as the nature of the achievement sank in, the U.S. reaction became more hysterical. The American media lost no time in pointing out that Gagarin's historic flight was closely linked with the USSR's burgeoning military power. We truly seemed to be winning the science and space race, and the United States was plunged into soul searching about the quality of American education and the heated competition with the Soviet Union. To me, the Gagarin flight was yet another sign that we were on the right track and that I was on the right side in the Cold War struggle. Now, looking back on those heady weeks following the first space flight, it's clear that Gagarin's achievement was the high-water mark of Soviet Communism. A few years afterward, with the dismissal of Khrushchev, my country would begin the long, slow decline that ultimately led to its collapse in December 1991.

Few world events in the early 1960s grabbed our attention as much as Cuba. In April 1961, our New York station was taken by surprise when Kennedy-backed Cuban exiles carried out the botched Bay of Pigs invasion. Realizing the U.S. administration's desire to overthrow the Soviet Union's Caribbean ally at any cost, Lubyanka immediately instructed KGB officers in the United States to strengthen ties to the Cuban exile community. Fortuitously, a friend of mine—a New York City bookstore owner involved in left-wing politics—introduced me to his daughter. She turned out to have a Cuban lover, a pilot, who secretly ferried Cuban exiles and arms back and forth to the island as part of a continuing attempt to overthrow Castro. I never met the Cuban, but the woman supplied, in great detail, information about his work: what planes he and his cohorts flew to Cuba, where they landed, where the exiles' Florida bases were. It all provided one more piece of the puzzle about the anti-Castro efforts. Later, I met a Peruvian writer, Katya Sachs, who introduced me to numerous Cuban exiles. Posing as a Russian émigré working for a New York City radio station, I chatted with the exiles, trying to put together a picture of their activities.

Moscow continued to bombard us with cables—"Tell us more about the Cubans. . . . When is the next invasion coming?"—and in late 1961 a golden opportunity arose for me to get to Florida to learn more about the situation. The annual conference of American trade unions was being held in Miami, and I received permission from the U.S. State Department to go there, ostensibly to cover the conference. Traveling with me was a KGB colleague, Mikhail Sagatelyan, who worked in the Washington bureau of TASS. We attended a few sessions of the union convention, then fanned out to the bars and restaurants Cuban émigrés were known to frequent. Posing sometimes as Russian émigré journalists, sometimes as journalists from Western Europe, we talked with numerous Cubans. Soon, we heard about a group of Cuban exiles planning another invasion of Cuba. After learning the group's address from one of the leaflets they were distributing, we rented a car and drove in the afternoon to the exiles' headquarters on the outskirts of Miami. On the way, I decided to pose as an Icelandic journalist, figuring no one in Miami—least of all in the Cuban exile community—would know that obscure Nordic language. Sagatelyan, an ethnic Armenian, posed as a Turkish correspondent.

A uniformed guard stood in the driveway of the tiny house, and let us in without questions when we told him we were Western journalists. We quickly found the leaders of the group on the second floor, and they launched into a tirade about how America and other Western governments had abandoned the Cuban exiles after the Bay of Pigs disaster. It came our turn to ask questions, and we decided to put the Cubans on the defensive.

"In Europe, we don't understand why it's taking so long to overthrow Castro," I said to the group's leaders. "When are you going to act? The whole world is waiting for you to take decisive steps to bring down this Communist dictatorship. We think you're just wasting American money here."

Determined to show us how forcefully they were moving to dump Castro, the exiles showered us with leaflets, memoranda, and literature that described their planning for a second invasion of Cuba. Sensing our interest was real, one of the leaders said he wanted to keep in touch with us and send more information.

"What's your address?" he asked.

We unwisely had not agreed on what Miami or New York address to give the exiles. In addition, we knew that giving out false names and addresses could lead to reprisals from U.S. authorities and possible expulsion. The exiles immediately sensed our hesitation. I quickly gave them the name of another Miami hotel, and they wanted to know the phone number. I told them I couldn't remember it. Several of the Cubans started mumbling something in Spanish, and one asked us, "Look, guys. Where did you say you came from?"

They told us to wait a minute. One of their leaders went into another room and got on the phone. We excused ourselves and began walking out, heading quickly but calmly for the front door. When we got to the street we dashed for our car, parked around the corner. As we roared off, we could see the Cubans running after us and gesturing angrily for us to stop.

Save for that close call, the Miami trip was a success. Our numerous conversations with Cuban exiles showed us that, while it was doing its best to mount another invasion, the Kennedy administration wasn't about to support a second attempt to use an exile army to oust Castro. The Cubans in Florida felt abandoned, and we came away convinced that, despite the anti-Castro fever gripping Miami, there was little chance his enemies would be able to topple him any time soon. Moscow was pleased with our trip, and we heard nothing more about our little foray into the heart of the Cuban exile camp.

Returning to New York, I hopped back on the treadmill of diplomatic receptions, press conferences, and meetings with students and other potential sources. Our station also became deeply involved in what we called "active measures," which essentially involved dirty tricks and disinformation campaigns. One of the most aggressive of our "active measure" campaigns was related to the emerging, postcolonial nations of Africa, where the United States and the Soviet Union already were locked in a struggle for influence. We in the KGB station in New York did everything we could to stir up trouble for the American side.

One of our dirty tricks involved a nasty letter-writing campaign against African diplomats at the United Nations—an idea cooked up by KGB headquarters in Moscow and approved by the Communist Party Central Committee. Our KGB staff, using new typewriters and wearing gloves so as not to leave fingerprints, typed up hundreds of anonymous hate letters and sent them to dozens of African missions. The letters, purportedly from white supremacists as well as average Americans, were filled with virulent racist diatribes. The African diplomats publicized some of the letters as examples of the racism still rampant in America, and members of the American and foreign press corps quoted from them. I and other KGB officers working as correspondents in the United States reported extensively on this rabid anti-black letter-writing campaign. I lost no sleep over such dirty tricks, figuring they were just another weapon in the Cold War.

Our "active measures" campaign did not discriminate on the basis of race, creed, or color: we went after everybody. Attempting to show that America also was an inhospitable place for Jews, we wrote anti-Semitic letters to American Jewish leaders. My fellow officers paid American agents to paint swastikas on synagogues in New York and Washington. Our New York station even hired people to desecrate several Jewish cemeteries. I, of course, beamed back reports of these misdeeds to my listeners in Moscow, who—tuning in to my broadcasts—no doubt thanked the Lord or Comrade Lenin that they had been born in a Socialist paradise, and not in a hotbed of racial tension like the United States of America.

Our active measures knew no bounds; we even had no respect for the dead. When the esteemed U.N. Secretary-General Dag Hammarskjöld died in a plane crash, I and my fellow officers did everything we could to fuel rumors that the CIA was behind it. I reported the rumors on Radio Moscow, saying that sources believed the CIA wanted Hammarskjöld out of the way because he was promoting too much freedom for black African countries.

In order to win propaganda points for the Soviet Union and further the Socialist cause, our active measures in New York also included the infiltration of left-wing and black nationalist movements. Several colleagues and I had good contacts in some black organizations, and even financed one Afro-American journal, *The Liberator.* We planted stories describing how America sided with the racist regime in South Africa and how the Soviet Union had solved its racial problems. I struck up a friendship with an editor from *The Liberator,* and went with him on several trips to Harlem, where I was the only white man in many of the clubs we visited. I knew our propaganda was exaggerating the extent of racism in America, yet I also saw firsthand the blatant discrimination against blacks. Again, I had no qualms about stirring up as much trouble as possible for the U.S. government. It was all part of the job.

One left-wing figure with whom I had close ties—and who unwittingly did the bidding of the KGB—was the publisher M. S. Arnoni, the editor of a journal called *Minority of One.* A Holocaust survivor, an ardent Zionist, and one-time editor at the *Encyclopaedia Britannica,* Arnoni was an eloquent and exuberant man. *Minority of One* was a highbrow magazine for the liberal American elite, and we decided to use Arnoni and his publication to further the Soviet cause in the United States. I was introduced to Arnoni in my capacity as Radio Moscow correspondent and we hit it off immediately, despite the fact he was decades older than I was. He was extremely knowledgeable about the situation in Israel—his circle of friends included such luminaries as Golda Meir and David Ben Gurion—and I often would forward to Moscow his assessment of events in the Middle East. At some point, I suggested that I should write an article for *Minority of One* and he agreed. In fact, the article on American militarism was written by the KGB propaganda department in Moscow. When I showed it to Arnoni, even this famed liberal found it too pro-Soviet, so I toned it down a bit. He published the piece under a pseudonym, and afterwards printed several more articles prepared by the KGB.

I told Arnoni that his audience was too limited and effete, and that my backers and I—to provide him with a larger national platform—would be happy to pay for an advertisement in *The New York Times* which would appear under his name. We worked together on the text of the ad, which criticized growing American involvement in Vietnam. After making a few changes, my superiors in Moscow gave their blessing and the KGB coughed up several thousand dollars for its publication. Several more *Times* ads were to follow, some of them signed by leading liberals who worked for such magazines as *The Nation*.

Arnoni frequently complained of financial problems, and I eventually suggested to him that some Soviet sponsors would like to make a donation to his magazine since it had been so faithful in presenting the Soviet view of world affairs. He declined at first, then eventually assented. The KGB gave him close to $10,000; at my suggestion, Arnoni broke it down into smaller sums attributed to anonymous donors throughout the United States. Thus did the KGB infiltrate a small yet influential American publication. Our smooth relationship with Arnoni continued until 1967, when Soviet support of the Arab side in the Six-Day War made him lose faith in our country and break off relations with our New York station.

Another one of my "active measure" projects was to contact the American author Charles Allen and help him in his research on Nazi war criminals living in the United States. It was a modest scheme, but perfect for the KGB: it made the United States look bad, and it was in our power to supply Allen information.

Allen, a former counterintelligence officer in the U.S. military, was doing extensive research on the dozens of Nazi war criminals who had fled Germany with the help of U.S. Intelligence organizations and emigrated to America. The U.S. government essentially forgave these men their war crimes; in exchange, the Germans promised to supply information about the Soviet Union or details of top-secret German rocketry and scientific projects. I heard that Allen was digging into this scandal and phoned him. Introducing myself as a correspondent for Radio Moscow and a Soviet whose family had suffered greatly at the hands of the Nazis, I offered Allen my services. He said he was lacking good documentary material, and I told him I might be able to help. Allen gave me the names of several war criminals living in the United States, and before long Lubyanka had dug up archival material on their crimes and forwarded it to me. With our help, he published a small book, *Nazi War Criminals in Our Midst,* which proved to be delightfully embarrassing to the U.S. government. Allen and I struck up a friendship; our families even took several excursions together to Long Island beaches.

Later, again with our help, Allen dug up proof that the NATO chief of staff, a German officer named Alfred E. Heusinger, had been involved in Nazi war crimes. He wrote a book on the case, *Heusinger of the Fourth Reich,* which proved to be another embarrassment to the United States and its NATO allies. Heusinger was later removed from his position, in part because of Allen's book.

Unlike my future assignments with the KGB, which would involve running spies and working with top-secret material, my job in New York at this time was more that of a troublemaker, propagandist, and low-level intelligence gatherer. I often hung out in a Russian émigré restaurant, Petrushka—sort of a New York version of Rick's Café in *Casablanca.* Owned by a charming and garrulous Russian singer, Marina Fedorovskaya, the restaurant was a hangout for New York's Russian community. Fedorovskaya attracted Russian artists, writers, businessmen, and a smattering of people from the émigré *demimonde* to her fashionable place at 78th and Madison. There were also KGB officers like myself, who hung out there not so much because we liked the vodka, food, music, and the other memories of home, but because Marina and others at Petrushka kept good tabs on émigrés we wanted to contact. She quietly helped us find several who we tried—with some success—to recruit. The KGB already had infiltrated numerous Russian émigré organizations: the New York–based, Russian-language newspaper *The Russian Voice* was a complete KGB operation, from financing to the appointment of the editor. We also had successfully penetrated virtually all the Soviet émigré nationalist groups—Lithuanian, Armenian, and so on. Later, when I became head of the KGB's Foreign Counter-Intelligence Directorate, I was to get more deeply involved in the subversion of these supposedly anti-Soviet groups.

One group that my fellow officers had under total control was Gus Hall's American Communist Party. One of our KGB case officers was assigned full time to the American Communists, delivering money and instructions from Moscow. I met Hall on several occasions, and was not impressed. We knew, for example, that he was as hypocritical as many of our Party bosses: Hall would denounce capitalist corruption while at the same time siphoning off Party money (Moscow money) to set up his own horse-breeding farm. We also knew that the American Communist Party had no chance of making serious inroads in the United States; indeed, when we got wind of a promising young American Communist who wanted to help our cause, we would contact him and warn him to stay away from Gus Hall's organization. FBI surveillance of the American Communist Party was so intense that it would have been foolish to have potential intelligence assets involved with the organization.

In the spring of 1962, the World's Fair in Seattle gave me an excellent opportunity to get out and see something of America. Joined by Stanislav Kondrashev of *Izvestia,* I headed to Washington State by rail, watching from the top of a glass-covered, two-tiered train as the spectacular scenery of the American West rolled past. The World's Fair was a great show, but what sticks in my memory even more vividly is a meeting I had with a local millionaire from Washington state. We were introduced at the fair, and he asked Kondrashev and me if we would like to see his business. We agreed, and he drove us to a small airstrip not far away. We watched in amazement as he clambered into a four-seater prop plane and beckoned us to follow. A half hour later, after flying over rivers and thickly forested mountains, we landed at his lumber mill. He showed us his tiny operation; then we ate lunch in a small wooden cabin with a group of lumberjacks. His pride in his work, the efficiency of his operation, and the seemingly good relations between the owner and his workers left an indelible impression on me. It was the first time I had seen small American business up close, and it was a far cry from the Soviet caricature of the cigar-chewing capitalist exploiting the unfortunate masses.

Kondrashev and I had not noticed FBI surveillance on the first leg of our trip, but when we rented a car and drove from Seattle to Portland, the FBI tail cars were unmistakably behind us. In Oregon we had an audience with the state's dynamic young governor, Mark Hatfield, then visited some Indian reservations, where I did the obligatory reporting about the disgraceful conditions in which Native Americans lived. We traveled to Reno, Nevada, and I vividly remember speeding through the desert at night, the scenery whipping past us at 80 miles per hour. The vast, empty desert and the enormous, star-filled sky left Kondrashev and me feeling insignificant and utterly alone . . . alone except for the headlights of the FBI tail car far behind us. We lost about $50 apiece in the Reno casinos, then flew on to Los Angeles and San Francisco. It was a fine trip, and made me wonder if the Soviet Union would ever be able to match America's vitality and prosperity.

That October, when the Cuban missile crisis erupted, I was on my way back to Moscow for vacation. The showdown over the placement of nuclear missiles had begun while I was still in the United States, and I knew from my reporting there—as well as from foreign radio broadcasts once I was back in Moscow—just how serious the situation was. But the atmosphere in the Soviet capital was strangely calm, in large part because our government was hiding the real danger of the crisis from the people. My KGB colleagues and I thought Khrushchev had acted recklessly, badly underestimating Kennedy's resolve and the severity of the U.S. reaction to the presence of the missiles. In the halls of Lubyanka, there was a collective sigh of relief when the crisis passed. There also was the sound of grumbling about Khrushchev, whose rash handling of the Cuban affair—and the humiliating about-face he performed after so many weeks of bluster—fueled the growing dissatisfaction with his leadership.

Upon my return to America later that fall, I watched Kennedy with renewed interest. His handling of the crisis had earned him great respect among my KGB colleagues, and we were instructed to continue supplying all possible information about his policies and private life. Like most Americans, I will never forget the day of his assassination and the hectic weeks that ensued. On that Friday afternoon, November 22, 1963, I was buying food and drinks for a reception at our apartment for foreign journalists. Suddenly, the shoppers around me stood stock still, then began shouting and heading for the door of the grocery. I was confused until I walked to the front of the store, where a radio blared the news that Kennedy had been shot and was being rushed to Parkland Hospital in Dallas. Arriving home, I turned on the TV and listened in disbelief as the announcer informed the country that Kennedy was dead.

I spent the rest of the day and night broadcasting detailed reports back to the Soviet Union for Radio Moscow. The next day, however, work for the KGB took precedence. By then, the news was everywhere about Lee Harvey Oswald's Russian wife and the months he spent in the Soviet Union. We began receiving nearly frantic cables from KGB headquarters in Moscow, ordering us to do everything possible to dispel the notion that the Soviet Union was somehow behind the assassination. In a long and unusually detailed cable, Lubyanka told us to report the simple facts: That Oswald had lived in Minsk, that he had never been trusted and was suspected of being a CIA agent, that he had been kept under surveillance, and that he left the Soviet Union and returned to America on his own, without KGB help. We were told to put forward the line that Oswald could have been involved in a conspiracy with American reactionaries displeased with the president's recent efforts to improve relations with Russia. The Kremlin leadership was clearly rattled by Oswald's Soviet connection, and in cable after cable the message we were to convey was clear: "Inform the American public through every possible channel that we never trusted Oswald and were never in any way connected with him."

I spoke with all my intelligence assets, including Russian correspondents and various U.N. employees, and told them to spread the official Soviet line. In the end, our campaign succeeded, and subsequent investigations have shown that the KGB—despite some contact with Oswald in the Soviet Union and Mexico City—had nothing to do with Kennedy's assassination.

One American correspondent with whom I spoke about the Kennedy assassination was a radio reporter for a local FM station, Ted Esterbrook; it would turn out that Esterbrook would be involved in the only serious American effort, while I was in New York, to recruit me. Esterbrook was a persistent and glib man who met me at a United Nations reception and afterwards pursued me with admirable—if annoying—diligence. He always wanted to take me out for a drink or dinner, and during our conversations he would ask questions about my life and the Soviet Union that went way beyond the bounds of normal curiosity. I was convinced Esterbrook was with the FBI or the CIA. So, in order to confuse the American side about my work and where my loyalties lay, I often praised America and criticized the Soviet Union while in Esterbrook's presence.

One day, Esterbrook showed up unannounced at my little summer house on Bayville, Long Island. He said he had a friend, a wealthy lawyer, who wanted me to stop by his nearby estate. We drove over to the friend's house, which turned out to be a mansion with a swimming pool and several acres of land. As we sipped cocktails, both Ted and his friend gently tried to feel me out about my views on the Cold War and our respective countries, and I again tried to leave them with an ambiguous impression.

A week later, Ted said he had another lawyer friend who wanted to have me over for dinner at his Park Avenue apartment. I accepted, and knew instinctively when I walked into the luxurious flat that the "lawyer" was a U.S. government agent, and that he and Ted were about to try to recruit me. I decided it was time to disabuse them of the notion that I was willing to betray my country. No sooner had we sat down at the table than I launched into a pro-Soviet diatribe about the USSR's stance in Berlin and East Germany.

"We suffered tremendous losses in the Second World War," I said. "In my family alone, five people were killed. Other families were wiped out completely. The Soviet people, as a nation of victors, are entitled to decide the postwar order in Germany. Any Americans who doubt our resolve to repel Western attempts at interference in Germany are deluding themselves."

Esterbrook looked crestfallen. So did his companion, who shot Esterbrook a look that said, "Hey, you said you'd bring me a guy who was willing to defect, and you brought me a Communist fanatic instead!"

That was the last I heard from the mysterious Mr. Esterbrook.

By this time, though I didn't know it, my five-year tour in America was drawing to a close. And the man who would force me to leave the United States was none other than Yuri Nosenko, one of the first Soviet defectors of the postwar period.

The word that Nosenko had disappeared in Switzerland came in February 1964. Our first information was that he had vanished under unclear circumstances. But several days later word came that he had defected while with a Soviet delegation in Geneva.

As defectors go, Nosenko was not a big fish: he was a captain in domestic Counter-Intelligence, meaning his main job was to investigate the actions of foreigners living or traveling in the Soviet Union. But he had apparently been planning to defect for some time and had squirreled away a fair amount of information. The fact was, however, that there had been few Soviet defectors in recent decades, and Nosenko's flight spread panic throughout the KGB. He was branded one of the great traitors of all time, and dozens of KGB officers stationed abroad who had had dealings with Nosenko were recalled: six officers in the New York station alone (including myself) were yanked back to Moscow.

There was another reason why the KGB reacted so vehemently

to the Nosenko defection. He was the son of a high-ranking minister in the Stalin government, and an investigation showed that this privileged officer—like so many other KGB officers—was a hard-drinking, philandering, and generally unreliable representative of our vaunted security service. Nosenko was having an affair with an attractive young woman who worked in the KGB archives. It turned out that she had been carrying on affairs with a small army of KGB men, and more than a dozen officers were subsequently fired for their association with her and Nosenko.

As the tremors from the Nosenko defection rippled through the New York station, I thought that I, at least, would not suffer from the actions of this traitor. But it turned out that Cook, the Thiokol scientist, would once again cross my path and affect my career. By sheer coincidence, Nosenko had, in 1963, arrested a well-known American leftist who was caught in a homosexual act with a Russian man in Moscow. Upon searching the American, they found a letter addressed to Cook's sister; it seemed that the leftist and Cook were friends, and the American visitor had agreed to deliver the letter. Nosenko began investigating the letter, and Cook's sister, and soon was told by the First Chief Directorate—Intelligence—to stay away from the case. He thus knew that Cook was involved with the KGB and probably was a spy, and Lubyanka feared he may have come across my name in connection with the case.

"As we have discovered, Comrade Felix [Kalugin] also was known to the traitor Nosenko," KGB headquarters said in a cable to the New York station. "As he has no diplomatic passport and is very active in intelligence work, it is better that his assignment be terminated and that he be brought home as soon as possible to prevent possible provocation."

So my first assignment as a KGB officer came to a close. It had been a fascinating, though frustrating, one. Indeed, I could see that our intelligence-gathering abilities were overrated: our New York station, for all the energy expended, produced very little in the way of first-rate information. But that was the spy game, and in my next assignment—Washington, D.C.—my record would improve.

Before leaving New York City in March 1964, there was one last, bizarre twist to the Nosenko case. Our station chief, Boris Ivanov—who later went on to head KGB operations in Afghanistan—called me in one day to discuss Nosenko.

"So many people are suffering from this traitor," Ivanov said.

"I know," I replied. "I am a victim of this treachery myself."

He gave me a strange look, and continued.

"This conversation is strictly confidential. I have an idea I am going to suggest to Moscow. During the next few days, a member of our embassy staff will meet with Nosenko in the State Department. It has been suggested that you participate in this meeting."

"If I must, I will," I replied. "Why not?"

There was a pause.

"I hope you haven't neglected your target practice," he continued. "Can you still shoot? Would you be able to finish off the traitor at this meeting?"

His question caught me offguard, but I quickly replied, "Of course I could."

"We could get you out of it later, of course," he went on. "You know, swap you for a Western spy. So there's no need to worry."

"I'm not afraid," I asserted. "I'm ready."

"I never doubted that," said Ivanov.

"Okay," I said. "Settled."

I was, indeed, prepared to go through with the plan. First, I was an officer and had to obey orders. Second, Nosenko was a traitor who had harmed hundreds of people and endangered the lives of some of our agents and spies. I was flattered they had chosen me for the job. But the longer I thought about my conversation with Ivanov, the more I realized how improbable his suggestion was. Why should the State Department allow a Radio Moscow correspondent into the meeting with Nosenko? And would Moscow really be willing to risk such a huge scandal, which the assassination of Nosenko was sure to have created?

Nothing ever came of Ivanov's scheme. In later years, I wondered why he had suggested it. Did he want to test my loyalty? Or was he merely trying to show he had enough admiration for my abilities to entrust me with such an assignment? I never found out. Ivanov and I never discussed the matter again, and as we both became more deeply immersed in the world of espionage, the case of the defector Nosenko receded further into the past.

FOUR

Washington Station

Moscow was even drearier than I had remembered. I had been spoiled—irretrievably, it turned out—by five years in New York City. Returning to the Soviet capital made me realize that worshipping Communism from afar was one thing. Living in it was another thing altogether.

Back in 1960, the KGB had given me a one-room apartment in the nether reaches of Moscow. Now that I was home again in the spring of 1964, the Committee for State Security thought that this cramped flat would do just fine—despite the fact that I now had a wife and two daughters. (Our second girl, ginger-haired Yulia, had been born in New York City. When we returned to Moscow and went to get her a Soviet birth certificate, an official at the birth registry office suggested we list her place of birth as Moscow. Putting New York City on her birth certificate could have an adverse effect on her future career, the official warned. "Record the truth," I told the bureaucrat, and to this day Yulia's capitalist origins have remained on her official record.) Desperate for decent living space, I turned to the State Radio Committee, my ostensible employer. They offered to sell me a three-room apartment, which I bought sight-unseen for 7,000 rubles. What a mistake! I was about to get a first-hand view of the "shining future" that Comrade Khrushchev and the Communist Party were building for the Soviet people.

Our apartment was located not far from the center of Moscow, in a new, five-story concrete building. Hundreds of these apartment complexes were built in Moscow in the Khrushchev era, and they were so distinctively horrible that they quickly came to be known as *khrushyobi*—little Khrushchev boxes. Walking into the apartment for the first time, Ludmilla and I nearly wept. Though brand new, it looked more like an old cattle pen—leaking walls, broken radiators, two tiny bedrooms, and a kitchen the size of a broom closet. Our instinct was to turn on our heels and flee. But where? Luckily, another fact of Soviet life saved us. We had terrific neighbors, and—stuck in the same miserable housing—we joined forces in true Soviet style and dreamed up several space-saving renovations, such as tearing down the flimsy wall between the toilet and the bathtub. That, at least, made it possible to turn around in the bathroom. The neighbor who helped make all this possible was Nikolai Kurnakov, an announcer for Radio Moscow's English-language service. He, too, knew America well: he had been born in Brooklyn to a White Russian officer who had fled his native land during the Russian Civil War. Kurnakov's royalist father experienced a change of heart in America, and during World War II he persuaded his son to return to the Soviet Union and join the army. Nikolai remained in Russia and was later joined by his parents, who unfortunately were subjected to intensive KGB interrogation for several months.

The country to which I had returned was in an odd state of limbo. Khrushchev's efforts to liberalize Soviet society had stalled, having run into implacable opposition from countless Party bureaucrats throughout the USSR's fifteen republics. His bungling of the Cuban missile crisis, his unceasing shake-ups of the Soviet Union's massive bureaucracy, and his general unpredictability had, by 1964, earned him powerful enemies. One of them was the KGB head, Vladimir Yefimovich Semichastny, who played a major role in the bloodless coup that would unseat Khrushchev just a few months later. Semichastny had been a Khrushchev protégé—a young, non-KGB, Communist Party official brought in to take firm control of the secret police—but he turned out to be a hard-liner who gradually turned against the Soviet leader. We didn't know it then, but our country was about to take a giant step backward, entering a period of retreat and stagnation that would last until Mikhail Gorbachev came on the scene two decades later.

I, too, was in a strange, suspended state. I was back in Lubyanka as a "burned" officer—meaning one who had to leave a foreign station for fear of exposure. As it turned out, Nosenko knew nothing about me and I could have remained in New York. But we didn't know that at the time, and so I returned to KGB headquarters, where I renewed old acquaintances and waited for my next assignment. I dreamed often of New York, of the bustle of Broadway, of the beatniks and underground life of Greenwich Village, of the emerald lawns of Riverside and of Fort Tryon Park in Upper Manhattan, which overlooked the Hudson River. I longed to return to America.

For the time being, I was officially stationed back at the State Radio Committee, on the foreign news desk. Just before resuming work there, a group of the First Chief Directorate—Intelligence—was asked to participate in a little war game with officers from the Seventh Directorate—Surveillance. I had to carry out three tasks while being tailed: meet an "agent"; carry out a "drop" of documents; and receive a package of materials from another agent. Luckily, I pulled off all three assignments without the rendezvouses or the document exchanges being noticed by my opponents from the Surveillance Department. They threw everything they had at me, but by darting in and out of crowded stores, subway stations, and underground pedestrian walkways I was able to lose the surveillance teams assigned to me.

No sooner had I settled into my work at the Radio Committee than I was summoned by the personnel department and told I would be attending what amounted to a training school for future KGB station chiefs. It was an honor to be chosen, for those selected for the advanced training were being groomed to head KGB operations around the world. I had reached the rank of major, and in September 1964, I joined thirty other young officers at a small, secluded compound just outside Moscow on the road to Gorky.

The head of the nine-month school was Ivan Zaitsev, a kind, savvy, and experienced officer who had served as KGB resident in Israel and Germany. We were well cared for: the food was excellent, our cottages were clean and cozy, and the school supplied us with cars to drive to Moscow whenever we wanted. We were taught psychology and other skills necessary to run a KGB station of anywhere from five to one hundred people. We also received instruction in the latest spy technology, be it long-range listening devices, miniature cameras, or sophisticated radio transmitters. There was a course in recent advancements in coding and decoding. But by far the most valuable aspect of the school was listening to instructors such as Zaitsev—and our fellow students—describe their on-the-ground experience in countries around the world. We discussed recruitments which had been successful and those which had gone awry. We analyzed the work of the CIA and other Intelligence services. And we talked about what the KGB could do to improve its performance in the spy war.

On the morning of October 14, 1964, I was heading to class when Alexander Feklisov, former head of the Washington station and now an instructor at the school, pulled me aside. Feklisov, who had known me since sending me off to Columbia five years before, confided that something strange was happening in Moscow.

"I just heard from Lubyanka that they're taking down all of Khrushchev's portraits at headquarters," he said in a whisper. "It looks as though it's curtains for him."

We listened all day for news of Khrushchev's removal, but there was silence until the following morning. Then it was announced that the Soviet leader was stepping down because of ill-health. The real reason, of course, was that the powerful members of the ruling Communist Party Politburo had grown tired of his helter-skelter efforts at reform and wanted to get Soviet Communism back on track. The Politburo summoned Khrushchev home from a Black Sea holiday and—with the heads of the KGB and the military lined up against him—informed the Soviet leader that his decade-long reign had ended. Khrushchev acquiesced and was sent into a comfortable retirement. As far as the Soviet masses were concerned, he might as well have died. There was no mention of him in the Soviet media until his death six years later, when *Pravda* published a small item saying that a pensioner, N. S. Khrushchev, had passed away.

I was depressed and disturbed by the news of Khrushchev's ouster. He had been far from an ideal leader. He was indeed unpredictable, getting caught up in harebrained schemes like his plan—dreamed up after his visit to Iowa—to plant corn the length and breadth of the Soviet Union. He had not done nearly enough to eliminate the Communist Party monopoly in all spheres of life or dismantle Stalin's totalitarian system. Toward the end, he was sanctioning the creation of his own "cult of personality"—the inevitable deification of a Soviet leader.

But he was the man who ended Stalin's reign of terror. It was Khrushchev who had tried to reform the lumbering, monolithic Soviet system. And Khrushchev, as well, who backed off the persecution of dissidents and ushered in an era of relative freedom in the arts and literature. And then, in the blink of an eye, the "Gray Cardinals" of the Kremlin had secretly met and decided to end Khrushchev's little experiment. It was shocking. I tried to tell myself that maybe it was all for the best, and even remember saying that

Leonid Ilyich Brezhnev—who succeeded Khrushchev as First Secretary of the Communist Party—looked like he might prove to be an energetic leader. How wrong I was!

Looking back, Khrushchev's ouster was a clear sign that the era of our long decline had begun. Even by the time of his removal, we had lost most illusions that our society would soon catch up with America's. Cynical jokes were already making the rounds, and by the time Brezhnev and Co. had gotten through with our country we would be left with little but cynicism. In one joke that poked fun at Khrushchev, one man asks another why the Khrushchevian mantra—"We will catch and overtake America"—could never come true.

"We can't catch and overtake the Americans," the joke went. "Then they'd be able to see our bare asses."

Another limerick went like this:

> *We caught up with America in the output of milk,*
> *But on meat, we fell behind: the bull broke his dick.*

In retrospect, it was not only Khrushchev who faded away during that bloodless October putsch. Our optimism, our hopes for a "shining future," went with him as well.

The KGB may not have been loyal to Khrushchev. But it remained loyal to the Communist Party, the Politburo, the Supreme Soviet—in short, to the Soviet state itself. Two months later, in an elaborate Kremlin ceremony, we were to be richly rewarded for our fealty.

In what can only be described as a big thank-you bash, our country's leadership invited more than two hundred stalwart KGB officers to the seat of Soviet power for an awards ceremony and a lavish banquet. I was one of those being honored, receiving the "Order of Merit" for my recruitment of Cook and my work in New York. If the Soviet leaders had cynically calculated that our morale would be boosted by this show of pomp, they were right. It was the first time in years there had been such a ceremony for the KGB, and I, for one, was elated as I walked into the Kremlin. I had never before entered this former fortress of the Czars, and standing under the vaulted ceiling of the Grand Kremlin Palace, waiting for a medal to be pinned on my chest, I felt a surge of pride and patriotism. Semichastny sat on the dais, as did Politburo member and former KGB head Alexander Shelepin. Representing the Soviet political leadership was Anastas Mikoyan, chairman of the Supreme Soviet. In a two-hour ceremony, we walked up to the stage, one by one, where Mikoyan's chief aide pinned the medals to our chests and shook our hands.

At the end of the awards ceremony, we officers—most in full dress uniform—were ushered into the gilded splendor of St. George's Hall. Row upon row of tables, laden with food and drink, awaited us. There was vodka and champagne, black caviar, sturgeon, and every imaginable kind of roasted meat. Semichastny, Shelepin, Mikoyan, and other leaders were there as well, and a hum of contentment and small talk filled the palatial room as we waded through the delicacies and drink. It was a splendid moment, and it is clear now that it was not only a thank-you for the KGB's loyalty during the coup. It was also a coming-out party, meant to show the KGB that—after years of scorn and travails under Khrushchev—the security ministry once again was ascending to its rightful place at the heart of Soviet society. Under Brezhnev, the KGB would become the "Party's Faithful Weapon," its "sword and shield." Our authority was, at last, on the rebound. And in 1967, when the forceful Yuri Andropov took over the KGB, our power would know no bounds.

In February 1965 I was summoned—out of the blue—by Boris Solomatin, the veteran KGB officer. He informed me that he was heading to Washington, D.C., as the new chief of station and was putting together a team to go with him. He said he had heard good things about me, had been impressed by my previous experience in the United States, and wanted me to accompany him as his deputy for Political Intelligence.

"You're going with me," he said.

"But what about my school?" I asked. "The course doesn't end until June."

"The hell with school," said Solomatin, and my fate was decided.

My colleagues agreed that Washington was the place to be.

"If you fail there, then having a scrap of paper saying you've completed this course won't mean a thing," one said. "If all goes well, no one will be interested in evidence of your qualifications."

My cover for my next American assignment was even better than my previous one as a Radio Moscow correspondent. This time I would be heading to the United States as a Foreign Ministry press officer, thus giving me a diplomatic passport and diplomatic immunity. To those who had known me in my earlier incarnation as a

Soviet correspondent, it would seem perfectly natural that I had decided to give up my career in journalism and begin working as a press attaché. And the KGB had infiltrated the Foreign Ministry to the same extensive degree that it had controlled the Soviet media. Nearly half the Soviet diplomats stationed overseas were officers of the KGB or Military Intelligence. Some of the genuine diplomats strongly resented that the long arm of the KGB had reached so deeply into their esteemed ranks. They could quietly fret and grumble about the situation, but the fact remained that they generally had to do what the KGB asked them to. Anyone who got too vocal about KGB control of the Foreign Ministry would not be sent overseas and might even be drummed out of the diplomatic service altogether.

Leonid Zamyatin, the head of the Foreign Ministry press section, took me under his wing during the four months I apprenticed there. He accompanied me to diplomatic receptions, where I occasionally saw Brezhnev—an energetic, bushy-browed man who had not yet taken on the fossilized look of his later years. I lunched once with the British ambassador in Moscow. And I got to know scores of foreign correspondents in my capacity as a "handler" of the foreign press corps, then under tight control in the Soviet Union. Once, I accompanied a group of U.S. correspondents from the *Los Angeles Times,* the *Baltimore Sun,* ABC News, and other media on a trip to the republic of Georgia—an excursion that, given the hospitality of the Caucasus Mountain people, turned out to be far more pleasure than work.

Before leaving for Washington in July 1965, I once again crossed the trail of Cook. My colleagues in Lubyanka informed me that in late 1964, the FBI—after receiving a tip from Nosenko—brought Cook in for interrogation. As it turns out, they were just fishing, for they had no evidence against Cook other than Nosenko's word that the scientist was involved with the KGB. The FBI accused Cook of being a spy, said they were about to arrest him, and urged him to confess. Cook kept his cool, however, and insisted he was no spy. They showed him pictures of dozens of men they claimed were KGB officers and Soviet Intelligence agents, but he could tell from the FBI's questioning that the Americans were casting about and had no proof of his contacts with me and the New York KGB station. Years later, when Cook and I met in Moscow, he told me he had done his best not to look directly at the photographs out of fear he might recognize me or another KGB officer and let slip that he knew us. Cook hung tough; but the interrogation left him rattled.

The Thiokol scientist immediately spoke to a lawyer, who advised him to leave the country for a while: he should purchase a ticket on Air France since, under de Gaulle, the French wouldn't let American authorities look at the passenger manifest. Cook followed the attorney's instructions and flew to Paris. There, he showed up at the Soviet Embassy, explained his situation, and asked the Soviet diplomats to inform Moscow of his arrival. Word came back that Cook was, indeed, a valuable asset, and the following morning he was on a plane to the Soviet capital. Cook settled down in the USSR, peacefully at first. In 1979, however, fourteen years after his arrival, Cook's case would develop into a full-blown scandal that would end with the scientist in jail and my career as a KGB officer in shambles.

Shortly before I was transferred to Washington, the KGB's chief of Intelligence, Alexander Sakharovsky, called me into his spacious, high-ceilinged room in Lubyanka to give me some encouragement and advice.

"You did a very good job in New York—we all know about it," said Sakharovsky, an energetic man who remained head of Intelligence for fifteen years. "We're putting you in charge of a lot of people now in Washington. You have to show them how to do a good job. Do not hesitate to set an example. By all means, don't treat it as a desk job."

And so, in July 1965, off I went to Washington.

Solomatin and I found a disorganized and demoralized KGB station. We had heard from KGB officers who had served in Washington that surveillance was so intense and security in our target institutions so tight that it was virtually impossible to work in the American capital. Indeed, when Solomatin and his new team arrived, the KGB station did not have a single American source supplying it with secret information. Solomatin set about to change that, and, with hard work and good fortune, he managed to do so.

The KGB operated in Washington out of the top floor of the Soviet Embassy—an imposing stone mansion on 16th Street. Of the hundred or so people stationed at the embassy, about forty were KGB officers. We were packed into a warren of offices, and driving us all was the intimidating—and inspiring—presence of Boris Solomatin.

Before leaving for Washington, I had heard that the new station chief was a hard man—unforgiving, demanding, and curt. That was accurate as far as it went, but it did not go far enough. He also was a real workhorse, with a keen intellect, a practical mind, and a talent for pulling off risky intelligence operations.

I will forever remember Solomatin wreathed in a cloud of smoke. He always seemed to have a cigarette in his mouth, and would sit in his small, bug-proof office from nine in the morning until nine at night, enveloped in a thick, choking tobacco fog. I can still see the smoke swirling over his desk and drifting slowly in front of the tall screens used to shield his office from FBI eavesdropping. If I ever develop lung cancer, I'll know where it came from. (I tried smoking once as a teenager. I lit up in our communal apartment in Leningrad, not expecting my father to come home. But he walked in, giving me enough time to toss the butt out the window. He sniffed the air and asked me if I had been smoking. I said that I hadn't, that the smell must have drifted up from the street. Without saying a word, my father marched downstairs, picked up the still-smoldering butt from the sidewalk, and returned to our apartment. He walked up to me, still silent, and slapped me so hard across the face that my ears rang. I have never since put a cigarette to my lips.)

Solomatin, whose cover at the Washington embassy was counselor, was probably the best station chief I ever worked with in my thirty-two-year KGB career. He was a glum, moody, stern-looking man with piercing, intelligent eyes. Forcing a smile or a laugh out of him was a Herculean feat, though I was able to do so occasionally as we spent more time together. We hit it off from the start, and I admired his ability—evident especially in the John Walker case— to mobilize people and unite them in carrying out a job. He was undeniably intimidating, and seemed perpetually unhappy with the way the station was run.

Solomatin's spoken English was far from smooth, but his command of the written language was superb, and few people were better at poring over a classified U.S. government document and figuring out its significance. He constantly hounded me to stay on top of a host of unclassified written sources and reports, as well, saying they were of invaluable help in intelligence gathering. His one weakness, if he had one, was that about once a month—in an effort to relieve the enormous stress of the job—he would get drunk. The following morning he would be back at his desk, apparently feeling fine. But occasionally during his drinking sessions his tongue would become too loose and he would criticize some top Soviet officials. Several times, Solomatin—who held tough, anti-American views—attacked Foreign Minister Andrei Gromyko for taking too soft a line with the United States.

His occasional drinking, and the ensuing outspokenness, may explain why Solomatin didn't climb higher in the KGB hierarchy. After leaving Washington, he became deputy chief of Intelligence for Asia and Africa. Solomatin was being considered for the enormously powerful job of chief of Intelligence, but the ruthless and cunning Vladimir Kryuchkov—who later became Gorbachev's KGB chief—derailed Solomatin's candidacy by whispering in Andropov's ear that Solomatin had a drinking problem. Kryuchkov then maneuvered himself into position to become chief of Intelligence, a job for which Solomatin was eminently more qualified.

Solomatin went on to become station chief in New York and Rome. In Italy he was involved in several successful recruitments of Western spies. But he never went as far as he should have, in large part because of an influx of Communist Party hacks like Kryuchkov who were increasingly shouldering aside qualified professionals. In 1987, when I began quietly criticizing the KGB and was trying to open a direct line to Gorbachev to discuss reforming the security agency, I turned to Solomatin for help. Like me, he had been put out to pasture as a reserve KGB officer, in his case overseeing the work of the State Planning Committee. When I told him I was thinking of going public with my criticism of the KGB—the first shoots of *glasnost* were just beginning to sprout—Solomatin urged caution.

"Don't do it now," Solomatin, who is ten years my senior, told me. "I agree with a lot of what you say, but if you try to wrestle with the KGB, they'll tear your arms off. They'll brand you as a crazy. They might do anything to you. You must leave the KGB with an impeccable record, and only when it's all over can you say anything you want. They won't be able to do anything to you then."

I took his advice, waiting until after I retired in 1990 to begin my public campaign against the KGB—a campaign that saw Kryuchkov and Gorbachev strip me of my rank and pension. And as I was working with the Soviet media to unmask the KGB, I asked Solomatin, then retired in Moscow, if he would be willing to help me. He said he would. So I sent reporters from several major Moscow newspapers to his apartment to speak with him. But when they got there, Solomatin (his hands shaking) told them he wouldn't talk.

The newspapermen called me to complain, and I got on the phone with my former station chief to say he had let me down. But the KGB had been listening to our conversations, and shortly after he had agreed to join me in my crusade against the security agency, Solomatin received a threatening call from a top KGB official.

"Listen," he told me over our tapped telephone line. "Head-quarters called and they told me, 'If you make a statement to the press, we'll do worse things to you than we've done to Kalugin.' They said they'd strip me of my pension, and worse. Oleg, you're ten years younger than I am. Maybe you can afford it. But I can't. I'm sixty-five. What'll I do if I'm left without my pension? I'm sorry, but I just can't do it."

I said I understood, and we hung up. This was not the same man I had known more than twenty years before.

But in Washington, our enemy was not the KGB; that fight would come later. It was the U.S. government. Operating right in the belly of the American beast, we set out to do battle.

I was Solomatin's chief deputy, with half of the Washington station's forty KGB officers reporting directly to me as head of Political Intelligence. Solomatin had three other deputies—for Counter-intelligence, Scientific and Technical Intelligence, and Illegals. The second most important branch was Counterintelligence, whose half-dozen officers in Washington were charged with trying to infiltrate agents into the CIA, the FBI, the Secret Service, and other police agencies. Counterintelligence also kept an eye on Soviet citizens in the capital, making sure they didn't defect or cooperate with the American side. In addition, Counterintelligence was assigned to infiltrate Soviet émigré organizations.

The Scientific and Technical Intelligence section had about five officers in our station, and their task was to obtain and analyze classified scientific information, as well as helping us with any technical problems, such as installing hidden microphones. The last of the four branches in the Washington station was the most secretive and, while I was there, the most unproductive. It was the section dealing with illegals—Soviet citizens or agents usually posing, under deep cover, as Americans. During my five years in Washington, including more than a year as acting station chief, I never learned of a single case of a Soviet illegal who had penetrated the U.S. government.

Officially listed as second secretary and press attaché of the embassy, I oversaw the work of about twenty Political Intelligence officers, their covers ranging from diplomat to doorman. Our three chief targets were the White House, the U.S. Congress, and the State Department. But we also targeted U.S. political parties, as well as think tanks like the Brookings Institution, whose scholars had wide contacts in the American government. Soviet Military

Intelligence—the GRU—was primarily responsible for penetrating the Pentagon. But when someone like John Walker strolled into our embassy and furnished us with top-secret information, the KGB—as the predominant Soviet Intelligence agency—played the lead role in running such an extraordinarily valuable spy.

A major part of my job, however, was to supply KGB head-quarters in Moscow and the Politburo with reliable information about U.S. politics and government policy. That dovetailed nicely with my cover job of press attaché, and as soon as I arrived in Washington I began to get to know some of the leading journalists and politicians in the capital. Among the journalists with whom I met were the columnists Walter Lippmann, Joseph Kraft, and Drew Pearson; Chalmers Roberts and Murray Marder of *The Washington Post;* Joseph Harsch of *The Christian Science Monitor;* Henry Brandon of *The Times* (London); and Carl Rowan, former director of the United States Information Agency. Speaking with them in their offices or at lunches or receptions, I would act like a good reporter, listening to their assessments of the political situation in the country. Rarely did I come up with a scoop for the Politburo, but the reporting of our section enabled Soviet leaders to have a better sense of American political realities—such as our prediction during the 1968 presidential campaign that Nixon would not be the anti-Soviet hard-liner Moscow feared.

I often went to my journalistic sources to get reaction to the latest events in Moscow—an exercise that sometimes bordered on the absurd. In March 1966, the Kremlin wanted reactions to what it considered to be the "historic" Twenty-Third Conference of the Soviet Communist Party, at which hard-liners and reformers fought over growing censorship in the country. In fact, few Americans had been paying attention to the Twenty-Third Party Congress. I went to see the eminent Walter Lippmann at home and asked him what he thought of the recent events in Moscow. To my dismay, Lippmann—who was quite weak by that time—knew absolutely nothing of the Party Congress on which I was supposed to be reporting.

"Really?" Lippmann said. "There was a Congress? You tell me what's going on over there. I must confess I am at a loss to understand your government's policy."

I couldn't simply cable back to Moscow that the gray eminence himself didn't give a damn about the Twenty-Third Party Confer-ence. So we chatted for a while, and I got his general thoughts on

Soviet-American relations and Soviet politics. Reports such as this one usually omitted any critical references to the Soviet Union so, at Moscow's request, I filed a bland cable about Lippmann's view of recent events in our country. Thus was the Soviet leadership lulled into thinking that the whole world followed the Congress with bated breath and applauded its outcome.

About a half-dozen times a year I would meet—usually at lunch—with the well-known leftist Washington journalist I. F. Stone. Before the revelations of Stalin's terror and before the Soviet Union's invasion of Hungary in 1956, Stone had been a "fellow traveler" who made no secret of his admiration for the Soviet system. After 1956, however, he had become a sharp critic of our government. Shortly after arriving in Washington, Moscow cabled me, saying we should reestablish contact with Stone. KGB headquarters never said he had been an agent of our Intelligence service, but rather that he was a man with whom we had had regular contact.

I called Stone, introduced myself, and we agreed to have lunch. Our first meeting was cordial, and we got together regularly after that. I came to view Stone as a sympathetic character, with insightful views on the U.S. political scene. Our relationship ended, however, following the Soviet invasion of Czechoslovakia in 1968. Shortly after the crushing of the "Prague Spring," Stone and I again met for lunch, but this time his manner was aloof. He warmed up somewhat as we ate and talked, but when I went to pick up the tab at the end of the meal—I usually bought our lunches since Stone was not a wealthy man—he angrily refused to let me pay.

"No, I will never take money from your bloody government," he said.

We split the bill and said goodbye. I never saw Stone again.

Another occasional source of "open" political information was Richard Valeriani of NBC News, who would give me his assessment of the Washington scene. But the news game is a two-way street, and occasionally I would try to help one of my contacts in the Washington press corps with a scoop. Such was the case when I told Valeriani about an upcoming meeting between President Lyndon B. Johnson and Prime Minister Aleksei Kosygin.

Occasionally I would openly try to recruit a reporter to supply us information in exchange for cash. Such was the case with two Japanese journalists, the first from the newspaper *Asahi Shimbun* and the second from *Kyodo Tyushin*. In the past they had given me some reliable information about China and their country's relations with the United States. I felt they were both sympathetic to me, and proposed bluntly that they feed me information in exchange for money. They declined. I was told later that both men went on to become top editors at their respective newspapers.

Indeed, among the Washington press there was more than a little suspicion that I might have been working for the KGB. Once, after Jack Anderson publicly identified me as a KGB officer, I went to a reception hosted by an Italian journalist, Girolamo Modesti, who had become a good friend. As I walked into the party at his office, Modesti saw me and shouted, "Here comes the famous spy!"

To which I replied, "Girolamo, I've always been a spy. How come you didn't know that before today?"

My staff and I, posing as diplomats, met frequently with leading members of Congress, including Senators Mike Mansfield, William Fulbright, Mark Hatfield, Charles Percy, Eugene McCarthy, George McGovern, Jacob Javits, and others. I once talked with Senator Robert Kennedy in his office, and he gave me a tie-pin replica of *PT-109,* the torpedo boat President Kennedy had captained during the war. Naturally, our relations were most cordial with liberals like Eugene McCarthy. Indeed, some conservative senators, such as Barry Goldwater, wouldn't give us the time of day. We didn't meet with these legislators to recruit them, but rather to divine the intentions and strategy of the U.S. government in the Cold War. Our superiors in Moscow—and their bosses in the Kremlin—also enjoyed getting cables saying that Washington's crack KGB staff had held a detailed conversation with a top senator such as Mansfield.

Though we didn't dare attempt to recruit a U.S. senator, we were not averse to trying to induce some of their aides to work for the KGB, although in my years in Washington we met with little success. At one point, it did appear that we had managed to recruit a senator's aide. One of our officers had struck up a relationship with the assistant, who briefed us on what was happening in the Senate and gave us some classified information from a research institution with which he was affiliated. But as I learned more about this aide, I became increasingly suspicious. The classified material he gave us was of little value. And his behavior seemed odd: he was easygoing, almost reckless, in arranging meetings with us, as if there was some power behind him protecting him.

I decided we had to find out if this man was genuine or not. So our technical people gave us a vial of sodium pentothal, or "truth serum." Our officer asked the aide to dinner, then slipped the serum—which generally made people feel weak and loose-tongued—in his drink. But evidently our officer slipped too much of the serum into the man's glass and, instead of loosening up, he began to throw up. He apparently suspected nothing, telling our officer the next morning, "I don't know what happened to me. Nothing like that ever happened before."

We tried another trick on this suspected double agent, and this time it succeeded. In Canada, we had a very highly placed agent in the Royal Canadian Mounted Police's (RCMP) Counterintelligence unit. Under a pretext I have now forgotten, we persuaded the Senate aide to travel to Canada. Before long, our mole in the RCMP reported that the aide was indeed an FBI agent. Shortly after the assistant returned to the United States, we broke off contact with him. And not long after that, my subordinate who had handled the botched recruiting job—he was officially in Washington as a TASS correspondent—was expelled from the United States. Shooting for so high a target as a senator's aide was a risky proposition.

Not long after I arrived in Washington, however, we began to have good luck in recruiting a variety of spies and moles, beginning with foreign diplomats in the capital, moving on to sources in the military and the CIA, and culminating in the astounding work of John Walker. Now, with the Cold War over and the United States the undisputed victor in the struggle, our efforts seem futile and sadly diminished. But a quarter century ago, with Soviet and American armies facing off around the world, the top-secret information my KGB colleagues and I were gathering seemed to us a matter of life and death: We never knew which purloined military plan or broken code might be the key to swinging a battle or a war in our favor.

In New York, with the exception of my dealings with Cook, I had had little experience with handling top-secret material and with the cloak-and-dagger aspects of the espionage business. Before heading to Washington, I was warned by colleagues, "Washington's just a small town where everything's controlled by the FBI. You can't move around, the government employees are scared of contact with Soviets, and the military shun all contact with foreign personnel." Strangely enough, KGB headquarters viewed Washington as one of the weakest links in our overseas intelligence chain, despite the fact that it offered far more intelligence and targets for us than any other capital in the world. Before Solomatin arrived, the officers at the KGB station in Washington were feeding Lubyanka straight political intelligence and little else. America's capital, it seemed, was not a good place for our Intelligence service to work. But with the arrival of Solomatin and his team, things started to change, and before long Washington would become *the* place to work. We discovered that we just had to be bolder and more aggressive and, with a little luck, we could get what we wanted.

Solomatin did not get off to a good start, quickly running into the kind of FBI trap that had been demoralizing the station for more than a decade. When we arrived, an officer in the scientific and technical section had been cultivating an agent in the U.S. Army, a supposed expert on military electronics. He had provided some interesting, though not terribly useful, classified information. But he was promising us far more. Then, the truth came out: Our mole was an FBI agent, and our efforts to recruit him were exposed in 1966. A scandal ensued, and the officer in the scientific section who had been handling the alleged mole was declared *persona non grata* and expelled from the United States.

Soon, however, the tide began to turn. We focused intensively on the other embassies in Washington, particularly those from NATO countries, and after several failed operations we cultivated some valuable sources in the diplomatic community.

One of my first assignments from Moscow was to contact the Norwegian Ambassador to the United States, who had worked for the KGB before his posting to America. Just as I was about to get in touch with him in 1965, he died of a heart attack. I then was assigned to the case of an ambassador from a large Arab country. This ambassador had been in the employ of the KGB for several years, and we met occasionally in Washington, where he passed me cables and other documents. He left within a year of my arrival. We also recruited several Asian and Latin American diplomats.

During my tenure, the most fruitful of our diplomatic spies was a top official from a Western European embassy, who furnished us with diplomatic cables, top-secret reports, recordings of his ambassador's conversations, and correspondence with the U.S. State Department. The diplomat, who had leftist political leanings, had earlier been stationed in Bonn, where KGB officers approached him on several occasions. But the relationship came to naught, apparently because our officers doubted his reliability.

Moscow instructed me to resume contact with the diplomat, which I did, meeting him on several occasions in Washington restaurants. I instinctively felt he was genuine, and so, after our second or third meeting, asked him bluntly if he would supply me with the latest annual report his embassy had sent to its Foreign Ministry.

He agreed, and in a few days I had the annual report—containing useful political information—in my hands.

I informed headquarters, and they quickly cabled back: "What have you done? This may spoil our relations with this country."

I sent back a reply that said, in effect, "What am I here for if not to do these kind of things? He gave me the annual report and you should be pleased, not angry."

Headquarters decided to let me run with the case, instructing me to ask him a long list of questions about NATO and the military and political situation in his country. He began supplying me with many useful, classified documents, mostly of a political nature. We saw each other frequently at diplomatic receptions, but he passed his material to me following prearranged meetings in the corridors of the old National Press Building. We would agree to meet at a certain time on a certain floor, and then each of us would walk the circular hallways until we ran into one another. It would have been impossible for FBI agents, if they had been tailing the diplomat, to have observed us without being observed themselves. I never took packages from him on the floor where we rendezvoused. Rather, we would head downstairs, where he handed me the documents before I ducked into the Press Club bar to have a drink with correspondents. Each time we met, I passed him a note with the date, time, and floor number of our next meeting.

We met for more than a year, and he received the relatively small fee of $500 to $1,000 for each package of information. He didn't seem to care much about the money, being one of that dying breed of spies who was betraying his country for ideological reasons. I lost touch with him after leaving Washington in 1970, but later heard from a colleague that he had continued working for the KGB into the 1970s.

We had another valuable diplomatic asset in Washington, a woman from a major European country, and we had snared her— as sometimes was the case—using sex and romance.

The woman had been posted to Moscow for two years in the mid-1960s. While she was there, the KGB's internal Counterintelligence Directorate—which was charged, among other things, with watching and recruiting foreigners living in the USSR—decided to try to recruit her. A young, handsome officer was assigned to the case, and soon he met the single woman (where, exactly, I am not sure) and began to court her. They had a passionate affair which continued up until the time the woman left Moscow for Washington in 1965. Before her departure, the KGB, knowing I was heading to America, had arranged for me to meet her at a diplomatic reception. I was introduced as a friend of her lover. He also was using a Foreign Ministry cover, so it seemed natural we would know one another. About two months later, the woman and I met at a picnic, and this time I informed her I was heading soon to our Washington embassy.

"Oh, really!" she exclaimed. "I'm going there too."

"Wonderful!" I replied in mock surprise, since she had told her lover months ago what her next assignment was. "Let's drink some champagne and celebrate."

Shortly after my arrival in Washington, we got together. She was an archivist at her embassy, and at first I told her that her lover in Moscow was working on a report and wanted some information about her country's foreign policy. We began meeting frequently at restaurants and receptions, and I asked her to bring me copies of diplomatic cables between her embassy and its Foreign Ministry. She promised to supply them, but at our next meeting she didn't bring them, protesting, "Oh, come on. I'd rather just tell you everything."

"Why waste time telling stories?" I replied. "Just bring the stuff to me and I'll stick it in my pocket. Won't that be easier?"

She was too fearful, however, and refused to bring copies of the cables. But she did agree to meet with me and recite what she had seen in top-secret messages and diplomatic correspondence. She had a good memory, and through her we learned the essence of some of the political issues being discussed at the top levels of NATO.

The woman must have suspected I was a KGB officer. But she wanted to help, in large part because she was still in love with our KGB man in Moscow and saw me as a link to that romantic past. We would meet in quiet, cozy restaurants and, though I never paid her, I did bring her scarves and jewelry and other presents. We would both have a few drinks, and I would sit there taking mental notes as she told me everything she could remember about the issues being discussed in secret at her embassy. It was valuable political intelligence, all made possible because of the conniving of our domestic Counter-Intelligence people and the play-acting of our handsome agent. I grew to like the woman, then in her early forties. After I left Washington I lost touch with her, to this day I don't know whether she continued working for us.

I was able to meet these diplomats freely because the FBI's

surveillance of me was spotty, at best. I didn't live in the Soviet diplomatic compound downtown, which was under constant FBI surveillance, but found a nice apartment for my family on Connecticut Avenue near the Maryland line. The FBI simply didn't have the manpower to tail me constantly, choosing instead to follow me intensively for a week or so. For weeks thereafter, there would be no surveillance whatsoever. My training at the KGB academies in Leningrad and Moscow came in handy, and I was able to spot a tail with little trouble. If I had a meeting with someone, such as the diplomat from Europe, I would take a circuitous route to our rendezvous site to make sure we weren't being followed. If I knew I was being tailed—and the FBI often made no effort to hide it—I would go about my normal business and do nothing to arouse the surveillance team's suspicions. I never contacted any of our spies or intelligence sources by telephone from my apartment, for it was a virtual certainty that our phones and apartments were bugged.

We worked hard at cultivating our moles in the Washington diplomatic community. But the fact remains that we never lifted a finger to recruit the most valuable spies we had in the American capital, culminating with John Walker: They literally dropped into our laps.

The first valuable American spy who came to us during my tenure in Washington was a man from U.S. Air Force Counterintelligence, an agency charged with ferreting out Soviet spies. He apparently was deeply in debt, and money seemed to be his sole motivation for passing us information. What he gave us turned out to be quite useful, including copies of U.S. Military Counterintelligence manuals. But his most valuable material concerned specific cases of Air Force personnel being investigated on suspicion of spying. Nearly all the people the Air Force surmised were Soviet spies were, in fact, not spies at all. But this man's information gave us a good picture of how the Air Force went about trying to identify and trap suspected Soviet agents.

One of the strangest experiences I had with an American spy involved a CIA man, once again a volunteer who approached us at great risk to himself. I am convinced that, in the beginning at least, he was not acting as a double agent. By the end of our brief relationship, however, he may well have been working again for the CIA.

The American agent came up to one of our officers at a reception, saying, "Listen, I know you're KGB," and shoved a package in his hand. As the man walked briskly away, he said, "You'll find all the instructions and meeting places inside."

Our officer immediately brought the package back to the embassy. We opened it and found several rolls of film of internal CIA memoranda and documents. It was clear the CIA man knew what he was doing and, from the material—which included a fascinating analysis of what sort of Soviet citizens were susceptible to recruitment—I concluded he was genuine.

"This is the right man!" I said, and ordered our officer to show up at the prearranged meeting and begin working with the CIA agent.

It turned out that he had been fired recently from the CIA—or so he said—and was looking for money. He passed us a lot of material, but the most valuable document was a long paper entitled "Detection and Approaches to Psychologically Vulnerable Subjects of the Enemy." In it, the CIA cited numerous examples of both successful and unsuccessful attempts to recruit Soviets around the world. The document also painted a portrait of those Soviet citizens most likely to become spies; later, when I became head of Foreign Counterintelligence, we used the CIA paper to attempt to figure out who might turn against the KGB. We even recalled several agents to the Soviet Union, fearing they so closely matched the CIA description of a potential turncoat that they were likely to be approached by the Americans and might even cooperate.

I have kept a copy with me to this day, and the CIA's portrait of Soviet defectors and spies was uncannily accurate, as the following excerpt shows:

> Soviet citizens are a highly disciplined group of people who have undergone extensive indoctrination, who are vigilant and extremely suspicious. Russians are very proud and extremely sensitive to any signs of disrespect. At the same time, many of them are adventurous, and they seek to break free from the existing restrictions.
>
> Acts of betrayal, whether in the form of espionage or defection, are almost in every case committed by morally or psychologically unsteady people. Treachery is essentially atypical of Soviet citizens. That can be concluded from the fact that of the hundreds of thousands of Soviets who have been abroad, only a few dozen turned traitors, and only several of those became our agents. Normal, psychologically-stable people—connected with their country by close ethnic, national, cultural, social, and family ties—cannot take such

a step. This simple principle is confirmed by our experience of Soviet defectors. All of them were single. In every case, they had a serious vice or weakness: alcoholism, deep depression, psychopathy of various types. These factors were in most cases decisive in making traitors out of them. It would only be a slight exaggeration to say that no [CIA] operative can consider himself an expert in Soviet affairs if he hasn't had the horrible experience of holding a Soviet friend's head over the sink as he poured out the contents of his stomach after a five-day drinking bout.

What follows from that is that our efforts must mostly be directed against weak, unsteady members of Soviet communities. Among normal people, we should pay special attention to the middle-aged. . . . People that age are starting their descent from the physiological peak. They are no longer children and they suddenly face the acute realization that their life is passing, that their ambitions and youthful dreams have not come true in full or even in part. At this age comes the breaking point in a man's career when he faces the gloomy prospect of pending retirement and old age. . . . The "stormy forties" are of great interest to a [CIA] operative.

This portrait of potential spies and defectors not only matched people from the Soviet side, but American traitors as well. Indeed, the report perfectly described the CIA man who furnished us with it.

Less than a year after the ex-CIA agent made contact with us, his KGB case officer was waiting for him one evening at a restaurant in Washington. Two men—either from the CIA or the FBI—approached our officer in the restaurant and said, "Look, we know who you're waiting for. He's not coming. Don't try to meet with him anymore. He's a crook and a scoundrel."

Not long afterwards, the retired CIA man contacted us again and asked for a meeting. One of our officers went, but this time the American handed us information of little value. We concluded that the CIA had probably reined him in and was trying to use him as a double agent, perhaps to stir up another spy scandal. In any case, it was clear the man was now useless to us, and we broke off contact with him.

Another spy who came to us and passed on reams of top-secret material was a soldier who worked at the National Security Agency

(NSA), which monitored and controlled communications throughout the world. Though not as famous or as valuable as John Walker, this young American handed over a significant amount of material to the KGB. The NSA, based in Fort Meade, Maryland, was not nearly as well known to the public as the CIA. Nevertheless, it was an enormous agency, crucial to America's espionage and counterespionage efforts. It monitored and decoded communications from around the world, including those of the Soviets, the Warsaw Pact, NATO, and other American allies. The young soldier was a "walk-in" who came to us in the mid-1960s, explaining that he was involved in shredding and destroying NSA documents and could supply us with a wealth of material. His motivation, too, was money and we set up a system—soon to be used again in the John Walker case—whereby the NSA soldier would leave his materials at "dead drop" sites in Maryland and Virginia. When he left the documents at a remote, prearranged rendezvous point, the soldier would pick up his payment—usually $1,000 per drop—as well as instructions on when and where the next drop would take place. Such "dead drops" enabled us to receive and pass material without ever risking the NSA man being seen with one of our officers.

The soldier's documents were highly classified; some even came to us partially shredded, as he obviously had to occasionally make a show of feeding the documents into the shredding machines. He handed us the NSA's daily and weekly top-secret reports to the White House, copies of communications on U.S. troop movements around the world, and communications among the NATO allies. He gave us whatever he got his hands on, often having little idea what he was turning over. A good deal of the material was of little value, and I spent countless hours poring over it in my cramped office in the Soviet Embassy, chucking out what we didn't need and translating valuable material to be cabled to headquarters in Moscow. I never once met the NSA soldier. Both his case, and the brazen espionage of John Walker, showed us how incredibly lax security was at some of the United States' top-secret installations.

The NSA soldier eventually left the agency and went to college, using the money he had received from the KGB to pay for his education. Eventually, he was handed over to the highly secret Department Sixteen of the KGB's Intelligence Directorate, which dealt with spies who had access to signal intelligence information, known as "sigint." For all I know, he may still be working as a mole inside the NSA or CIA.

*   *   *

By far the most spectacular spy case I handled in the United States was that of John Anthony Walker, a chief warrant officer who had access to top-secret communications at the headquarters of the United States' Atlantic Fleet submarine base in Norfolk, Virginia. Walker began spying for us in 1967. By the time he was unmasked by his wife eighteen years later, he had provided us with so much material that the Soviet Union was able—in the course of nearly two decades—to decrypt an estimated 1 million U.S. messages. His information was so good that our side had access to the battle plans of the U.S. Atlantic Fleet. Because of Walker, we knew in advance of U.S. naval exercises, and our ships—much to the amazement and consternation of the American admirals—sometimes showed up as the allegedly top-secret maneuvers were about to begin. Thanks to Walker, we often knew in advance the timetable of U.S. B-52 bombing runs in Vietnam. His material enabled us to break many of the United States' most secret codes.

I first heard of Walker on the day he showed up at our Washington embassy in late 1967. He had driven up from Norfolk, looked up the address of the Soviet Embassy in the phone book, and literally walked in the front door. Once inside, he told someone at the front desk, "I want to see the security officer or someone connected with intelligence."

At the time, our security officer at the embassy was a former deputy chief of the Latvian KGB, Yakov Lukasevics. In America, he worked under the alias Bukashev. He spoke little English. Walker had brought with him classified material about U.S. Navy operations in the Atlantic, as well as information enabling us to decipher the submarine fleet's communications. Even Lukasevics realized the material was valuable, and thankfully had the good sense to phone station chief Boris Solomatin.

"I have an interesting man here who walked in off the street," Lukasevics told Solomatin over a secure internal line. "Someone must come down who speaks better English."

We all were wary of "walk-ins"; for every one true intelligence asset there were a hundred crazies or CIA plants who came in off the street. Many Soviet embassies were downright afraid of these volunteers, also known as "well-wishers." There had been several instances where legitimate spies were at first turned away because KGB personnel thought they were acting as U.S. or NATO agents.

The most notorious case occurred in the KGB's Mexico City station in the early 1970s, when CIA officer Philip Agee walked in and offered to tell all about American Intelligence. Our officers there thought he was a CIA plant and chucked him out; later, Agee would go to the Cubans and supply invaluable information about CIA operations and agents worldwide.

After a while, discerning who was genuine and who was not became easier, though by no means were one's instincts foolproof. But from the start, it was clear to us that Walker was the real thing. His material was simply too authentic and too valuable for the Americans ever to use it in a double agent ruse.

One of our English-speaking officers went down to see Walker. The American told our man point-blank, "I'm a naval officer. I'd like to make some money and I'll give you some genuine stuff in return. I want to make arrangements for cooperation."

"Wait a second," our officer replied. He took Walker's material and came upstairs, where Solomatin and I were sitting in the station chief's office. The officer handed us the documents which, though we didn't know it at the time, included a month's key settings for a top-secret cipher machine. We had never seen anything like this material—about the only remotely comparable documents we had laid eyes on were brought to us by the soldier from the NSA. We compared the language and the classifications with the NSA material and it was clear that what Walker was passing to us was real. In addition, Solomatin, who had grown up in the Black Sea port of Odessa, was a navy buff. His eyes widened as he leafed through the Walker papers.

"I want this!" he cried. "What are the conditions?"

Our officer returned downstairs, where he gave Walker an advance of several thousand dollars and arranged a meeting with him later in the month at an Alexandria, Virginia, department store. Walker was warned never to come back to the Soviet Embassy; then he was dressed in an oversized hat and coat, placed on the floor of a car between two large KGB men, and driven out of the embassy. When our officers were far away from the embassy and certain they had not been followed, they let Walker out of the car.

Though I would become deeply involved in the Walker case over the next two years, I never once laid eyes on the man. As instructed, he never came back to our embassy. In the future—using a plan devised by Solomatin, me, and Walker's case officer, Yuri Linkov the Navy officer would drop off his material at remote sites in the

Washington area. It was at these sites, too, that he would receive some of the more than $1 million we eventually paid him. Though we only vaguely sensed it at first, Walker would become one of the most daring and damaging American spies in the history of the Cold War. I had no idea just how big he would be, nor how high he would launch my already soaring career in the KGB.

At the Washington station and at KGB headquarters in Moscow a small group of people anxiously awaited the next batch of information from Walker. We knew how valuable he would probably be, so, for security reasons, only three of us began to work with the American spy—Solomatin, myself, and Walker's case officer, Linkov. At Lubyanka, only a handful of the most senior officers knew of Walker's existence.

Several weeks after Walker came to the embassy, Linkov rendezvoused with the American at the department store, paying him $5,000 for a series of cards that would enable us to break the code on the Atlantic Fleet's ciphers. Such a sum was enormous at the time, for we were a surprisingly cheap organization when it came to paying spies. Eventually, on specific authorization from Moscow, we paid Walker $10,000 for each drop.

Walker said later that his meeting at the department store was the last face-to-face rendezvous with Linkov. I believe there was one more. In any case, realizing the meetings were too risky, we quickly switched to a system of "dead letter boxes" or "dead drops." We put countless hours of planning into these dead drops, and in the two years I helped handle Walker—and, I believe, in all the subsequent years—not one of the drops went awry. They worked in the following manner.

In his last face-to-face meeting, Walker was given a time and an exact location where to make his next drop to the KGB. That set off a chain of drops in which he would deposit his material, while at the same time collecting his money and instructions on the next drop. Say, for example, Walker had been instructed that the next drop would be on January 20. Prior to assigning him that drop, Linkov and I would have scouted out a remote location, usually in the woods, where the drop could take place. At the start of our work with Walker, I drove all over the Maryland and Virginia countryside looking for places that were at once remote, yet at the same time accessible to Walker and the KGB. Later, Linkov would take over the search for the drop sites, and he would spend many of his weekends on such scouting missions. On the map, a place might look fine for a drop. But in reality it might be in the midst of a rural black community, where the presence of white men would be suspicious. Or it might be near a police station. Or a military base. So we put an enormous amount of thought into the location of the drop sites.

Once a site had been selected and Walker notified at the previous drop, on the date arranged the Navy man would leave Norfolk—making sure he was not being followed—and head to the location. Later, we would supply him with detailed photographs of where to drop his material, but in the beginning he did fine following written instructions and a map. In the beginning, also, before we gave him a camera, he delivered entire bags of documents, so the drop sites were always in remote woods where we were sure no one would stumble upon the bags. After making his drop and picking up his money and instructions, Walker would drive away. According to a prearranged plan, he would then leave a sign that he had made his drop. He might draw an "X" on a certain telephone pole, or drive to a McDonalds restaurant and leave a mark on page 500 of the Virginia telephone directory.

Then, some fifteen to thirty minutes after the drop, Linkov would show up at the location where Walker had left the mark. Linkov would see the "X" or the telephone book notation and, knowing Walker had deposited his material, would proceed to the drop site and pick up the bag. Linkov then drove to another prearranged site, where he made another "X" on a telephone pole or a mark in a telephone book, showing Walker that the material had been collected. Walker would drive to that site, see the sign that Linkov had picked up the documents, and then head home, knowing the drop had been completed successfully. A few weeks later, the whole process would be repeated.

My job was, first, to go over every aspect of the drops to ensure they were foolproof. Walker was a huge catch, and we knew that if we fouled up and lost him it would not only be the end of one of the great spies of the Cold War. It also would be the end of our careers. Solomatin and I both had to literally sign off on the "dead drop" plans, a clear signal from Moscow that our jobs were on the line. We sweated over the sites, and thankfully did not slip up.

My second—and most time-consuming—task in the Walker case was to sift through the mountains of material supplied by the American, translating what was urgent and cabling it to Moscow. The remainder of the material we would either translate later or forward to Moscow by diplomatic pouch.

The sheer volume of Walker's information was staggering. In the beginning, he would dump hundreds or thousands of pages on us at every drop. Later, when he became proficient in the use of a tiny Minox camera, he delivered rolls of filmed documents, which he would hide at the drop sites in Coke cans. As a communications watch officer on the staff of the commander of the U.S. Navy's submarine forces in the Atlantic, Walker got his hands on an astonishing variety of material. First, there were documents on the movement and activity of the Atlantic Fleet. Then there was information that enabled us to break the United States' codes. In addition, since Norfolk was a center of U.S. Naval Intelligence, Walker had access to communications and documents from the CIA, the State Department, and other agencies. It was a real cornucopia, and what amazed us was how easy it was for Walker to simply stuff top-secret documents in his clothes or briefcase and walk out of the communications center of such a crucial American naval base. Later, he was able to photograph the documents with similar ease, often doing so on the night shift, when he was the only person on duty. After his arrest, Walker would remark that "K-Mart has better security than the Navy."

Trying to make sense of the documents, especially at the beginning, was an ordeal. They were filled with incomprehensible Navy and Pentagon abbreviations and communications jargon. Using dictionaries and a few American and Soviet reference books, Solomatin and I gradually were able to make sense of all the gibberish and figure out what information the documents contained. Initially, I would spend an entire week just translating the most urgent material from a drop and cabling it to Moscow. Some of Walker's material was, indeed, urgent, for it might contain information about ship or troop movements around the world—information that was of great value to the KGB and the Soviet armed forces. We would then forward material to Moscow that was not of immediate operational value, and a team of experts at Lubyanka would study it. Our code specialists would utilize the cipher keys and other information from Walker to crack the U.S. Navy codes. Breaking the codes was, of course, invaluable in case of a military buildup or war situation, not to mention the enormous peacetime advantage it gave our side in intelligence gathering and monitoring the Atlantic Fleet's activities.

Being present at the creation of such an important spy and being one of only three KGB officers handling his material in Washington was a thrill, though the crush of work from Walker often left us exhausted. He was, in fact, the kind of spy one encounters once in a lifetime. After I left Washington in 1970, I lost touch with the Walker case, though occasionally—in my capacity as head of Foreign Counterintelligence—I would receive snatches of information that showed Walker was still alive, well, and active. His case, as with the NSA soldier, was transferred to the top-secret Sixteenth Department, which oversaw the handling of agents involved in classified communications. Department Sixteen did such a good job keeping Walker a secret that even high-ranking KGB defectors didn't know about the American spy. Vitaly Yurchenko was one such defector who, though security officer at the Washington station from 1975 to 1980, never heard of Walker.

Walker went on to recruit his son, his brother, and a close friend, brazenly creating a large spy ring. He even tried, and failed, to recruit his own daughter. After meeting with KGB officers in Washington in 1967, Walker went ten more years before meeting one of our officers face to face. That subsequent rendezvous took place in Casablanca in 1977, when he met his handler from the Sixteenth Department. Later, having retired from the Navy and hired his Navy friend Jerry Whitworth to continue the spying, Walker met twice a year with his KGB handler in Vienna. Once, Walker's controller told him that Moscow considered his work so valuable that the Soviets had made him an honorary admiral in the USSR Navy.

Finally, in 1985, Walker's ex-wife—who had suffered years of abuse at his hands—reported him to the FBI. His spectacular eighteen-year career as a spy was at an end. Walker was sentenced to life in prison.

For those of us involved in the case, Walker was a great coup and gave our careers a tremendous boost. Solomatin received the Order of the Red Banner and promotion to deputy chief of Intelligence, though Kryuchkov eventually derailed his career. Yuri Linkov, Walker's first handler, was awarded the Order of Lenin. Walker's second handler, a man named Gorovoi, became the first KGB officer in decades to win the country's highest award, Hero of the Soviet Union.

As for myself, I was awarded the prestigious Order of the Red Star. And my participation in the safe handling of Walker was undoubtedly the major factor that led to my becoming, in 1974, the youngest general in the postwar history of the KGB.

Long after Walker was exposed, people would ask me if I looked down upon or detested such spies as John Walker or Kim Philby. In all honesty I did not, though I readily admit to having a double standard. I had nothing but contempt for my fellow countrymen, such as Yuri Nosenko and Oleg Gordievsky, who defected. They were traitors whose actions weakened the Soviet Union and jeopardized the lives and careers of my fellow officers. Even though I was one day to become a staunch critic of the KGB, I never considered defecting and working for the CIA. Perhaps it was my superpatriotic boyhood, perhaps it was because I had lost so many relatives during the war, perhaps it was the memory of my father, who would certainly have personally shot me had I gone over to the other side. I loved my country and was deeply attached to it. And though, as the years passed, I grew ever more critical of my government, I thought—until the bitter end—that it could be reformed. Besides, I had no desire to run to another country, be pumped dry of everything I knew about the Soviet Union and its Intelligence service, and then be cast aside, to live a life of isolation. I liked America a great deal, but felt I would always be a second-class citizen if I moved there. No, for better or for worse, the Soviet Union was my homeland. For me, defection was unthinkable.

When it concerned defectors from the other side, however, my harsh moral scruples disappeared. It was the defectors' business if they wanted to turn against their own country. I, for one, was delighted that people like Walker or Philby had decided to help our cause. Naturally, I had more respect for someone such as Philby who became a spy out of the deep ideological conviction that the Soviet system was superior to capitalism. But even spies motivated purely by money, such as Walker, earned my respect. I understood what risky lives they led, and also knew that once they had been milked for every bit of information, it was inhuman—and ultimately foolish—to cast them aside like an empty vessel. Such was the fate of Philby, and I am proud to say that I would later play a pivotal role in rehabilitating the famous British spy.

Our activities in Washington were hardly confined to cultivating and handling spies such as John Walker. In my five years there, we also were deeply involved in "active measures" (dirty tricks), efforts to locate and re-recruit—or even assassinate—Soviet defectors, and attempts to expand electronic surveillance of U.S. institutions. Nothing matched our scheme to place a bug in the U.S. Congress.

The attempted bugging of Congress was a reflection of the aggressive, "can-do" attitude Solomatin brought to the Washington station. In our first two years in the American capital, we had talked from time to time about the tremendous intelligence value of a well-placed bug in the U.S. Congress. But we hatched our plan slowly, primarily because of the scandal that might ensue if we were caught planting or using the bug. At first we considered installing a microphone in the U.S. Senate Foreign Relations Committee, hoping to listen in on its closed sessions. But our officers, including a TASS correspondent who spent a lot of time on Capitol Hill, advised us that security was too tight in the Senate committee, making the bugging too risky.

Finally, we decided it would be possible to bug the House of Representatives' Committee on Armed Services. The committee, at its closed sessions, was known to discuss top-secret issues relating to all aspects of America's military. A bug in the committee room would be an absolute gold mine, and we decided to give it a try.

The best way to bug the room, we decided, would be to send the TASS correspondent to an open hearing. Then, when the hearing was over and reporters and congressmen lingered to talk to one another, the TASS man could plant the bug in a hidden spot and leave. The bug had to be wire-less and have a sufficiently strong battery to transmit for an extended period of time.

We contacted the KGB's technical department, the scientific whizzes in Moscow who could do anything from installing poison darts in umbrellas to spying on someone from a satellite. We told them our problem and, before long, they had sent us what we needed: a battery-powered, wire-less bug concealed in a thin, wood panel. On the top of the panel were small, sharp metal spikes enabling an agent to affix the bug to the underside of a table. The bug looked perfect. In the summer of 1967, we decided to put the plan into action.

After studying a detailed diagram of the Armed Services' Committee hearing room, the TASS correspondent went to an open hearing, the device in his pocket. When the hearing adjourned, he milled about for a while, then stealthily withdrew the bug and quickly affixed it to the underside of a table.

We had placed agents with a receiver in a car just a few blocks from the Capitol. But they were unable to pick up anything. The bug didn't work. At the time, we didn't know why, figuring the device was faulty or had been discovered. Decades later, when I returned to America in 1991 as a critic of the KGB, a member of the American Intelligence community told me they had found the bug, had disarmed it, and left it in place.

"Mr. Kalugin, we know it was your idea to bug the House committee," the American said.

"Yes, of course," I replied.

"Well," the American said, smiling, "we found the bug."

"Hmm," I replied, also grinning. "I didn't know that."

At the time, we had been afraid to retrieve the bug from the Armed Services Committee, worried the FBI would be waiting for us and would turn the matter into an international incident. So we never went back for the wooden panel, and it was a good thing: Years later, the American Intelligence source said the FBI *had* been waiting for us.

We had better luck with a more far-reaching attempt at electronic eavesdropping. Our technical people in Moscow had devised a state-of-the-art series of antennae capable of intercepting all open airwave communications. In 1967, we placed the antennae on the roof of our embassy, and suddenly we were able to overhear the communications of the Pentagon, the FBI, the State Department, the White House, the local police, and a host of other agencies. These communications all were broadcast on open, non-secure channels, but nevertheless a surprising amount of useful material was relayed over the airwaves. Transcripts of the conversations, when compared with other classified sources of information at our disposal, enabled us to piece together everything from the Secretary of State's travel schedule to the latest crimes being investigated by the FBI.

Over the course of several years, one of the most amusing conversations we overheard—and one which delighted our superiors in Moscow—was an intercepted phone conversation between the national security adviser at the time, Henry Kissinger, and his fiancée, Nancy. He apparently had just given a speech and, in his egotistical manner, was asking her what she thought of it. He was saying, in effect, "How did I look? You really thought I sounded well?" The transcript showed Kissinger to be a vain and boastful man. We forwarded it to Moscow, not thinking much of it. Then word came back that Yuri Andropov, chairman of the KGB, loved the intercepted conversation. He had reported on it to a regular meeting of the ruling Communist Party Politburo, proudly showing the Soviet Union's leaders that his KGB officers in Washington were so on the ball that they were plucking out of the air the intimate conversations of Richard Nixon's national security adviser.

*   *   *

The Washington station, like its New York counterpart, also was engaged in a series of "active measures" to counter what we saw as anti-Soviet propaganda emanating from the United States. We even dreamed up some anti-American propaganda of our own. While I was in Washington, the Soviet Union was under increasing attack for its discrimination against Jews and refusal to allow some Jews to emigrate. Our bosses in Moscow branded these attacks as an "ideological diversion" and ordered us to fight them. We did so by once again flooding American Jewish organizations with anonymous, rabidly anti-Semitic materials, as well as by hiring people to desecrate Jewish graves and paint swastikas on synagogues. Then, of course, the Soviet media faithfully reported on the wave of anti-Semitic activity sweeping America.

In the late 1960s and 1970s, one of our station's more innovative dirty tricks campaigns involved the doctoring of purloined American documents. We would take CIA, Pentagon, or State Department documents—obtained from a variety of sources—insert sinister phrases in them, stamp them "TOP SECRET," and pass them on to leftist journalists in America or around the world. For example, we might obtain a State Department document about the threat of Communist takeovers in Italy or France. The document might primarily have been an analysis of left-wing movements in those countries, but we would insert a sentence such as "The United States government, after assessing the situation, suggests that the U.S. must put its troops on alert." It was all a lie, and the American media didn't fall for such ruses. But the media around the world often regurgitated our disinformation, and our own media would have a field day with the KGB-doctored documents showing that America was an aggressive, imperialistic nation. None of these "active measures" had a determining effect on the outcome of the Cold War, but they were a nuisance for the United States and played a role in our ongoing propaganda battle.

Under Solomatin, our station also stepped up efforts to locate Soviet defectors from the postwar era. In some cases, such as that of Yuri Nosenko, our assignment was to carry out the death sentences handed down by Soviet courts. These assassination efforts were known as "wet jobs," and in my time in Washington our superiors in Moscow were extremely reluctant to order such killings. I'm certain that had we found Nosenko we would have received permission to kill him, but it was a moot point. We never located him. We did, however, manage to find other defectors. Our goal was to re-recruit them or lure them back to the Soviet Union to score a propaganda coup against the United States.

Nikolai Popov, who came to Washington around 1967 as the new chief of Counterintelligence, worked closely with Solomatin and me to locate Soviet defectors on American soil. Perhaps the most intriguing case was that of Nikolai Fyodorovich Artamonov. The effort to bring Artamonov back to Russia was a convoluted affair involving double and triple dealing; before it was over, Artamonov's case would also be the only time, in all my years with the KGB, when I was present at the death of one of the spies with whom I had become involved.

Nikolai Artamonov was a tall, handsome seaman who had served with a Soviet naval squadron in the Polish port of Gdansk in the 1950s. He was extremely bright and regarded by his superiors as one of the finest young officers in the Soviet Baltic Fleet. While only in his early thirties, he became commander of a torpedo-carrying destroyer. He was being considered for transfer to the Naval Forces Staff, where he would have undoubtedly been promoted to admiral in due time. Artamonov, however, fell in love with a Polish woman, and in June 1959 he commandeered a launch and defected with his lover to Sweden. He left behind a wife and young son. In Sweden— and later in America—Artamonov told the CIA everything he knew about the Soviet Navy and its Baltic operations. The damage he caused was considerable, though not catastrophic.

A Soviet court sentenced to him to death *in absentia,* and KGB stations around the world were alerted to keep an eye out for Artamonov. Through various intelligence channels, the KGB received word that Artamonov had moved to America and was working as an analyst for the Office of Naval Intelligence. By the time I arrived in Washington in 1965, the hunt for Artamonov had dragged on six years. When the new Counterintelligence chief, Popov, arrived, we redoubled our efforts to locate Artamonov. We put out feelers to members of the émigré community in Washington, but to no avail. Then, around 1967, one of our sources in the academic community informed us that a former Soviet naval officer was giving a series of lectures at Georgetown University on Soviet military policy. We sent an agent to one of the lectures with a picture of Artamonov and, to our surprise and great satisfaction, the lecturer turned out to be none other than the dashing defector himself. He was lecturing under the name of Nicholas Shadrin.

We found his address, and began discreetly tailing him. Soon, we had a good idea of his schedule and habits. Simultaneously, in Leningrad, the KGB met with his wife and son. They were persuaded to write heart-tugging letters to Artamonov, pleading with him to return home. The boy was just about to enter college, and the KGB told him to write that his father's treachery had ruined his life. I do not have a copy of the son's letter, but it went something like this: "Father, I want to become a navy officer like you, but because of what you've done my dream will probably never come true. Father, we love you dearly! You still have a chance to repent and serve your country and do your duty by your family. Please come home!"

Moscow sent a special agent, working under diplomatic cover, to Washington to make the initial contact. We had long ago decided it would be best not to assassinate Artamonov, but rather to persuade him to work for us and then return to the Motherland to expose his appalling treatment at the hands of the CIA and the decadence of life in the West. We knew that approaching him would be highly risky, since he had already been working for years for the CIA.

We decided to make contact with Artamonov in a public place—there would be no risk of a bugged office or apartment—and chose a suburban supermarket. Armed with two letters, one from Artamonov's spurned wife and one from his son, the Moscow KGB man walked up to the defector in a grocery store aisle and said in Russian, "Hello, sir. We've been looking for you. I think we need to have an important chat."

Artamonov was stunned and visibly shaken. But he pulled himself together, and he and the Moscow KGB officer went to a nearby restaurant and began to talk. The officer handed Artamonov the two letters, which he read with a stricken look on his face. In a matter of minutes, Artamonov agreed to turn against the CIA and begin working with us.

The Artamonov case, from all sides, was marked from the start by Byzantine duplicity. I only recently learned that the KGB officer from Moscow who approached Artamonov was already working for the CIA. He was Igor Kochnov, a KGB colonel, who contacted the CIA in Washington and volunteered his services. He undoubtedly alerted the Americans from the start about our approach to Artamonov. Later, when I was head of Foreign Counterintelligence in the 1970s, we would strongly suspect Kochnov of being a CIA agent and put him under surveillance. But we were never able to prove it. Kochnov, the son-in-law of the USSR's Minister of Culture, died of a heart attack before his treason was revealed in a recent American book. We had nothing to do with the death of the man, who was a well-known womanizer. What was interesting about Kochnov was, despite the fact that he supplied the Americans with valuable information, the CIA's notoriously paranoid head of Counterintelligence, James Jesus Angleton, never believed that Kochnov and several other defectors were for real.

At the time, we thought we had a major accomplishment on our hands in the rerecruitment of Artamonov, whose code name became "Lark." On the very day he was first approached by our Moscow officer, Artamonov wrote an impassioned letter in which he promised to do "everything" to pay for the crime he had committed against the Soviet Union and to work wholeheartedly for the KGB. The letter was a moving one and, though we in Washington and our superiors in Moscow were skeptical of Artamonov, we were impressed by his repentance. We waited to see what he would deliver.

Artamonov had been promised a pardon and restoration of his military rank if he honestly cooperated with us. In addition, his son was to be admitted to a Soviet naval academy. That, in fact, happened, and Artamonov and his family were pleased. The KGB assured the son that his father was not a traitor, but rather a hero who had been playing a double game all these years. The KGB also began giving Artamonov's wife and son a monthly allowance.

At first, we had no reason to suspect that "Lark" was deceiving us and had become a double—or was it a triple?—agent. Our plan, which he carried out, was to keep him working as a consultant for the Office of Naval Intelligence, using his position to supply us with classified material. He came through, handing us a variety of classified documents. He furnished us, for example, with U.S. assessments of Soviet naval capabilities, including analyses of our latest missile tests in the Black and North seas. We pushed him to pinpoint the source of the information on our missile testing; by getting more specific, Artamonov might have been able to help the KGB determine whether there was, for example, an American spy on the missile-testing range itself. But Artamonov was never able to give us more detailed information. His data and reports were good, but not of blockbuster quality. In hindsight, this should have aroused my suspicions.

In the Washington station, and at KGB headquarters, we were excited about Artamonov's cooperation for another reason: He said he knew the defector Yuri Nosenko and had a general idea of where Nosenko lived in the United States. The KGB had been searching for Nosenko for years; perhaps, in our zeal to get our hands on Nosenko, we were too trusting of Artamonov.

I continued to help oversee and analyze Artamonov's work while I remained in the American capital. It wasn't until several years later, when I was back in Moscow in Foreign Counterintelligence, that I became convinced "Lark" had once again turned against the Soviet Union. I would set in motion an elaborate ruse to lure this double dealer back to his homeland—a plot that would come to a bad end along the Austrian-Czech border on a cold, moonless night in 1975. But that was yet to come.

Our search for defectors led us, in the late 1960s, to another famous Soviet turncoat—Alexander Orlov, one of the top men in Stalin's NKVD secret police. After serving as NKVD chief in Spain, Orlov fled to America in 1938. He, too, had been sentenced to death *in absentia,* and the KGB had been searching for him for decades.

Finally, Counterintelligence located Orlov in Ann Arbor, Michigan. In 1969, a KGB officer from Moscow traveled, again under diplomatic cover, to the University of Michigan, where he tracked down Orlov at his apartment. The goal was not to shoot the aging defector, but rather to bring him back to Moscow and use him in the propaganda war, with headlines like "NKVD Warhorse Returns to Motherland After Unhappy Life in America." After all, by the late 1960s, things were not going well on the public relations front. Almost all the Cold War defectors—including Stalin's own daughter, Svetlana Alliluyeva—seemed to be streaming out of the Soviet Union. We were desperately seeking to counteract this negative propaganda, and persuading an old Bolshevik to return home after three decades abroad seemed like just the thing.

After the initial shock of being discovered wore off, Orlov—despite implacable resistance from his wife—agreed to return to the USSR. It was a real coup, made possible by the persuasiveness of the KGB man who had contacted Orlov (Mikhail Feoktistov) and the persistence of our Counterintelligence people in Moscow and Washington. We informed headquarters of Orlov's decision, and waited for permission to spirit him out of the United States and back to the Soviet Union. We waited nearly a month and, when Moscow spoke, their message was a huge disappointment: Leave him alone, Lubyanka instructed us. Let him live out his life in peace.

Shortly afterwards, I returned to Moscow on vacation and asked my superiors what had happened with the Orlov case. They said the decision on his fate had been kicked all the way up to the Politburo, whose members finally decided that the old defector wasn't worth the fuss. The Politburo said it would be foolish to treat a traitor as a hero, and he was too old and the case too stale to trick him into coming back and then put him on trial. No, our leaders said, leave him alone. And so we did, after wasting an enormous amount of time and money hunting for the Stalin-era spy. He died in 1973 of heart failure, at seventy-eight.

Toward the end of my tour of duty in Washington, I undertook yet another unsuccessful bid to entice one of our countrymen back to the USSR. In retrospect, I am amazed we wasted so much energy on such silly exercises designed to give us a brief—and transparently artificial—victory in the propaganda war with America.

This case involved a Soviet couple from Armenia who had emigrated years ago and gone to work for the CIA, all the while secretly serving as agents for the KGB. The man was a double agent, working for KGB Foreign Counterintelligence. He had barely started to work for us when a high-ranking KGB officer, Anatoly Golitsyn, defected in 1961 and we became concerned Golitsyn might expose the Armenian double agent. The Armenian laid low; it later turned out that Golitsyn knew nothing of his existence.

The Armenian died of cancer in the early 1960s, and we lost touch with his widow. Counterintelligence instructed me to find her to see if she would be willing to work for us or return to the Soviet Union. After hours and hours of searching, I located the woman at her Alexandria, Virginia, apartment. I knocked, and she reacted with horror when I told her I was from the Soviet Embassy. She was convinced I was from the FBI and that the U.S. government had finally discovered that she and her husband were spies. Negotiating through a tiny crack in the door, I did my best to calm her down. Finally, I managed to slip a letter from her brother through the tiny opening.

"This is your brother writing to you," I said. "This comes straight from Yerevan. How could the FBI get its hands on this?"

At last, the woman relented and opened the door.

"What do you want from me?" she asked.

"To talk to you," I said. "To find out how you're doing. We couldn't resume contact for some time because we were afraid for your safety. Now the time has come."

I still had to spend another twenty minutes proving to her I wasn't from the FBI. Finally, I won her trust and she began describing her husband's long illness and the loneliness she had experienced in recent years. She said she longed to return to her native Armenia to be reunited with her family. After several hours of coaxing, she agreed to return to the USSR, where we planned to use her to condemn the CIA and to describe her husband's feats as a KGB officer. I gave her money for the plane ticket and for the cost of shipping her belongings back to the Soviet Union.

Then, literally on the eve of her departure, we met and she told me hysterically, "I can't leave here. I could never leave my husband's grave. I want to be buried beside him. I will stay here forever."

In vain, I tried to persuade her to go. She wouldn't budge. By the time of our last meeting, she had apparently grown fond of me. As we bade farewell, she handed me a ring, saying, "This is a gift from the heart. Give it to your wife. I love my country, but I cannot leave my husband behind."

I walked away feeling sorry for the woman, for she and her husband had led a troubled life. Intelligence work is not always a dry affair; inevitably, one gets emotionally involved in the often-twisted lives of those who become caught up in the world of espionage.

In the midst of these intrigues involving defectors and former agents, one of my former recruits from my New York days—"Pompei"—came back to haunt me. I had spent roughly $15,000 setting up the Greek, John Makris, in the travel business, hoping he would use it as a front to attract women we could later infiltrate into the State Department, United Nations, or the FBI. The Greek had been a singular failure, and in 1966 we found out why.

An FBI informer told us that Makris was, in fact, a double agent working for the FBI. I was already in Washington, and the matter might have died quietly were it not that the FBI, apparently fed up with the KGB's increasing aggressiveness, wanted to expose me.

After hearing from the FBI informer that "Pompei" was working for the U.S. government, I waited anxiously for several months, fearing an imminent announcement of my expulsion. Luckily,

Makris had been so inept that the FBI had little grounds on which to bounce me out of America. One day, as I was walking near our Washington embassy with a Soviet colleague, I saw Makris heading my way. He came closer, and I could see his eyes giving me a tentative, frightened look through his big glasses. I glowered and wagged my finger at him, and he walked away. A few weeks later he was back, pretending to wait nonchalantly at a bus stop near our embassy. Once again, I steered clear of him. The FBI didn't know that we had been tipped off, and the Americans were making a clumsy effort to draw me back into a relationship with their agent.

All was quiet until 1967, when I drove one Sunday with the TASS bureau chief, Vladimir Vashedenko, to a beach resort in Rehoboth, Delaware. We had brought with us a pile of fat Sunday American newspapers and were working through them and sunning ourselves when a *Washington Post* story caught Vashedenko's eye. The front-page article was written by Stephen Rosenfeld, and recounted a "strange" espionage case in which a Soviet agent had hired a Greek man to recruit young women and place them in jobs at the U.S. State Department. The name of the Soviet agent? Viktor Kraknikovich—the alias I had used in my dealings with "the Greek."

"Look at this stupid article," said Vashedenko, who though not a KGB officer nevertheless worked closely with us. "It's all about Soviet intrigues again. Looks as though they're about to launch another wave of spy mania. Do you think we ought to react in some way or just ignore it?"

I was facing a dilemma. If I had told him not to report it—and if my political officers had kept quiet about it—Moscow probably would have been blissfully ignorant of the story. But the piece was about me, and I didn't want anyone accusing me of covering up a scandal in which I was involved.

"I don't know what this stupid stuff is about," I told the TASS man, "but you can put it on the wire."

The next day, the TASS report on the affair was on the desk of KGB Chairman Vladimir Semichastny. He immediately called the Intelligence Directorate and demanded an explanation. They gave him the whole, sordid story: the botched operation to plant women in the State Department, the squandered money, the Greek turning out to be a double agent.

"This is a typical example of the wastefulness and stupidity on the part of our field officers in America," Semichastny wrote in a memo about the case. "Fifteen thousand dollars was wasted for nothing. Investigate, and punish the gulity parties."

I knew nothing of this until months later, when I returned to Moscow on vacation. As it turned out, fate was kind to me. Within weeks of ordering an investigation that could have badly damaged my career, Semichastny was sacked by the Politburo. His dismissal meant, in effect, that I was granted a reprieve for my bungling. In hindsight, the KGB officer who originally cultivated Makris obviously exaggerated the man's usefulness as an agent—something typically done in the KGB. For all I know, our officer may even have pocketed the money meant for the Greek. When I came along, a neophyte in the espionage business, I was so anxious to develop a good agent that I overlooked Makris's many shortcomings and failed to recognize that his behavior was highly suspicious.

Unfortunately, *The Washington Post* article was only the first of three volleys fired by the FBI.

The next came in 1968, when the FBI fed columnist Jack Anderson information about the case involving the Greek. Anderson, unlike Rosenfeld, used my name.

"A Soviet intelligence agent here has failed in one of his primary missions," Anderson wrote in the opening paragraph of his article. "His name is Oleg Kalugin, second secretary at the Sovict embassy. For some time, he has been trying to place a female acquaintance of his as his agent in the State Department. He also instructed an aide to cultivate a girl who works at the FBI. Neither attempt succeeded. Both girls have been leading him on under the direction of the FBI."

The article ended with the following words: "But even though much spying is now done by cold computers, there is still room in it for a charming man like Oleg Kalugin."

There was a picture of me, looking every bit the suave young spy in trenchcoat and scarf.

As if that wasn't enough to kill any hopes I had of becoming the KGB's Washington station chief, a follow-up article by Anderson in his "Washington Merry-Go-Round" column buried my chances for good. Headlined "SOVIET SPY ALLOWED TO REMAIN IN U.S.," the Anderson article—fed directly to him by the FBI—recounted the entire case. It said I had committed a "serious act of espionage" and that the "handsome, lotharian Kalugin . . . became entangled in a web of espionage and romance."

"His undercover activities in this country are known to the FBI,"

Anderson wrote, fairly demanding that I be expelled. "But only the State Department knows the reason he is still here. Other spies caught in the act have been declared *persona non grata* and have been given 48 hours to leave the country."

Anderson described the plans I had hatched with the Greek, including infiltrating secretaries in the State Department and penetrating anti-Castro Cuban groups in New York. "But one by one, each new conspiracy fell apart out of confusion and exaggerated caution."

I had to laugh at that line; Anderson was parroting the FBI's little professional digs. The columnist—or, I should say, the FBI—also misrepresented my plans with the Greek, alleging that I was the one who charmed and bedded down a woman we were trying to insinuate into the FBI. The allegation wasn't true, but the FBI apparently figured that if it couldn't persuade the State Department to expel me, at least it could stir up some domestic trouble in the Kalugin home.

"He [Kalugin] would romance the lady while his wife tended the home fires in their apartment," wrote Anderson.

Nothing ever came of Anderson's articles, though it was clear that after their publication there was no way I could be appointed station chief. Not only did the KGB not like its station chief to be in the limelight, but in the wake of such stories Lubyanka was afraid I might be expelled at any moment. Why I wasn't kicked out of the country is a mystery, though I imagine it had something to do with the flimsiness of the evidence against me, as well as the budding *détente* between our two countries. In the long run, not being named station chief was a boon for my career, for otherwise I would never have become—at such a young age—head of Foreign Counterintelligence. But at the time, I was fuming that the third-rate misadventures with the Greek had blown up in my face. KGB headquarters, afraid of a provocation or expulsion, sent me orders to lie low and to keep trips outside the embassy to a minimum.

My wife, by the way, was not chagrined by the articles. But for weeks after the stories appeared, members of the Soviet Embassy community would tease me, saying how honored they were to have such a "Lothario" in their midst.

No matter how deeply I became involved in the machinations of espionage, I still had to live my cover life as Soviet Embassy press officer and carry on as a member of the embassy community. We were extremely fortunate to have Anatoly Fyodorovich Dobrynin as

Soviet Ambassador to the United States. An intelligent, tough, and able professional with owlish looks and a kindly manner, Dobrynin presided over the Soviet Embassy in Washington for an extraordinary twenty-four-year term, from 1963 to 1986. Inside the embassy, he was a friendly, fatherly figure who did his best to smooth out the conflicts that inevitably arose in the pressurized environment of a small diplomatic community. The ambassador let the KGB do its job, and seemed favorably impressed when we began showing the intelligence information we were receiving from such assets as John Walker.

Dobrynin also was well liked by the Americans. At times, as he defended the official Soviet line, he may have seemed to the West like a hard-liner. But Dobrynin was, in fact, a comparatively progressive man who came under attack from orthodox Communists in Moscow for being too soft on America. He knew the United States well, and scoffed at the ideas of the arch conservatives in Moscow that there was some sort of American cabal—composed of Jews, the military-industrial complex, and evil capitalists—determined to bury the Soviet Union. Dobrynin had another enemy in Moscow— Foreign Minister Andrei Gromyko, who saw the ambassador as a rival and tried to diminish his achievements and stature in Washington.

By the time Gorbachev came to power, replacing Dobrynin in Washington and moving him into the Central Committee of the Communist Party, the ambassador looked like a representative from the old order. But when I knew him in Washington, Dobrynin was very much a man of "new thinking"—as would be evidenced by his reaction to the Soviet invasion of Czechoslovakia in August 1968.

I continued to have great respect for our station chief, Boris Solomatin, though I began to see in 1967 and 1968 that he was, like most Soviet bureaucrats, afraid to rock the boat. During the November 1967 celbration of the fiftieth anniversary of the Russian Revolution, I went to the reception given by Ambassador Dobrynin. The entire diplomatic corps, as well as scores of American politicians and journalists, attended. People drank rivers of vodka and champagne, and by the end of the evening the embassy was filled with inebriated Soviet diplomats. As the guests began to head home, I passed the embassy's secretary, Vladimir Bykov, on the main stairway. He was clinging to the bannister, obviously bombed. Bykov was a smarmy, insolent man, and as I passed him I made a casual remark which he interpreted as an insult.

"People like you aren't needed around here!" Bykov bellowed, obviously referring to KGB officers. "It would be much better without you."

"And better still without drunks like you!" I shot back.

The next morning Solomatin called me in for a chat.

"Bykov complained about you to the ambassador," the KGB station chief said. "Things will have to be smoothed over. Go and apologize to him. Don't forget that his father-in-law is Abrasimov, head of the Central Committee department for overseas cadres."

I was taken aback by Solomatin's counsel, for he was plainly afraid of incurring the wrath of the Communist Party functionaries in Moscow.

"I have no intention of apologizing to that boor," I replied. "That would be an unacceptable humiliation for me and for the entire service. Don't forget that his insults were not directed just at me. You, too, are a representative of the KGB, and they affect you just as much."

"Well," Solomatin replied gloomily, "you've only yourself to blame if Bykov does complain to Abrasimov."

Just a few months earlier, I had caught one of our officers embezzling hundreds of dollars intended as payments to some of our operatives. I reported the case to Solomatin, and recommended we take tough action. But there was a hitch. The officer was the son-in-law of Viktor Alidin, a Brezhnev crony and the powerful head of the Moscow KGB. Rather than risking offending Alidin, Solomatin limited himself to a mere reprimand of the KGB officer.

When I returned to Moscow for vacation in 1967, I heard nothing about my run-in with Bykov. What struck me most about Moscow was the coolness with which many of my colleagues greeted me—a reception I soon came to attribute to jealousy. Word had gotten around headquarters that we were developing an extensive network of agents in Washington, something many people had said was impossible. The overwhelming majority of the Intelligence staff had never laid eyes on a top-secret document, let alone seen a real, live American agent. I was in my early thirties, already a major and participating in some of the KGB's most important operations. This didn't sit well with some people.

Back in Washington, I became immersed in my duties as press attaché. In June 1967, at the start of the Arab-Israeli Six-Day War, I attended a reception at the home of *Washington Post* columnist Chalmers Roberts. We were drinking and chatting when Secretary of State Dean Rusk showed up. Many of the guests were journalists, and they rushed to the lawn to meet Rusk and pepper him with questions about the war.

Rusk answered a few questions. Then, after hearing that a Soviet diplomat was at the reception, he walked up to me, glass in hand. Draping his arm around my shoulders, he turned to the assembled reporters and said, "The Soviet Union and the United States will not be fighting in the Middle East. Right?"

He looked at me and I nodded in affirmation. Rusk and I talked for several minutes about the war and U.S.-Soviet relations. After the Secretary of State departed, the reporters gathered around me, wanting to know what he said. In true diplomatic fashion, I replied that it was clear from Rusk's statement that the United States had no desire to become involved in the Arab-Israeli conflict and that the two superpowers would stay out of it.

The following year, 1968, was one that rocked the United States and the Soviet Union. Indeed, for me, 1968 was a watershed year that forever changed the way I looked at my country and left me deeply pessimistic that the long-awaited reform of Soviet society would ever take place.

In America, within the space of two months, Martin Luther King, Jr., and Senator Robert Kennedy were assassinated. I was a great admirer of King's, viewing him as the person who had done more than anyone else to fight racism in America. As a man, I was saddened by the wave of rioting that swept the country after King was gunned down in Memphis, Tennessee. As a KGB officer, however, I welcomed the disturbances, which we viewed as the inevitable consequence of decades of smoldering racial tension in America. The KGB played no role in the riots. We didn't need to, for America's blacks were setting the cities on fire all on their own, with no encouragement from anyone.

But there was little time to gloat. For just as the fires were dying down in America, the Soviet Union got involved in its own disaster: Czechoslovakia.

Throughout the early months of 1968 I watched with hope and amazement as Czech Premier Alexander Dubcek attempted to liberalize and democratize his nation. Dubcek was not talking about doing away with Communism, but rather reforming socialism to give it a "human face," with power being transferred from a monolithic

Communist Party to the Czech people. Khrushchev had tried to liberalize Soviet society, but his ouster in 1964 and the ensuing four years of inaction had convinced me that our Soviet attempt at reform was dead, that the Communist Party *nomenklatura* was doing everything it could to maintain its hold on power. The heartening events of the "Prague Spring" awoke in me the hope that the process of democratization would spread from Czechoslovakia to Eastern Europe and, eventually, to the Soviet Union itself. I secretly wished Dubcek and his allies success in their peaceful revolution.

The first word I had that the "Prague Spring" was to be snuffed out came on August 20, 1968, in a top-secret cable from Moscow. By that time, I had been promoted to acting station chief and was reporting directly to the ambassador. Shortly before the invasion began, I received a coded message to be read only by myself and the ambassador. The cable said that counterrevolutionary activity in Prague—supported by American and NATO secret services— had forced the USSR and "fraternal" countries of Eastern Europe to take "decisive steps to defend the achievements of socialism in Czechoslovakia." In view of these "decisive steps"—i.e., invasion— Moscow advised us to take timely measures to reinforce security at the embassy, to ensure the safety of Soviet citizens in the United States, and to justify the Warsaw Pact action to the American public as an unavoidable step to safeguard international stability and foil the aggressive schemes of reactionary Western circles.

I held the cable in my hand, stunned and deeply depressed. I had been following the events in Czechoslovakia not only through the press but also through National Security Agency and CIA documents received from our American assets. In addition, the head of Czechoslovak Intelligence in Washington had given me regular briefings. From all of these sources, I knew that our supposed reasons for intervention were nothing but lies: It was absolutely clear that the CIA and other Western intelligence agencies were not fomenting unrest in Czechoslovakia. The "Prague Spring" had risen up from below, from the Czech people themselves.

Cable in hand, I walked downstairs to Ambassador Dobrynin's office.

When he finished reading it, I muttered, "This is monstrous folly! It's idiotic. There is no other word for it."

I had no idea how Dobrynin would react, but he, too, did nothing to conceal his outrage.

"They are absolute fools!" Dobrynin hissed. "This is a terrible business, and it will be a crippling blow to all our good beginnings with America. To sink to something like this! We'll have to brace ourselves for a lot of unpleasantness."

On August 21, when Soviet troops entered Prague in force, I dropped in to see the *Pravda* correspondent Boris Strelnikov. Volodya Til, from the Czechoslovak Press Agency, was already there. The announcement of the crackdown in Czechoslovakia had not been made, and I kept sneaking apprehensive glances at the clock: word of our invasion was expected to come any minute. Finally, American TV broke in with a special announcement about our occupation of Czechoslovakia. Til's face turned stony, and as soon as the bulletin ended he walked out.

Soviet propaganda kept citing instances of U.S. and Western involvement in the Czech events, alleging that CIA and NATO agents had infiltrated the country to foment revolution. *Pravda* and other Soviet media reported that Warsaw Pact troops had found CIA arms caches and that thousands of NATO troops, disguised as tourists, had flooded into Prague. I knew it was all nonsense, and that any signs of CIA involvement were sure to have been fabricated by the KGB's "active measures" experts—as turned out to be the case.

As expected, the outcry around the world was deafening. In Washington, we unenthusiastically spread the official Soviet line, though I privately told my friends in the American press corps that I was dismayed by the crushing of the Prague Spring. The day after the announcement of the invasion, my counterpart in the Czechoslovakian Intelligence Department phoned me and asked for an urgent meeting at a nearby restaurant. No sooner had I sat down than the Czech resident, tears welling in his eyes, launched into an attack on the Kremlin.

"Your leadership has committed a crass error in using force against a nation which has always respected the Soviet Union," he told me. "In my mind, Oleg, I can probably understand the reasons which motivated Brezhnev to resort to armed force. But in my heart, I cannot accept any justification for it. My children will hate you for what you've done to my country. They will never forgive you for what happened."

I was deeply moved by the resident's words. All I could say, in response, was that not every Soviet agreed with what had happened. I said I was immensely sorry and that I hoped our friendship would survive, despite everything. I embraced him as we said goodbye. We never saw each other again.

In the days following the invasion, I sat in my office in the embassy and pored over hundreds of pages of purloined U.S. Intelligence reports on Czechoslovakia. Not one of them gave a hint that the CIA or other U.S. agencies had done anything nefarious in Czechoslovakia in recent months. On my own initiative, I prepared a detailed analysis of the activity of American Intelligence in the weeks preceding the invasion. The analysis conclusively showed that, while America was closely monitoring the situation in Czechoslovakia, the CIA had taken no steps to destabilize the country. I addressed the report to KGB Chairman Yuri Andropov, certain he would want to see it. Later, I learned that when my report arrived in Moscow, Andropov ordered its immediate destruction.

Eventually, the furor over the Czech invasion died down. Dubcek and his aides, after being hauled away to the Soviet Union by the KGB, were returned to Czechoslovakia. They served briefly as a puppet government before a staunch, pro-Moscow regime was installed. These lackeys would reign another two decades, before the whole house of cards came tumbling down in 1989.

It's clear now that Brezhnev and the Politburo knew precisely what they were dealing with in Czechoslovakia. They realized that, had they let the Prague Spring continue to flower, the logical end would have been the spreading of revolution to Hungary and Poland and the Baltic states and—ultimately—to Russia itself. What was going on in Prague had to be crushed in its early stages. Otherwise, the entire Communist edifice would crumble.

For me, the invasion of Czechoslovakia was one of the two or three milestones on my road to total disillusionment with the Soviet system. I suppose that had I been bolder, had I been more of a dissident, I might have resigned shortly after Soviet tanks rolled into Prague. But I was no dissident, no Sakharov or Solzhenitsyn. I was a product of the system, a patriot, and defection was absolutely out of the question. I suppose I also was a slave to my ambitions, and to the illusion that this system—despite the increasing proliferation of Communist Party hacks at all levels—could be reformed. So I stayed in the KGB; indeed, I continued to rise rapidly through its ranks. I was a professional, and I knew we were involved in a bitter power struggle with the United States. I was not prepared, despite even the colossal blunder of Czechoslovakia, to abandon my country or its Communist system. But the crushing of the Prague Spring had profoundly unsettled me. I would never be the same again.

By this time another unsettling trend also was becoming evident in the KGB. At all levels, Communist Party *apparatchiks*—shallow, fawning, and unprofessional—were moving into positions of power. Though I respected Andropov's astuteness and toughness, he, too, was responsible for bringing in legions of Party hacks who ultimately weakened the KGB. In the late 1960s and, especially, in the 1970s, Communist Party bureaucrats such as Vladimir Kryuchkov—who went on to lead the KGB and the ill-fated 1991 coup—moved into positions of power. The members of the ruling Politburo viewed these *apparatchiks* as a stable and reliable force, especially considering the frightening counterrevolutionary trends that had popped up in Czechoslovakia.

But this influx of Party bureaucrats into the KGB was disastrous. They knew little about the nuts and bolts of intelligence, and even less about the world outside the Soviet Union. We disparagingly called them "encyclopedists"—men who knew a little about everything. They could do anything, run any organization. And they ruined the country. In the KGB, officers increasingly were promoted because of who they knew, not what they had accomplished. Men of strong character and high professional ability became suspect, while obsequious "yes men" climbed higher and higher.

Perhaps in part because of the influx of Party bureaucrats, the KGB—like virtually every organization in the country—began to suffer from gigantism. Right before my eyes, in the late 1960s and 1970s, I saw the KGB steadily grow both larger and more ineffective. When I started working with the KGB, there were three major directorates: Intelligence, Counterintelligence, and Codes. By the 1970s, there were a dozen—each a little fiefdom unto itself.

When I began working for the KGB, Political Intelligence was divided into eight geographic regions. By 1980, there were twenty geographic departments. When I started my career, there was one advanced KGB school in Moscow. By the 1980s, there were three. In my early days, the KGB Intelligence Directorate was headquartered in Lubyanka and a nearby, smaller building. By the late 1970s, Intelligence had virtually been given its own city, the sprawling compound at Yasenovo on the outskirts of Moscow. Yasenovo contained a twenty-two-story building, an eighteen-story building, and a nine-story building.

One fact alone tells the story of the KGB's growth: By 1990 there were more KGB employees in Moscow alone—47,000—than all of the CIA and FBI employees combined. And the bitter truth was that this sprawling organization turned out to be far less effective than its earlier counterpart.

This gigantism had another result which should not be overlooked, for it was one of the main reasons why the Soviet Union ultimately self-destructed. The KGB—like the army, the Communist Party, and the gargantuan military-industrial complex—was siphoning off an enormous percentage of the Soviet Union's financial resources. These authoritarian institutions were draining the country dry: nothing was denied the KGB, the Party, or the defense industry. The average Soviet, meanwhile, was living virtually a Third World existence with appalling food, backward medical care, and laughably shoddy consumer goods. There was indeed some truth to the old joke that the Soviet Union was little more than the Congo with rockets.

These problems weighed on me in Washington, but the truth is I was so busy trying to balance my dual existence as a KGB officer and press *attaché* that I did not have the luxury to dwell on such cosmic matters. As 1968 progressed, especially after the Czech events, our station—and particularly my political intelligence line— got deeply involved in analyzing the presidential race between Republican nominee Richard Nixon and Democrat Hubert Humphrey. In fact, the KGB did more than analyze: We forged a close, backchannel tie with Henry Kissinger that not only changed our view of the race but also opened up a direct line between Brezhnev and Nixon that was to significantly improve U.S.-Soviet relations.

As the election heated up in the fall of 1968, the conventional Soviet view—and the one held by Ambassador Dobrynin—was that a Humphrey victory would be far better for the Soviet Union. Dobrynin believed that Humphrey and the Democrats were more predictable and would guarantee more stable relations between our two countries. The ambassador and many other Soviet officials feared Nixon, viewing him as a staunch anti-Communist. Dobrynin also thought Nixon was unpredictable and something of a scoundrel.

We in the KGB, however, took a different view. We liked Nixon. We knew, of course, that he was unpredictable, but we also thought that—unlike the Democrats—Nixon could take giant steps that could lead to a marked improvement in Soviet-U.S. relations. Early on, we saw that the very fact that Nixon was a conservative and a fervent anti-Communist could work to our advantage: Such a man would have the power to improve relations between our countries, for no one would ever dare accuse Nixon of being soft on Communism.

We also had a little help in our intelligence assessments, thanks to a fascinating relationship that developed between one of our officers and Henry Kissinger.

The KGB officer was named Boris Sedov. Officially, he was in Washington as a reporter for the Novosti Press Agncy. In fact, he was one of my underlings in the KGB's political intelligence line. In the course of his Novosti work, Sedov had met Kissinger, who was then at Harvard University. They hit it off, and began meeting with each other frequently. We encouraged Sedov to cultivate his relationship with Kissinger, because we knew the German émigré professor was well connected and held widely respected views on foreign affairs. We never had any illusions about trying to recruit Kissinger: he was simply a source of political intelligence.

When Kissinger became a close political adviser to Nixon during the campaign, however, we knew that we had a very important relationship on our hands, one that could go well beyond what Sedov and Kissinger had enjoyed before. In fact, both sides began rather quickly to use this contact as a fruitful back channel between the leadership of our two countries.

For his part, Kissinger—clearly acting on instructions from Nixon and plainly aware that Sedov was more than just an average Soviet reporter—began to convey to us that Nixon was no anti-Communist ogre and that he wanted improved relations with the USSR. Again and again in meetings with Sedov, Kissinger told us not to under-estimate Nixon's political abilities, not to overestimate his anti-Communism, and not to take Nixon's hard-line campaign pro-nouncements at face value. Kissinger told Sedov that Nixon, if elected, would strive for a new era of improved relations between the two superpowers. That message was conveyed to Lubyanka, which passed it on directly to Brezhnev and the Politburo. Later, Nixon—through the Kissinger-Sedov channel—sent an unofficial letter to Brezhnev in which he set out his views on the international situation and said he would do all he could to improve relations between us.

The message was well received in the Kremlin, in large measure because Brezhnev and his Politburo cronies were anxious to be-gin repairing the damage that had been done after the invasion of Czechoslovakia. In reply to Kissinger's overtures, Brezhnev sent back a message, relayed through Sedov, that the Kremlin would welcome the chance to work with Nixon and had no ill feelings toward him.

Dobrynin was apprised in general terms of the content of the confidential communications between Brezhnev and Nixon. He was not thrilled about the back channel, but accepted it because the election campaign was under way and it was still improper for the Soviet Union to open up direct contact with Nixon.

The Republican was overwhelmingly elected the thirty-seventh President of the United States. Even before sending an official message of congratulations, Brezhnev forwarded a confidential congratulatory note to Nixon through Sedov. In it, he expressed the hope that Nixon's election would usher in new changes in the superpower relationship. For more than a month afterward the Soviet regime and the president-elect communicated through the Sedov-Kissinger back channel.

Finally, Dobrynin had had enough. He said it was time to begin all communication through proper, diplomatic channels. Dobrynin sent a cable to Brezhnev, saying in effect that he appreciated the service done by the KGB in establishing communications with Nixon but, considering that the ambassador was alive and well, all contact with the new administration should go through the Foreign Ministry and the embassy in Washington. Brezhnev agreed. Dobrynin himself began to meet with Kissinger, and Sedov was relegated to the background.

That, however, was not the end of Sedov's and the KGB's contributions to the dialogue between the U.S. and the Soviet Union. Once Kissinger became national security adviser to Nixon, Sedov began to meet frequently with one of Kissinger's top aides, Richard Allen. I, too, later met Allen at a small party given by Sedov. As with Kissinger, Sedov met regularly with Allen to exchange information. Allen must have been aware that Sedov was from the KGB, but both sides nevertheless found it beneficial to use these informal meetings to probe one another, ask questions, exchange ideas, and float trial balloons. Sedov once considered trying to recruit Allen as an agent, and even went so far as to look into Allen's financial affairs and inquire whether there might be some compromising material that could be used to recruit the National Security Council deputy. But I quickly quashed the idea, saying it was useless—and could jeopardize our improving relations—to go after such a man.

Sedov and Allen's relationship continued until I left Washington in 1970. Allen eventually went on to become national security adviser to President Ronald Reagan.

* * *

In December 1968—exhausted from a combination of the Czechoslovakian events, the campaign, the Walker case, and my job as acting station chief—I decided to take a rest. Customarily, KGB officers stationed in America vacationed in the Soviet Union. But I knew a home trip was out of the question since it would be virtually impossible to find a replacement for me as acting station chief on such short notice. I was then gripped by a wild notion: Why not vacation in Florida? No KGB officer had ever done that before, figuring the Americans would flatly reject the idea. Remarkably, I got the okay I needed from Dobrynin, KGB headquarters, and the Americans themselves.

Delighted that I had somehow managed to outfox the sprawling bureaucracies of the world's two great powers, I piled my family into our green Volkswagen "Beetle" on a cold December day and headed south. As expected, the beaches were delightful. But by far the most memorable part of the trip were the friendly—even touching—encounters with the FBI agents who followed me to and from the Sunshine State.

The road from Washington to Florida was a long one, and in our case it was made even longer by the tortuous route we had to take because of FBI security regulations. U.S. officials weren't taking any chances that I might do a little snooping around on my vacation, so they chose a route for me that steered well clear of military bases and other "top-secret" installations. Leaving Washington, I saw two FBI cars on our tail, assuming they would be with us the whole way. But the FBI had decided to let all their agents in the southern states have the fun of tailing a Russian spook, so every time we crossed a state line we waved farewell to an old surveillance team and picked up a new one. The trip south was uneventful, and it felt great to be out of the Washington rat race and traveling through the picturesque, slow-paced world of the American South.

Arriving in Fort Lauderdale, FBI agents in tow, we quite randomly selected the Hacienda Motel—a typical, modest 1950s American motel that had the supreme advantages of being relatively cheap and right on the beach. Hardly had I finished checking in when one of the FBI agents approached me and politely asked when I would be returning to Washington. I told him the exact date and time, two weeks hence, and he thanked me and disappeared. Except for a brief side trip to Miami, our FBI surveillance ceased until we got ready to head back to Washington.

We lounged around Fort Lauderdale for several days, then took the prearranged trip to Miami. We were only allowed to travel by train or plane, so early on in the morning of the appointed day of our excursion we arrived at the Fort Lauderdale railroad station. Two FBI men were wandering up and down the platform, and we nodded politely. The train was delayed, virtually no one else was on the platform, so I decided to talk to our FBI escorts. Normally, while being tailed, we are supposed to ignore the men following us and go about our business. It certainly wasn't advisable for KGB officers to begin talking to agents of a hostile Intelligence service without first receiving permission from headquarters. But it was vacation, no one else was around, and I decided to ask one of our FBI men about hotels and public transportation in Miami. He was extremely friendly, filling us in on where to stay and what sites to see. I asked him if he would be accompanying us to Miami, but he said he wouldn't, that another surveillance team would pick us up when we got there. We bade farewell and hopped on the train. With me were Ludmilla and our youngest daughter, Yulia.

Word must have spread among the FBI that we weren't bad folks. We spent twenty-four hours in Miami, and the following morning— after having rushed out of our hotel without breakfast—we arrived at the station to catch our train back to Fort Lauderdale. I wandered down a side street in search of a quick place to eat. After I had gone a few yards, one of the surveillance team—a jovial, middle-aged man—asked me what I was looking for. When I told him breakfast, he hurried back to get Ludmilla and Yulia and led us to a decent cafeteria. After a quick meal, we got on the train, our little Russian family smiling and waving goodbye to the G-Men.

I was beginning to like these guys.

Two weeks later, rested and refreshed, we pulled out of the Hacienda Motel at the appointed hour. Two FBI cars were parked nearby, ready to roll. The occupants smiled at us as if we were old friends, and we set off on the long road back to Washington.

That night, it was already dark when we decided to pull into a roadside motel. As we entered the parking lot, my old "Beetle" sputtered and died. Nothing could get it to start again. I began pushing the Volkswagen into the parking lot when one of the FBI men leaped out of his surveillance car and gave me a hand. He couldn't get it started either, but assured me there was a garage nearby and that we would get the car fixed.

We washed up at the motel, then set off on foot in search of dinner. In the distance, a flashing neon sign—"Howard Johnsons"—beckoned. We had walked no more than 30 yards when a blue Dodge, tires whispering, pulled up beside us. A car door slammed, and a tall, young FBI agent approached us.

"Where are you going in the dark?" he asked. "It's not all that safe around here. Hop in. I'll drive you wherever you want to go."

I hesitated for a second, then we piled into his car and drove to the Howard Johnsons restaurant. I asked him to join us for dinner, but he politely declined, saying he and his partner had already eaten.

We emerged from the restaurant an hour later. The Dodge was there waiting for us, its driver holding open the door for Ludmilla and Yulia. This was getting to be a bit much, but I enjoyed it nevertheless.

"Have you been with us all the way from Fort Lauderdale?" I asked the young man, settling down in the front passenger seat.

"No," he responded. "We picked you up halfway. We'll be with you as far as St. Petersburg, and then we'll hand you over to someone else."

He hesitated, perhaps remembering that FBI rules also forbade agents talking to KGB men without approval. Then he continued.

"We don't get many Russian visitors, although once I escorted a fellow countryman of yours."

"We're very grateful to you for your help and courtesy," I said. "Even though relations between our countries are not too friendly, we've encountered only good feelings on this trip. Perhaps some day we'll be friends. And maybe the time will come when our respective services will work together in peace."

"Well, I don't know about that," he replied. "But people should help each other when they're in trouble . . . By the way, don't worry about your car. Everything will be all right."

He said goodnight to us outside our motel door, then disappeared into the darkness.

The next morning when we walked out to the Volkswagen, we discovered that our FBI surveillance team had gotten up early and taken the car to be repaired. It started on the first try, and we headed back to Washington.

I was so impressed with the friendliness of the FBI agents that, back in Washington, I had the urge to write J. Edgar Hoover and praise the men who had accompanied us on our trip. But then I realized that if my letter were to somehow make it into the American or Soviet press, life wouldn't be worth living back in Moscow. The impulse passed.

Not long after my return, I passed up another chance to probe the limits of *détente*. I was at a dinner given by Joseph Harsch of *The Christian Science Monitor*. At one point, Allen Dulles, the retired CIA director, appeared at the party. I was tempted to talk with him, but I knew he was ill. I also had already been identified by Jack Anderson as a KGB agent, and I was still acting station chief. So I never approached the aging cold warrior, figuring the last thing I needed back in Moscow was an item in the Washington press about my having an intimate dinner-party conversation with the retired American spymaster.

Early in 1969, as the months ticked by, I knew that my time in Washington was drawing to a close. Headquarters already had made it clear that, due to the publicity that had appeared about me, there was no way I could be named station chief. Moscow already was working on a replacement for me, and I was trying to sort out where I might like to go next. I clearly had little time left. Nevertheless, I still kept trying to develop agents in the United States—and the FBI still kept trying to entrap me, usually with a woman as bait.

In February 1969, I attended a party at the West German Embassy, where I met an attractive young woman who had fled Hungary after the 1956 uprising. That in itself interested me, but when I found out that she worked at the State Department, I just had to take a stab at recruiting her. We stayed at the *Fasching* (Shrove Tuesday) party until four in the morning, dancing and talking, and even kissing a bit. We agreed to meet again the following day. But when we rendezvoused and I asked if I could see her again, she told me it would be impossible.

"Oleg, I like you very much as a man, but I've been warned to stay away from you," she said. "I'm a government employee, and my Hungarian past may damage my reputation, especially if I meet with you again."

I tried to talk her into having dinner with me later in the week, but she made it clear that State Department security people had sternly warned her not to have anything to do with me.

A fellow KGB officer also had been at the West German party, had met a secretary in a senator's office, and was pursuing her, as well. That same week, the FBI warned her about my colleague, and their budding relationship ended. Clearly, FBI Counter-Intelligence had been at the party, keeping close watch on us.

Before I left the nation's capital, the FBI was to make one last effort to entrap me. This final episode occurred in the summer of 1969, when a large group from the Soviet Embassy rented a boat and invited dozens of American journalists and politicians to join us on a four-hour cruise down the Potomac River. During the trip, a rather plump but attractive woman approached me and began chatting. It turned out that she was an American descendant of Austrian aristocrats, and that she worked as a public relations officer at the U.S. State Department. She seemed unusually friendly, which put me on guard. Then, the following day, she phoned me at the embassy and invited me to come to her house for a dinner party that evening. I was sure it was a set-up, and I was right.

That night, I drove to her apartment in one of Washington's most fashionable neighborhoods, on Massachusetts Avenue. As I parked in front of her building, I noticed a U.S. government car parked nearby. It was unmistakably the FBI.

She answered the door in a sexy dressing gown. As I kissed her on the cheek, I once again thought to myself: "Can the FBI really think I'm that stupid?"

There was no one else in her beautifully furnished apartment. Candles burned on the dining-room table, which had place settings for just two people. The woman fixed me a drink, and I asked her, "But you said you were having a party. Where are the other guests?"

"Oh, they'll be along later," she assured me.

"Jesus Christ!" I thought to myself. Unable to get me expelled from the country by planting articles with Jack Anderson, the FBI now wanted to entrap me and arrest me on a rape charge. I could see how it would unfold: The woman would start screaming and federal agents, listening through the hidden microphones in her apartment, would burst in and lock me up. I even walked over to her third-floor balcony and tried to figure out a possible escape route. I cursed myself for showing up, unsure how far the FBI wanted to take this game.

In any event, we sat down to dinner, and I made small talk with the woman, waiting for her next move. As we were finishing, there was a knock at the door, and she let in another couple. I don't remember now who they said they were, though I was convinced they, too, were from the FBI. The couple had a drink, then announced they had to leave. I had had enough of this intrigue, and announced that I was going.

"Why are you running off?" said the hostess. "Please do stay. Let them go. It's not late."

She followed me into the corridor, trying gently but insistently to restrain me. I was politely adamant and, walking onto Massachusetts Avenue, I swore I would steer clear of all such situations in the future.

In mid-1969, a new station chief—Mikhail Polonik—arrived. A career KGB officer, Polonik had been in charge of Political Intelligence in New York. He was a professional, but it was clear from the start that, compared to Solomatin, he was mediocre.

It was time to go. I had been in Washington nearly five years, during which time Solomatin and I had turned around a lackluster KGB station and run some of the most valuable spies the Soviet Union had during the Cold War. But the long hours and constant pressure—particularly since my exposure by Jack Anderson—had left me weary. In late 1969, I heard rumors that Alexander Sakharovsky, the head of Intelligence, was considering me for the job of station chief in Tokyo. It was an appealing prospect, especially considering Japan's growing economic power and world prominence. I waited anxiously for official word of my transfer.

Then, just before Christmas, a ciphered message arrived for me from headquarters. It caught me totally offguard: I was being offered the job of deputy chief of Foreign Counterintelligence. I was flattered, but skeptical whether this was the right move for me. Becoming deputy chief of an entire section was an undeniable step up. And the leaders at KGB headquarters assured me that they wanted to vastly enlarge and improve the department, charged with penetrating foreign intelligence services and keeping an eye on Soviets abroad. But at that time, Foreign Counterintelligence had a reputation for being staffed with people far inferior to those in Political Intelligence. While many of the officers in Political Intelligence were cosmopolitan people with good language skills, the personnel in Foreign Counterintelligence often were unsophisticated men from regional KGB offices, men with little knowledge of the world or its languages.

I mulled over the offer. The cipher clerk told me that Polonik had held the cable concerning my promotion for a week in his safe. Perhaps Polonik had been irritated that I was jumping over his head in the service hierarchy, and would in fact be one of his bosses in Moscow. In any case, when we talked about the offer, Polonik tried hard to dissuade me from taking the job.

"Don't go," he said. "You have such a great reputation in Political Intelligence. You'll be promoted yet. Why move to Counterintelligence? Think of who you'll have to work with, these hicks from the domestic service. You'll hate it. Why mix with this crowd? Think about it."

I did, though I knew it would be foolish to pass up the opportunity.

Washington was lovely that December. The city glimmered with Christmas lights and shoppers filled the streets, and I asked myself if I really wanted to give up the pleasures and thrills of life overseas and return to the Soviet capital. I stalled, in part because I had just bought my wife a fur coat, had not paid off my subscription to the *Encyclopedia Britannica,* and wanted to pull down my prized hard currency salary a few more months. But early in January 1970 I received a new ciphered cable: the time for a decision had come.

"The vacancy has to be filled at once due to the necessity of concentrating all forces in one section to counteract the main efforts of the enemy's special services," the message said. "Cable reply."

So I was going. I had to take back the fur coat and sell the *Encyclopedia Britannica* because we were running low on money. In late February, the day came to say goodbye to my co-workers in Political Intelligence. We gathered in a small, stuffy room in the embassy, and several of the officers who had worked for me gave valedictory speeches. My turn came to speak, and I urged everyone to treasure the experience they had gained in the last five years, to keep running risks and bringing a gambler's instinct to the espionage business. Our work would come to nothing, I told them, without the aggressive style and daring tactics we had used in recent years. Polonik looked displeased, as if I were trying to plant a mine underneath all his well-crafted, conservative plans.

"The main thing is to always be on the lookout," I told the men of my section. "It's like fishing or going on a hunting expedition. You have to be on the alert all the time and never miss an opportunity."

On February 26, 1970, my family and I boarded an Aeroflot flight for Moscow. I wouldn't set foot in America again for another twenty years, and upon my return I would no longer be the same loyal servant of the KGB. All told, in New York City and in Washington,

I had spent a decade in the United States, and those years had a profound effect upon me. I grew as an intelligence officer, and I tasted the freedom of American life.

After Washington, I would return to Moscow and spend another ten years in the very heart of the Soviet Union's intelligence apparatus. I would serve my country faithfully and put everything I had into battling the United States, the CIA, and the West. But that decade in America had changed me irrevocably. I had learned to speak my mind and I had learned not to cringe. In the 1970s, as the Soviet Union became more deeply mired in the stagnation of the Brezhnev era, these were not highly prized qualities. Ultimately, my outspokenness, my reluctance to kowtow to superiors, would lead to my break with the KGB.

And for that, I am grateful to America.

Oleg Kalugin at a Young Pioneer summer camp near Leningrad in 1947. Kalugin, who is 12 years old in the photo, is in the top row, fourth from the left.

Kalugin (left) with a friend on the eve of graduation from high school in Leningrad in 1952. The frozen Neva River is in the background.

Kalugin, age 17, just after his high school graduation.

Kalugin (third from right) at KGB summer training camp near Leningrad in 1953.

Lyudmilla on the eve of her wedding to Oleg

Kalugin's father, Daniil (right) in 1955. Behind Lyudmilla is her father.

Kalugin's mother, Klavdia, in later years with Kalugin's daughter, Svetlana.

The young journalist/spy at Columbia University School of Journalism in 1958.

Kalugin second from left at Columbia in 1959. At right is
Alexander Yakovlev, who went on to become a close adviser
to Gorbachev and one of the architects of perestroika.
(credit: George E. Yoseph)

STUDENTS PRAISE SOVIET EXCHANGE

Continued From Page 1, Col. 5

are studying at five American universities, and twenty-one United States students, all men, are attending two Soviet institutions. Over the week-end a group of scholars met at Columbia University to pick the bulk of the twenty-eight American students who will go to the Soviet Union for the program's second year next fall, when thirty-three Soviet students are scheduled to arrive here.

Complaints voiced by Soviet students in this country have centered mainly on the restrictions on their right to travel beyond a twenty-five-mile radius from their schools. Similar complaints have been voiced by their American counterparts in Russia. In both cases, however, some exceptions to the rule have been made, permitting wider travel.

Some Soviet students here have complained that the $250 a month allowance they receive is inadequate for all the things they would like to do. American students in Russia receive 1,500 rubles ($150 at the tourist exchange rate) monthly.

David C. Munford, head of the Inter-University Committee on Travel Grants, which administers the United States program for the State Department, had warm words last week for the cooperation of Soviet educational authorities. The difficulties and problems that have arisen, he said, have generally been over matters outside these officials' area of responsibility.

The program is part of the broad Soviet-United States cultural exchange program signed into effect early last year. The United States share of the program is being financed mainly by funds from the Ford Foundation and from a government grant.

The Soviet students and the universities they are attending are:

Columbia: Gennadi P. Bekhterev, Oleg D. Kalugin, Y. N. Tonhkov, and Aleksandr N. Yaovlev.

Harvard: Anatoly F. Glushchenko and Oleg D. Brykin.

California: Yanis Y. Abelinash, Oleg A. Bondin, Vil M. Bykov, Oleg D. Knab, Valentin A. Levin, Sergei G. Shcherbakov, Aleksandr S. Shchukin and Aleksandr V. Zhuravchenkova.

Chicago: Konstantin I. Nesen. Washington: Elgen P. Grigorev and Yuri N. Sokolov.

The Americans studying in the Soviet Union, fifteen at Moscow University and six at Leningrad University, are: Patrick L. Alston, Jeremy R. Azrael, Alton S. Donnelly, Richard A. Gregg, Thomas J. Hegarty, Richard W. Judy, Peter Juviler, Michael M. Luther, David Mackenzie, Mark Hannll, Charles A. Moser, Dennis O'Connor, Alexander V. Lasanovsky, Alfred J. Rieber, Thomas Riha, Ernest H. Sway, Robert N. Taaffe, Howard L. Bronson, James O. Bailey Jr., Willis A. Konick and Albert C. Todd Jr.

One American, Walter C. Clemens Jr., had to interrupt

A Popular Russian
Oleg Danilovich Kalugin

"Real personality kid"
The New York Times

ONE of the results of the Soviet-American student exchange is that the student council of Columbia University's School of Journalism now includes a Soviet citizen, elected by his classmates. He is 24-year-old Oleg Danilovich Kalugin of Leningrad.

"Brilliant" and "a real personality kid" are typical of the terms Columbia professors and students apply to Mr. Kalugin. With an engaging smile and fluent English, this blond, slim, jaunty young man has won many friends since he arrived on the Columbia campus six months ago.

Part of the reason for his popularity at the School of Journalism has been his willingness to enter into the spirit of the work there. Typical was the time several weeks ago when he and a student-photographer went to the Metropolitan Opera House and took pictures of the Bolshoi Ballet's ballerinas during their rehearsals, sometimes in ungraceful poses. Mr. Kalugin was not daunted by the fact that he and his colleague were thrown out of the Metropolitan when their unauthorized presence was discovered.

Many Tastes in Common

Another reason for Mr. Kalugin's popularity is that he has many tastes in common with his fellow students. He is a jazz fan, favoring the music of Glenn Miller and Harry James. He does not like rock 'n' roll.

"The United States is just what I expected it to be," Mr. Kalugin says, stoutly denying that the Soviet press distorts American realities. A member of the Young Communist League, he expects to join the Communist party. Since arriving here he has had many discussions on political matters with Americans who disagree with his Communist views. He has also expressed his views before an audience of school children in Darien, Conn.

Mr. Kalugin spends much of his spare time at the movies, a habit he has brought from home, where he usually saw more than 100 pictures yearly. So far he has seen about seventy films here, all of which he has carefully listed and noted. "The Old Man and the Sea," is his favorite American film so far.

He thinks Soviet journalists can learn some things from American practice, particularly the speed of sending the main news of a story of the abbreviated form used in cables for transmitting messages. He has enjoyed the School of Journalism, but has some criticisms too, saying: "I think the courses are too practical. There should be more courses, giving background information."

Majored in U. S. Literature

Mr. Kalugin specialized in American literature at the University of Leningrad. For his visit here he was selected by his professors and Soviet educational authorities on the basis of his knowledge of English and general ability. Born in Leningrad Sept. 6, 1934, Mr. Kalugin was evacuated from that city soon after the German attack in 1941 and spent most of the war years with his mother in the Siberian city of Omsk. His father, a clerk in Leningrad's city government, stayed in the city throughout the siege. Mr. Kalugin is an only child.

Like many a young American, he began dating his wife, Ludmilla, early, when he was 16, and married her four years later. His wife, who has remained in Leningrad, is a mathematics teacher. Mr. Kalugin, noting the wide differences between his own and his wife's interests, says, "I was afraid it might be boring, but so far it hasn't been." The Kalugins have a 3-year-old daughter, Svetlana.

American students became tired of joking comments that they did not play basketball, although they came from the nation where basketball was invented. They organized a pick-up team, practiced, brought in a marine from the United States Embassy guard as a re-

dormitory without an elevator, crowded four to a room. Lack of heat during the winter, no hot water and of other facilities has produced some discomfort. The university bill of fare is monotonous and of poor quality by American standards.

At Leningrad there

lazy students too, Al Glushchenko, a 24-year-uate of the University reported here.

A graduate student al Harvard University Glushchenko said he Russian classmate found American graduate dents working hard. "But graduates are less student commented.

The classmate is Brykin, 26, a graduate Moscow Pedagogical In Mr. Brykin is a teacher lish, and at Harvard is izing in American dialect is working toward a por interpreter.

Both Russians said the along well with their students from this country abroad. The two men small rooms at William Hall, a dormitory for graduate students. Mr. said he sometimes found severely functional do depressing and not quiet.

Both men are married Mr. Glushchenko has one Their wives remained Soviet Union.

The Soviet students de the exchange program distinctly worth while. Th rived here late in Novembe will remain through the summer to complete their course.

"The courses are good Brykin said, "but somet do not agree with the ide pressed—in an economics for example. I think our is preferable to yours, be on the whole it does me the people."

Dr. Carroll F. Miles, a special students at Ha said the Russians were scholars. Because they a taking courses for cred explained, there is no w evaluate their work.

"They are very popular their fellow students," Miles said. "In fact, the lionized."

Kiev Man Likes Chic

Special to The New York Tim

CHICAGO, May 8—How Konstantin Ivanovich Nes Kiev like the student exc program?

His square, high-cheek face broke into an infec grin. "Okay," he said.

Mr. Nesen, 25-year-old uate student in physiolc the University of Ch thinks, moreover, that th gram should be extende addition to students, he a full-fledged scientist sho included. But the progra said, should be "more ized."

He commented that it impossible to tell from t versity catalogue the exa ture of courses given an caliber of the men tea them.

An adviser to the prog plained that it was not Mr. Nesen had been on campus for some time an gone from one course to a that he understood what be of most value to him, specializing in physiology.

Ленинградец знакомится

с жизнью

в Соединенных Штатах

Симпатичному Олегу Даниловичу Калугину 26 лет; он один из первых четырех советских студентов, зачисленных в Колумбийский университет на основе советско-американского соглашения об обмене в области образования. Всего в пяти университетах США 17 советских студентов, высшие учебные заведения в СССР посещает 21 американский студент. Во время своего пребывания в Колумбийском университете, где у него осталось много друзей, Олег Данилович был избран членом студенческого совета факультета журналистики и выступал перед учащимися. По окончании учебного года Калугину, как и другим советским студентам, была предоставлена возможность поездить по стране и обогатить свои знания об Америке и ее народе.

A 1959 Soviet magazine article featuring Kalugin and portraying him as a simple exchange student.

Kalugin (second from left) during a summer break in 1961 from his cover job as Radio Moscow correspondent. He is pictured in Bayville, Long Island, with future Soviet foreign minister Alexander Bessmertnykh (at right).

Oleg and Lyudmilla at a 1969 Soviet Embassy reception in Washington, D.C., for foreign journalists. At the time, Kalugin had begun working with American spy John Walker.

The author as a KGB lieutenant-colonel in 1970.

Kalugin (left) as deputy chief of Foreign Counterintelligence, with heads of the Romanian security service at a 1972 banquet in Bucharest.

Kalugin receives the Order of the Red Banner from Bulgarian security minister Dimitri Stoyanov at a 1974 ceremony in Moscow. Looking on in the background (center) is Kalugin's mentor, KGB chairman Yuri Andropov.

The legendary British spy Kim Philby (center) with Kalugin at intelligence headquarters at Yasenovo in 1976. Kalugin played a major role in rehabilitating Philby in the 1970s.

Kalugin with Lyudmilla (center) and a family friend at Karlovy Vary, Czechoslovakia, in 1976. He worked closely with all of the intelligence services of the Warsaw Pact countries.

A 1976 meeting between Kalugin (right) and a Czech double agent who had penetrated the CIA.

Cruising Hungary's Lake Balaton in 1977 with top security officials, including chief of Hungarian Intelligence Janosh Bodie (left).

Hungarian interior minister Andrash Benkai awards KGB Foreign Counterintelligence chief Kalugin a state decoration.

FIVE

P h i l b y

ne morning in March 1970, I sat in the inner sanctum of the KGB in Moscow, just a few feet from the bulky, imposing figure of Yuri Vladimirovich Andropov. I was attending a meeting of the KGB's ruling body, the Collegium, which was being chaired by the legendary Andropov. Arrayed in front of me in the spacious, wood-paneled room were a dozen of the "Gray Cardinals" of the dreaded Soviet secret police and espionage apparatus. At its regular monthly meetings, the Collegium decided all matters of importance to the KGB, and on this cold March morning the powerful, poker-faced members of our agency's ruling council were assembled around a long table discussing—among other things—my promotion.

The staff in the personnel department had instructed me to keep my head up and my mouth shut, and that's what I did as the Collegium considered my nomination as deputy director of Foreign Counterintelligence. Alexander Sakharovsky, the KGB's chief of Intelligence, summarized my achievements in New York and Washington. All the while, Andropov slumped in his chair, his eyes fixed on the papers in front of him. When Sakharovsky finished his talk, Andropov finally raised his head and asked me one question.

"Do you agree to take the position you've been offered?" the chairman asked.

"I do," I replied, with all the solemnity of a man taking his wedding vows.

"Do any members of the Collegium have any objections?" asked Andropov, his eyes surveying the room.

"No objections," he said. Then, nodding in my direction: "You can go."

And with that I was inducted into the upper reaches of the KGB and sent off to do battle with America and its NATO allies.

What I found on the front line of the espionage wars was disconcerting. My new directorate, a section of the Soviet Intelligence apparatus, had a dizzying array of responsibilities and was—atypically for the KGB—woefully understaffed. Foreign Counterintelligence had several major duties. We were charged with penetrating the Intelligence, Counterintelligence, and police agencies of the United States, its NATO allies, and other non-Socialist countries. We were supposed to penetrate and subvert Soviet émigré organizations, as well as anti-Soviet "centers of ideological subversion" such as Radio Liberty, a U.S. government station that beamed its broadcasts into the USSR. We were assigned to keep watch on thousands of Soviets working overseas to make sure they were not recruited by hostile Intelligence agencies and did not defect. And we had to ensure that the more than twelve thousand officers and employees of Soviet Intelligence did not go over to the other side and begin spying against the USSR. In short, Foreign Counterintelligence had a pivotal job in the KGB, and when I came on the scene in 1970 we were not doing it particularly well.

Now, in hindsight, it seems almost comical that KGB Intelligence and Foreign Counterintelligence should have been viewed around the world as a terrifying juggernaut. Perhaps the CIA saw us as a cold, efficient spying machine, though somehow I doubt it. For anyone close to the KGB's foreign operations, what seemed most immediately obvious were the tremendous problems we faced and the sloppiness of our work, not our valiant achievements. And as I settled into my new job at Lubyanka, I was painfully aware of how much work there was to be done, though I was at the same time proud of the heritage of Soviet Intelligence. After all, it was Foreign Counterintelligence, that had set up in the 1930s and 1940s one of the most spectacular spy rings of the century: Kim Philby and the "Magnificent Five" from Cambridge University. Following World War II, Soviet Intelligence had helped steal America's atomic bomb secrets, thus speeding up by several years our development of nuclear weapons. In the 1950s and 1960s, Foreign Counterintelligence had managed to penetrate deeply into the French, British, and Italian Intelligence agencies. In America, we had developed John Walker into a superspy.

But there was, in the halls of Lubyanka, a growing feeling that our glory was a thing of the past. And as I spent more time in Foreign Counterintelligence, rising to head of directorate in 1973, it became increasingly clear why we were lagging behind America in the field of espionage: Virtually no one believed any more in the Soviet Union. Almost to a man—or woman—the great spies of the early Soviet days, the Philbys or the Rosenbergs, came to us because of what they saw as our noble Communist experiment. The USSR and Communism looked like the wave of the future, and our best spies—such as the handful of men at the top of French Intelligence and the military—came to us in the 1930s, 1940s, and early 1950s out of ideological conviction.

All that began to change in 1956, when Khrushchev exposed the cruelty of the Stalin regime and showed that our "Socialist achievements" had been built on the bones of our own people. True Communist believers, such as Philby, began to dry up and disappear. And by the time we invaded Czechoslovakia in 1968, only the most fervid ideologue could hold any illusions that the Soviet Union was striving to build a Socialist utopia. CIA Director William Colby put it well when he said in the 1970s: "The Russians sometimes succeed in recruiting Americans on a material basis, making one-time payments for information passed on. They will only be able to recruit people on an ideological basis when they can present convincing proof that their country is the model society of the future, both politically and socially."

That, of course, was not going to happen.

As disillusionment with the Soviet Union set in, the number of KGB defectors also began to skyrocket, further damaging our operations. When I first started working in Foreign Counterintelligence in 1970, the KGB was experiencing a trickle of defections from the ranks. Unfortunately, I was Foreign Counterintelligence chief when two KGB officers defected during the 1970s. After I left the directorate in 1980, the number of turncoats in our ranks swelled to a torrent as more and more KGB officers became disenchanted with our system and fled to the West.

In my first few months on the job I felt forlorn as I sat at my desk and looked over the annual reports of Foreign Counterintelligence officers from around the world. Much of what these KGB professionals fed to us in the center was half-baked information, rumors, old wives' tales. My unit, known as Service Two of the Intelligence Directorate, had no moles in the CIA or FBI. Our agents in Western European Intelligence agencies were dying out. We had managed to penetrate the secrete services of many Third World countries, thus boosting the sheer number of spies working for us and meeting or over-fulfilling our annual quotas. But buying up agents in Asia and Africa was no great achievement, and I quickly realized we had to redouble our efforts and focus them on penetrating the CIA and NATO Intelligence agencies.

My welcome at Lubyanka, after spending a decade in America, was not the warmest, and my new boss and co-workers struck me as an unimpressive lot. The head of Foreign Counterintelligence, Vitaly Boyarov, was a pushy, argumentative, and self-righteous man who had been expelled from the KGB's London station in 1969. At first, staring at his puffy face, I thought I was in for a long, unpleasant relationship with my new chief. Yet I slowly came to respect Boyarov, realizing he was highly intelligent and tough but fair. He turned out to be a stubborn, sophisticated man who wouldn't kowtow to his superiors; in the end, under Kryuchkov, that was Boyarov's undoing.

There was little nice to say about the other deputies in Foreign Counterintelligence, all of whom were at least a decade older than I was. One was a chain-smoking, profane man who constantly berated his underlings. Another was a fussy, indecisive man who had no business being in the KGB, let alone in a relatively high position. The third was an utter nonentity. All three looked suspiciously upon the thirty-six-year-old *Wunderkind,* fresh from a successful tour of duty in Washington.

Shortly after I returned to work in Lubyanka, I received an unexpected call from Sergei Antonov, an old KGB friend. Antonov then headed KGB Directorate Nine, which protected all top Soviet officials. It was a large and powerful organization, and Antonov wanted to know if I would like to come to work for him and take charge of the section which recruited agents in the Kremlin among the entourages of the country's leaders. The section I was to head had more than one thousand five hundred officers whose job was to make sure no harm came to our Kremlin leaders and to keep an eye on—and recruit informers among—drivers, cooks, housekeepers, and other employees. I would have great power—and great perks—Antonov assured me, and he did his best to persuade me to leave Foreign Counterintelligence and come to work for the domestic side of the KGB.

"I've made inquiries, Oleg," said Antonov. "You don't even have a good place to live; your apartment doesn't even have a telephone.

We'll give you the biggest section in Directorate Nine. You'll have more than a thousand people working for you and a network of agents. We protect the Politburo. You know that work. You'll get everything—an apartment in the best building in Moscow, a car by your door every morning, and first-class food. You might make general in a year or two. Who knows? Come on, Oleg, be a good boy."

For a second, given the rocky state of affairs in Foreign Counterintelligence, I was tempted by Antonov's offer. But I knew that, although I would enjoy tremendous privileges and would rub shoulders with the country's leaders, the work I would do at Directorate Nine would not be nearly as valuable as the work in Foreign Counterintelligence. Had I gone to work for Antonov I would have been little more than a courtier. And the thought of bowing and scraping before the members of the Politburo, the thought of the endless court intrigues, was repulsive to me. I politely declined. One additional factor was my knowledge of the role the protection department played in the overthrow of Khrushchev in 1964, when the Soviet leader's immediate entourage and bodyguard plotted with the Politburo and betrayed him. Twenty-seven years later, the same scene would be played out again, this time with Mikhail Gorbachev: In the botched coup of August 1991, the Soviet president was betrayed by the chief of his bodyguard and several dozen other KGB officers assigned to protect Gorbachev and his family.

Boyarov had gotten wind of my conversations with the protection department, and asked me if I was negotiating behind his back to leave. I told him I was not interested in working for Directorate Nine, and we got down to work.

One incident that occurred early in my career there showed how disorganized and poorly prepared the section was. The KGB was getting ready to build a top-secret Intelligence headquarters at Yasenovo, on the outskirts of Moscow. Within the agency, there was a debate as to whether the buildings at Yasenovo should be taller than seven stories, which might make the supposedly supersecret facility visible from nearby roads. One official argued that the CIA's headquarters at Langley, Virginia, was no more than seven stories and that, for security purposes, Yasenovo shouldn't be either.

Sakharovsky, the Intelligence chief, phoned me and asked me to dig up a picture of CIA headquarters. I got on the phone with our people in records, thinking they would have the photograph to me in a matter of minutes. The fact was that, for nearly twenty-four hours, our crack experts in archives couldn't *find* a picture of Langley. How were we supposed to recruit CIA agents if, in our Moscow offices, we couldn't even locate a picture of CIA headquarters? Finally, our records people turned up a photograph. I resolved to straighten up the mess there, and eventually our section was one of the first in the KGB to become computerized.

Knowing the difficulties in recruiting CIA agents in America itself, Boyarov and I set in motion a plan to enlist CIA officers posted overseas. Many KGB stations, particularly in the Third World, had been satisfied to recruit dozens of local army officers, politicians, and intelligence operatives, all the while giving CIA men a wide berth. Boyarov and I resolved to take the fight directly to the CIA, and within a year of my assuming office an excellent opportunity to recruit an American Intelligence officer presented itself in India. Boyarov decided I should fly to New Delhi to attempt the recruitment myself.

The CIA agent was a third secretary at the U.S. Embassy in New Delhi. His last name was Leonard. Over the course of a year, Leonard—then in his early thirties—had carried out a series of extraordinarily careless meetings and recruitment attempts with Indian politicians, army officers, and security agents. We had gotten wind of his hamhanded actions for a simple reason: We had scores of sources throughout the Indian government—in Intelligence, Counterintelligence, the Defense and Foreign ministries, and the police. It seemed like the entire country was for sale; the KGB—and the CIA—had deeply penetrated the Indian government. After a while, neither side entrusted sensitive information to the Indians, realizing their enemy would know all about it the next day.

We, however, had been more successful than the Americans. Using bribes, confidential ties, and liberal financing of election campaigns, the KGB had played an important role in keeping India among the Soviet Union's friends and partners on the international scene. Corruption was so widespread in India that one top minister offered to pass us information for a fee of $50,000.

"Do we need him?" Andropov asked his subordinates.

"Not really," one replied. "We've got all the documents from the Foreign and Defense ministries. Anyway, why pay fifty thousand dollars to him? There might be a scandal."

During the 1960s and 1970s, the KGB gave hundreds of thousands of dollars in campaign contributions to Indira Gandhi's Indian Congress Party. The Indian Communist Party got wind of our under-the-table "gifts" and was understandably upset, but we were not naive and put our money on the party that was likely to continue leading India. The KGB had several agents and informers in Indira Gandhi's entourage, and they told her that the large contributions came from sources in the Soviet Union, though her aides may not have told her the money was actually from the KGB.

In any case, India was a model of KGB infiltration of a Third World government. And when Mr. Leonard from the CIA began violating elementary rules of secret meetings and unwittingly exposing his Indian informers, we quickly had detailed accounts (and sometimes photographs) of Leonard's rendezvous. By the time I got into the act, the file documenting Leonard's sloppy espionage work was a thick one.

I flew out of Moscow on a frigid January day in 1971. I calculated my chances of recruiting the CIA man at about fifty-fifty, and could only hope that he would be so worried about our exposing his missteps to the Indian press and the CIA that he would agree to cooperate. For a high-ranking KGB officer to attempt to directly recruit a CIA agent was an uncommon and risky proposition; I knew if I failed that a scandal might ensue, one that could jeopardize my chances of ever serving again in the United States. I was uneasy, yet at the same time excited about the opportunity of confronting my adversary face to face in an effort to win him over. My plan was to meet him in comfortable surroundings and use a forceful but friendly approach. A lot would depend, I realized, on Leonard's personalilty. Our KGB officers on the scene had said he might make a good recruit.

Flying into New Delhi's Palam Airport late at night, I was immediately struck by the poverty of the country. Stick figures warmed themselves around fires that smelled of dung and burning grass. The streets teemed with rickshaws and figures swaddled in dirty robes. Compared to Western Europe, Moscow looked worn and gray. But compared to New Delhi, Moscow seemed like a world-class capital.

Settling into the embassy compound, I read the dossier on Leonard and met with our Counterintelligence officers. My stay in New Delhi had been kept quiet so as not to draw the attention of the CIA, which monitored the movements of certain Soviets in and out of India. I met with our ambassador to let him know I was in town to attempt to recruit a CIA officer. All I told the ambassador was that I was going to be tough on the CIA man because he had been aggressively trying to recruit our people.

Several nights after I arrived in New Delhi, the KGB station chief held a small party for me, attended by some men from our agency and from the GRU, Soviet Military Intelligence. At the party, our resident let drop that I was in town to "shake a fist" at the Americans because they had been behaving increasingly aggressively in India. At no time did the station chief or I mention that I was in town to recruit a CIA man. One of the guests at the party was the GRU resident in New Delhi, a man named Polyakov. Years later, we would learn that he was already working for the Americans.

My subordinates had arranged for me to meet Leonard at the home of one of our KGB officers. Our officer was an acquaintance of Leonard's and suggested he come to dinner. Leonard may have told his superiors about the invitation, and the CIA probably decided it would do no harm to dine at the Soviet diplomat's house and see what developed. I arrived at my colleague's bungalow well before the CIA agent was scheduled to show up, and we worked out the details of the recruitment approach. When Leonard appeared, I donned sunglasses and began smoking a cigarette, all in an effort to make it hard for the CIA to identify me. The three of us had a few drinks, and Leonard seemed to be in a fine mood, laughing loudly at our—and his own—jokes. My KGB colleague's wife served us dinner, and after the main course my fellow officer retired to another part of his bungalow, leaving Leonard and me alone.

I got right to the point.

"Listen," I said. "I have something to tell you. I know you're with the CIA. I represent Soviet Intelligence. So we don't have to hide things from each other. We are both professionals. And I'll tell you, young man, in your career you have made so many mistakes that you'll probably lose your job soon."

I pulled out his dossier, showing him detailed reports and photographs of his meetings with a host of Indian sources. He blanched and began to protest, but I cut him off.

"This is all of your work," I continued. "Besides endangering a dozen Indian military men and politicians who are on the CIA payroll, you have done your government a disservice. You have compromised your organization, your agents, and your government. When we have all this information published in the Indian press, it will be a nice gift to the Indian and American governments. Can you imagine? The local press will have a field day when they learn that you paid their officials to work for you. When the local public finds out about what you did, U.S. positions in India will be seriously undermined and you will pay for your sins with your job. Do you understand that this is the end of your career? The CIA will throw you out right away."

The man who just ten minutes ago had been roaring at his own jokes and uttering silly platitudes about U.S.-Soviet relations was now a sorry spectacle. He looked stunned, frightened, and utterly flustered. Sensing I was making progress, I pushed on.

"I'm offering you a deal. You will provide me information about CIA activities against the USSR and I, in return, will give you information which you can feed to your superiors and which will be useful in your career. We will obviously pay you for your services."

"How much would you be willing to pay?" he asked.

"I can give you twenty-five thousand right now," I responded. "If you work well, I can give you a hundred thousand down the line, and more after that if our relationship continues."

I was not bluffing, and had the twenty-five thousand dollars with me. Leonard's jaw literally dropped; he was dumbfounded that the KGB was actually trying to recruit him.

"You understand that this is an unbelievably serious thing you just told me," he said. "I have never been in a situation like this before. Your proposition is tempting, and what you have told me will be a lesson to me. But I cannot make a decision at once. Betraying my country would be contrary to my convictions, to everything I've done in my life. I am a patriot . . . I have to think it over."

He was virtually pleading with me.

"I understand it's not an easy decision to make," I replied. "What do you want?"

"I want time to think it over," he said. "Your offer is very enticing, but I need to think about it. I'm willing to meet again. Give me until tomorrow."

We parted, and I thought I might have succeeded in persuading him to cooperate. But the next day at 6:00 P.M., Leonard didn't show up at our appointed meeting place in New Delhi. The following day, the American ambassador sent a strongly worded letter of protest to the Indian Foreign Ministry and the Soviet ambassador, Mr. Pegov. The American ambassador met Pegov to protest our attempted recruitment, but our ambassador replied, "Yes, I know about this case. Your people have been trying to recruit my staff and I told this man who came from Moscow to stop it."

The protest went nowhere. We, meanwhile, gave the material to the Indian press, though we left out Leonard's identity. After all, we didn't want to irritate the CIA too much or they might start acting in kind. The leaked story of this brazen CIA agent created the predictable stir in India, with Indira Gandhi even publicly lashing out at the CIA. I sometimes wondered why the Americans didn't decide to use Leonard as a double agent; perhaps they decided that they couldn't keep him under tight control.

One mystery remained—a mystery I pondered as I made a short inspection trip around India to Bombay, Jaipur, and Madras. When the American ambassador sent his letter of protest, he mentioned me by name as the KGB officer who had tried to recruit Leonard. How could the Americans possibly have known my name, since I flew into the country as an unregistered diplomat? There must have been a source in our embassy, and we set about to find it.

We had no luck. But fifteen years later, the issue was resolved. Edward Lee Howard, a CIA defector, fled to Moscow and provided the KGB with reams of information on U.S. moles in the KGB and GRU. Howard usually didn't know the names of the moles, but he knew enough about their circumstances that we were able, in many instances, to uncover the spies. And one of those men exposed by Howard was none other than Polyakov, the GRU resident who had toasted me in New Delhi. Polyakov, after leaving New Delhi, had risen to the rank of general, and over the course of roughly fifteen years he fed the United States top-secret information. Our well-connected assets in French Intelligence kept telling us in the 1970s that the CIA had a mole inside the GRU. We repeatedly went to our Military Counterintelligence people, saying we had it on impeccable authority that the GRU had been penetrated at a high level.

"Come on, Oleg," my colleagues in Military Counterintelligence would reply. "What nonsense!"

"These sources have never lied to us," I replied. "They may not know enough, but they aren't lying. There must be a joint effort to find the mole."

Military Counterintelligence made halfhearted attempts to ferret out the spy in the GRU, but never could locate him. Then along came Howard, and in a matter of months Polyakov was arrested, interrogated, and shot. He was one of several Soviet turncoats exposed by Howard and executed in the late 1980s.

When I returned from India to Moscow, the corridors of Lubyanka were buzzing with rumors of my unsuccessful recruiting attempt.

Some friends tried to console me. Other colleagues thought my career was washed up, since such a rare and risky recruitment effort had blown up in my face. I thought they were wrong, saw nothing at all harmful in what I had done, and was even thinking of new ways to approach CIA agents. I threw myself into the effort to reorganize and strengthen Foreign Counterintelligence. And I took solace in the words of Kim Philby, who told me, "If one attempt in fifty is successful, your efforts won't have been wasted."

And it was to Philby that I was devoting a great deal of my time in the early 1970s, nurturing a relationship that would prove to be one of the most rewarding and fascinating in all my years in the KGB.

I came to know the legendary spy in a roundabout way, following one of the most publicized defections by a KGB officer in the Cold War era. In September 1971, Oleg Lyalin, a KGB major on our London station, went over to the other side after working six months for British Intelligence. But Lyalin was no ordinary Intelligence officer, and what he revealed to British authorities created an international scandal that seriously undermined our espionage activities in England.

Lyalin, an expert marksman and parachutist, was assigned to one of the KGB's most shadowy sections—Department V—whose duty was to prepare contingency plans for assassination and sabotage in the event of war. Every large KGB station throughout the world had one officer representing Department V. We had one in Washington, who did everything from plotting ways to poison the capital's water system to drawing up assassination plans for U.S. leaders. No one from Department V had ever defected before, and what Lyalin divulged—which was eventually made public—created a stir. He disclosed that Department V's wartime plans in England included plots to shadow leaders and assassinate them, flood the London Underground, blow up military installations, and generally wreak havoc. The sabotage would be coordinated by Lyalin and carried out by Soviet special forces troops and Soviet illegals and agents living in England.

The furor created by Lyalin's revelations led the British government to expel 105 Soviets from the country. In addition, the English clamped down on the KGB by denying visas to known Soviet Intelligence officers. Our intelligence-gathering activities in England suffered a blow from which they never recovered, and the Lyalin defection sent shockwaves through Lubyanka. An investigation showed that Lyalin's behavior was suspect and should have been curtailed, but that the KGB resident in London, as well as our Counterintelligence man, covered up Lyalin's misdeeds. Lyalin had seduced the wives of several Soviet officials in London. Our people knew about his shenanigans and, very likely, British Intelligence did, too. But no one reined in his increasingly wild behavior because they did not want a scandal and, as often was the case, KGB officers in the same station covered up for one another.

The upshot of the Lyalin affair was that dozens of KGB officers were fired or demoted. Department V was shut down. And Andropov demanded that something be done to stem the growing tide of KGB defections, while at the same time luring more Western defectors to the Soviet Union.

Andropov called in my chief, Boyarov, and ordered that a new program be developed to make defection to the USSR attractive— not an easy assignment. The KGB chairman suggested that we lure defectors to the Soviet Union with offers of large amounts of money, fancy apartments and country houses, and complete freedom of movement in the USSR and Eastern Europe. According to Boyarov, Andropov told him, "Lyalin has disgraced our organization. We must make people want to defect to us. Why do our people always defect to the West? We should have a program that would entice Western spies to come to us. We need to seduce them into coming here with financial remuneration, a better life, perhaps ideological reasons. Spare no effort."

Andropov, still thinking in terms of the old Communist International, was deluded if he thought that as late as 1971 we could persuade defectors to come to us for ideological reasons. But he was on the right track when he suggested that we needed to make life better for those people who had spied for the Soviet Union and defected to our side.

"How many defectors do we have?" Andropov asked Boyarov. "Are they living well? Are they treated all right? Make a life for them so that everyone will envy them. Everyone should know about it."

Boyarov called me in and said he was entrusting me with the job of improving the lot of foreign defectors in Moscow, most notably Kim Philby.

"You'll take care of these people," Boyarov said. "You're perfectly suited for it. You have the experience of working in the West. You deal with these people. Give them anything they want. Do anything. I won't interfere."

And so, early in 1972, I found myself heading to the apartment of Harold Adrian Russell "Kim" Philby, a living legend in the espionage world. I had read reports and heard rumors about Philby's life in Moscow—his drinking, womanizing, bouts of depression and squalid existence. Driving to his flat, located on Yuzhinsky Pereyulok, just off Gorky Street in the very center of Moscow, I had butterflies in my stomach, not knowing what to expect. I entered the faded, pre-Revolutionary building and was assaulted by the smell of urine. A dark, rickety elevator haltingly carried me up seven floors. I got out, walked up one flight of stairs to the top floor, and rang the buzzer next to Philby's reinforced steel door. Nothing had prepared me for what I was about to see.

Someone fumbled with the lock. The door opened, and I stepped inside. There, in the twilight of the entrance hall, was a wreck of a man. The bent figure caromed off the walls as he walked. Reeking of vodka, he mumbled something unintelligible to me in atrocious, slurred Russian.

Hunched over in front of me was one of the great spies of the twentieth century. Philby, along with four Cambridge University classmates, had decided in the 1930s to devote his life to the Communist cause, and he concluded that he could best serve it by becoming a Soviet spy. Philby and his cohorts infiltrated the British Army, the Foreign Ministry, and the Secret Intelligence Service (SIS), where, for more than a decade, they passed along invaluable information to the Soviet Union and exposed scores of agents within the USSR. Four of the so-called "Magnificent Five" have been identified: Philby, Guy Burgess, Donald Maclean, and Anthony Blunt. Speculation has been rife about the identity of the so-called "Fifth Man," though numerous people are claiming that he was John Cairncross. In any event, Philby and the Cambridge spies were true Communist believers. Appalled by the rise of fascism in Nazi Germany, dismayed over the collapse of the Labour Party in Britain, and impressed by Stalin's Socialist experiment and his bold industrialization drive, the young men became convinced that Soviet Communism was the wave of the future.

After graduating from Cambridge in 1933, Philby went on to quietly make contact with leftists in England and on the Continent. In 1937, he went off to the Spanish Civil War, where he made a name for himself in England by writing for *The Times* (London) and distinguished himself in the eyes of the Soviet secret police by supplying them with detailed reports about Franco's regime and the involvement of the Germans and Italians on the side of the Spanish Fascists.

When World War II broke out, Philby, with Guy Burgess's help, landed a job in Counterintelligence with Her Majesty's Secret Intelligence Service. He gave his Soviet handlers excellent information, including two books detailing the work of British agents against the Soviet Union. In 1944, Philby managed to maneuver himself into position to head up the SIS unit assigned to hunt down Soviet agents in England. He truly became the fox guarding the henhouse, and passed along to Moscow priceless information about anti-Soviet intelligence efforts in Great Britain. From 1947 to 1949, he was the SIS's chief in Turkey, handing over information about the attempts of anti-Soviet agents to enter the USSR. And from 1949 to 1951, he served in Washington as the SIS's chief liaison wit the CIA. That job placed him in an extraordinarily sensitive position, and the damage he did to the West was enormous. Among other things, he passed along precise information about Western efforts to parachute Russian-speaking illegals into the Soviet Union. The information, along with many of his other tips, led to the capture and execution of dozens of Western agents in the Soviet Union, a byproduct of his work that (on the surface at least) never seemed to bother Philby. In Washington, Philby became close friends with the future CIA Counterintelligence chief, James Jesus Angleton, who trusted Philby implicitly and was stunned when the Englishman turned out to be a spy. Angleton was so badly burned that for the rest of his life he saw evidence of far-reaching Soviet plots everywhere and remained paranoid about Soviet "volunteers."

The extraordinary espionage careers of Philby and the Magnificent Five began to unravel in 1951 when the CIA broke the Soviet Intelligence code and began to close in on Maclean. Guy Burgess and Donald Maclean both fled to the Soviet Union as the CIA and SIS noose was tightening. Philby, who had been closely associated with Burgess, immediately came under suspicion and was tossed out of the SIS. But he bluffed his way through several inquiries, remaining in England until 1956, when he moved to Beirut as a journalist. Finally, in 1963, the SIS had convincing proof of Philby's espionage and sent an officer to confront him. The British spy then fled on a ship from Beirut to Odessa, beginning his quarter century of exile in the Soviet Union.

He was exhaustively debriefed in Moscow. But after every bit of information had been wrung out of Philby, he was essentially tossed aside. The KGB gave him a comfortable flat and a handsome pension, but almost never tried to use his expertise. Many KGB officials remained—idiotically and utterly without proof—suspicious of Philby. I had read Philby's file before visiting him, and discovered an analysis by one intelligence officer who argued that Philby was actually a British double agent seeking to misinform the Soviet Union. The head of the KGB security group, who brought me Philby's dossier, opined that Philby might well be a double agent sent to Moscow to penetrate the KGB. Philby's phone and apartment were bugged, his mail opened, and his visitors screened. Though he undeniably was one of the great spies for the USSR, he was never promoted in the KGB and remained, until the end, a rank-and-file officer, known by his code name "Agent Tom."

By the time I ascended the stairs to Philby's rundown apartment, the famed spy, who had risked his life to serve what he believed was a noble Communist cause, had been driven half-mad by the paranoia and idiocy of the KGB. No doubt he also was driven to despair as he saw the cause to which he had devoted his life transformed into the shabby reality of modern-day Soviet life. Philby was as disillusioned as any of us, perhaps more so. And in the late 1960s, his despondency had led him to legendary bouts of drinking and womanizing. It was a miracle he was still alive.

As the gray-haired, puffy-faced, but still handsome, legend stood swaying in the hallway, a wave of pity swept over me. And then, realizing I was from the KGB, Philby began wildly cursing the secret police, the Soviet government, and the world at large. I was rescued by Philby's long-suffering Russian wife, Rufa, who led him away and then fussily helped me off with my coat.

"Mr. Kalugin, I'm very sorry about the way my husband behaves, but what can I do?" said the striking, red-haired Mrs. Philby.

She led me into their apartment. It was spacious and sparsely furnished, with an ascetic feel to it. The ceilings were high and leaky. A few lithographs hung on the walls. The only room that exuded a feeling of warmth was Philby's study, which was lined with English books. Philby's ranting about the KGB settled down into an occasional mumble, and I tried to make small talk with the British spy and his wife. After twenty minutes, I excused myself and left, promising to return soon. On the way out, I was cursing to myself, incredulous that I had been assigned to baby-sit this broken-down drunk. "Jesus!" I said to myself as I walked out of Philby's building. "This is not my job."

I described the situation to Boyarov, and we both agreed that the KGB had better do something soon for Philby, otherwise he would drink himself to death as his fellow member of the Magnificent Five, Guy Burgess, had done in Moscow a decade before. It was plain to see that what was ruining Philby was not simply alcoholism—that was only a symptom. What was really ailing the man was the lack of purpose to his life, the sense that he had been used up by the Soviet system and cast aside. He had lost any reason to live. So Boyarov and I devised a two-pronged strategy to save Philby. The first, and least important, was to improve his material lot. The second, and most crucial, was to make him feel useful again, and I quickly came to see that Philby could still be of service to the KGB and the Soviet Union.

I began visiting him regularly, and gradually succeeded in convincing him and Rufa that I was not one of the KGB goons who had effectively placed him under house arrest. On one visit, when Philby was relatively sober, I asked him to write a detailed analysis of how he thought our Foreign Counterintelligence section should work, as well as a description of CIA and SIS operations against the Soviet Union. He said he'd rather just tell me about it, but I insisted he write it down.

"No, no," I said. "If I just listen, I may miss something or forget something. Just sit down and write it up for us. After all, you're a free man. You don't have to go to work. Please do it for us."

He agreed, and produced an astute and—for me—useful tract on how we should structure our operations against the CIA and Western intelligence services.

A key aspect of my plan to rehabilitate Philby was to end the isolation which the KGB had imposed upon him. First, I persuaded my superiors to scale back on the electronic eavesdropping, and they agreed to bug only his telephone. We concurred that, when the time was right, he could start seeing some foreigners, especially correspondents. After all, the goal set out by Andropov was to significantly improve Philby's life and show other potential collaborators in the West that he was living happily in the Soviet Union. Slowly, over the course of several months, we began to sober up Philby and introduce him to a wide range of KGB officers and trainees.

I brought over officers from our English section, Foreign Counter-Intelligence, and our "Active Measures" department to talk informally with Philby. We would sit in his living room discussing current events and problems in the KGB. At first, I think Philby was disoriented by what was going on; he had grown accustomed to the quiet of his apartment, and now it was filled with loud conversation, jokes, and laughter. He was also by nature cautious, and it took him months to accept that I was genuinely there to help him. On our first few visits, he offered us vodka and we never refused him. But in an effort to get Philby off the hard liquor, we began to bring him wine and champagne. Soon, he was only offering us wine or champagne, and we noticed that Philby was beginning to dry out and become more responsive.

I decided to use Philby to talk with young intelligence officers and students from the KGB Higher School. Officers who were bound for England, Australia, or New Zealand were invited to his apartment for "teas," during which the veteran spy would expound primarily on life and social mores in England, occasionally throwing in some reflections on the espionage business. Both he and the students seemed to get a lot out of these meetings. On several occasions, we took him to talk with the players from the "Dynamo" hockey team, which was sponsored by the KGB. Once he received a standing ovation from the players before they departed for the World Championship.

But Philby's duties went beyond mere lecturing or public relations. His English and knowledge of the world of espionage made him perfectly suited for use by the "Active Measures" department. We brought numerous CIA and U.S. State Department documents to his apartment. He would insert sinister paragraphs into the documents—something, perhaps, about plans for U.S. military involvement in Asia or Latin America—and we would stamp them "TOP SECRET" and deliver them to journalists in the Third World or Europe who were sympathetic to the Soviet cause.

I also called on Philby for advice on operational matters and sought his opinion on whether some "volunteers" who had come to us were genuine or not. In one case, an Australian sent a letter to our embassy in Canberra, enclosing top-secret documents and requesting that payment be made to a post office box in the capital. The anonymous "volunteer" promised to supply us with more information if we sent the money. Fearing a set-up by Australian security services, we debated whether to send the cash to the donor. Finally, we decided there was no harm in transferring the funds anonymously to a post office box. Thus began a fruitful relationship in which the anonymous Australian—apparently someone in their Intelligence agency—supplied us with extremely useful information about the Australian Secret Intelligence Organization and its American and British partners. At some point, I showed Philby the Australian's letters and the classified material he had supplied us. I had blacked out any references to the country, so as not to compromise the security of the operation, but Philby quickly surmised that the "volunteer" was from Australia and that he was genuine. Eventually, our Australian began passing on so much material that we set up a series of "dead drops" similar to those used by Walker. Although I lost touch with the operation after 1980, I don't think the Australian ever was caught.

At one point, Philby was doing so much for us that I offered him an honorarium of several thousands rubles—a large sum, roughly equivalent to his annual pension. Philby proudly refused my offer, telling me, "You know, old man, that I've never taken money. My pension is enough for me and I don't need anything else."

Eventually, we arranged for Philby to travel to our fellow Socialist countries, where the warm receptions he received provided a needed boost to his ego. Before I arrived on the scene, he had traveled once to the Soviet republic of Georgia, where his hosts—showing true Caucasian hospitality—had kept him drunk around the clock. I asked him if he'd like a return engagement to the Caucasus, to which he replied in horror, "Oh, come on! When I recall their public toilets, I'm simply disgusted. I don't remember ever experiencing anything like that . . . No, never again!"

So we arranged several trips for him to Hungary, Czechoslovakia, Mongolia, and Cuba. These were private visits, during which he would meet with local intelligence officers and be fêted at banquets. The trips mainly offered the worldly Philby a chance to escape the drabness of Moscow, and they did seem to give him a lift. I remember him returning from Cuba with a mountain of gifts, including carpets, weapons, and vases. The only Communist country he steadfastly refused to visit was East Germany; he never was able to forgive the German people for supporting Hitler and Nazi fascism.

At the same time as we were getting Philby out and about, we also spent sizable sums of money—with Andropov's blessing—to improve his life materially. Using hard currency, we bought him books, appliances, clothing, and scarce foods. We supplied him with a housekeeper. My assistant provided him with whatever train, theater, or plane tickets he needed. On special order from Andropov, Philby was given a 100-ruble-a-month credit at one of the private groceries for the Soviet elite—not a bad perk considering that a tin of black caviar cost only 5 rubles then. Mikhail Lyubimov, the KGB resident in Denmark who had befriended Philby during his debriefing, brought the Englishman delicacies and clothes from Scandinavia.

Philby's apartment was in bad need of repair, and I suggested that he consider moving to a new place. I showed him three: one was in the very center of town, right on Gorky Street; a second was in a comfortable complex for KGB big shots (I lived there); and a third was spacious but far from the center of town. In those days, good apartments were terribly scarce, and the KGB's offer to show Philby three excellent flats was a measure of how serious the agency was in improving his life.

He rejected my apartment complex and the one far from the center, saying they were in bleak, modern residential areas.

"Listen, Oleg. I like to take walks in the evening," Philby told me. "What will I do in a place like that?"

It was true. Philby, particularly as his mood improved, loved to amble at night through the center of Moscow, past the high brick walls of the Kremlin and down the small streets, such as the Arbat, that exude a sense of the beauty of pre-Revolutionary Russia.

We looked at the apartment on Gorky Street, just a few blocks from his place. It was in good shape, and bigger than the one in which he and Rufa lived. Nevertheless, Philby decided he'd rather stay put.

"I'm a conservative at heart, though I'm not one of those people who would like your country to go back to Stalin's times," Philby said with a wry smile. Later, he told me, "If we could just have my old apartment repaired, that would be fine."

So the KGB sent in a special work crew, which labored several months repairing ceilings, replacing plumbing, and generally sprucing up the place.

After Philby refused to take any money for the help he was providing us, I decided to take some funds we had set aside for him and replace his shabby furniture. Unbeknownst to Kim, I took Rufa to a special shop for the Kremlin elite, where she picked out some handsome contemporary furniture from Finland. Several days later, the furniture was delivered, much to Philby's delight.

"When Kim saw the luxurious armchairs, sofa, tables, wardrobes, and bookcases, he was amazed," Rufa told me later. "He walked around them in circles for a long time, stroking the rosewood sides and the soft upholstery. Once I awoke at three in the morning.

Kim wasn't in the bedroom, so I got frightened. I got out of bed, opened the door a crack, and saw the lights were on in the living room. When I went in, Kim was sitting on the new sofa, looking admiringly at the cut glass in the cupboard. 'I feel so happy,' he said. 'How nice the apartment looks now. Why didn't I think of it before?' "

I was happy, too, helping bring Philby back to life.

Unlike many other spies and defectors, Philby seemed to me an unselfish man who cared very little about money and creature comforts. He spent his days reading, writing, and listening to the BBC, whose English-language broadcasts in the Soviet Union were not jammed. Once I mentioned to him how much I enjoyed listening to Alistair Cooke's "Letter from America" on the BBC, and Philby said it was one of his favorite programs, too. We knew that Philby spent a great deal of time writing; the man in charge of bugging his apartment said it was obvious that Philby often was at his desk scribbling away. This naturally made the KGB suspicious, as the agency wondered whether he was compiling reports to British Intelligence. The fact was that Philby was doing little more than writing letters and working on his memoirs.

Over time, my wife and I became close friends with Philby and Rufa. On his birthday or on state holidays, such as the November 7th anniversary of the Russian Revolution, we often went to visit him. Sometimes he would cook for us; he was an excellent chef, preparing delicious, spicy recipes he had picked up in Spain or Lebanon. He was a warm, witty man, and a great raconteur. For me, it was gratifying to see the steady transformation of Philby from a pitiful drunk into a sociable, sober human being. Slowly, the anguish and indifference I had seen in his eyes when we first met was replaced by a liveliness, even a sparkle. My profession is not known for its humanitarianism and good works, and being able to actually help someone put his life back together—particularly someone of Philby's stature—was a source of immense satisfaction to me.

Over time, Andropov did score the propaganda points he was looking for in the rehabilitation of Philby, though I doubt it did the Soviet Union much good. By 1980 few, if any, Western intelligence agents were scrambling to jump to the other side of the Iron Curtain. Soviet television showed a film about Philby's life. We put out the word in Moscow and in the West that Philby was living well, and numerous foreign correspondents and Western authors came to see the legendary spy. Philby even published his own memoirs, over the objection of Politburo member Mikhail Suslov, who remained suspicious of the Englishman. We tried to persuade Andropov to award Philby the rank of general, but never succeeded. We instructed Philby to tell Western reporters he had been made a KGB general, which he did, and I assured him, "With what you've accomplished, you're more than justified in feeling that you are a general."

To which Philby replied with a smile, "I know I'm a general."

In my years with Foreign Counterintelligence, I also worked with two other famous British spies who had fled to Moscow: George Blake, a Secret Intelligence Service agent who began spying for the Soviet Union in the 1950s; and Donald Maclean, a member of the Magnificent Five.

I met Blake in 1971, just a few days after I was first introduced to Philby. Blake's history was, in its own way, as bizarre and tumultuous as Kim's.

Born in Rotterdam to a Dutch mother and a Jewish father who was a naturalized British citizen, Blake went on to join the SIS in the late 1940s. He was posted to Seoul, South Korea, where, at the start of the Korean War, he was captured by Chinese forces. The Chinese turned him over to Soviet Intelligence agents, who had little trouble persuading Blake—who already held far-leftist views—to return to England and work for the KGB.

Blake was repatriated in 1953 and spent the ensuing eight years working as a KGB spy in London and Berlin. Perhaps his most famous accomplishment was his disclosure to the Soviets in 1955 that the British and Americans had dug an underground tunnel into East Berlin that was used to plug into top-secret Soviet and East German communication lines. Blake also provided the Soviets with information that led to the exposure—and execution—of dozens of Western agents working behind the Iron Curtain. In 1961, using information provided by a Soviet and Polish defector, British Intelligence discovered Blake was a spy and arrested him. He was sentenced to forty-two years in jail but, in a bold rescue attempt carried out by several pacifists and anti-nuclear activists, Blake was sprung from jail after six years and bundled off to Russia.

In 1973, two years after meeting Blake and shortly after I was named head of Foreign Counterintelligence, I made a chilling discovery about Blake's rescue.

Settling into my new job, I began to read the top-secret files that had been sitting in the safe of the former head of Foreign Counter-intelligence. I was studying dossiers from the 1950s and 1960s when I came across a sealed envelope marked *"Never to Be Opened Without Permission."* Since there was no indication about whose permission was needed, and since I myself now headed the directorate, I opened the envelope. The papers inside were headed "SPECIAL OPERATION" and they described the fate of an Irishman, Sean Burke, who helped Blake escape and who fled with him to Russia. The document explained that Burke was extremely dissatisfied with his life in the Soviet Union and was planning to return to the United Kingdom. Alexander Sakharovsky, chief of Intelligence, said the KGB feared that Burke would describe to British Intelligence how he and Blake were smuggled into the USSR and would divulge Blake's whereabouts in Moscow, thus making him vulnerable to assassination. Sakharovsky therefore ordered that Burke be surreptitiously given a drug that would damage his brain and give the appearance that he had suffered a stroke. The drug was administered, and Burke returned to England in a debilitated condition. A few years later, he died—apparently a result of the KGB's drugging and his alcoholism.

When I first met George Blake, he was in far better shape than Philby. Blake rarely drank, held a good job at the Institute of World Economics in Moscow, and had a devoted Russian wife and a young son. The Englishman was friendly, and grateful for the extra money and perks we gave him. We discovered, through electronic surveillance of his apartment, that Blake also was a religious man who enjoyed reading the Bible, particularly the Gospel According to John. I later talked to him about his belief and asked whether he thought it was in contradiction with his Communist faith.

"What's wrong with it?" he replied. "Communism is the same as Christianity, only put on a scientific basis."

Blake was an easygoing man, and our two families hit it off and began to socialize. He wasn't near the challenge that Philby was, yet we considered him less reliable than Philby. I essentially trusted Blake, though there was one episode that aroused my suspicions. We learned that a British Intelligence officer was coming to Moscow under diplomatic cover, and we asked Blake if he would help us attempt to recruit the man. Both Philby and Blake knew him, but Philby was ailing and we thought we had nothing to lose by sending Blake to talk with his former SIS colleague. But Blake refused.

"Oh, no, Oleg," he said. "I'm not a recruiter."

"You don't have to go in for the kill," I replied. "Just scare him. Make him vulnerable. See how he reacts."

After much arm-twisting, Blake agreed to meet the man. We arranged it so that Blake would bump into the man in a hotel in Moscow, but the visiting British Intelligence officer refused to speak with Blake and our effort flopped. Blake's resistance to the recruitment made some people suspicious, and the electronic eavesdropping in his apartment was continued. My reading of the situation was that Blake was simply a far shyer person than Philby. Unlike Philby, Blake shunned the limelight, fearing that since he was a fugitive he was vulnerable to an abduction attempt.

Perhaps because of his religious beliefs, Blake also seemed more disturbed by the consequences of his espionage activities. He told me several times that Soviet Intelligence promised him that none of the people he identified as agents in the USSR had been shot. He clung naively to that belief; I didn't have the heart to tell him that his work led directly to the deaths of dozens of agents behind the Iron Curtain. Philby knew that his spying and tips to the KGB had doomed many men, and it didn't seem to haunt him: he wrote off the victims as casualties of the Cold War. Neither did Philby ever say he was sorry for what he had done. Blake, however, did tell NBC News in 1991 that he realized he had made a mistake. But, said Blake, at the time he began spying for the KGB he strongly believed in the Communist cause and felt sure he was doing the right thing.

Blake still lives in Moscow, and from time to time we get together and talk about the old days and the enormous changes that have swept over Russia since we first met.

The last of the great English spies I was to meet was Donald Maclean. Maclean had penetrated the British Foreign Office, rising after World War II to First Secretary of the U.K. Embassy in Washington. He provided the Soviets with excellent material on British and American foreign policy and intelligence operations, including information on the U.S. nuclear weapons program. Maclean, whose KGB code name was "Homer," was forced to flee England along with Burgess. The two men lived in Moscow, where Burgess—a homosexual and wild binge drinker—died from complications of alcoholism in 1963.

By the time I met Maclean in the mid-1970s, he was a bitter, acid-tongued man battling alcoholism, personal demons, and disillusionment with life in the Soviet Union. His wife of many years,

Melinda, left him in 1965 when she began having an affair with Philby. After the notoriously philandering Philby essentially stole Maclean's wife, the two men never spoke to one another again.

Maclean had heard from Blake, with whom he worked at the Institute of World Economics, that the KGB was working hard to improve the existence of defectors in Moscow. Through Blake, Maclean asked Andropov if my Foreign Counterintelligence Directorate would be willing to take over his case from domestic Counterintelligence. The domestic side was only too happy to be rid of Maclean, and so he, too, became my charge.

The first time I met him at his spacious apartment in central Moscow, Maclean—like Philby—launched into a vicious attack on Brezhnev and the Soviet Union. Knowing his apartment was bugged, I urged him to restrain himself, but to no avail. I shared many of his views on Brezhnev, and even surprised him several years later when I said of the Soviet leader, "Don't you see he's an old fool, good for nothing."

Maclean gradually grew to trust me, and I increasingly came to respect his erudition and knowledge of international relations. He never asked for much, and lived quite modestly. I did help him with two requests: The first was to arrange the emigration of his daughter's fiancé, a Soviet citizen, to the West. The second was to arrange emigration papers for a friend of his, a Soviet artist. He always remained extremely grateful to me for those two favors.

By the time I met Maclean, he was suffering from kidney disease brought on by his drinking. He was weak, but still mentally alert and never missed a chance to criticize the Soviet system. His disillusionment with our way of life knew no bounds. I once arranged a lunch with Maclean and Kryuchkov, who was then head of Intelligence. I thought our Intelligence chief would enjoy meeting the experienced and scholarly foreign service officer, and the lunch was pleasant enough. But Maclean, who spoke good Russian, couldn't help but get in a barb about Soviet Communism, telling Kryuchkov at one point, "A nation that reads *Pravda* every day is invincible!" Unsure if Maclean was joking, Kryuchkov looked perplexed, though there was no doubt in my mind in what spirit the Englishman had made the remark. I laughed heartily, and finally, after looking at Maclean and me, a nervous smile forced its way onto Kryuchkov's face.

Once, a colleague of mine brought me a Czechoslovakian Communist's diatribe against Alexander Solzhenitsyn, entitled *The Spiral of Solzhenitsyn's Betrayal.* I passed it on to Maclean, and he returned it to me the next day with a note saying: "Thanks for the gift. But please don't send me any more trash. It's an insult to me."

I last saw Maclean in 1983 when he and Blake visited me in Leningrad. A short while later, Maclean died.

None of the great British spies worked their way into my heart, however, like Kim Philby, and I continued to see him regularly until he died in May 1988. Unfortunately, after I stepped down at the end of 1979, my replacement in Foreign Counterintelligence did not share my enthusiasm for the "Magnificent Five." After I talked to my successor about the special care we were giving Philby and the others, he could only say, "Why do we have to pay so much attention to these people? Why drink and talk with them? We've given them everything already."

My replacement didn't understand the enormous complexity of men like Philby, who were living with the weight of betraying their countries and forging a new existence in a strange land. During the 1980s, Kim still lived well and in relative freedom, but he never again enjoyed the support and friendship that I and my underlings had given him. When I visited him during my trips to Moscow, he and Rufa complained about the callousness of their new KGB handlers. He also became more vocal in his criticism of the Soviet Union, though, like me, he wanted to continue believing in the Communist dream that had inspired him since his youth. But he, too, saw the dream was crumbling. He spoke to me of his trips to the Russian provinces, where he was disgusted by the squalor of life, the dirt, the shoddy upkeep of buildings, and the ubiquitous rudeness and boorish manners of the Soviet masses. He detested the increasing passivity of the people, the sense that no one, at any level, wanted to take responsibility for what was happening in the country. Nevertheless, he still kept his sense of humor. And never once did he say he regretted what he had done.

I last saw Kim Philby in April 1988, a month before his death. Doctors had found polyps in his intestines and were planning to operate. He looked wan and fragile and spoke little, though he greeted me cheerily enough, saying, "Welcome, old boy. Glad to have you back."

Despite his obviously deteriorating health, Philby found time to ask about my career, which was then near the bottom of its downward slide. I had been put out to pasture as the KGB's security officer at the Academy of Sciences, and Philby tried to commiserate, saying he was sure I would once again be reinstated to a high position in Intelligence. I stayed for a little more than an hour.

"I hope we get together again after I'm back from the hospital," Philby said as I left his apartment. "We'll discuss things at length then."

The operation supposedly was a success, and Rufi called us twice to convey Kim's best regards. She mentioned that the doctors were trying to find Kim some fortified red wine to enrich his red blood cells. It was the wine traditionally used during communion at the Russian Orthodox Church, and through my contacts at the Moscow Patriarchy I was able to obtain three bottles. Rufa called to say the wine had worked wonders for Philby and that he was feeling much improved. Three days later, he died of heart failure.

Philby lay in state at the Dzerzhinsky Club, an ornate KGB meeting hall in downtown Moscow. The memorial service was to begin at noon. I arrived at 11:00 A.M. and waited in the corner for Kryuchkov and other KGB officials to show up. Shortly before noon, they walked in, and one of the Foreign Counterintelligence people motioned for me to come forward. I found myself at the head of the procession filing past Philby's body.

Walking up to the coffin, which was strewn with flowers, I paused for perhaps ten seconds. Looking down on the thin, craggy, still-handsome face, I was overcome with a sense of grief and loss. Philby had become a true friend, and I would miss him. But my melancholy went deeper than that. Philby had been a symbol of that generation that believed in Communism. He had been a romantic who embraced the Soviet Union in an era—a half century before—when many in the world thought that the "shining future" lay with us. Now, in 1988, Philby was stretched out before me, and the dream we had both believed in was as dead as my good friend. We had both been betrayed. We had *all* been betrayed.

I often think about Philby, and realize that—no matter how well I thought I knew him—he remains a mystery. To me, he was a hero who served the Communist cause, yet he did something I would never dream of doing: he turned against his country. I suppose he was haunted by that until his dying day, for he was a tried-and-true Englishman. He loved the country he had betrayed, and surrounded himself in Moscow with its books, its radio programs, its mementos. There was, after all, something ineffably sad about Philby, something in his expression, in his bearing, that told you this was a man carrying a heavy burden. He never said he had made a mistake, never suggested that he should have lived his life differently. He was too proud for that.

I prefer not to remember the melancholy Philby. Instead, I like to think of the man I knew in the late 1970s, a man who was sober—most of the time—and who displayed a wry, knowing sense of humor. I like to think of the Kim Philby who, when asked to do some assignment for the KGB, would flash me a smile, nod his head ever so slightly, and say in his elegant Cambridge accent:

"I am at the service of your Service."

ſIX

The Spy Game

By the mid-1970s, there were more KGB officers in Moscow alone—50,000—than all the employees of the CIA and FBI combined. The KGB was nothing less than an enormous army of a half-million men. About 220,000 of them guarded the Soviet Union's borders. Most of the rest served the KGB at home, comprising that huge totalitarian apparatus that hounded dissidents and troublemakers, opened mail, tapped telephone lines, eavesdropped on apartments and offices, shadowed foreigners, investigated crimes, and generally kept an iron grip on our sprawling and—just below the surface—unruly land. We in the KGB's foreign operations were a relatively small, elite unit, and we were proud that we trained our sights on foreign enemies of the Soviet Union, not on our own people. In fact, most of us in Intelligence viewed the domestic KGB as an unsavory, cruel, and totalitarian organization, and we were glad to have as little to do with it as possible.

In March 1973, Yuri Andropov called on me to head the KGB's Foreign Counterintelligence operations. The following year, at age forty, I became the youngest person in the postwar history of the KGB ever promoted to the rank of general. By that time, I was overseeing a dizzying growth in our Counterintelligence operations overseas, a growth that was mirrored in many other sections of the KGB. My relatively small organization, which had come to be known in 1972 as Directorate K of the Intelligence branch, was in the process of expanding from two hundred to seven hundred officers. We also were opening a broad attack on the CIA and Western intelligence services, while at the same time trying to significantly tighten the control we had over a burgeoning number of Soviets working abroad.

On the KGB's sprawling organizational chart, Foreign Intelligence (known as the First Chief Directorate) was one large branch on an otherwise enormous tree. There were about twelve thousand of us working in the First Chief Directorate. To get a feel for the immensity and bureaucratic complexity of the KGB, one need look no further than my unit, Foreign Counterintelligence. Though we only had about seven hundred officers, we were divided into eight departments that ran the gamut of KGB operations.

Department One was assigned to penetrate the CIA, the National Security Agency, the FBI, and various branches of American Military Intelligence. As later sections of this story will show, we worked around the globe to achieve that goal, probing and attacking U.S. Intelligence from Ghana to Greece to Finland.

Department Two was assigned to penetrate NATO and Western intelligence services; we enjoyed respectable success primarily because of an aging but loyal group of spies who had burrowed into French and English ranks around the time of World War II. Our East German brothers made sure we had thoroughly infiltrated West Germany's secret services.

Department Three was assigned to penetrate other intelligence agencies around the world, from China to Latin America. In many countries, such as India, we were successful in our mission, though the results helped us only marginally in our primary struggle—that with the United States.

Department Four was charged with infiltrating Soviet émigré organizations and centers of "ideological subversion," and that—as readers will soon see—we did well.

Department Five was responsible for internal security. Its task was to monitor the twelve thousand employees of the Intelligence Directorate to ensure they did not spy for the West or defect. To this end, our Foreign Counterintelligence officers in embassies around the world or in Moscow monitored the activities of Soviet Intelligence personnel. As time passed, our record on defections and internal security lapses grew worse, and now it is clear we were swimming against the tide of history. Department Five also was responsible for security at all the USSR's intelligence installations outside the country's borders.

In addition, we were assigned to keep an eye on all Soviets

traveling and working overseas, from diplomats to tour groups to troupes of artists. We didn't have the manpower to infiltrate every group, but instead relied on informers who were liberally sprinkled among the delegations that went abroad.

Department Six was in charge of transportation, which essentially meant that we had to keep an eye on every boat, truck, or plane that traveled outside the USSR. When two Soviet truck drivers delivered cargo to Europe, one or both of them would report to the KGB. When a Soviet merchant marine or scientific vessel sailed overseas, at least a quarter of the crew were KGB officers or informers. At least one of the officers on board invariably was with the KGB. When Aeroflot planes flew around the world, the flight crews were riddled with KGB informers.

No matter what mode of transportation, if it was Soviet and chugged, steamed, rumbled, or jetted overseas, we controlled it.

Department Seven was our information and analysis section, which by the end of the 1970s had become the most exhaustive and up-to-date source of intelligence data and analytical reporting in the KGB. Using our own sources of information, as well as those from Eastern European intelligence agencies and Soviet Military Intelligence, we put together daily, weekly, monthly, and yearly bulletins. They described the activities not only of the CIA and NATO Counterintelligence services, but also of the secret services from Indonesia to Peru. We looked at the methods used to recruit our people in foreign ports and capitals, and sent our summaries to Soviet Counterintelligence sections throughout the USSR and the world. Domestic Counterintelligence officers used our top-secret reports to get a sense of what was happening in the espionage world beyond the Soviet Union's borders. We also reported on terrorism, drugs, and international crime.

Relying heavily on American and NATO sources, our annual report reviewed events of the previous year in internatoinal politics and in espionage, and made predictions about the future. We also produced a highly classified book entitled *Who's Who in the CIA*. It was about as thick as a Manhattan phone directory and contained biographical information on ten thousand current and former CIA agents. I plopped it on Andropov's desk in 1977, saying it was my present to him in honor of the sixtieth anniversary of the Russian Revolution. Andropov was delighted, and I even suggested going public with the book to embarrass the CIA.

"Give me the appropriate order and we'll publish this all over the world," I told Andropov. "Every CIA officer around the world will become known."

"Don't do that," replied Andropov. "Just use it for our work. It will be more valuable to us that way."

Finally, Department Eight of Directorate K was set up to fight economic espionage and sabotage abroad. We took control of this realm after several scandals involving Soviet employees overseas who had embezzled or stolen money from Soviet banks and foreign trade organizations. By the early 1980s, the KGB had placed qualified officers into high positions in most Soviet banks doing business abroad.

So that was Directorate K, and by 1973 we were reorganized, reinforced, and ready to do battle with the CIA. We also had a new Soviet Intelligence doctrine, which called for a more aggressive stance against Western intelligence agencies. The preamble of the new doctrine stated, in part, "Under the conditions of a world split into two hostile camps, with our adversary possessing weapons of mass destruction and with instantaneous reaction attaining maximum importance in a possible nuclear war, the main task of [Soviet] Intelligence is to find out the strategic military plans of the states opposing the USSR and warn the government immediately about emerging crises to prevent a sudden attack on the Soviet Union or its allies."

In late 1974, Andropov called in the heads of the various Intelligence directorates to introduce us to our new boss, Vladimir Kryuchkov. At that meeting, Andropov criticized the agency for not being sufficiently aggressive and imaginative, and urged us to use the intelligence agencies of the Warsaw Pact and Third World countries in our struggle against the CIA. He said our agents had done a good job ferreting out information about the United States' B-1 bomber program and other military projects, but that we knew very little about our adversary's space program. In a calm, matter-of-fact tone, Andropov set forth his view that *détente* was not going smoothly because reactionary circles in the United States and the West were sabotaging the Soviet Union's peace overtures. I sat there wondering how Andropov could hold the naive, one-sided view that the problems in Soviet-U.S. relations were the fault of right-wing Americans, and not, in part, because of our intransigent, hard-line leaders. But that was his outlook, and it was to change little after he became the head of our country.

I, then, had a mandate to go after the CIA as aggressively as possible, and I returned to the offices of Foreign Counterintelligence and instructed my subordinates to draw up plans to press our offensive against the West. In addition to continued attempts to recruit current and former Western intelligence officers, I had in my arsenal many other weapons, including the increased use of Soviet double agents. Among them was a man whose case I had come to know in Washington, the spy with the code name "Lark." Soon, the "Lark" affair would blow up into a major international incident.

"Lark" was Nikolai Fyodorovich Artamonov, the Soviet naval officer who had commandeered a torpedo boat in 1959 and fled with his Polish girlfriend to Sweden. He ultimately defected to the United States, where my officers, after a long search, found him lecturing at Georgetown University. Using the name Shadrin, he was working as an analyst at the Office of Naval Intelligence, and we decided to attempt to re-recruit him as a double agent. After promising to grant him a full pardon, to help his Russian family financially, and to arrange the admission of his son into a Soviet naval academy, Lark agreed to work for us secretly while pretending to continue working for the Americans. When I left Washington in 1970, Artamonov had been supplying us with some useful information about U.S. military operations.

After taking the helm of Foreign Counterintelligence in 1973, I decided to press Artamonov for more valuable information; there was a nagging feeling at headquarters that he was not living up to his potential. Sakharovsky, the head of Intelligence, had been skeptical of Lark from the moment we tried to re-recruit him. When I first returned to Moscow in 1970, a colleague informed me that Sakharovsky was suspicious of the meager quantities of material coming from Artamonov, and was fearful he was playing a trick on us and still working for the CIA. I, however, never doubted Artamonov's sincerity and was convinced he was genuinely on our side once again.

But when, as head of Directorate K, I sat down and painstakingly went over Artamonov's file, I also began to experience doubts. There was something strange about his case. "Lark" had supposedly been working for us in Washington since 1967, but a close inspection of what he had furnished the KGB showed that although much of the material was marked secret, it shed little light on U.S. military and Intelligence operations. He had made numerous promises to us, such as turning up the whereabouts of the defector Yuri Nosenko, but all Artamonov ever told us about Nosenko was that he was probably living near Washington, D.C. Artamonov wasn't pulling his weight, and I instructed our people in Washington to tell him to pass us some rudimentary documents that would show whether he was genuinely working for our side. One document I asked for was the classified internal telephone directory of the Office of Naval Intelligence—something Artamonov should have had no trouble procuring.

At their next meeting in Washington, Artamonov's KGB handler asked him to provide us with a copy of the phone directory. He danced around the request, saying he could get his hands on the phone book but that copying it was out of the question; too many people used it, he said, and he would be unable to take it away and Xerox it unnoticed. Our officer said we would give him a special miniature camera for the job, but Artamonov retorted that he would never be able to smuggle a camera into his office. Then our officer replied that we were going to supply him with a Minox camera, disguised as a pack of cigarettes, and that all Artamonov needed to do was run the end of the cigarette pack over the phone book, thus automatically photographing the pages. Artamonov finally agreed, and several weeks later his handler gave him the camera.

When Artamonov handed back the Minox, we developed the film and found that it was dark and unreadable. Artamonov swore that he had worked the camera correctly and that it had malfunctioned, so we gave him another "cigarette pack" and sent him back to the Office of Naval Intelligence. For the second time, none of his film turned out. Our specialists tested the camera and found it working perfectly. Sitting in Moscow, I became increasingly convinced that Artamonov had once again double-crossed his country.

"There's one way to find out if he's genuine," I told one of my assistants. "Let's invite him to Canada."

We had a high-ranking mole inside the Counterintelligence section of the Royal Canadian Mounted Police and there was a good chance that if we could get Artamonov to Canada, we could find out who he really was working for. I knew by then which buttons to push at the CIA and the FBI, so we devised a pretext for Artamonov's travel north of the border that we thought the Americans would find impossible to resist. Artamonov's KGB handler in Washington told him that we wanted him to travel to Canada to meet the KGB man in charge of illegal operations in North America. FBI Counterintelligence salivated whenever it got the chance to learn anything about illegals—people posing as American citizens who actually were deep-cover KGB agents. Artamonov quickly agreed to go to Canada, where he met one of my assistants from Moscow who had flown in posing as our handler for illegals.

Several weeks later, our fears were confirmed. Our mole in the Royal Canadian Mounted Police provided us with a report clearly stating that a Soviet working for the FBI recently had come to Montreal to meet with a KGB agent. The RCMP also said that the FBI's Soviet agent had recorded some of his conversations with the KGB man.

Now, it was clear: "Lark" had fooled us for six years and was still working for the Americans. The next question was: What to do with him? His death sentence, which had been annulled after he began working for us, was reinstated. But I had other ideas about how to handle Artamonov. The tricky part was getting our hands on him.

We knew that U.S. Intelligence customarily allowed defectors to meet with Soviets only in America and Canada. But our plan involved luring Artamonov to Austria, where we could abduct him, drive him into Czechoslovakia, and whisk him off to Moscow. Once again we needed some bait, and once again we devised a scheme that we figured the Americans would find irresistible. We spent months working on the plan and waiting for the right moment. Finally, in 1975, Artamonov's KGB handler met him and said he wanted him to travel to Austria, where he was to learn how to operate a secret radio that would enable him to contact his new handler in the United States. To make our trap even more inviting, we told Artamonov that his new handler would be an "illegal" living undercover in America. And, to top it off, we promised Artamonov that he would have the chance to meet this "illegal" in Vienna so that the two could become acquainted and work out the best way to contact each other in the United States. As further justification, we told Artamonov that there was growing surveillance of our operations in North America and that it would be far safer to meet in Vienna.

U.S. Intelligence officials, desperate for information about our network of "illegals," gobbled up the bait and gave Artamonov permission to travel to Vienna.

In December 1975, Artamonov, accompanied by his wife, arrived in Austria, ostensibly on a ski holiday. Two U.S. officials were assigned to keep an eye on him. Meanwhile, I was on my way to the Austrian-Czech border.

For two days, our officers in Vienna met with Artamonov and taught him how to use a secret radio transmitter. They also began talking with him in vague terms about "illegal" operations in the United States. We promised Artamonov a meeting on the third day with the "illegal" who would be his new U.S. contact. For some reason, be it laziness or the fact that the Americans had been lulled into thinking all was well, Artamonov's U.S. handlers had stopped following him. Our people didn't spot any tails, and our informers in the Austrian police also told us that the Americans—probably from the CIA—were rarely venturing out of their hotel. They trusted Shadrin, and apparently they were satisfied that we trusted him, too, and wouldn't attempt to abduct him.

So on the evening of the third day, several KGB officers picked up "Lark" on a Vienna street. Among the officers was a tough, hulking, man who went on to become security officer at the Soviet Foreign Ministry. Several minutes after Artamonov sat down, the husky KGB man slapped a chloroform-soaked cloth over the agent's face. "Lark" himself weighed about 220 pounds and began struggling in the backseat. Our man then pulled out a syringe filled with a powerful sedative and jabbed in the needle. Artamonov stopped struggling, and lost consciousness. Indeed, the Vienna KGB team, concerned about Artamonov's size, had administered twice the normal dose needed to knock out a man.

The KGB car sped out of Vienna, heading for the Czechoslovakian border.

Several colleagues from Moscow and I had been at the border for two days, scouting out locations where our officers from Vienna could cross with Artamonov. We told the head of the Czech border police that we were meeting on the frontier with an illegal, and the Czech gave us free rein. Dressed in camouflage fatigues, my colleagues and I had spent two days pretending to hunt along the border, all the while scouting a good rendezvous site. We soon found one—an old asphalt road that ran through a wooded area. The road was seldom used and had no border checkpoint, but it was still possible to drive to the frontier from the Austrian side. On the Czech side, the road ran through a no-man's-land where we were planning to meet the KGB car from Vienna. Several hundred yards behind the no-man's-land were the barbed-wire fences and lookout towers of the Czech border guards.

The night of the rendezvous was cold and moonless. Though it was below freezing, there was no snow on the ground. In front of us were the woods and a field. It was pitch black, and the only sound was the faint whispering of the wind through the dry leaves that had remained on the trees from autumn.

We waited in some bushes, my stomach churning in anticipation. Our plan was to get Artamonov back to Moscow, where he would be informed he had two choices: Either tell us everything he knew about U.S. Intelligence operations and other agents working against the Soviet Union, or face a firing squad. We were certain he would tell all, at which point we would parade him before the press in Moscow, where he would describe his many years of working as a loyal Soviet mole inside the dastardly United States Intelligence community.

Suddenly, we saw the headlights of a fast-moving car heading down the road on the Austrian side. The lights illuminated the Austrian border markers, about 20 yards in front of us. The car roared up the road, then came to a halt a few yards from our position in the bushes. Car doors slammed, and we heard the excited whispers and curses of our three KGB colleagues.

When I walked up to the car, our colleagues from Vienna were huffing and puffing as they dragged Artamonov out of the vehicle and plopped him on the road. He was breathing heavily and occasionally letting out a moan.

"A stretcher!" someone called out. "There's no other way we can carry this boar!"

Fortunately, someone had brought a large canvas poncho, and we slid it under the unconscious Artamonov. Four of us began the arduous task of hauling "Lark" back to the Czech border point and our car. We made it halfway there when we decided to take a break. We laid him on the ground, and someone pulled out a pocket flashlight to see how our prisoner was doing. Illuminating his face, we saw, to our horror, that he wasn't breathing. We massaged his chest, then forced open his clenched jaws and poured brandy down his throat. Nothing worked.

We hustled to the checkpoint, where we instructed the guards to call a doctor. We already knew, however, that we didn't need a doctor to make this diagnosis: "Lark" was dead. The Czech doctor arrived and tried in vain to revive him with injections and a heart massage. After several minutes he gave up, saying with a shrug, "It's useless. He's gone."

Spreadeagled on the poncho, his arms flung out wide, Artamonov looked peaceful, as if he had forgiven everybody—including himself—for the damage done and the pain he had caused. He would be telling no one now about the arduous life of a double agent, about the furies that had hounded him ever since he fell head-over-heels for some Polish beauty sixteen years before and chucked everything—his wife, his son, his homeland—and headed West. Artamonov was dead. And so was an excellent opportunity to learn about U.S. Intelligence and to use "Lark" as our main character in a stirring propaganda show. I felt bad for Artamonov, but worse for myself. He was, after all, a traitor and probably had it coming. Now, because one of our men had had a heavy hand with a sedative, we had lost a valuable espionage prize we had spent years trying to snare.

My officers went through Artamonov's pockets, finding a hotel registration card, $700 in cash, and the name and telephone number of an American woman in Vienna, apparently his CIA handler.

We returned to Moscow with Artamonov's body, where Yevgeni Chazov—the head of the Kremlin Medical Department and a future USSR Minister of Health—performed an autopsy. Artamonov had died of heart failure as a result of the sedative overdose, though the autopsy showed he also had the beginnings of kidney cancer. He was buried secretly in a Moscow cemetery under a Latvian alias.

Within weeks, an international storm broke over "Lark's" disappearance. Artamonov's Polish wife in Washington appealed to President Gerald Ford to help find her husband. Ford and his Secretary of State, Henry Kissinger, asked Brezhnev to find out what had happened. Other American officials and Sovietologists accused the KGB of abducting and executing the defector. In typical Soviet style, Brezhnev stonewalled Ford, saying the USSR also would like to know what became of Artamonov. The accusations and recriminations went on for more than a year, and no one could say where the man had gone. Several books were published worldwide, concluding that it was impossible to say what had happened to Artamonov and for whom he had been working.

Finally, the KGB struck back, using one of our "pet" Soviet journalists who always did our bidding. He was Genrikh Borovik, who published an article entitled "Overdriven Horses Are Shot, Aren't They?" in *Literaturnaya Gazeta* faithfully setting forth the KGB's view of the case. The article, purportedly relying on documents and inside information, described how the CIA had actually killed Artamonov when it realized he was playing a double game and working for the Soviets. When I was feeding Borovik our account of what had occurred, he asked me several times, "Now, Oleg, are you sure that this is the way it really happened? Artamonov was really working for us?"

"Absolutely, Genrikh," I answered. "It's the truth, I swear."

In all the years I was in Foreign Counterintelligence, *Literaturnaya Gazeta* was our prime conduit in the Soviet press for propaganda and disinformation. Whenever we called the editor, Alexander Chakovsky, and asked him to print an article, he complied. Sometimes we wrote the stories and put them under the names of nonexistent authors. Sometimes journalists such as Borovik or Iona Andronov wrote the stories themselves, using information supplied by the KGB. But whatever the method, *Literaturnaya Gazeta*—which oddly enough went on to become one of the leading publications during *glasnost*—was one of our preferred publications.

I viewed the "Lark" case as a badly botched job on our part, and though I certainly wasn't responsible for his death, I felt some measure of blame and considered the failed abduction one of the low points of my career. I was, then, quite surprised when Kryuchkov summoned me to his office a few month's after Artamonov's death and asked me, "Which medal do you want—the October Revolution or the Combat Red Banner?"

I was speechless. Were we now receiving awards because we had, however inadvertently, carried out the death sentence against Artamonov?

"Well, why are you acting so confused?" said an impatient Kryuchkov. "Which one do you like better? I already have Andropov's approval. Go on, take your pick."

I mumbled that it would be best for the leadership to decide which award I deserved, and Kryuchkov dismissed me with a wave of his hand. A short while later, the Presidium of the Supreme Soviet of the Union of Soviet Socialist Republics issued a decree announcing that I and several other officers involved in the Artamonov case had been awarded the prestigious Order of the Red Banner.

Until now, the full story of Artamonov's fate has never been told. In 1992, Artamonov's Polish wife telephoned me after hearing from sources that I had supervised the abduction of her husband.

"You took part in the operation," she told me. "Did my husband die?"

"Yes, he did," I replied.

"How did he die?" she asked.

"I feel sorry for you," I answered, "but I can't tell you anything over the telephone. I can only confirm that he died, and that we didn't intend to kill him."

I never heard from her again.

After the "Lark" affair, we continued our efforts to go head-on with the CIA and recruit some of its agents. One of our most successful operations came near the end of my tour in Foreign Counterintelligence, with the recruitment of a former CIA man named David Henry Barnett.

Barnett was a veteran CIA officer who had served for years in several Asian countries, including South Korea and Indonesia. In 1978 or 1979, shortly before he was planning to retire, Barnett contacted one of our KGB officers in Jakarta, Indonesia. He divulged several enticing bits of information, then told our officer he would supply us with detailed material about CIA operations worldwide. Barnett demanded an up-front payment of $80,000, to be followed by more money if our relationship continued.

This proposal landed on my desk, and I knew immediately it would have to be approved at the highest level—by Andropov himself. Not only would I need Andropov's signature to secure the princely sum of $80,000 for a volunteer, but I also knew the KGB chief would want to be apprised that a high-ranking CIA man had made contact with us. Kryuchkov and I talked to Andropov, and I told the chairman that I thought the man was genuine and worth the money. The case was sufficiently important, I told Andropov, that I wanted to personally meet the American in Vienna.

"Okay," Andropov said. "But don't give it to the man all at once. Just give him half at first. Maybe he isn't worth eighty thousand."

Andropov signed a letter authorizing the dispersal of the money from our accounting office, which kept millions of dollars of cash on hand. The money was used for every conceivable operation, from paying informants such as Barnett to shelling out money to spies who provided us with samples of Western scientific, military, and industrial technology.

Accompanied by an assistant who helped carry the mountain of cash—all in twenty-dollar bills—I flew to Austria, which had become the KGB's most popular spot for rendezvousing with Western spies. The country bordered the Eastern Bloc, and Austrian officials gave us a free hand to roam the city and carry out the clandestine meetings that had brought us there. As usual, I traveled to Vienna on a diplomatic passport as counselor of the Soviet Foreign Ministry. I flashed my green diplomatic passport at the immigration booths and an official waved me through. No one checked my bags. Austria was a comfortable place to be a spy.

Our officers in Vienna had arranged to meet Barnett on the street, then bring him to one of several houses used by the Soviet Trade Mission, which had well-appointed guest rooms and a nice sauna. When I first met Barnett in the living quarters of the mission, I was struck by his extreme nervousness and agitation. Of his appearance I remember little other than that he was middle-aged and of average build. But I will never forget his emotional state: He was a man who exuded desperation. He had come to us, it was clear, not because of ideological convictions—by 1979 it was far too late for that—but because he was in desperate need of money and seemed to be going through an acute psychological or midlife crisis.

"Let me guess," he said to me. "You're from Intelligence."

That was close enough. "You got it," I replied. As was customary, I did not tell him my name.

I knew we had to settle Barnett down and break the ice. Besides, I never believed in diving right into business without first having a drink and some food. So we threw down a couple of vodkas and toasted to peace and friendship. Barnett loosened up a bit, and then we repaired to the dining room, where the mission's cooks served us an excellent dinner and some good wine. Barnett, my assistant, and I talked informally about our respective services. After tea and coffee, I suggested we get to work.

"Are you ready for a serious conversation?" I asked Barnett. "Relax, wash up, and we'll head into another room."

We had come with a list of hundreds of questions about CIA operations in Asia and around the world, and so, with a tape recorder on a table, we launched into our interrogation. At first, I went over some of the aspects of the CIA's Asian operations that Barnett already had discussed with our agents in the Orient. All the while, I was gently testing him to see if I could find any discrepancies in his story. It was a rare opportunity to get our hands on an experienced CIA agent who had just left the service, and beginning that night we spent two straight days pumping him for information on all aspects of U.S. Intelligence. He filled in gaps in our knowledge about the structure of the CIA, described in detail operations in South Korea, Indonesia, and other Asian countries, revealed the names of dozens of CIA Intelligence officers, and disclosed the identities of informants recruited by the CIA.

As we were finishing our session that first night, Barnett looked disturbed. I asked him what was wrong.

"We haven't completed our financial arrangements yet," he said.

"What financial arrangements are you referring to?" I said.

"I asked your people for eighty thousand dollars," Barnett replied, growing increasingly edgy.

Remembering Andropov's admonition to give him only half the sum at first, I told Barnett, "Look, for what you've told me so far I can only give you forty thousand. No more."

I wasn't prepared for the explosion that followed.

"What are you talking about!" he yelled, on the verge of hysteria. "You're putting me on the rack! That forty thousand is good for nothing. It won't solve my problems. I don't need any fucking forty thousand! If I don't pay my debts and restore my social standing, I'm going to put a bullet through my head. If you don't want me to do that, keep your word. I've told you all I could. Now it's your turn to deliver."

I realized that if we wanted him to continue cooperating with us, I had no choice but to ante up the entire $80,000.

"If you expect me to pay you eighty thousand, I need more exhaustive answers than I have been getting up to now," I said.

"If I don't get the money," Barnett told me, "I don't work with you at all."

I handed over $80,000. Barnett let out a sigh of relief, shook my hand, and slumped back in his chair. We talked a short while longer, then I showed Barnett to his guest room.

We talked all the next day, and after extracting every bit of information from him, we discussed the possibility of Barnett—who was then in his forties—continuing to work for the CIA as a consultant or landing a job on the House or Senate Intelligence committees. I gave Barnett detailed instructions on how to meet his handler in Washington, and we parted. His information, while not documented, was extremely useful, and I was excited about the prospect of Barnett landing a new position in U.S. Intelligence. When I returned to Moscow, we sent instructions via coded cable and diplomatic pouch on the first rendezvous. I was confident we were developing an excellent American spy.

Barnett met several times with KGB officers in Washington.

Then, out of the blue, word came that the FBI had arrested him. The U.S. Justice Department said later that American agents had observed Barnett meeting the KGB in Vienna, but that was a cover story. In fact, Barnett had been exposed before then. Several years later, when the CIA agent Edward Lee Howard defected, we learned that the Americans had recruited a high-ranking KGB officer in our station in Jakarta, Indonesia. When Barnett approached our people in Indonesia, it's likely that the Jakarta station was buzzing with talk that a CIA volunteer had come to us. His name would not have been known to most of our officers in Jakarta, but all the CIA needed to know from its mole within our ranks was that a U.S. Intelligence officer had volunteered his services to the KGB in Jakarta. After that, pinpointing Barnett—he was retiring, he was in financial trouble—would not have been difficult.

In October 1980 Barnett pleaded guilty to espionage and was sentenced to eighteen years in prison. After Edward Lee Howard's defection, the KGB discovered the mole who had served in Jakarta; by the mid-1980s he had already been promoted to Party secretary of the KGB's Andropov Institute in Moscow. He was arrested, tried, and executed. The contrasting fates of Barnett and our own KGB spy vividly demonstrated that, while the CIA dealt harshly with traitors, we were infinitely more severe.

It was also in Vienna that I met another valuable American source—this one from U.S. Military Intelligence. The man was a high-ranking officer stationed with American forces in West Germany, and we successfully recruited him after one of our informers in Germany told us the officer might be open to a KGB approach. On several occasions I traveled to Vienna to meet the American, who handed us classified documents that contained, among other things, battle plans for NATO forces. The American officer also had access to CIA documents and communications, which he dutifully passed along to us. His motivation was strictly financial, and we paid him $5,000 each time he "dropped" us material every few months. In our last meeting, he complained about his meager payments, but in my time we never increased them simply because what he gave us wasn't as valuable as the material provided by someone like John Walker. As far as I know, the intelligence officer was never caught by the Americans.

We pulled off another intelligence coup against the Americans in the 1970s when we succeeded in bugging the headquarters of an American Air Force base in the Mediterranean. We got inside by recruiting a local employee of the base, who later planted the listening devices for us. The bugs worked for more than a year, during which time we gathered a substantial amount of information on NATO operations in Europe.

Among the bolder assaults we planned on the CIA while I was chief of Foreign Counterintelligence was a scheme to abduct a CIA officer in Beirut. We planned the operation over a six-month period in 1977 and 1978. The plot was relatively simple: We would pay the Palestinians to do our dirty work. The KGB had close ties with Palestinian groups in Lebanon. Indeed, we had for years been using our own officers and intelligence officers from the Warsaw Pact to forge strong ties with Palestine Liberation Organization leader Yassir Arafat. After receiving preliminary approval from Andropov, we instructed our Palestinian operatives in Lebanon to begin tailing the CIA man, who was posted to the U.S. Embassy in Beirut as a military attaché. Our plan was to pay the Palestinians to abduct the CIA agent and then, under duress but not outright torture, to interrogate him. We would supply the Palestinians with the list of questions, and we also planned to instruct them on how they might recruit the American. The Palestinians were told that they could threaten him with death, but that under no circumstances were they to kill the man or physically torture him. From the start, it would be a KGB job, though our fingerprints would not be on it.

The plan was set in motion. The Palestinians were constantly watching the CIA officer and informed us they could pick him up at any time. They had picked out a safe house in Beirut in which to detain and question him. I then went to Boris Ivanov, my one-time station chief in New York, who had since become deputy chief of Intelligence.

"Everything's ready," I told him.

"I have to clear it," Ivanov replied. "It's a major operation. I have to talk to Andropov."

"Why talk to him again?" I argued. "I already have his written permission."

"It's a delicate matter," said Ivanov. "I have to ask him again."

Ivanov telephoned Andropov, and we both spoke to him on a secure Lubyanka line. I described the plot and said we were ready to abduct the CIA agent.

"A kidnapping!" barked Andropov. "Are you crazy?"

"But you gave your permission," I said.

"Maybe I did," Andropov replied, "but I am against it now. We shouldn't do this kind of thing. What if your plan goes awry and somehow the Americans find out about it? Are you going to start a war? They would start kidnapping our people all around the world, and they're better equipped for nabbing our people than we are for kidnapping theirs. It will turn into a war of Intelligence services. It will do us no good whatsoever."

"The Americans won't find out," I replied, still confident it would have been a sanitized way to get our hands on a CIA officer and interrogate him. "The Palestinians can pull it off. I know it."

"No, I don't trust these Palestinians," said Andropov. "Don't do it. I forbid you."

A one-minute phone conversation with Andropov had wiped out six months of planning and preparations.

Nearly a decade later, Iranian-backed Hezbollah terrorists kidnapped the CIA station chief in Beirut, William Buckley. Under horrible torture, they extracted from Buckley everything he knew about CIA operations. The American died from the interrogation. By then I was no longer involved in foreign operations, but I am confident the KGB had nothing to do with Buckley's abduction or torture, though it is a virtual certainty that the transcript of Buckley's interrogation—the Hezbollah butchers recorded it—was eventually sold to the KGB, and probably for a very handsome sum.

One of my last meetings with a U.S. Intelligence agent took place in 1979 in Helsinki, which nearly rivaled Vienna as a stomping ground for Soviet spies. To this day, I don't know whether the American was genuine or a CIA plant.

The man was a retired captain of a U.S. nuclear submarine. He, too, was a volunteer who had contacted one of our stations in Europe. In the beginning, he looked too good to be true—not only did he seem to have extensive knowledge about the United States' submarine fleet, but when he contacted us he claimed to be a contract, or part-time, worker for the CIA. As often was the case when we were presented with what looked like an intelligence prize, I decided to meet the man in person to judge whether he was for real.

In the spring of 1979, I traveled to Helsinki to meet the American naval officer. Though I initially was very skeptical, I soon grew to believe that he was genuine. He may have just been a good actor, but his story was convincing. The American told me he had come to us because he wanted money, and also because he was angered that, after his tour on the atomic submarine, he had not been promoted and transferred to naval headquarters in the Pentagon. His information was good, but not great: in several meetings in Helsinki over the course of two days, the American told me in some detail about the operations of the United States' atomic submarine fleet and its activities against the USSR. He provided me with no documentation, saying he no longer had access to Navy materials and that his contract work for the CIA had just gotten under way. We paid him modestly, no more than $10,000 while I was Foreign Counterintelligence chief.

I wanted the captain to land a permanent position with the CIA. At the end of our meetings, I suggested that he write Admiral Stansfield Turner, director of the CIA, and explain that he was a retired submarine commander doing contract work for the CIA and seeking a full-time position with the agency. The captain, who kept in touch with us, later said through an intermediary that he had written the letter but received no response.

To this day, I still have my doubts about the American. That was one of the great challenges of Counterintelligence—trying to figure out when a "volunteer" was real and when he was doing the bidding of the CIA or NATO. In the case of the captain and many other volunteers, I turned their stories over and over in my mind, trying to divine the truth. It was an exasperating—and thrilling—aspect of the job.

Regardless of who the American captain was, he left me with a warm and memorable parting shot. One of our Finnish meetings took place over lunch at a café in a remote, wooded area 35 miles from Helsinki. At one point, the American asked me, "Did you ever try *real* Scotch whiskey?"

"Well, yes," I replied. I hesitated because I made it a point never to engage Americans or British people in a debate about their whiskeys; it was their domain, just as surely as vodka was a Russian's.

"Have you ever drunk Glenfiddich?" the American asked.

"No," I replied. "I've never heard of it."

"Oh, you haven't!" he exclaimed. "Then you don't know what real whiskey is. I will send you a bottle or two through my case officer."

A month later, my KGB subordinate who was handling the American sent me a bottle of Glenfiddich via diplomatic pouch. I opened it and was just about to take a sip when my innate, intelligence paranoia set in. What if he was working for the CIA? Would the Americans be so diabolical as to try to poison a KGB general with a bottle of Scotch? No, I concluded—even *we* wouldn't do that. So I took a sip, and it went down like nectar. Within several weeks, my colleagues and I had—a sip or two at a time—polished off the lovely Scotch whiskey. Ever since I have been a devoted fan of Glenfiddich.

Returning home from Finland that spring of 1979, I had an experience that—looking back—was a premonition of things to come. In the late 1970s, running one of the KGB's most important directorates, I can honestly say that I loved my work. My job was always challenging, placing me at the heart of the Cold War competition between the Soviet Union and the United States. I traveled the world, overseeing Counterintelligence operations, and when I was in Moscow, my KGB work consumed me six or seven days a week. I strongly believed that what I was doing was necessary and useful. I was not so blind that I didn't see how far we were falling behind the West, how corrupt were the upper reaches of the Communist Party, and what a senile fool Brezhnev had become. But I had not given up on my country, nor on the idea that it could be reformed. The great illusions which had determined my worldview since birth still stayed with me, tattered as they might have been.

Traveling home on the Helsinki-Moscow train, I was in good spirits. Our long green train stopped at the Finnish border town of Vainikala, where the sun shone warmly into my compartment. Shoots of early grass were pushing through the ground beside the railroad tracks. Suddenly, for no apparent reason, I was overcome by feelings of sadness and foreboding. I looked out at the neat Finnish cottages and my heart sank when I thought of crossing into Soviet territory at Vyborg, a gray and gloomy town. The prospect of returning to Moscow, where the media would be prattling on about Five-Year Plans and the triumph of socialism, made me ill. I felt that something bad lay ahead and, as will soon become clear, I was right. I had the disquieting feeling that I was returning not to my homeland, but to prison. And I sensed that I would not be back in the West for a long while. I was right about that, too.

But I am getting ahead of my story.

Our struggle in Foreign Counterintelligence was not only against the CIA. We devoted significant resources to penetrating the Intelligence agencies of NATO countries, and to a lesser degree the secret services in the Third World. All told—piecing together information from CIA, NATO, and other sources—we were able to draw a fairly comprehensive picture of U.S. and Western strategy and their activities against the USSR. Meanwhile, the CIA and NATO intelligence services were doing the very same thing, and probably more successfully. During my ten years in Foreign Counterintelligence, I frequently felt as if I were participating in some sort of Great Game, in which a defection or intelligence leak from our side would put us behind, while in the next breath a source like John Walker or David Henry Barnett would appear and place us back in the running. It was a constant, dizzying to and fro, as we took a piece out of them and they took a piece out of us. The whole frenzied scrum was obscured and complicated by the layers of deception, the double agents, the maddening sense of often not knowing who we could trust. It was, in short, espionage, and when my decade in Foreign Counterintelligence was finished, I felt we had done our best to hold our own in a struggle that we were gradually and inexorably losing.

When I took over as head of Foreign Counterintelligence in 1973, the extent of our penetration of NATO and other Western intelligence agencies became clear, and it was impressive. Reading through files, talking to my subordinates, and handling the day-to-day duties of the office, I realized that—often thanks to spies who had come to us for ideological reasons in the 1930s and 1940s—we had an extensive and highly placed network of agents in France, West Germany, Canada, Italy, and the Scandinavian countries, among others. England, which in the heyday of the Magnificent Five had been a bulwark of our intelligence efforts, had slipped badly following the unmasking of Oleg Lyalin and the expulsion of more than one hundred KGB officers and diplomats from London. But our strength in other countries helped make up for that loss.

Though I knew before I joined Foreign Counterintelligence that we had an impressive network of agents in France, I was nevertheless surprised at the sheer number of high-ranking moles we had in French Intelligence, Counterintelligence, and the military. During my time, we boasted about a dozen excellent spies in France, most of them operating at the top rung of their agencies. These agents had, for the most part, been firm believers in Communism who first approached our people in France in the 1940s. Our officers had discouraged them from joining the Communist Party in France or in any way betraying their ideology. Then, these moles and their KGB handlers patiently waited as the Frenchmen rose to positions of high responsibility in Intelligence and the military. By the 1960s and 1970s, the French secret services and military leaked like a sieve; indeed, things were so bad that the Americans eventually stopped trusting the French with secrets of any kind.

Some of these French moles were uncovered. One of the most notorious was Georges Pacques, who worked at the French General Staff and at NATO headquarters in Paris (NATO was located in Paris until the French severed their ties with the organization in 1966) and who supplied the KGB with NATO's battle plans for Western Europe. But many more French Communist agents were never discovered. Most were in their fifties and sixties by the time I became Foreign Counterintelligence chief, and undoubtedly they had retired by the time the Soviet Union collapsed in 1991.

I traveled to Paris in the mid-1970s to meet one of our top agents in French Intelligence, who had begun working for us in 1946. We smuggled him into our embassy in the Soviet ambassador's car, its windows darkened. The French officer arrived in the early evening, and he and I talked until dawn. My purpose was not solely to debrief the man, who had been working for us for decades and was a tried-and-true agent. We thought he would enjoy meeting the head of Soviet Foreign Counter-Intelligence, and mainly I praised him for the help he had provided us over the years. I also questioned him at length about the activities of French Intelligence—what operations they were running against us, which double agents they employed, and how the French were working with the CIA.

In addition, we talked at length about information he had picked up from CIA sources that the Americans had a high-level spy in the KGB or Soviet Military Intelligence (GRU). I got the distinct impression from the Frenchman that the mole was in the GRU, and years later I would be proven right when Edward Lee Howard gave us information that led to the arrest of GRU General Nikolai Polyakov. The GRU man had been spying for the Americans for fifteen years, passing on key information on Soviet military strategy. He was executed in 1986.

At the time, the Frenchman's information touched off a major investigation that led to us picking up damaging information on several top GRU officials, though none was the real culprit. Looking for an unidentified mole is like looking for a needle in a haystack, but using the Frenchman's scant information we tried to check out likely KGB and GRU collaborators. If we suspected someone, we would tap his phone, place him under physical surveillance, insert an agent into his department, and check out his friends and acquaintances. Our investigation showed, for example, that a GRU station chief (a general) in a major Far Eastern country was a homosexual. He was dismissed on the grounds that he was a security risk. Several other GRU and KGB officers were dismissed when our taps showed that they were talking too freely about top-secret operations.

My meeting with the French Intelligence man in Paris was a memorable one, and we drank, ate, and talked until the sun came up. Toward the end of our conversation, the Frenchman pulled out a pistol and told me, "If something happens to me, I always have this."

"Nothing is going to happen to you," I assured him, for indeed he and others like him had been operating with near impunity for a long time.

While in Paris, I met with one of our key officers there, who shall be known only as Evgeny. He was officially working for UNESCO in Paris, but in fact Evgeny was our main handler of the moles inside French Intelligence. He traveled around the French capital with ease and impunity, meeting his French sources and collecting crucial information for the KGB. Evgeny, a devastatingly handsome man, was eventually made a KGB general as a result of his excellent work with the French spies.

We had so deeply infiltrated French Intelligence that we were able to see clearly just how ineffectual that agency was. The French had a network of scores of agents worldwide, including such cities as New York and London, but there was little evidence that the French spies accomplished much. Without doubt, French Intelligence was the weakest and most wasteful of all the hostile secret services we faced.

Our penetration of the Intelligence services in Scandinavia has been widely reported, especially our close links with Finnish President Urho Kekkonen, who was in office from 1956 to 1981. It is indeed true that Kekkonen was a kind of agent of ours, in the sense that he met regularly with a KGB case officer and would listen closely to our advice on a wide range of issues. But there was a strange paradox in our relations with the Finns: Even though the top levels of Finnish government were riddled with Soviet agents, these very same moles often were Finnish patriots who would help us when they thought it was in Finland's interest, but wouldn't hesitate to snub us if they thought it necessary. While I was in Foreign Counter-intelligence, the Finns on several occasions expelled KGB officers they thought had acted too boldly in recruiting one of their fellow countrymen or an American. Once, when our people from Intelligence were boasting at a meeting about our deep penetration in Finland, I responded, "What kind of agents do we have there if they don't let us work aggressively against the U.S. Embassy in Helsinki? Real agents would help our work, and the Finns don't do that."

The truth was that the tiny Finnish nation had to walk a fine line in its relations with the Soviet giant next door, and Finnish leaders did a skillful job of catering to our desires while at the same time maintaining their country's independence.

We had good sources in Sweden and Norway, as some Scandinavians came to work for us because they were committed Socialists. In the mid-1970s, I traveled to Vienna to meet a top Swedish police official who was working for us and—as it turns out—several other Intelligence agencies. I paid him $10,000 for providing us with Swedish police and Foreign Office documents. He was later imprisoned on charges unrelated to the spying he did for the KGB.

The KGB also had excellent sources in Australia and Canada, including a valuable mole in Royal Canadian Mounted Police Counterintelligence. We had productive moles in Australian Intelligence who passed us documents from the CIA and British Intelligence, as well as providing us with information on subjects as varied as the peace movement and the Australian military.

One of the more outlandish episodes in the KGB's European operations during my tenure occurred in the mid-1970s in Portugal, not long after the overthrow of the Salazar dictatorship. The Portugese Communist Party was the third largest in Europe (after those of Italy and France), and in the mid- to late 1970s socialism and Communism enjoyed wide support in Portugal. Indeed, we had agents throughout the Portugese Intelligence service, and in the chaos that followed the Socialist revolution that overthrew Salazar, our agents came up with a bold stroke. One night, with the help of moles and sympathizers inside the security apparatus, Portugese working for the KGB drove a truck to the Security Ministry and hauled away a mountain of classified intelligence data, including lists of secret police agents working for the Salazar regime. The truckload of documents was delivered to our embassy in Lisbon, then sent by plane to Moscow, where analysts spent months poring over the papers. Portugal was a member of NATO, and there was some material of limited interest on American military operations in Europe. But the really valuable material was the list of the thousands of agents and informers who worked for the Salazar dictatorship—information that our officers later used to force some of these agents to work for us. In the history of Cold War intelligence coups, the Portugese operation was not a signal achievement; but for sheer audacity— making off with a truckload of material right out of the Security Ministry—it had few rivals.

As for NATO's strongest European power, West Germany, we also had access to huge quantities of intelligence—and virtually without lifting a finger. The East German Foreign Intelligence agency, headed by the brilliant Markus Wolf, had so deeply penetrated the West German government, military, and secret services that about all we had to do was lay back and stay out of Wolf's way. KGB Intelligence naturally had close ties with the secret services of all of the "fraternal countries" of Eastern Europe, though none would be as fruitful as our relationship with East Germany and Wolf. In my seven years as head of Foreign Counterintelligence, I would spend a great deal of time working with and visiting my counterparts in the Warsaw Pact countries. Our Communist colleagues provided us with some invaluable help in our fight against the U.S. and NATO powers. My Eastern European colleagues also showed me some of the finest hospitality and hunting I encountered in all my years in the KGB.

Shortly after taking over Foreign Counterintelligence in 1973, I made my first trip to Berlin and met Wolf, a tall, dark-haired man with a humorous glint in his eyes. We had a lengthy talk in his office, followed by a lunch at East German Intelligence headquarters with his deputies. Later, Wolf arranged a banquet for us at the KGB's residency in Karlshorst. Wolf immediately struck me as the most capable and shrewd of all the Intelligence professionals I had known; his skill and expertise put someone like Kryuchkov, our Intelligence chief, to shame. When I first met Wolf, I sensed that he and some of his deputies were skeptical of this young Soviet Intelligence officer, perhaps fearing I was not a true enough believer in Communism. But I broke the ice with them when, at our first lunch, I proposed a toast and recalled Stalin's words that the creation of an East German state "was a turning point in the history of Europe, and the existence of a peace-loving, democratic Germany beside the peace-loving Soviet Union rules out a new war on the European continent."

As I sat down after the toast, Wolf looked pleased, and one of his deputies said something about me being a member of a "new generation" of Soviets. I don't know whether the deputy meant that I was merely young, or whether he had in mind that I was one of a "new generation" of Stalinists. My toast wasn't just empty words: I truly believed then that if the Soviet Union and East Germany worked closely together, there was a chance that a united, Socialist Germany might emerge one day. In that case, the USSR and Germany would dominate Europe. My bitterness over our invasion of Czechoslovakia had diminished, and in 1973 I still had faith in our system. (The problems of dissidents of the political opposition in Russia were not my concern.) That was the business of the domestic side of the KGB, and I steered clear of it. I was focusing all my energy on one goal: our struggle with the United States and the West.

Wolf had created a model Intelligence agency that had achieved spectacular results. His greatest coup was the selection and training of East German agents who moved to West Germany and penetrated the highest levels of the West German government. Wolf's task was unquestionably made easier by the fact that he was using Germans to infiltrate opposing German security structures. Yet despite that advantage, the East German's achievements still looked dazzling. Hundreds of East German agents penetrated the West German government and military at the height of the Cold War; the most famous was Günther Guillaume, who became one of West German Chancellor Willy Brandt's most trusted aides and passed reams of material to East German Intelligence.

Wolf also masterminded the technique of using East German "illegals" to seduce middle-aged, single West German women who worked in government agencies, such as the Foreign Office. These "Red Casanovas," as they came to be called, provided Wolf—and us—with valuable material on NATO, among other things. I remember sitting in my office in Moscow and reading with awe, and amusement, the field reports of some of the East German Intelligence gigolos. These agents not only described the intelligence information they were receiving from the West German women, but they also—in typically Teutonic, detailed fashion—described their sexual encounters. The accounts read like pornography, and I found myself sympathizing with some of the married agents who described the disgust they felt at having to make love to older women to whom they were not at all attracted.

The most successful "Red Casanova" had managed to seduce a

woman, fifteen years his senior, who worked for one of the top men in West German Intelligence. He wined and dined her and gave her expensive gifts. Inevitably, the time came to sleep with her. In the reports I read, the East German agent described the wild passion of this sex-starved woman. In pornographic detail he talked about their oral sex sessions, about the moans and groans she made in bed, and about how hard it was becoming for him to maintain an erection with his *Fräulein*. He posed as a nationalistic, anti-Communist West German businessman, and broached the subject of acquiring intelligence material by claiming he was worried that the West German government was angling to make peace with East Germany. Using the argument that patriotic German groups needed to know what was going on inside their government, he persuaded his lover to begin passing him materials from West German Intelligence.

We had an extraordinarily close relationship with Wolf and the East Germans, though it was not without its tensions. Nowhere in the world did the KGB have an operation like that in East Germany. In East Berlin alone, our station numbered some 450 officers; dozens more were scattered about East Germany's provinces. (Most Eastern European countries only had about fifteen to twenty KGB officers.) Our East Berlin station acquired the status of a regular KGB directorate, and the station chief assumed the rank of a deputy chief of Intelligence. For KGB officers, particularly those who had been expelled from Western countries for spying, East Berlin was a plum assignment, offering regular trips to West Berlin and a salary that was paid partly in hard currency.

Toward the end of my time in Foreign Counterintelligence, there were growing complaints from some East German politicians that the KGB presence in their country—particularly in the provinces—was too large. We made contingency plans to move some of our agents into less conspicuous positions, with joint ventures and trade missions, for example. But the East German leadership never pressed the point, and large numbers of agents remained in the country. Our relationship with the East Germans was, in fact, a complex one in which they helped us a great deal, but never played the role of a subservient younger brother. We could never merely dictate to the East Germans, as we did with such Warsaw Pact countries as Bulgaria. Nor did the leaders of East Germany's security services bow and scrape in front of their Moscow colleagues. I met East German Security Minister Erich Mielke on several occasions, and he was self-assured to the point of arrogance. Once, at a party at the East German Embassy in Moscow, the stout, hard-drinking Mielke carried on in a loud, boisterous manner, seemingly unintimidated by the presence of KGB Chief Andropov and other members of the Politburo. It was clear that Mielke, the second-ranking East German official after Eric Honeker, had been seduced by the dictatorial powers that he and Honeker possessed.

Whenever possible, we did what we could to help out the East Germans, since it seemed they were always doing far more for us than we for them. One incident in which we came to Wolf's aid occurred in 1978, when an informer betrayed several East German Intelligence agents living in West Germany. Two of Wolf's agents took refuge in the Soviet Embassy in Bonn and two in our military mission in Wiesbaden, West Germany. Our problem was how to get them out of West Germany, where they were wanted for espionage, and back to East Berlin.

In Moscow, I argued strenuously that the only way to extricate the four was to give them fake Soviet diplomatic passports and smuggle them out of West Germany in cars with USSR diplomatic license plates. Others in KGB headquarters in Moscow retorted that there would be a major scandal if we were caught smuggling East German spies out of West Germany using phony Soviet passports. The KGB station chief in Bonn agreed, contending that the four should surreptitiously be allowed to abscond from the embassy and the military mission and then find their way back to East Germany on their own.

"That won't do," I said to the station chief over a secure line. "The East Germans have confidence in us. They give us all the intelligence secrets they get. We must help their people. We have no right to abandon them."

I pressed my case, and eventually Andropov agreed, saying it was highly unlikely that the West Germans would stop a Soviet diplomatic vehicle. So our technical people counterfeited four Soviet passports for the East Germans, sent the documents to our embassy and military mission in West Germany, and in a matter of days Wolf's agents were joyfully embracing their colleagues on the East German border.

The one East German activity that made my superiors at KGB headquarters squirm was that country's support of international ter-rorists, such as the infamous Carlos. We knew full well that a wide variety of terrorists—including those from the PLO, the Italian Red

Brigades, and the West German Bader-Meinhof gang—were receiving refuge and support in East Germany. I didn't know of any actual incidents in which the East Germans trained such terrorists or helped them carry out specific terrorist attacks, but I realized that Wolf and his agency were doing more than providing R&R for these international outlaws. My superiors in Moscow viewed this East German "hospitality" more as a sign of solidarity with forces struggling against world imperialism; but the fact remained that none of us delved too deeply into what the East Germans were doing with these unsavory characters.

Carlos, responsible for some of the most heinous Middle Eastern terrorist acts in the 1970s and 1980s, came to the Soviet Union twice while I was in charge of Foreign Counterintelligence. On both occasions, I was notified that he had applied for a Soviet visa at one of our consulates in Eastern Europe. We gave him permission to come to Moscow—where he had been a student at Patrice Lumumba University in the 1960s—but kept him under close surveillance. When he arrived on his first visit, our officers met him at Sheremetyevo Airport and took him to his hotel, where he was questioned extensively about his trip to the USSR. He claimed that he was in the Soviet capital to visit old friends for a few weeks, and our tight surveillance of him turned up nothing that contradicted that assertion. In fact, our surveillance officers were astounded that this infamous international criminal would turn out to be such a playboy; he seemed to spend almost all of his time in Moscow at parties, and our agents marveled at the number of women Carlos courted in the Soviet capital. After a couple of weeks Carlos left without incident.

In 1976, knowing that we could not remain forever immune from the growing terrorist threat, I formed a small unit to do research on the world's leading terrorists and terrorist organizations. Using published Western documents as well as our own extensive network of sources in Eastern Europe, the Middle East, and other regions, we compiled a handbook identifying more than two thousand international terrorists. The book was sent to all Soviet border posts in an effort to stop terrorists from entering the USSR.

In addition, our officers in Eastern Europe set out to discover how deeply involved our Socialist neighbors were in sponsoring international terrorism. We learned that not only East Germany, but Yugoslavia, Czechoslovakia, and Romania all were giving support to a variety of terrorist groups. The Romanians were supplying terrorists with training and weaponry, and the Czechs were selling them large quantities of light weapons and plastique explosives. We discussed the idea of trying to penetrate these terrorist organizations, but backed off out of fear that—should our agents be discovered—we would be accused of participating in terrorist acts. Andropov even once suggested that we attempt to penetrate the Mafia. It wasn't a bad idea, but we pointed out that an international scandal would arise if it ever became known that we had anything to do with Italian organized crime.

"You're probably right, but you should look into it,'" said Andropov. "There is a risk involved, but you have to keep an eye on all these groups. We can't let them grow without our knowledge."

As close as our relations were with Markus Wolf and East German Intelligence, we had an even tighter relationship with the secret services of Bulgaria. That Eastern European country, headed by Todor Zhivkov, was so firmly bound to the USSR that people in both countries referred to Bulgaria as the sixteenth Soviet republic. The Bulgarian Interior Ministry was little more than a branch of the KGB. Our station chief in Sofia for many years, General Ivan Savchenko, virtually ran Bulgaria's secret services; no general in Bulgarian Intelligence or in the Interior Ministry dared do anything of consequence without first picking up the telephone and checking with Savchenko.

I went to Bulgaria on numerous occasions in the 1970s, and though some business usually was transacted, the trips turned out to be far more pleasure than work, thanks to the legendary hospitality of the Bulgarians. Compared to East Germany, Bulgaria was of little intelligence interest to us, though the Bulgarians did give us some useful information about Greece, Turkey, and the southern front of NATO. At our urging, the Bulgarians also worked aggressively in their Black Sea resorts and in the port of Varna to recruit foreigners. Shortly before I left for Leningrad in 1980, Bulgarian Intelligence agents struck up a relationship with a young West German woman who was the wife of a West German legislator. Her husband also served on the legislature's security committee, and the Bulgarians kept in touch with her after the couple returned to Germany. I never found out whether the relationship bore fruit.

Mostly what I remember about Bulgaria is being squired around in chauffeured limousines to the country's beautiful mountains and beaches, where—sometimes accompanied by my wife—I was treated like a pasha. I have never encountered hospitality like it, before or since. The Bulgarians drowned us in their delicious wines. They laid out enormous feasts at the finest Communist Party retreats. They put on hunts for deer, duck, and pheasant at the game preserves reserved for President Zhivkov and the Bulgarian elite. On several occasions, their desire to please their elder Slavic brothers reached absurd proportions.

Once, on a bird shoot with some officers from the Interior Ministry, a Bulgarian gamekeeper walked up to our party carrying a large sack. He dumped the contents on the ground, and out scrambled a dozen barely fledged pheasants. The dazed birds scampered a few yards away and hid in a cornfield.

"Go ahead, shoot!" said one of my hosts, flashing me a proud smile.

It was clear that my Bulgarian colleagues were so bent on showing me a good time that they wanted to spare me the embarrassment of a missed shot. But I could hardly execute these young birds as they crouched in terror on the ground. My hosts tried to kick a few of the pheasants up, but to no avail. I scared up one young bird, and he frantically beat his wings but only managed to get off the ground for a few seconds before dropping back to earth. The Bulgarians were eagerly watching me: if I declined to shoot these adolescent pheasants, I obviously would be deeply offending my hosts. So I took aim at one of the poor creatures on the ground and pulled the trigger. The Bulgarians seemed relieved. It was the last young bird I shot that day.

On another occasion, this time during a deer hunt, I once again ran into all-consuming Bulgarian hospitality. A group of beaters had driven a deer out of a patch of woods, and my Bulgarian host and I stood in a clearing, ready to down the animal. The deer bounded out of the forest and paused for a second. I raised my gun and was preparing to fire when my host said, "Oleg, give me your gun. I'll shoot him for you."

"No," I replied. "I didn't come all this way to let you do all the work."

"No," the Bulgarian insisted. "I'll shoot him for you. What if you miss!"

"I don't care if I miss!" I barked back, the two of us nearly wrestling for the gun.

By the time I fended off my host and was ready to fire, the deer was long gone.

All my memories of Bulgaria and the Bulgarians are not so amusing, however. Another kind of hunt—this one for a human being—turned out to be the most infamous example of cooperation between our two Intelligence services and the blackest mark on my career.

In all my years in the KGB, I have only once been involved in what we call in the business a "wet job"—an assassination. It occurred in 1978, and though I didn't have a pivotal role in the killing, I nevertheless did not try to talk my superiors out of the plot to kill the Bulgarian dissident Georgi Markov.

The case first came to my attention in early 1978. Kryuchkov, our Intelligence chief, had just received an urgent cable from General Stoyanov, the Bulgarian minister of the interior. The Bulgarian had a blunt request: He wanted the KGB's help in carrying out President Zhivkov's express order to liquidate Georgi Markov. Unquestionably, Andropov had to approve the plan, and Kryuchkov asked me to accompany him to a meeting with the KGB chairman.

I had heard about Markov from my colleagues in Bulgarian Intelligence. He was a former close associate of Zhivkov's who had turned against Communists, fled to England, and was beaming back strong criticism of the regime to Bulgaria through his position with the Bulgarian radio service of the BBC. During my most recent visit to Bulgaria, my colleagues there had several times mentioned what a nuisance Markov had become.

"He lives in London and slanders Comrade Zhivkov," one Bulgarian Intelligence officer told me. "Our people are very unhappy about him."

The meeting where the Bulgarian request to murder Markov was raised took place in Andropov's spacious, wood-paneled office in Lubyanka. In attendance were Andropov, Kryuchkov, Vice Admiral Mikhail Usatov—first chief deputy for Intelligence—and myself. After discussing several, unrelated matters, Kryuchkov spoke up.

"We have a request from the Bulgarian Interior Minister Stoyanov that we help them with one of the opponents of the regime who lives in London, the writer Markov," Kryuchkov said. "They want us to help them in the physical removal of Markov. This request was made by Comrade Stoyanov, but it comes from President Zhivkov himself."

We sat there in silence for a few seconds. I will never forget the tidy euphemism Kryuchkov used for Markov's assassination—"physical removal," *fizicheskoye ustraneniye* in Russian. I felt a chill go down my spine, then thought to myself: "To hell with these Bulgarians. Let them do whatever they want to their political opponents. Why are they dragging us into this mess?"

Andropov also was taken aback. He abruptly stood up from his desk and started nervously pacing back and forth. The chairman seemed lost in thought for a few seconds, then said, "I am against political assassinations. I don't think it's the right way to deal with these problems. The time when this sort of thing could be done with impunity is past. We can't revert to the old ways. I am really against it."

Again, there was silence, save for the faint hum of traffic in Dzerzhinsky Square. Finally, Kryuchkov spoke again.

"But Comrade Andropov," said Kryuchkov (who would later lead the 1991 coup against Gorbachev). "It's Comrade Zhivkov's personal request. If we deny him our assistance, Zhivkov may think that Comrade Stoyanov has fallen out of favor with us or maybe that his own reputation in the eyes of the Soviet people has been tarnished. Comrade Zhivkov may interpret it as a sign that we are distancing ourselves from him. I repeat: This is a personal request from Zhivkov. We have to deal with the problem somehow."

Andropov continued pacing around the room.

"All right, all right," he said, stopping suddenly. "But there is to be no direct participation on our part. Give the Bulgarians whatever they need, show them how to use it, and send someone to Sofia to train their people. But that's all. No direct involvement. I won't permit any more than that."

Kryuchkov nodded in agreement. I listened and watched without saying a word.

Over the next half year, using the "talents" of KGB scientists schooled in the art of poisoning and other methods of murder, we and the Bulgarians stumbled toward the assassination of Markov. It was a wrenching trial-and-error process, right out of the pages of the blackest comedy. But in the end, even the Soviets and the Bulgarians couldn't screw it up: We got our man.

When Kryuchkov and I returned to Yasenevo, the Intelligence chief set the plot in motion. "Well, what shall we do about this?" Kryuchkov asked me as we settled into his office at Yasenevo. Unfortunately, I knew the answer.

"Sergei Golubev deals with problems like this," I replied.

Golubev was summoned to Kryuchkov's office and ordered to contact the Operational and Technical Directorate, the successor to the top-secret *Kamera* created by Joseph Stalin. The directorate had a laboratory that invented new ways of killing people, from poisons that could be slipped into drinks to jellies that could be rubbed on a person to induce a heart attack. A KGB agent rubbed just such a substance on Alexander Solzhenitsyn in a store in Russia in the early 1970s, making him violently ill but not killing him. That was the handiwork of the Operational and Technical Directorate, and they would be in charge of coming up with a solution to Zhivkov's problem: Finding a way of "physically removing" Markov without leaving a trace of what brought about his death. The more it looked like a heart attack the better. Even a despot like Zhivkov didn't have the stomach to shoot someone in the head on a London street.

Sergei Golubev was in charge of security for the Intelligence Directorate, and part of his job description included carrying out "wet jobs" (the term has obvious roots: killing people is messy). By the late 1970s, the KGB had virtually stopped pulling off "wet jobs," but Golubev—a quiet, dour man—still had a unit of a half-dozen men whose job it was to try to locate KGB defectors. So Golubev, working with Laboratory 12 of the Operational and Technical Directorate, was the perfect man to help the Bulgarians get rid of Markov.

After consulting with our scientists, Golubev and an assistant, Yuri Surov—head of the search team for KGB traitors—flew to Sofia. There, Golubev described to the Bulgarians three main ways of liquidating Markov silently: the poison jelly, poisoning his food, or shooting him with a poison pellet.

The Bulgarians at first liked the idea of the poison jelly, and considered rubbing it on the handle of Markov's car door, but dropped the idea when they realized they could just as easily kill Markov's girlfriend as Markov himself. The Bulgarians weren't so much concerned about accidentally wiping out the girlfriend as they were about scaring off Markov.

Our Bulgarian allies then learned that Markov was planning to vacation at a seaside resort in Italy. They hatched a plan to follow him there and have an agent "accidentally" bump into him on the beach and smear him with the poison jelly. But this plot was scrapped because the weather was cold, the beach was half-empty, Markov was clothed, and the agent couldn't figure out a way to rub cream on the victim inconspicuously on a deserted beach.

Yet another plan was discussed by the Bulgarians, this one to poison Markov's food during a trip to Germany. A Bulgarian agent did follow the dissident to Germany but, for reasons that were unclear, could not pull off the poisoning.

What had looked like a simple plot to kill an unarmed dissident was now turning into a comedy of errors. In the summer of 1978, the head of Bulgarian Foreign Counterintelligence—General Todorov—suggested we come up with a new way to kill Markov. After the failure of the poison jellies plots, Todorov and Golubev decided that the best way was by shooting Markov with a tiny poison pellet, no bigger than the head of a pin. The poison to be used was ricin, an extraordinarily toxic substance made from castor-oil seeds. I can't imagine how in the world our scientists ever figured out that castor-oil seeds could be turned into a deadly poison; I suppose that's what they were paid to do as they worked feverishly, year after year, in their top-secret KGB lab.

Golubev returned to Sofia with the ricin pellets. One was shot into a horse, which died. The Bulgarians then decided to try out the ricin on a human being. The unfortunate victim was a Bulgarian prisoner who had been sentenced to death. As Golubev later explained it, an officer from the Bulgarian Interior Ministry approached the prisoner with an umbrella, the tip of which our scientists had converted into a gun that would silently shoot the ricin pellet into its victim. The officer shot the poor prisoner with the umbrella, and the fellow yelped as if stung by a bee. Apparently he was hysterical, realizing that his death sentence had just been carried out in a most unusual manner. But the poison wasn't released from the pellet, and the prisoner remained in good health.

Golubev returned to Moscow with the disconcerting news of this failed attempt. Our laboratory went back to work on the ricin pellet, assuring Golubev and the Bulgarians that it would work.

In September 1978, a Bulgarian agent hunted down Markov in London. The agent approached the handsome, gray-haired Markov on Waterloo Bridge, prodded him with an umbrella on the right thigh, then apologized and walked off. As he was dying in a hospital on September 11, Markov told doctors of the incident on the bridge. But doctors couldn't immediately determine the cause of Markov's death, and it wasn't until news of his strange demise spread that the Bulgarian exile community began to piece together what had happened.

A few weeks before Markov's death, a Bulgarian defector in

Paris, Vladimir Kostov, had felt a sting while riding the Métro and seen a man with an umbrella standing close to him. After hearing of Markov's death, Kostov alerted officials in London that Markov might have been the victim of an assassination attempt. A month after the attack on Kostov, French doctors extracted a still-intact ricin pellet from his body; he had been saved either because the poison had been old and ineffective or had not been released. Officials in London then exhumed Markov's body, and an autopsy showed a tiny pellet lodged in a small wound in his right thigh. By the time of the autopsy, the ricin had decomposed.

Though Bulgarian exiles were sure that Zhivkov was behind the assassination of Markov and the attempted assassination of Kostov, no one could prove the involvement of the Communist dictator and the KGB. I felt sick when I heard of Markov's assassination, and few of us in Foreign Counter-Intelligence said much about the killing.

Returning to Bulgaria shortly after the Markov affair, I met Interior Minister Stoyanov, who gave me an expensive Browning hunting rifle with a brass plaque on the stock that read: "From Minister Stoyanov to General Kalugin." Though he did not specify the reason, I understood Stoyanov had given the gun to me in appreciation for the help we rendered his agency in "physically removing" Markov. Every time I looked at the rifle I was reminded of the Markov affair, and eventually I stuck it in a closet. Several years ago I pulled the plaque off the stock and, with great relief, sold the gun. I still have the plaque.

After the fall of Communist regimes in Eastern Europe in 1989 and the arrest of Zhivkov, the truth about Markov's murder began to emerge. In 1990, I became the first person to publicly divulge details of the plot. In 1992, two years after I had publicly broken with the KGB, the Bulgarian Embassy in Moscow telephoned and invited me to come speak with them. Embassy officials informed me that Bulgaria's new leader, President Zhelev, wanted me to come to Bulgaria as his personal guest to tell investigators what I knew about Markov's assassination. I readily agreed, in part to assuage my conscience but also to continue my task of exposing the inner workings of the KGB. Before I flew to Sofia, Yevgeny Primakov—the new head of Russian Intelligence—telephoned me and asked why I was going to Bulgaria. I told him that President Zhelev had invited me.

"Are you going to say anything about Markov's case?" Primakov asked.

"If they ask me, I will," I replied.

"What are you going to say?" Primakov inquired.

"The same as I have said about the case publicly before," I replied.

I couldn't understand why Primakov, who was appointed by President Yeltsin, seemed so concerned. The plot against Markov occurred well before his time and Primakov bore no responsibility. I told him that the best thing he could do was to call a press conference and announce, "This did happen under a previous regime, this is how it happened, and it will not happen again."

I felt uneasy as I flew into Sofia. But I was overwhelmed by the warm reception I encountered there. The president and vice president received me, and I spent several days testifying in closed session before the Bulgarian prosecutor's office. I supplied them with as many details as I could remember, including the names of all the Russians and Bulgarians I knew to be involved in the Markov assassination. Later, I held a press conference for Bulgarian and foreign correspondents. I appeared on Bulgarian TV to talk about the Markov murder. By the end of my week there, I was being recognized on the street and treated not as a criminal but as a national hero. Several people stopped me in downtown Sofia and gave me presents. Others asked for my autograph. I even met Markov's brother, who had flown in from London to confer with the prosecutor and talk to me. Meeting the brother, I felt awkward and ashamed. But he, too, was gracious enough to forgive me, and like most Bulgarians he was more interested in finding out which of his countrymen was involved in the assassination of his brother.

I told Markov's brother I was sorry about what had happened, and he replied, "No, Mr. Kalugin, I want to thank you for what you have disclosed."

His gratitude made me uneasy; I certainly didn't deserve it.

Though Bulgarian officials know the identities of all the people involved in the murder of Markov, they have yet to bring anyone to trial.

Markov's murder was a nasty affair that to this day leaves me with feelings of remorse.

Fifteen years after the assassination, the Markov affair would come back to haunt me as British authorities tried to charge me with conspiracy to kill the Bulgarian.

On October 30, 1993, I flew into London to participate in a BBC

Panorama program about British Intelligence. I first had an inkling
something was wrong when an immigration oficer at Heathrow Airport dallied over my passport, then instructed me to sit in a nearby
waiting area. Nearly an hour passed, and then a man in plainclothes
approached me and said, "I am from Scotland Yard's Counterter-
rorism Unit and you are under arrest on charges of conspiracy to
commit murder."

I was floored. "What are you talking about!" I protested, but
the man instructed me to follow him to a nearby room. There, two
more men were waiting.

"You must come with us on charges of conspiring to murder Mr.
Markov," said one of the men, and with that they handcuffed me
and led me down darkened corridors to a waiting car.

The policemen drove me to the Belgravia Police Station in central
London, where I was stripped to my underwear, searched, and my
possessions confiscated. One of the officers even took a look inside
my underpants.

"What are you looking for—explosives between my legs?" I
asked. By now, my earlier disorientation had turned to cold anger.

"Mr. Kalugin," said the Scotland Yard detective. "You are a
professional. Am I doing anything improper?"

"No, you are not," I told him. "Go ahead."

I was taken to a brightly lit cell that contained a bed and a toilet,
but no sink. There were no bars, only a heavy door and a steel-
reinforced window high up on the wall. After a while, I was led to
an interrogation room, where a woman inspector asked me if I had
any complaints. I forcefully protested my detention, and told her it
would be nice to have some toilet paper and to dim the lights in my
cell.

The woman left, and a few minutes later there was a stirring in
the hallway. The door to the interrogation room swung open, and
in walked a distinguished-looking man. It was Christopher Bird, the
superintendent of the Metropolitan London Police. The time was
eleven o'clock, Saturday night, and Bird said he wanted to question
me about my involvement in the Markov murder.

"This is absolute bullshit," I said. "I will not utter a word or
answer a single question until there are representatives of the Russian Embassy here."

Bird seemed taken aback, but granted my request. A few minutes
later, I received a phone call. It was a diplomat from our London
embassy, and he assured me he would send someone to speak to

me first thing Sunday morning. Superintendent Bird retired for the night, and a few minutes later a lawyer, hired by the BBC, showed up at the Belgravia station and announced he was there to defend me.

I didn't sleep a wink that night, not because I was worried I might be put on trial for the Markov murder, but because I was still furious over the heavy-handed tactics of the police, particularly the handcuffs and the overnight stay in jail. The next morning, Bird, the BBC lawyer, two representatives from the Russian Embassy, and I gathered in an interrogation room. A secretary was taping the session as I made an opening statement.

"I understand why you might want to question me about the Markov murder, but why did you have to treat me in this way?" I asked Bird. "I would gladly have come in and answered any questions you had. But if you are trying to intimidate someone, you have picked the wrong fellow. Trying to bully a Russian will have the opposite effect."

I then agreed to answer questions, and we sat in the room until six-thirty that evening going over my role in the Markov affair. I told Bird what I had told the Bulgarians: That I knew of the plot and that my subordinate, Golubev, was working with the Bulgarians. But my role had been peripheral, and it was Kryuchkov—not I— who had given the order to Golubev to travel to Sofia and assist the Bulgarians. And then it became clear why I had been brought in for questioning by Scotland Yard. Bird produced a copy of the British tabloid, *The Mail on Sunday,* which had interviewed me in the spring of 1993 about the Markov case. The police inspector showed me the headline, and I could hardly believe my eyes: "I ORGANIZED THE ASSASSINATION OF GEORGI MARKOV."

"Bastards," I muttered.

We had listened to the tape of my interview with *The Mail on Sunday,* and nowhere had I said anything about organizing Markov's murder. The reporter had utterly distorted my words, as the tape of our interview—which had been obtained by Scotland Yard— showed perfectly well.

"Mr. Kalugin, you must be more careful with our press," Bird said.

The appearance of the story that April had led to a minor scandal, with Lord Bethel saying in Parliament I should either be arrested for murder or publicly acknowledge that I had lied about my involvement in the Markov affair.

"People saw the story and they were wondering how we could let such a criminal roam our streets," Superintendent Bird said.

"I understand," I replied. "But why did I have to be hauled in here and treated in this fashion?"

Bird didn't answer. It seemed clear I would not be charged in the Markov case, but Bird told me to stay in the country until Thursday, at which time a formal decision would be made about my future.

I was released Sunday night, and the BBC found me a room at the Kensington Hilton under the assumed name, "Harry Dean." It wasn't that I was trying to hide from the authorities; the BBC was trying to protect me from the British press, who indeed took an intense interest in the case. The BBC's lawyer thought I should assume a low profile until the matter was settled.

That Monday I met with our ambassador to England, Boris Pankin, whom I had come to know in Moscow. The KGB station chief sat in on the meeting, and we planned what we would do if I were detained again. Our KGB station chief thought the worst fate would be expulsion, and he doubted that the British would take such a step.

As it turned out, my BBC lawyer called me Wednesday evening to announce that Bird had said there would be no charges filed against me in the Markov assassination and I was free to leave the country. I was relieved, but still fuming at the heavy-handed way the matter had been handled. And with that, the Markov case—for me at least—was closed.

Besides Bulgaria, we cooperated closely with the Intelligence services of other Warsaw Pact countries, though thankfully during my remaining years in Foreign Counterintelligence none of our Communist allies asked for our help with other "wet jobs." In several instances, our Eastern European allies helped us unmask CIA moles within the Soviet Union. One such case occurred thanks to the Czechs, and we found the spy in our midst with the help of a man whose allegiance was never clear to me.

Czech Intelligence had been decimated by the purges following the Prague Spring of 1968, and their secret services never really recovered. When I worked with Czech Intelligence in the 1970s, the agency was demoralized and hamstrung by the corruption of top Communist Party bosses. Cronies of Prime Minister Gustav Gusak and the Czech Interior Minister constantly pressured Intelligence Chief Milos Gladek to give up some of his precious hard currency reserves. The Communist bosses then used the money for everything from purchasing prostitutes to cars. So Czech Intelligence was a wounded organization, and during our visits there, despite the smiles with which our Czech colleagues greeted us, we felt the lingering anger and bitterness over the 1968 invasion.

In the mid-1970s, the Czechs managed to reestablish contact with one of their agents who had fled to America following the events of 1968. The Czech immigrant had taken a job as a contract employee of the CIA, and he had access to internal CIA communications as well as messages intercepted by the agency around the world. The Czechs made contact with the man in Washington, and he agreed to resume working for them. Most of the information he supplied to the Czechs was of little value, but he forwarded one CIA communication that listed the names of three Soviets in Columbia who were targets of CIA recruitment. One was a diplomat named Ogorodnik.

Ogorodnik had been transferred back to Moscow, where he held a senior post at the Soviet Foreign Ministry. We turned over our information to the KGB's Internal Counterintelligence section, which conducted an investigation of Ogorodnik. But bugs on his phones and surveillance turned up nothing, and Internal Counterintelligence was just about to drop the inquiry when we got a break. The KGB's Seventh Directorate, in charge of physical surveillance, was doing a routine tail of an American diplomat when they noticed the American car and a Soviet-made Volga driving next to one another. The Volga driver apparently made a strange movement, as if trying to signal the American, and our surveillance people took down the license plate of the Soviet car. It turned out to be Ogorodnik's.

The investigation was revived, this time far more thoroughly. His apartment, office, and country house were bugged and secretly searched. All his telephones were tapped and he was placed under round-the-clock surveillance. Eventually, Internal Counterintelligence found evidence that he had been spying for the CIA for several years, turning over classified Foreign Ministry documents to the Americans. Our agents confronted him with the evidence, which at first he denied. He finally acquiesced, however, and asked for a piece of paper to write out a statement of confession. Ogorodnik pulled out a fountain pen, extracted a cyanide pill hidden in the pen top, and popped the poison in his mouth. Our officers tried to pluck the pill out, but he had already swallowed it. The diplomat died on the spot.

Though the Czechs' CIA mole in Washington helped ferret out Ogorodnik, they remained skeptical of him. I suggested that, to test his loyalty, they contact the mole and tell him he had done a superb job in America and that Czech Intelligence now wanted him to return to his homeland to work. The Czech responded that he could still be useful to his country in America and didn't want to return to Prague. His superiors did persuade him to visit Prague with his wife, during which time I and several officers from Czech Intelligence questioned him closely. He seemed evasive to me. And when I began showing him some snapshots he had sent us which purported to identify his CIA co-workers at a party, he could not remember the names of most of the people in the pictures. I was fairly certain he was a double agent working for the CIA, and advised the Czechs to drop him. They apparently did not. But my doubts about the man may not have been justified. In 1991, I heard that a Czech couple that perfectly fit the description of the man and woman I met in Prague had been suspected of spying in America and expelled. The Czech may have been genuine after all.

My last visit to Czechoslovakia was in April 1979, to attend a conference of Intelligence officials from the Eastern Bloc and other Communist countries. Our delegation included Viktor Chebrikov, who went on to head the KGB from 1982 to 1988. Our Czech hosts put us up in a grand, two-hundred-year-old hotel in the heart of the capital, and there—in the midst of a splendid Prague spring—the leaders of the secret services from the Communist world discussed cooperating in a fight against the growing dissident movements in our countries. We discussed how best to penetrate and weaken the various dissident and émigré organizations, and many of those present seemed to naively believe that just by gathering to talk about this problem we might somehow be able to solve it. I was skeptical, and welcomed the move to reform our failing Communist societies. But I didn't fully grasp then what a foolish endeavor the meeting was. We would hardly be able to stop the flow of history by launching a campaign of harassment against émigrés and dissidents. We didn't know it at the time, we were sitting on a volcano. A decade later it would blow, bringing down the entire Communist edifice in Europe.

As I traveled throughout Eastern Europe in the late 1970s, being wined and dined by my Warsaw Pact colleagues, there were signs everywhere that the foundations of our Communist system were beginning to crumble. The situation wasn't alarming, but there was a sense of foreboding. It was, as W. H. Auden once put it, like the sound of distant thunder at a picnic. Only a fool could ignore the stirrings of discontent; unfortunately, in places like Poland, there were fools aplenty.

Our colleagues in Polish Intelligence were a wild, carefree bunch. They had earned our respect by aggressively penetrating the large Polish émigré circles abroad and using those foreign agents to steal military, commercial, and technical secrets from the West. But they had a devil-may-care attitude about unsettling events in their own country, such as the rise of Solidarity. Our Polish colleagues always met us in big Mercedes and squired us around to the country's resorts. Though the Polish economy was in dire straits, their Intelligence agencies seemed to have no shortage of hard currency. But many of my Polish colleagues were blind to life in their own country.

I vividly remember my last trip to Poland in 1979. Our delegation included Kryuchkov and other high KGB officials, and after several days in Warsaw we decided we wanted to see Gdansk and its enormous shipyards. Arriving in Mercedes limousines at the gates of the shipyard, where Solidarity was in the process of being born, the shipyard manager came out to meet us and said, "Please don't drive your cars inside the shipyard. People don't like bosses driving around in black cars. You'd better walk. You won't be so conspicuous that way."

We left our cars at the gate and toured the massive shipyard. We were undeniably impressed by this huge industrial enterprise; but equally impressive was the surly, gloomy demeanor of the shipyard workers, whose eyes bored into us with looks of disdain and animosity. I was relieved when we finally left.

Back in Warsaw, at our farewell banquet, I proposed a toast to our Polish colleagues, wishing them well with their "current difficulties." It hardly seemed an intemperate remark, given the obvious problems looming with the workers at Gdansk. But State Security Chief Miroslav Milewski took offense. Milewski had long been a KGB asset, and was well versed in Soviet ways. His reports to us and to his own leadership were a clever mixture of truths, half-truths, and lies—all of which led to a disastrous underestimation of the power of Lech Walesa and Solidarity.

When the time came for the Polish side to make a toast, Milewski struck back.

"I don't know why Comrade Kalugin is so concerned about the

effectiveness of our work," Milewski said to the assembled Security and Intelligence officers. "I could count all our dissidents on the fingers of my two hands. We know every dissident by name, and we can deal with this unrepresentative handful of loudmouths any time we want. Our Soviet comrades can be sure of that. We keep these dissidents under tight control and can put them in prison whenever we wish. We're just not seeking an international scandal."

Within a year, Milewski's "handful of loudmouths" had turned into an army of Solidarity members and supporters. And by the end of the decade, these rabblerousers had risen up and swept Milewski and his smug colleagues from power.

In Romania, I had had an inkling years earlier that all was not well with the regime of Nicolae Ceaucescu. Though Ceaucescu had severed contact with the KGB, I headed a delegation of ten KGB officers and their wives on a trip to Romania in 1972 that was part vacation, part official visit. We stayed in a luxurious Interior Ministry villa at the Black Sea resort of Mangalia, where we were warmly received by the chief of Romanian Intelligence. Later, the Interior Minister himself met with our delegation in Bucharest. Following that meeting, one of the minister's assistants led me down endless dark corridors, finally ushering me into a large room with expensive Western furniture and an enormous Chinese rug. Suddenly, through an open door, an old friend appeared: Viktor Dorobantu, whom I had known when we both worked together in Washington.

He had become deputy Intelligence chief, he told me as we drank coffee and brandy. Then, apparently confident that his office was not bugged, Dorobantu launched into a diatribe against Ceaucescu.

"Do you know what is going on in this country?" Dorobantu asked. "Don't trust the official smiles. Ceaucescu ordered that we break completely with the KGB. You are the last group we are receiving in Bucharest. Ceaucescu is a traitor and an egomaniac. His wife and his whole entourage are power-loving, corrupt scum. They don't give a damn about the country and its people, about socialism or about friendship with the Soviet Union. We in the security organs are beginning to realize that Ceaucescu will have to be deposed."

I sat there stunned. I didn't know whether the deputy Intelligence chief's passionate monologue was a cry for help or a provocation. All I could do was occasionally nod my head and utter platitudes about how these difficulties would be overcome and how our two countries would once again live in harmony.

Upon my return to Moscow, I notified our people who handled Eastern Europe that they must immediately open up communications with Dorobantu so as to better understand the bizarre goings-on in Romania. The head of our Eastern European desk promised he would, but I never checked back with him and to this day don't know the fate of Dorobantu. One thing is clear: his talk about ridding Romania of Ceaucescu never went anywhere, for the megalomaniacal leader remained in power until he was overthrown in a popular uprising in 1989 and executed.

In the Communist sphere outside of Europe, we worked closest with the Cubans, who displayed a revolutionary fervor that we had long since lost. I knew the Cuban Intelligence chief, Jose Mendez-Cominches, quite well, and his style was characteristic of the entire Cuban Intelligence organization: he was wild, naive, and unpredictable, but somehow managed to get a lot done. When you play without rules, sometimes you get into trouble. But sometimes you achieve unexpectedly good results. Mendez-Cominches was a heavy-set, flamboyant high-flier. I still remember his behavior at the 1979 meeting of Intelligence chiefs in Prague, where he spent most of his time drinking and chasing local women. Cominches, who would later run Cuban operations in Angola, even came to some of our sessions drunk. I didn't approve of his behavior, but it typified the wide-open Cuban style.

The Cubans, in a sense, were even closer to us than our brother Slav Communists, who had been battered by the Hungarian uprising of 1956, the 1968 events in Czechoslovakia, and the rise of Solidarity in Poland. In Cuba, there was pure, revolutionary zeal, and when I visited the country in 1977, I was struck by the enthusiasm of the Cubans as they tried to spread Communism to their neighbors in Central and Latin America. As a Soviet, I also couldn't help but be impressed by the Cubans' fanatical anti-Americanism, and it was this desire to wound America at any cost that made them an effective intelligence ally. Castro and Mendez-Cominches had thoroughly infiltrated the anti-Castro Cuban exile movement in the southern United States, to the point of virtually neutralizing the regime's exile opposition.

The Cubans' ardor also spurred them to take chances that we, a conservative superpower, were reluctant to take. A perfect example occurred shortly after I became head of Foreign Counterintelligence in 1973. CIA agent Philip Agee approached our KGB station in Mexico City, offering us reams of information about CIA operations. But our station chief in Mexico City thought Agee was a CIA plant spreading disinformation, and rejected him. Agee then went to the Cubans, who welcomed him with open arms. As it turned out, Agee was absolutely genuine, divulging the names of hundreds of CIA agents and informants, and providing the Cubans with mounds of information about U.S. Intelligence. Agee proved to be one of the most damaging CIA turncoats in history. The Cubans shared Agee's information with us. But as I sat in my office in Moscow reading reports about the growing list of revelations coming from Agee, I cursed our officers for turning away such a prize. I sent out orders for our stations to work carefully with such volunteers and reject them only after we were certain they were not genuine. In any event, the Cubans never let us forget that they were the ones who had discovered Agee. In the 1970s and 1980s they continued going after current and retired CIA officers and enjoyed some success, though none of the future recruits would ever be as spectacular as Agee.

Finally, we enjoyed limited cooperation with one other Communist country: Vietnam. In the early 1970s, as the Vietnam War was winding down, we asked a KGB liaison officer in Hanoi to approach the North Vietnamese on a sensitive matter: We wanted to recruit some American POWs being held by the Vietnamese. For half a year, we received no answer from Hanoi. Finally, the Vietnamese said we could send a KGB representative to Hanoi. I sent one of my subordinates, Oleg Nechiporenko, who was permitted to see transcripts of some interrogations of American prisoners. From those documents he focused on several POWs as possible recruits. On that trip, however, the Vietnamese did not permit Nechiporenko to interview the Americans, and he returned to Moscow empty-handed.

In 1973 or 1974, when the Vietnam War was winding down and all American prisoners supposedly had been repatriated, the Vietnamese again contacted us and said we could send a representative to Hanoi. Nechiporenko returned and stayed at least a month. This time he was allowed to question a CIA agent and two American pilots. The CIA officer gave us some information on his agency and even told Nechiporenko he would cooperate with us when he returned to America. Nechiporenko flew back to Moscow and the CIA man apparently returned to the United States. But in 1975 or

1976, when KGB officers in Washington attempted to contact him, he was nowhere to be found. With that, our halting efforts to recruit American POWs from the Vietnam War came to an end.

Though it didn't play a pivotal role in our struggle with U.S. Intelligence agencies, we caried on a low-level campaign to infiltrate numerous anti-Soviet émigré organizations, as well as so-called "centers of ideological diversion." Virtually all of the large national groups in the Soviet Union—Ukrainians, Armenians, Lithuanians, Latvians, and Estonians—had vocal émigré organizations abroad that fought for the independence of their countrymen at home. Our job in KGB Foreign Counterintelligence was to insinuate agents into these groups who would keep abreast of émigré activities, let us know which leaders were likely targets for recruitment and, if possible, soften the anti-Soviet thrust of these usually rabid anti-Communist organizations. Our ultimate goal in working with these groups was to find agents who might eventually go to work for Western intelligence and security services.

We enjoyed some success in penetrating the Baltic émigré organizations, particularly in Sweden. And we had a good network of agents among the Ukrainian émigrés, particularly in Canada, where several million Ukrainians had settled. But the émigré organization we most thoroughly infiltrated was the Armenian exile group, *Dashnak Tsutyun*. Once, *Dashnak Tsutyun* had been a staunchly nationalist group that campaigned for an independent Armenian state. Over time, we placed so many agents there that several had risen to positions of leadership. We succeeded in effectively neutralizing the group, and by the 1980s *Dashnak Tsutyun* had stopped fighting against Soviet power in Armenia. The organization and some of its members had been co-opted by the KGB. Years later, in 1992, when *Dashnak Tsutyun* leaders and other Armenian nationalists were attacking Armenian President Levon Ter-Petrosyan for not being sufficiently nationalist, I got a call from the president—with whom I had had several friendly conversations—at my Moscow apartment. He asked me for help in fending off the attacks by *Dashnak Tsutyun*, and I provided him and the Armenian press with information about the KGB's deep penetration of that émigré group in the 1970s.

We also recruited agents among the hundreds of thousands of Soviet Jews who fled to Israel and American in the 1960s, 1970s, and 1980s. When I worked in Leningrad in the 1980s, I knew of at least two hundred Jews from that city alone who worked with us before leaving the Soviet Union. Many promised to work for us abroad, but almost invariably forgot their pledges as soon as they crossed the Soviet border. A few did help us, keeping the KGB informed about the plans and activities of Jewish émigré and refusenik groups. Our ultimate goal was to place these Jewish émigrés, many of whom were scientists, into sensitive positions in Western government, science, or the military-industrial complex. But we enjoyed little success, and by the time I stepped down as head of Foreign Counter-Intelligence in 1980 I didn't know of a single case in which a Jewish émigré had become a valuable mole in the West for the KGB.

That didn't discourage us from trying to slow emigration to Israel in any way possible. One "active measure" we employed was to concoct letters, attributed to nonexistent émigrés, and then publish the correspondence in *Pravda* and other newspapers. I still have one of the published letters, supposedly from a man in Tel Aviv.

"Modern Israel is a country of peddlers, money changers, crooks, and demagogues," the fake letter said. "Culturally, it's like the remote provinces of Russia, if not worse. . . . Now I have everything, but I miss our parties, our noisy apartments. Who will I eat and drink with? My next door neighbor from Morocco? . . . Local Socialist Party activists are illiterate bureaucrats whose education ended in the fourth grade. They masturbate to the ideas of Marx and Herzel and try to build socialism."

We made out far better when it came to getting our agents inside one of the most damaging, anti-Soviet propaganda organizations—Radio Liberty. The radio station, funded and controlled by the CIA well into the 1970s, beamed a steady stream of pro-American and anti-Communist news back to the USSR in several different languages, driving Soviet leaders crazy. Our government jammed Radio Liberty broadcasts, though not with total success. My job was to attack Radio Liberty at the source—at its European headquarters in Munich—by placing agents on its staff. If we couldn't control what Radio Liberty was broadcasting, at least we could know what it was up to, learn something about the CIA, and perhaps soften the station's blows against us.

In my ten years in Foreign Counterintelligence, we had several good agents at Radio Liberty, whose staff included many émigrés from the USSR. But by far our best agent there was a man named Oleg Tumanov, who had a twisted history of involvement with the KGB that continued into the 1990s.

Tumanov's saga began when, as a young sailor with the Soviet merchant marine, he jumped overboard in the Baltic Sea and swam to Sweden. He settled there for a while, later traveling to Austria. But Tumanov apparently was just as unhappy in the West as he had been in the USSR, and he began writing letters to relatives back home expressing his dissatisfaction. We knew this because the KGB had an enormous department, employing thousands of people, whose job was to open most of the mail going in and out of the Soviet Union. The department read millions of letters annually, and among them one year was a disgruntled missive from Tumanov in which he told a relative, "Maybe I have made the greatest mistake of my life."

It was clear that the letter was from an émigré or a defector, and the officers responsible for interception of correspondence passed along the letter to us. We knew of Tumanov's case, and sent an officer to visit the relative to whom Tumanov had been writing. The KGB officer acted as if he knew nothing of the letters, but merely pretended to be making inquiries about the fate of this Soviet traitor. Our officer asked to see any letters the defector had written and, as it ws the early 1970s and Soviets were not in the habit of saying no to the KGB, the relative turned over several letters. Our man began reading the correspondence, commenting to the relative that "everyone makes mistakes."

In a return visit, we persuaded the relative to write Tumanov and tell him that the security services had paid a call and said it wasn't too late to make amends for what he had done. One of Tumanov's relatives, who actually was working for us, took the letter to Austria, located Tumanov, and asked him to read the correspondence.

"Listen, if you want to come back and start a new life, why don't you do something for your country," our agent told Tumanov. "Help our people and they will help you. It's not difficult."

Tumanov said he was interested in working for us and returning to the Soviet Union, and our agent introduced him to a KGB officer stationed in Vienna. Our officer told Tumanov that before he returned to the USSR, we wanted him to take a job at Radio Liberty. His credentials were good—he was, after all, a defector—and before long Tumanov was hired as a low-level analyst for Radio Liberty. He proved to be extremely capable, and rapidly rose to the head of Radio Liberty's Russian-language service—a promotion that gave us much satisfaction in Moscow, knowing that a KGB agent was now in charge of the most fiercely anti-Soviet, Russian-language radio program.

Tumanov remained head of the Russian service for several years.

In meetings with his KGB case officers in Germany, he kept us well informed about activities at Radio Liberty and the CIA's involvement with the station. He subtly helped us spread rumors and disinformation, and did what he could to create conflict among the staff members. Among other things, we wrote anonymous anti-Semitic letters which caused a rift among some station employees. He also told us which of his colleagues might be ripe for recruitment or which—because of their homosexuality, philandering, or thievery—might be susceptible to blackmail. Through Tumanov, we recruited two other Radio Liberty employees, including one man from the Baltic states. Polish Intelligence also had two Polish émigré agents on the staff of Radio Liberty. Though he had to be careful not to seem pro-Soviet, Tumanov did manage to avoid airing blatantly anti-Soviet material.

Perhaps Tumanov's most notorious act was the help he gave us in planting a bomb at Radio Liberty's Munich headquarters. The explosion was my idea, and my aim was not to hurt anyone but rather to stir up sentiment to move the rabble-rousing station out of Munich and Germany. We began planning the explosion in 1979, but didn't actually carry it out until two years later, when I was already in Leningrad. With Tumanov's help, an East German agent planted a small bomb which did minor damage, but made an awful racket and shattered windows in the neighborhood. Unfortunately, even though the KGB set off the explosion in the early hours, one person sustained an eye injury.

There is a postscript to the bombing story. In 1991, just three days before the August coup, I visited Radio Liberty in Munich to talk about the need to reform the KGB. While there, I told the Radio Liberty staff that it was I who had masterminded the idea of the bomb. I thought they would pounce on me, but most took the news calmly and said they were happy I was now on their side.

Tumanov eventually had to flee Munich and Radio Liberty when a high-ranking KGB official with knowledge of Tumanov's KGB ties defected to the West. Tumanov received a big welcome in Moscow, where the KGB portrayed him as a hero who had infiltrated and exposed that foul purveyor of anti-Communist propaganda, Radio Liberty. Our masters of deception claimed he was a KGB officer who had risked life and limb to work in the West. No mention was made of the fact that twenty years earlier he had defected from the USSR.

I was to run into Tumanov again, in almost comical circumstances. In 1990, after I publicly denounced the KGB, Tumanov—still a stooge for the security apparatus—attacked me. When I ran for the Soviet parliament, he published scathing articles about my career and even traveled to my legislative district in southern Russia to lambast me.

"I denounce this man!" Tumanov said at one meeting. "I know him. He betrayed everyone at Radio Liberty!"

I let everyone know just who, in fact, Tumanov was, for I found it unpalatable that the very man I had helped bring home to the USSR—a traitor and double defector—was now accusing me of treachery. Even today, Tumanov is a hard-liner, spouting nationalist, pro-Communist cant.

Our long arm overseas even extended into the inner confines of the Russian Orthodox Church. Indeed, the KGB's near-total control of the Russian Orthodox Church, both at home and abroad, is one of the most sordid and little known chapters in the history of our organization. I had only a passing knowledge of our church operations while I worked for Foreign Counterintelligence, though I later learned in depressing detail just how—through threats, bullying, and blackmail—the KGB had co-opted the church in the Soviet Union.

During my numerous trips to Eastern Europe, I met many of the somber, bearded, black-robed Russian Orthodox priests who worked with Soviet and Russian émigré communities there. The KGB's notorious Fifth Directorate, in charge of ideology and dissidents, had a stranglehold over the church inside the Soviet Union, and also had recruited scores of priests in Russian émigré communities throughout the world. The Russian Orthodox Church in America was split, but the faction that remained loyal to Moscow was riddled with KGB agents.

The KGB used Orthodox priests living abroad to keep an eye on émigré communities in various countries, as well as Soviets stationed overseas who might be churchgoers. In Foreign Counter-Intelligence, we found that Russian Orthodox priests occasionally would supply us with valuable information. A prime example was the priest at a church in West Germany who first alerted one of our case officers about a possible recruit from American Military Intelligence. The priest befriended the American, and eventually put him in touch with one of our officers, who recruited the man. The material the American officer provided us was described earlier in this chapter, but the priest's help in spotting a potential recruit is precisely the reason we in the KGB wanted agents inside the church. One Russian Orthodox priest in East Germany was actually a KGB colonel, who was so skilled in deception that he could perform church services and chant the haunting Orthodox prayers. Most of the priests, however, were not actual KGB officers, but informers who would do our bidding.

But, as I soon found out, the KGB's infiltration of the church had gotten way out of hand. Many of our officers were abusing their power. Numerous Russian Orthodox priests in Eastern Europe complained to me that KGB officers would come to them, drink up the church communion wine, steal church property, and demand bribes or payments. A sizable number of the priests were homosexual, and one of the main ways the KGB recruited priests was by catching them in homosexual acts or relationships and then blackmailing them into working for the security services. Many KGB agents, both at home and abroad, looked upon the priests with disdain and abused them whenever they got the chance. The priests, for their part, were disgusted that they had to dance to the tune of the boorish KGB officers.

"I can't go on like this," one priest told me in his church in East Berlin, referring to KGB officers boozing it up and extorting gifts from him. "It will put me in a ridiculous position if my parishioners ever learn about it. My reputation will be lost."

There was little I could do to help the priests stationed overseas, for they had been recruited and were under the control of two notorious officers from the KGB's Fifth Directorate—Romanov and Timoshevsky. These were despicable men, who ran the church for the KGB. For all practical purposes, they controlled it, deciding who would rise in the church hierarchy, who would become a bishop, and, ultimately, who would be anointed Patriarch. I met Timoshevsky—a protégé of future KGB Chairman Viktor Chebrikov—only once, and he struck me as an evil, gray-faced mediocrity. His and Romanov's specialty was digging up incriminating evidence on priests and then using it to exert control over them. They treated the priests and church leaders like marionnettes, and Timoshevsky was deeply hated by many in the Russian Orthodox Church, though none dared speak out against him.

One of Romanov and Timoshevsky's underlings was a Major Kostikov in Rostov-on-Don, whose abuse of priests and extortion of money became so egregious that even the KGB couldn't continue to ignore him. He was arrested for extorting 150,000 rubles in bribes from priests, and promised a lenient sentence if he confessed. He did, and was promptly executed. Several of my colleagues said that Kostikov implicated high-ranking officers of the Fifth Directorate in the extortion and bribery schemes, and that he was killed to cover up the affair.

Toward the end of my years in Foreign Counter-Intelligence I got to know Patriarch Pimen and his entourage, and over time several high-ranking officials divulged the shameful truth about Timoshevsky and Romanov's all-pervasive power.

I recall one bizarre and humorous incident involving the church that took place in the late 1970s. The British spy George Blake, who was quite religious, told me he wanted to attend the church's Easter service—a grand show that our Communist leaders cynically used to prove to the world that, yes, we Russians really did have religious freedom. As it turned out, I was able to take Blake behind the altar at Epiphany Church to see Patriarch Pimen before the services began. Suddenly, the procession began moving into the church, which was ablaze with the light of thousands of candles reflecting off golden icons. Blake managed to squeeze into the throng of worshippers, but after a half-dozen steps I found myself marching down the aisle at the head of the procession; I was unable to move into the crowd because the aisle was now fenced off. I didn't want to look like a fool rushing frantically to and fro, so I had no choice but to solemnly lead the procession. Patriarch Pimen walked a few paces behind me, and behind him came the synod, its members holding staffs and crosses. It seemed like the eyes of thousands of people were upon us. I moved slowly, staring at my feet so as not to meet the glance of any acquaintances in the crowd. What a scandal it would have been—a KGB general leading the Russian Orthodox Church's Easter services!

Fortunately, the worshippers were focused on Pimen, though some people, after seeing me in my black leather jacket, whispered, "Look, that's Pimen's bodyguard walking in front."

The procession finally came to a halt and the Patriarch intoned three times, "Christ Has Risen!" Just then my eyes met those of Boris Kolomyakov, the head of the KGB's Latin American Department. He didn't seem to be too surprised to see me next to Pimen and, just to be on the safe side, I tried to look as mysterious as possible, as if I were carrying out the orders of the KGB chairman himself.

That night, after the service, Patriarch Pimen invited us to the

Easter celebration in the attic of the Epiphany Cathedral, where dozens of church leaders, priests, guests, and KGB officers were sumptuously wined and dined.

My relationship with the Russian Orthodox Church didn't end after I left the KGB in 1990. In fact, it continues to this day.

When I ran for a seat in the Soviet parliament in 1990, I once again ran smack into the church and its KGB-controlled leadership. During campaigning in my district, in the southern Russian region of Krasnodar, the local bishop spoke publicly and denounced me as a traitor. I couldn't sit silently, particularly because I knew that the Krasnodar bishop, Isidor, had cooperated closely with the KGB for years and was one of the church's more despicable informers. During one of my speeches, I lit into Bishop Isidor.

"You in the church hierarchy are all KGB stooges and you have the insolence to brand me as a traitor?" I said. "I know, Bishop Isidor, that you are a longtime KGB agent and I know who your case officer is."

The attack made headlines, and I went on to tell local reporters of the involvement of Isidor and other Orthodox bishops with the KGB. During my successful campaign, and for months afterward, I received scores of letters from irate Krasnodar citizens providing detailed accounts of Isidor's misconduct, including allegations of shady business dealings, drinking parties, even orgies. In 1991, I decided the matter had to be brought to the attention of the new Patriarch of the Russian Orthodox Church, Aleksei II, and so I wrote him a letter about Bishop Isidor. For months I heard nothing. In the meantime, some top dissident priests and Russian journalists had gathered incontrovertible information that the Patriarch himself had been working with the KGB for more than twenty years, and that his code name within the agency was "Drozdov." Insiders had long known this was the case, since a priest didn't rise to the top of the church hierarchy without collaborating with the KGB.

Because Aleksei himself was seen as something of a reformer, the journalists and dissident church leaders had entered into a conspiracy of silence. They let the Patriarch know that they had proof of his KGB ties but would not publicize them if he continued to try to open up the church. But when, after nearly half a year, I had still heard nothing from Aleksei II concerning my complaint about Bishop Isidor, I started quietly telling a few church acquaintances that I might blow the whistle on the Patriarch.

"The Patriarch isn't acting properly," I told several members of the church hierarchy. "If he continues to hide all the scandals in the church, I will have something to say about him, too."

Within a matter of days, I received a call from one of the Patriarch's aides, saying he would like to see me. Soon, I found myself sitting with the august church leader, a man in his sixties with long gray hair and beard and cool blue eyes.

"My son," Aleksei II said, "what did you write about the Bishop of Krasnodar?"

"You have my letter," I replied. "I have nothing to add to it. I think it's a scandal that people like him are not removed. You can't remove them all, I understand, but if it becomes a public scandal, it will be bad for the church. It's in your interest to do something. You're in charge and I'm not trying to pressure you. I'm just telling you my opinion."

"But some people defend him," said the Patriarch.

"I know who these people are—old Communists," I said. "You have to understand that this scandal affects the church. Something must be done to clear the church of this filth."

"I agree with that," Aleksei replied.

We discussed the political scene for a while, and then the Patriarch—a man well schooled in the arts of deceit and diplomacy—subtly got to the point of our meeting. Though he never once asked me not to publicly expose his history of involvement with the KGB, the gist of his remarks was clear.

"You know, many clergymen had to cooperate with the KGB," Aleksei said in a cool and composed fashion. "Would you deny that we were right to defend Soviet foreign policy, which was aimed at world peace? Were our clergymen wrong to support the removal of American missiles from Europe? Were our clergymen wrong to go overseas and try to enlighten our Western colleagues about Soviet foreign policy? It was peaceful foreign policy, wasn't it? So I expect you not to make any public statements about the people who did that."

"I have no intention of doing so," I responded. "I just told you about one man who was asking for it. He put himself in such a position that I had to hit him back."

We parted on friendly enough terms, and a few months later the Patriarch invited my wife and me to the church's Christmas dinner at the Patriarch's Moscow headquarters. Eventually, however, the details of Aleksei II's links to the KGB leaked out in a few small magazines, though it hardly created a scandal among a public that all along had assumed the church was under the control of the secret police. Bishop Isidor was not replaced. But there was one bright spot in efforts to reform the church: At my urging, Vadim Bakatin, who briefly headed the KGB after the failed coup of August 1991, disbanded the section charged with overseeing the church and fired the hated colonels Romanov and Timoshevsky.

One of our most important, difficult, and exasperating jobs in Foreign Counterintelligence was our search, both inside and outside the KGB, for Western moles and potential defectors. In our struggle with the CIA, nothing did as much damage to our operations and to Soviet security as the diplomats and Intelligence officers who went over to the other side. But preventing it was virtually impossible, particularly as the absurdity and backwardness of our system became more apparent to everyone in the late 1970s and 1980s. In the decade I spent in Foreign Counterintelligence in the 1970s, two KGB officers defected. During the 1980s, literally dozens of others jumped ship, as did numerous diplomats and other Soviet officials. By the time the Soviet Union collapsed in 1991, the KGB's foreign operations had been collapsing for years as a result of ceaseless defections and the ensuing exposure of Soviet agents working abroad. It was like rats leaving a sinking ship. The KGB's decades-long struggle with the CIA had turned into a rout.

I had dozens of officers whose job it was to ferret out and identify the spies and potential defectors in our midst, but the truth is that only rarely did our efforts produce results. The KGB usually only found out about moles within its ranks when a Western defector, such as Edward Lee Howard, fled to our side with information about Soviet traitors. In Howard's case, his information led to the arrest and execution of several KGB officers who had been spying for the United States. One of those KGB officers was our man in West Germany in charge of cultivating "illegals"—Soviets who spoke German and who were to be infiltrated into the West German government, army, or Intelligence agencies. The turncoat KGB officer was forcibly abducted from West Germany, returned to the USSR, tried, and put to death.

We were flooded with information about possible moles in our midst. Indeed, the Soviet people had been so deeply inculcated with informing on one another that the sheer volume of material we received about suspected foreign agents was overwhelming. In my time, we checked hundreds of suspected spies—bugging their apartments, tailing them, opening their mail. But only in rare cases, such as with the diplomat Ogorodnik, did we turn up anything. Along the way, we would collect untold amounts of useless information, some of which wound up hurting several good officers. Such was the case with an excellent KGB colonel, Alexander Khylstov. He happened to be dining one night at a restaurant that had been thoroughly bugged because of suspicions that a Soviet official who dined there might be a spy. Khylstov was eating with several friends and during dinner he made a disparaging remark about Brezhnev—the kind of remark that all of us were making in private by the late 1970s. But KGB microphones picked up his comment, and several weeks later our personnel department summoned Khylstov and fired him on the spot, ending his twenty-year career.

A typical case in which we correctly suspected someone of misconduct but were unable to prove it involved an officer named Vladimir Vetrov, who worked in the KGB's science and technology section. Vetrov served in Montreal, and while he was there we received a tip from our source in the Royal Canadian Mounted Police that Vetrov was involved in some illicit business deals with Canadian businessmen. In fact, our RCMP source told us that one of the businessmen was an informer for Canadian Intelligence who was trying to recruit Vetrov by involving him in lucrative business deals.

Under a suitable pretext, we recalled Vetrov to Moscow, where he continued to work in the science and technology section. We investigated him, bugged him, and followed him in Moscow, but found no evidence of wrongdoing. As it turns out, however, shortly after our investigation stopped, Vetrov made contact with the French military attaché in Moscow and sold him intelligence secrets connected with Soviet scientific projects. On several occasions, Vetrov met with the French military attaché in one of Moscow's busiest and most prestigious neighborhoods, just down the street from Leonid Brezhnev's apartment.

Vetrov might never have been caught were it not for a foolish blunder on his part. He had begun an affair with one of his secretaries, and apparently told her of his involvement with French Intelligence. They had a quarrel, and—fearful that she might inform on him—he tried to kill his lover by pushing her out of his car. She survived, but Vetrov killed a passer-by in the process. I was already in Leningrad by that time, but apparently the woman never reported on him, and Vetrov went to jail for killing the man and attempting to kill the woman. While Vetrov was serving his sentence in Siberia, the KGB discovered he had been spying for the French. The KGB version was that he finally decided to confess in jail, but it is equally likely that our sources in French Intelligence identified Vetrov to us. In any case, he was tried and shot—no thanks, however, to our efforts in Foreign Counterintelligence.

The treachery of our own people sometimes caught us utterly by surprise, as was the case with the 1979 defection of one of our top officers in Toyko, Stanislav Levchenko. Just months before his defection, I had visited our Tokyo station and been introduced to the young officer. The station chief, Oleg Guryanov, had raved about Levchenko.

"Listen, you must talk to this man," Guryanov told me. "He is great. He has terrific sources and assets in political circles, among Socialists and other left-wingers and newspapermen. He also has access to some Japanese Counterintelligence people in the national police."

I met Levchenko and was suitably impressed by both his character and the quality of his work. Then, a few months later, he defected to the United States, taking with him detailed information about our operations in Japan and the Far East. I was stunned and angry, for it was precisely this kind of defection that my directorate was supposed to prevent. But how could we have known? We had thousands of people to keep an eye on, and Levchenko gave us no reason to suspect him. He may have made a few politically cynical comments, but it was 1979 and we were all increasingly critical of Brezhnev and the system. He wasn't living beyond his means, he wasn't an alcoholic, and he wasn't a womanizer—all signals that usually send up red flags. His treachery came utterly out of the blue.

In 1992, I had the opportunity to meet Levchenko in Washington. He had a new wife and was working for a Russian émigré newspaper. Hearing I was in town, Levchenko phoned me and asked to meet in a bar. We had downed a few drinks when he asked me, "Listen, what do you think of me?"

"I liked you when I met you in Tokyo, but you're scum," I replied. "You're a traitor. Why did you do that, betray your own country? Forget it, I don't really want to know."

"Oleg, you don't understand," he replied, a wounded look in his eyes. "Life is a complex thing . . ."

But I politely cut him off. We continued talking for an hour or so, parting on cordial terms. As much as I may have agreed with his criticism of the system, I would never turn against my country as he did.

The most galling defection was the infamous case of Vitaly Yurchenko. Not long before I stepped down as head of Foreign Counter-Intelligence, I was summoned by Vice Admiral Mikahil Usatov, the first deptuy chief of Intelligence. Usatov knew Yurchenko personally and wanted me to bring him into my directorate. As almost always was the case, I lived to rue the day that I caved in to KGB cronyism and allowed an unqualified—and unsuitable—person into our unit.

"Oleg, I know Yurchenko—he was in Navy Counterintelligence in the Black Sea Fleet," Usatov said. "Take him in. I'm sure he will do a good job."

I had little use for most military Counterintelligence people— whom we disparagingly referred to as "boots"—because they usually behaved with the inflexibility of soldiers and not with the cunning required of Foreign Intelligence officers. I told Usatov that I thought Yurchenko was a mistake, saying, "You're giving me another provincial."

"No," Usatov assured me. "He speaks English. He served in Egypt. He's a good chap."

I agreed to meet with him, and disliked him on sight. He had empty, evasive, pale blue eyes. He spoke poor Russian and was cocky. I phoned Usatov and told him I didn't want Yurchenko, but the vice admiral insisted.

"You won't regret it," Usatov said.

How wrong he would turn out to be.

I took Yurchenko on as as security officer trainee, and we began trying to whip him into shape. Soon, there was an opening in Washington, and Usatov was once again pushing his protégé.

"Why don't you send him to Washington?" Usatov said. "Give him a chance."

I objected again, but it was all in vain. Yurchenko went to Washington under the cover of a first secretary at the Soviet Embassy, where he was an unmitigated disaster. He committed several minor transgressions, such as having an affair with the wife of one of our diplomats. But that was nothing compared to his greatest blunder in Washington.

A retired CIA officer, Edwin Gibbon Moore, Jr., clandestinely contacted our Washington station chief, Dmitri Yakushkin, at his apartment in Washington in 1976. The former CIA officer left a note in Yakushkin's mailbox saying that he had a substantial amount of top-secret CIA documents which he wanted to sell to Yakushkin. The CIA man instructed Yakushkin to leave a mark on a notice board in the apartment building to show he was interested. Our station chief, however, was jittery, for two of our officers had just been arrested in New York for receiving secrets from an American spy about the United States' B-1 bomber program. So Yakushkin cabled KGB Center in Moscow seeking permission to pursue the "volunteer's" approach. Andropov, however, fearful of an FBI set-up, denied Yakushkin permission

The American left another note in Yakushkin's mailbox, saying he had extremely interesting material and wondering why the KGB station chief had remained silent. But Yakushkin obeyed Andropov's orders and did not contact the American.

Out of desperation, Moore took his sack of material and threw it over the wall of the Soviet Embassy in Washington. He left instructions on how to contact him in the future, evidently certain that once the KGB saw the material he had flung into the embassy compound, the Soviets would immediately contact him. But unfortunately for Moore, the man who was handed the bag was Vitali Yurchenko. And rather than opening the sack and discovering a trove of Intelligence documents, Yurchenko called the Washington police: He was afraid the bag contained a bomb! So he summoned U.S. authorities and turned it over to them, simultaneously losing dozens of top-secret documents and exposing an American "well-wisher." The hapless CIA man was arrested, tried, and sentenced to fifteen years in jail, all because of Yurchenko's indescribably stupid error. The incident did us enormous damage, for all the world knew from the trial that a CIA volunteer had come to us with excellent material, only to be rejected and essentially handed over to the FBI.

That, however, turned out to be moderate damage compared with what came later from the bumbling security officer.

Yurchenko stayed in Washington until 1983, when he was transferred back to Moscow and—because of high connections like Usatov—was made deputy chief of security for Foreign Intelligence, a highly sensitive post in Directorate K. Not only did he learn about our efforts to ferret out defectors and spies, but he also became familiar with some of the more scandalous cases our directorate had been involved in, including the kidnapping of Artamonov from Vienna and our participation in the murder of Georgi Markov. Later, he was transferred to the Intelligence directorate, where he held the post of deputy chief of the department that directed operations against the United States and Canada. Yurchenko learned of the existence of some of our top spies in the United States, including Edward Lee Howard and Ronald Pelton, a National Security Agency employee who for six years fed us detailed information about that top-secret organization. So, despite the fact that I and numerous other officers viewed Yurchenko as a sloppy, unreliable officer, he had risen to a high position in the KGB and knew details of secret agents and operatons.

Then, while on a trip to Italy in 1985, Yurchenko defected to the United States. It was an enormous blow to us as the disgruntled KGB man exposed Pelton, who was arrested, and Howard, who had to flee the country. He also told the CIA about the Markov assassination, the Artamonov abduction, and many other operations. The damage was considerable.

After several months in America, however, Yurchenko grew increasingly unhappy with his treatment at the hands of the CIA. Though U.S. officials had promised to keep his defection a secret, word leaked out about the CIA's great catch, causing Yurchenko anxiety about the fate of his family in the USSR. He also was kept in near-total isolation and treated more like a prisoner than a prize intelligence asset. So Yurchenko began making plans to re-defect, an act for which there was some precedent. Oleg Bitov, a correspondent for *Literaturnaya Gazeta,* defected in 1981 and then re-defected when he, too, grew unhappy with his new life in America. Upon his return to the USSR, Bitov was not punished and was paraded before a press conference to denounce the CIA and life in America.

Yurchenko managed to slip away from his American handlers and made his way to the Soviet Embassy in Washington. Instead of being tried and executed upon his return to the Soviet Union, he was treated like a hero by KGB Director Kryuchkov. The KGB maintained that Yurchenko had been abducted and then had valiantly escaped to freedom. The greatest insult came a few months after Yurchenko re-defected when Kryuchkov gave him an award, pinning the medal on his breast in a ceremony in front of his former Intelligence and Foreign Counterintelligence colleagues.

"Mr. Yurchenko," said Kryuchkov, "your bravery, your courage, and your determination earned you this decoration."

I was in Leningrad at the time, but my former colleagues in

Moscow said they were disgusted by such a farce. Yurchenko is retired from the KGB and still lives in Moscow today.

During my years in Foreign Counterintelligence, we also experienced the defection of several non-KGB officers. Two cases were particularly intriguing. The first involved a Military Intelligence man who eventually returned to the USSR; the second was the much-publicized defection of United Nations diplomat Arkady Shevchenko.

I was swept up into the case of the Military Intelligence (GRU) officer when an urgent ciphered cable arrived one night from our embassy in Washington. Our security officer there explained that a former GRU officer named Chebotaryov had shown up at the embassy, explaining that he had defected to America less than a year before and now wanted to return home. Chebotaryov's case had never been publicized in either the United States or the Soviet Union, but his mysterious disappearance several months before had created a stir at KGB headquarters. He had been stationed in Brussels, where he was involved in intercepting NATO communications. He was not a high-ranking officer, but he knew enought about GRU and KGB operations to do some damage. We were virtually certain that he had gone over to the other side.

Now, with the message from Washington, our fears had been confirmed. I cabled our security officer in Washington and ordered him to detain Chebotaryov, interrogate him, and ensure the defector's safe passage back to the Soviet Union.

The next morning began with a barrage of phone calls to my office as the KGB and GRU—longstanding rivals—jockeyed over who would detain and interrogate the turncoat. Throughout Soviet history, intelligence gathering and espionage activities had been handled by these two powerful agencies, with the GRU concentrating on military and scientific intelligence. But the inescapable fact was that we were the dominant agency; the KGB even had a Military Counterintelligence unit that operated clandestinely inside the GRU, recruiting officers and soldiers to work for us. During my time, one of the Soviet Union's top admirals—a commander of one of our four fleets—worked for the KGB. So our colleagues in the GRU often resented our dominance and our penetration of their agency. In the eyes of Military Intelligence officers, the stereotypical KGB man was sly, dishonest, and a potential traitor. For our part, we looked down on GRU men, viewing them as crude, provincial, and unprofessional.

This friction was the backdrop of the maneuvering over the fate of Chebotaryov. My phone rang off the hook that morning. The GRU wanted to get their hands on Chebotaryov first, perhaps to establish that he had been the victim of an abduction. He had disgraced the GRU, and it was possible the military wanted to hush the matter up and concoct a story—just as we had done with Yurchenko. Ultimately, however, the KGB appeared to prevail: Andropov ordered that my directorate detain Chebotaryov when he arrived in Moscow and interrogate him at the KGB safe house in the country.

There was little trouble getting the GRU officer out of Washington, as he told immigration and State Department officials he was returning to the Soviet Union of his own free will. Meanwhile, I arrived with an aide at Sheremetyevo Airport to meet Chebotaryov's flight. But when I showed up, I was greeted by a group of senior GRU officers, including a lieutenant general.

"Chebotaryov is coming with us," the lieutenant general told me peremptorily. "Orders from [GRU chief] General Ivashutin."

"No, he's coming with me," I replied. "Andropov's order."

The GRU officers eyed us mockingly, seeing they had us vastly outnumbered. I excused myself and walked away. But once again I would rely on KGB cunning to outfox the flat-footed "boots" from Military Intelligence. Aeroflot was under our control, and before leaving for the airport I had telephoned one of our officers who worked at Sheremetyevo. He had arranged for me to drive right up to the plane and meet Chebotaryov, who was accompanied by our security officer from Washington. We intercepted them as they disembarked, and whisked Chebotaryov away. The GRU officers watched, crestfallen, as we drove up to them. Not wishing to poison relations with people who theoretically were my colleagues, I got out to speak with them. The lieutenant general, now addressing me in a conciliatory manner, asked if we might first visit GRU General Ivashutin. I refused.

"Come on," the lieutenant general implored. "Do we have to quarrel over some scumbag?"

I agreed to call Army General Tsinev, Andropov's first deputy. I suggested that, for the sake of improved relations with the GRU, we first take Chebotaryov to see Ivashutin for half an hour.

"All right," Tsinev agreed. "But don't let him out of your sight for a second."

We drove in convoy to GRU headquarters on Khoroshevskoye Chaussée. I had never set foot in the place before, and was surprised—particularly in comparison with the relative splendor of Lubyanka and Yasenovo by the shabby condition of the building. It looked more like a barracks than an Intelligence headquarters. We walked down dark, comfortless corridors, passing beat-up wooden doors, as we made our way to Ivashutin's office. When we arrived in his antechamber, one of Ivashutin's aides announced our presence. I started to go in but an aide stepped in front of me and said haughtily, "You're not allowed inside."

"What do you mean, 'not allowed'?" I said, brushing him aside and grabbing the door handle. "I have orders from deputy KGB Chairman Tsinev and you have no right to prevent me from entering."

Ivashutin evidently heard the dispute and flashed me a hateful look as I entered his office. "I don't care what you think of it, but I won't let Chebotaryov out of my sight even for a second," I announced.

The tall, husky, square-jawed Ivashutin had once worked for the KGB as deputy chairman and undoubtedly knew that Tsinev—a Brezhnev protégé—had a violent temper. So the GRU chief, realizing I had the upper hand and not daring to cross Tsinev, let me stay.

General Ivashutin clearly was hoping that Chebotaryov would confirm he had been abducted and coerced into working for the CIA. But things would not turn out that way. As the GRU chief listened in disgust, Chebotaryov recounted how he had left the Soviet Trade Mission in Brussels to meet an agent and had been stopped for a traffic violation. He was taken to the nearest police station because he didn't have his driver's license, and there—under questioning from men who obviously worked for Belgian Counterintelligence—Chebotaryov began to talk about his work for the GRU.

"Were you tortured or beaten?" Ivashutin asked.

"No," replied the cowering Chebotaryov.

"Why did you confess?" Ivashutin asked him.

The miserable GRU officer said he had been given a glass of water and that perhaps it had been laced with sodium pentothal. In any case, he said he felt as if he had lost his will, and couldn't help but talk about his GRU activities in Belgium. After meeting with the Belgian police, he then asked for and received asylum at the American Embassy. In Brussels and later in Washington, the CIA debriefed him extensively. He provided them with information about GRU operations against NATO, as well as some material about the KGB.

Ivashutin grew gloomier by the minute. Finally he yelled at the hapless officer, "You're just a coward—nothing more!"

"Yes," replied Chebotaryov. "What can I say?"

"Well, what are we to do with this man?" Ivashutin said to me in a friendly manner. "He's all yours."

The GRU chief's attitude had changed completely, and as I was leaving he thanked me for the KGB's cooperation. I told him I would supply him with the details of our debriefing and then turn Chebotaryov over to a military court.

The next day, we took Chebotaryov to a well-appointed country house outside Moscow, where he was treated warmly and fed well. We didn't want to scare this obviously weak man, and figured he would be far more forthcoming if he wasn't treated like a prisoner. I interrogated him the first day, then turned him over to our investigators for a week's questioning. Not only did we want to know what he had told the CIA about Soviet Intelligence operations, but it was helpful to us to determine exactly what our opponents were interested in learning from him. That way, we might be able to get a sense of what the CIA knew and didn't know about our activities.

The interrogation went well, and afterwards I recommended to my superiors that Chebotaryov be shown leniency. The damage he had done was moderate, and I argued that pardoning Chebotaryov would send a signal to other defectors that they could return to the fold without fear of dire consequences—provided they confessed and had not done us irreparable harm. Yurchenko had not yet defected, and it seemed to me that Chebotaryov's was a case that would best be handled with mercy, not stern punishment.

A military tribunal convicted Chebotaryov of espionage. He served several months in jail and then, upon our recommendation, the Presidium of the Supreme Soviet pardoned him. The KGB quietly spread the word that Chebotaryov had been shown leniency, and helped him land a job as a French teacher in the provincial city of Ryazin, a few hours south of Moscow. If he's still alive today, he no doubt recalls those days in Brussels, Washington, and Moscow as an absolute nightmare.

*   *   *

Perhaps the most infamous defection with which I had to deal was
that of Arkady Shevchenko, who became one of the highest-ranking
Soviet diplomats ever to go over to the American side. The loss of
Shevchenko was a case where we in the KGB had grown suspicious
and were doing our job, but were ultimately thwarted because Shevchenko was so well connected that few people took our concerns
seriously.

Shevchenko was the Soviet Union's deputy ambassador to the
United Nations and a rising star in the Foreign Ministry. He served
as an assistant to Foreign Minister Andrei Gromyko, primarily writing speeches for the wily cold warrior who had guided Soviet foreign
policy for decades. Shevchenko was articulate, charming, and bright,
and there was every expectation that he would one day rise to the
position of Soviet Ambassador to the United Nations or the United
States.

I had met Shevchenko in the mid-1970s, about a year before he
was posted to the United Nations. The reason for our chat was that
an anonymous letter-writer had accused him of taking a bribe in
exchange for helping a woman emigrate to the United States. Shevchenko and I sat in my office and, over brandy and coffee, had a
friendly talk in which I mentioned the letter. He strongly denied
the accusations, and there was no evidence to back them up. I
promised I would try to figure out who had written the slanderous
letter, though I never did. I was impressed with Shevchenko, and
figured that with his personality, brains, and distinguished looks he
would go far.

In 1978, I received an alarming letter from the KGB station chief
in New York, Yuri Drozdov, in which he said he had reason to
believe that Shevchenko had been recruited by the CIA. He said
that Shevchenko was drinking heavily and behaving strangely: he
was taking unexplained trips to places like Florida, was avoiding his
fellow diplomats, and was not showing up in the office. I found it
hard to believe that a diplomat of such promise and high standing
could turn out to be a spy. And it was clear from Drozdov's letter
that the KGB station chief was extremely hostile toward Shevchenko.
Nevertheless, Drozdov's assessment could not be ignored. I forwarded the report to Kryuchkov, who appears to have shelved it.

About a month later, Drozdov sent me another cable about Shevchenko. The station chief's tone had changed from alarm to panic.

"I have told you on many occasions that I have reason to suspect Shevchenko of being an unreliable, untrustworthy man, and now he's drinking so hard he doesn't even show up at the office," Drozdov wrote. "We must do something, otherwise the case will explode into a major scandal."

I immediately forwarded this cable to Kryuchkov, Gromyko, and the Central Committee of the Communist Party. Drozdov's warnings could no longer be ignored—it was clear something had to be done. The Foreign Ministry at last swung into action, but unfortunately they acted so clumsily that they succeeded only in scaring away Shevchenko.

Gromyko reluctantly ordered his personal department to summon Shevchenko to Moscow for consultations. The Foreign Ministry cable was so blunt and unexpected, however, that it immediately put the diplomat (who already was working for the CIA) on alert. Had we composed the cable, we would have dreamed up some credible pretext to lure Shevchenko back without arousing his suspicions. We had experience in doing that, and might have cabled, for example, that a close relative was gravely ill. Then, we could have cut off the relative's phone or removed him from his apartment for several days, making it impossible for Shevchenko to check the story. But the Foreign Ministry cable, which merely said he must return "for consultations," set off alarm bells in Shevchenko's mind. Shortly after receiving it, Shevchenko talked with a visiting Soviet diplomat, who told him he was being recalled because something strange was going on behind the scenes. That was enough for Shevchenko. He decided to defect.

I was awakened around 1:00 A.M. by a call from the Foreign Counterintelligence duty officer. He said we had just received a cable with extraordinarily bad news: Shevchenko had gone over to the Americans.

I called my driver and went immediately to my office at Yasenovo. At least once a month I was summoned to the office late at night because of a defection or discovery of a mole or some other calamity, like the sinking of a Soviet merchant marine ship. In the case of Shevchenko, I wanted to get to my office immediately so I could instruct the New York station what to do and then prepare a list of actions—or reactions—for Kryuchkov and Andropov. This was no ordinary defection. In fact, as far as I know, Shevchenko was the highest-ranking Soviet diplomat to defect during the Cold War era. The cable from the New York station confirmed that he had gone over to the CIA. I called the Soviet deputy foreign minister at home over a secure line and told him what had happened.

"You've got to be kidding," he said.

He then asked me to read the cable, and listened to its contents in stunned silence.

Shevchenko's defection was a bombshell. It wasn't just that he had been passing the CIA diplomatic materials from the highest levels. (The year before, I had heard that the CIA had gotten its hands on our Washington ambassador's annual report. Now it seemed clear how the Americans had obtained it.) Shevchenko's defection, and ensuing denunciation of Soviet foreign policy, was a serious moral blow, for he had worked at such a high level.

The recriminations between the KGB and the Foreign Ministry began almost immediately. I felt that our New York station chief had done his duty and that we gave top officials in Moscow more than ample warning that Shevchenko was a potential problem. I also told Andropov that the reason Shevchenko wasn't recalled sooner was that he was a protégé of Gromyko. But when Andropov spoke to Gromyko, the Foreign Minister told the KGB chief that he had worked with so many assistants at the Foreign Ministry he could scarcely remember Arkady Shevcheno. Andropov returned from his talk with Gromyko and began chiding us for spreading unsubstantiated rumors about Shevchenko's close ties with the Foreign Minister.

Soon, however, we were proven right. KGB officers searched Shevchenko's Moscow apartment and, in addition to finding dozens of sheepskin coats that Shevchenko's wife was selling through her mother's shop, we found some interesting photographs. They showed Shevchenko and his wife eating shashlik (shishkabob) with Gromyko at the Foreign Minister's *dacha.*

After being shown the pictures, all Andropov could do was shake his head and say, "Oh, Andrei Andreyevich [Gromyko]."

Not long after Shevchenko's defection, I gave a lecture at the KGB's Higher School. In the course of my talk, a KGB officer asked me, "Comrade Kalugin, how would you explain this top diplomat's defection to the West? What did your department do to prevent him from fleeing?"

"We did our best," I replied. "But the man was a personal assistant to the Foreign Minister, and you probably realize how hard it is to deal sometimes with people who have close ties to top government officials."

I later heard that my comments had been repeated to Gromyko, and had made him extremely angry. Roughly a year later, when I was removed as head of Foreign Counter-Intelligence, some fellow officers speculated that I had been sacked because of my intemperate remark about Gromyko. But they were wrong. I was sacked because, in coming to the defense of Cook, the spy I had recruited years ago in New York, I took on the top brass of the KGB and lost.

During my years in Foreign Counterintelligence, I was constantly running up against the nepotism, cronyism, and corruption that increasingly was plaguing our Communist system. By 1980, only the most dottering Party bosses still believed the rubbish about the Soviet Union building a true, egalitarian system. Our Communism had degenerated over decades into a farce, a system in which the Party elite divided up the spoils and the plum jobs while the masses were left with cheap vodka, fatty sausage, and the chance to go once a year to a third-rate resort on the Black Sea. As Foreign Counter-intelligence chief, I was frequently forced to hire inferior officers because they were relatives or friends of Party big shots. And because the conduct of Soviets living abroad was my responsibility, I encountered numerous instances of blatant corruption and miscon-duct on the part of well-connected diplomats and ambassadors. Year by year, it became more depressing to see the spread of nepotism and officially sanctioned graft and thievery. The last years of the Soviet Union validated the old saying: A fish rots from its head.

Cronyism abounded. Everywhere top Soviet officials were hiring relatives and friends and then engaging in a giant game of scratching each other's backs and covering each other's tracks. Tsinev, the first deputy KGB chairman who was good friends with Brezhnev, not only forced upon us the defector Yurchenko. He also fobbed off on me a young man named Yartsev, the son of an old friend. The younger Yartsev was an undistinguished KGB officer who showed little promise, yet Tsinev wanted me to send him to England—a posting where we had few openings following the expulsion of 105 Soviet officials and the ensuing restrictions on the number of Soviet diplomats in the country. I told Tsinev that we had an opening in Foreign Counterintelligence in Denmark and that, if absolutely nec-essary, we could place Yartsev there. But Tsinev insisted on England, saying his "adopted son" had always dreamed of going there and he wanted to help the young man's dream come true. I had no choice. Finally, I managed to find a spot for the ne'er-do-well Yartsev as the Soviet Film Export representative in London. His salary would be paid by that organization and he would do legitimate work for them, all the while reporting to us. I thought I had made the best of a bad situation.

Yartsev, as feared, was a disaster. After the young man had been on the job less than a year, our London station chief received word from a confidential informant that British Intelligence was very interested in recruiting Yartsev. We placed him under surveillance, and it turned out that he was having an affair with an English woman suspected of being an agent for the British. Once the affair was discovered, the station chief—without letting on that he knew about the woman—suggested to Yartsev that he stay in the Soviet diplomatic compound during the evening hours, since the British were known to be tailing all Soviet officials. Yartsev promised to do so, then promptly went out and spent the night with his girlfriend. The next morning he said he hadn't gone anywhere, but a check of his car mileage showed that he'd been cruising around London.

Further investigation showed that Yartsev embezzled Soviet Film Export money and falsified expense reports. We also knew that he was stealing hardware and antiques from the London mansion in which the organization's offices were located. We recalled him to Moscow, opened up his luggage when he landed (making it look as if a customs officer had made a mistake and searched a diplomat's bag), and found enough old knickknacks to fill an antique shop. Under questioning, Yartsev admitted he had done everything from sleeping with the British woman to stealing door handles. Even Tsinev couldn't help Yartsev. He was fired from the KGB and expelled from the Communist Party.

In another instance of cronyism, the son-in-law of Ukrainian KGB Chief Vitaly Fedorchuk smashed up his car while driving drunk in Uganda. The son-in-law was a TASS correspondent there and occasionally did work for us, though he was not one of our officers. The young reporter tried to persuade TASS to pay the $1,700 car repair bill, but TASS refused. So what did Fedorchuk do for his daughter's husband? The Ukrainian KGB chairman sent a memo to Andropov saying that the TASS journalist (who he implied was a KGB officer) couldn't afford to get his car repaired and might become a target for recruitment by Western special services because he was in financial trouble. Andropov agreed to pick up the bill.

"We wanted to fire this good-for-nothing drunk." Sergei Losev, a good friend who was director of TASS, said to me. "Your office did TASS a disservice by paying his debt."

A short while later, Fedorchuk and the KGB would force Losev to give the worthless young correspondent another foreign assignment.

Corruption at high levels often amounted to a lot more than the paltry sum of a $1,700 car repair. Once, on a trip to check our operations in Italy, I was pulled aside by the Soviet ambassador, Nikita Ryzhov. He informed me that the KGB had done nothing about a report he filed on massive corruption involving a Ministry of Foreign Trade official named Sushkov. The ambassador told me that Sushkov was purchasing vast quantities of clothes and consumer goods and apparently shipping them back to high-ranking officials in the Soviet Union.

"I have told your people several times that every time Sushkov comes to Italy he returned with a railroad car full of stuff," the ambassador told me. "He can't possibly have that much money. He has to be stealing it from somewhere. Where's it all coming from? I told your colleagues several times, but nothing has been done."

I promised to look into it and wrote Andropov a report when I returned to Moscow. There was no reaction. Several years later, in 1983 or 1984, Sushkov's thievery apparently got so out of hand that it could no longer be ignored. He was arrested on corruption charges and thrown in jail.

Even more scandalous was a report we received from our station chief in Italy. He said that several sources had told him of a large-scale art fraud at the Soviet ambassador's residence in Rome, the Villa Garibaldi. Top embassy officials were reportedly involved in a scam in which they would send paintings by old Italian masters—paintings owned by the Soviet government—to Moscow for alleged restoration. Instead of refurbishing the paintings, Soviet artists would copy them and ship the fakes back to Rome to hang in the ambassador's residence and the embassy. The originals were then either given or sold to members of the Politburo and other top Soviet officials. We reported the scam to Kryuchkov, but heard nothing further about it.

We frequently had problems with our ambassadors, most of whom were well connected politically at home. In my ten years in Foreign Counterintelligence, we took steps that led to eight ambassadors being recalled—sometimes for corruption, but often for sexual misconduct. In dealing with the ambassadors and all well-connected officials, we had to tread very lightly. Often, we didn't open an official investigation or leave a paper trail. Instead, we would work behind the scenes with the Foreign Ministry or the Communist Party Central Committee (which approved all ambassadorial posts) to remove the envoys quietly.

In one case, a Soviet dancer on tour in Australia complained to us that the Soviet Ambassador to Australia had visited her in her hotel room and then sexually assaulted her. An investigation supported her claim, and when the woman threatened to make a scandal, the KGB reported the alleged assault to the Central Committee. The ambassador was recalled.

The Soviet Union's Ambassador to East Germany, Pyotr Abrasimov, was involved in shady dealings, as were his daughter and son-in-law. But the ambassador, a longtime friend of Leonid Brezhnev's, was never punished despite being at the center of an investigation that led to the arrests of both East Germans and Russians. Abrasimov, working with a West German businessman, smuggled clothes and consumer goods from East Germany into Russia. Abrasimov once asked a KGB officer who worked undercover at the East Germany Embassy to pick up 150 men's shirts from the businessman and ship them to Moscow, where they were to be delivered to members of the Central Committee and other top officials. Where Abrasimov got the money to buy all these consumer goods and what he did with them never became clear. His involvement in the smuggling was hushed up.

Abrasimov's daughter was married to a Soviet diplomat named Ragulin, who served as counselor at the Soviet Embassy in Warsaw. We received credible reports from Polish Intelligence that Ragulin and his wife were involved in orgies and spouse-swapping in Warsaw, which left them wide open to blackmail. The daughter also was involved in smuggling goods in and out of Poland, according to Polish Intelligence. Later, the Poles reported that Ragulin was meeting frequently with British and American diplomats—more than customarily would be called for his job. Fearing that he had been blackmailed and might be working for Western intelligence, we wrote a report to the Central Committee, laying out the sordid details of the lives of Abrasimov's daughter and son-in-law. The Central Committee had to act and urged the Foreign Ministry to recall Ragulin, which it did. The material we had gathered on the couple was so serious that even Brezhnev could do nothing. Ragulin was sacked. His wife was brought back to the USSR as well, where a search of her luggage showed that it was crammed with contraband from Poland. Abrasimov raised hell and wrote a letter to Brezhnev, saying her "human rights" had been violated. She was briefly allowed to return to Poland, but came back to the USSR shortly thereafter and divorced her disgraced husband. Abrasimov went on to run the Soviet tourist agency, Intourist, where he had access to huge sums of hard currency.

Once, the Soviet ambassador to a small African country was having an affair with his secretary that was creating a scandal among embassy employees. My directorate found out about the affair and brought it to the attention of the Foreign Ministry, which transferred the ambassador to Costa Rica. But the ambassador, who personally knew Kryuchkov and had good connections in the Foreign Ministry personnel office, also managed to have his mistress sent with him. Our station chief in Costa Rica said that despite the ambassador's flimsy precautions—he would meet her on a street away from the embassy—the affair was becoming widely known in the capital.

I told Kryuchkov, who had gone to school with the ambassador.

"Okay, Oleg, when he comes home on leave, talk to him," said Kryuchkov. "I don't want to talk to him myself."

The ambassador was summoned to Intelligence headquarters, where I sat down with him over coffee and cognac and had a man-to-man chat.

"We have information from the CIA [I made that up to scare him], from an impeccable source, that you're having an affair with your secretary," I told the paunchy, gray-haired diplomat. "They know about it and they are watching you."

"Oh, no," he replied. "Why didn't your station chief tell me?"

"He didn't wish to expose his source, so he reported it to me," I replied.

"Does Kryuchkov know about it?" the ambassador asked.

"Yes, he does," I said, "and he wants me to talk to you about it."

I had his attention now, and he was plainly frightened.

"Well," he said, "what should I do?"

"Just be informed that Western intelligence agencies know about the affair and they may very well try to make use of it," I said. "They may try to intimidate you, recruit you. Just be very careful, and I suggest that you either send the girl home . . . Well, as a man of the world, you know how best to deal with the situation."

He thanked me, and in a few weeks returned to Costa Rica. Eventually, he was recalled and assigned to a desk job in Moscow.

Perhaps the thorniest case of sexual misconduct on the part of our ambassadors involved our top diplomat in Mauritania. It was a case that went all the way to the top of the KGB and the Politburo as we sought to get rid of what can only be described as a dirty old man.

My Foreign Counterintelligence officers stationed in embassies overseas occasionally monitored the mail of Soviet Embassy employees. In Mauritania, one of our officers opened a letter from a twenty-year-old girl who had just come to work at the embassy as a secretary. The girl wrote her mother that she was having a terrible time, not because of the African heat or the mosquitoes, but because the aging ambassador kept trying to molest her. The letter described in graphic detail how the old pervert would summon the young girl to his office to take dictation, whereupon he would pull out his penis and begin chasing her around his desk.

My officer sent me the letter, which I read with growing anger and disgust. I told my people to write to the Central Committee of the Communist Party and report, without going into gory detail, that the ambassador was behaving in an improper fashion and should be recalled. Andropov signed the letter himself and forwarded it to the Central Committee.

I had numerous friends on the Central Committee staff, and about a week later one of them called me.

"What are you doing, Oleg?" he said. "This ambassador is very friendly with top Soviet leaders."

"So what?" I said. "He has to take responsibility for his actions."

"But don't you know that he sends Mauritanian carpets and other gifts to Politburo members?"

"Maybe he does, but what's that got to do with me?" I responded. "I'm just reporting to you what we know, and you decide what to do with the man."

Shortly afterward, I met the KGB's deputy chief of Intelligence for African affairs, who told me, "Come on, Oleg, you'll never be able to break this man. It's impossible. Don't you understand that these people all defend each other? He sends them expensive gifts. They will never turn against him."

I told him I had an obligation to report what I knew. A month or two passed, and no action was taken against the ambassador. Then, we intercepted another letter from the girl. She was hysterical now. She described how he kept exposing himself and trying to seduce her, and she threatened to kill herself if the sexual harassment continued.

That was the last straw. I picked up the phone and called Kryuchkov.

"I have another letter from Mauritania about this scoundrel," I told the Intelligence chief. "The girl is about to commit suicide. Do we want to be responsible for that?"

Kryuchkov hated being responsible for anything, so he told me, "Okay, call Andropov and report it to him."

I phoned the KGB chairman and told him I had to see him in person. He instructed me to come at eight that evening.

"Okay, what is it now?" Andropov asked when I arrived at his office.

"Remember you signed that letter to the Central Committee about that guy in Mauritania?" I said. "Well, nothing has been done about him."

"What can I do about it?" the chairman replied. "That's for the Politburo to decide."

"I have received another letter from there," I said. "Will you please read it? I think this is a matter of life and death and we cannot sit on our hands."

Andropov took the letter and began to read. His face hardened, and I could feel his anger rising. Without saying a word, he picked up his direct line to Foreign Minister Gromyko.

"Andrei Andreyevich, do you remember that case in Mauritania?" Andropov asked. "Let me read something to you from this secretary. . . . It's time to make a decision."

The KGB chairman read the most emotionally charged passage to Gromyko, said a few words into the receiver, and hung up.

"All right," Andropov told me. "Everything will be settled. He is being recalled. Cable Mauritania."

Within a week, the ambassador was recalled for consultations. When it became clear he was back in Moscow permanently, he began to protest, writing Brezhnev and other top Soviet leaders to complain of a KGB plot against him. The Central Committee reviewed the case for several months, but even I was confident that such blatant perversion would end the old man's career—no matter how good his connections. He was forced into retirement, but only after being awarded the highest pension given to ambassadors.

I was forever amazed at how much trouble people got into over sex. The CIA and Western intelligence services used sexual blackmail against our people, and we employed it even more frequently against our adversaries. Catching people with their pants down was a prime way of compromising and recruiting them. As long as men would be men and women would be women, lust would play a role in the spy wars.

In all my years in the KGB, the case of the Soviet wife and her big dog topped the list of bizarre sexual escapades.

The year was 1979. My office received a report from a highly placed source inside the Counterintelligence agency of a large Asian state. He informed us that we had an unusual problem on our hands. It seemed that the wife of the Soviet Military Intelligence (GRU) station chief in this Asian country was having sex with the family's male dog. Our Asian source said that his agency's surveillance officers had numerous times watched the large animal copulating with its Russian mistress. The real problem was that the Asian Intelligence agency was planning to use the woman's perversity to blackmail the husband into spying for them and the West. As far as we knew, the husband—a well-respected GRU officer—had no inkling of his wife's strange sexual predilections.

Normally in such a case we would immediately recall the officer who had been targeted. But this was no normal case. First, we didn't want to make a fuss over the situation, since it might compromise our Asian Intelligence asset. More importantly, this case would be so profoundly embarrassing to the GRU man that we had to handle it with extreme care so that neither he nor his colleagues would know about the woman's perverse behavior.

The problem was so sensitive that it was quickly kicked all the way up to Andropov. He, Kryuchkov, and I all gathered in Andropov's office to discuss the weighty issue of what to do with this oversexed dog and her crazed Russian partner. We briefly discussed the situation, then Andropov fell silent.

Suddenly, the solution came to him.

"Kill the dog!" the KGB chairman said, and we all concurred that this was, indeed, the Solomonic way out of the situation. The GRU officer was due home soon for his vacation, and when he came back to Moscow we would suggest that he not return because we had information that an undisclosed provocation was being planned against him.

My department talked with our technical specialists, the same ones who masterminded the poisoning of Markov. Oddly enough, they couldn't immediately decide which poison and what dose should be administered to the animal. Finally, they hit upon what they said was the right formula, and we sent the poison to one of our KGB officers in the Asian country. He knew the GRU station chief, and on a visit to his home slipped the dog some meat laced with the poison. Unfortunately, our technical people screwed up: the amount of poison they prescribed didn't kill the dog, but only partially paralyzed him. Luckily, he was paralyzed from the waist down, and was rendered impotent.

Our Asian Counterintelligence source said their bugs in the GRU officer's house showed that the woman was inconsolable when the dog became ill. The GRU man and his spouse soon came back to the USSR, where his superiors told him that he couldn't return to his old posting for security reasons. The Asian Intelligence service didn't try to blackmail him, and he wasn't sent overseas again. Apparently, he never discovered that his wife had been intimate with the dog.

I never found out whether she replaced the family pet.

On the sexual espionage front, we usually got the better of the CIA and hostile Intelligence agencies for the simple reason that we were far more willing to use sex as a weapon, and generally had fewer scruples. The KGB had a department called Territorial Intelligence whose job was to recruit tourists and foreign businessmen. Territorial Intelligence used two main hooks to catch and compromise foreigners—illegal currency transactions, and sex. During the decade I was in Foreign Counterintelligence, the Territorial Intelligence unit usually recruited several dozen foreigners a year. The problem was that, after being caught in a compromising position and agreeing to work for us, the foreigners would return home and almost always break off contact with us.

I read dozens of files involving the sexual entrapment of male foreign tourists and businessmen, and our *modus operandi* was usually the same. Territorial Intelligence would target a foreigner for recruitment, then introduce him to an attractive Soviet woman at a bar, a hotel, a tourist agency, or a government office. The KGB preferred to work with actresses, dancers, teachers, and other professional women rather than prostitutes, because they generally were more intelligent and therefore more credible to foreigners. The women would be recruited for such work with promises of a promotion, a nicer apartment, overseas employment, or outright payments. Some women occasionally would make love to a stranger for love of country, but they were the exceptions. Territorial Intelligence also used gay recruits to entrap homosexual foreigners.

Once our woman had met the foreigner, she would (usually with little difficulty) lure him to a KGB love nest, where their lovemaking could be photographed. Sometimes we would merely approach the foreigner after the fact, show him pictures of his passionate night, and threaten to send the photographs to his wife back home. Other times, when we wanted to shock a man into cooperation, we would wait until the couple were entwined in a passionate embrace and then send one of our agents into the room, playing the part of the outraged husband. Occasionally the agent/husband would smack around the foreigner just to scare him; other times he would merely scream and threaten the unfortunate visitor with death or castration. But in all cases, he would phone the police, who would arrive in a matter of minutes and go through an elaborate, staged ritual. The policemen, who actually were KGB officers, would say things like, "We're sorry to have to do this, but you're a foreigner and we'll have to open an investigation . . . Oh, you're an American? That's not good. Not good at all."

By the end of this charade the businessman or tourist would usually be a blithering wreck. Then, a few hours later, another of our officers—posing as the good guy—would talk to the man and suggest that the matter could be hushed up if he would do a few things for us when he returned home. The victims often agreed to work for us, but the truth was that few if any could be persuaded to fulfill their promises once they were back in their native land. As a rule, we didn't pursue them aggressively, partly out of fear of angering the local Counterintelligence officers, but also because agents coerced into working for us often proved to be of little value.

We did, however, enjoy some success in our sexual warfare with the West.

In the mid-1970s, in a case that was highly publicized, one of our women operatives seduced a driver for the Canadian Embassy and later got him involved in some black-market business transactions. We confronted him, threatened to expose him to his embassy, and he agreed to work for us. He returned to Canada and began cooperating with us while holding down a job in the federal government. Soon, however, he and several other KGB agents were exposed in a major spy scandal in Canada and arrested.

In the late 1970s, in an Arab country, one of our female officers— using the cover of a teacher—became acquainted with a French military attaché. The Frenchman clearly liked her and wanted to take her to bed. We told her to go ahead.

"But that will be a violation of the rules," she said.

We told her, in effect, "If you feel like doing it and you like him, go ahead."

She began an affair with the man. What happened later, I don't know; shortly afterwards I was transferred to Leningrad.

I always told my officers, male and female, "Don't be afraid of sex." If they found themselves in a situation where making love with a foreigner could help our work, I advised them to hop in bed. And I always instructed them that if they were caught *in flagrante delicto* by another Intelligence service, they should never act flustered and always call their adversary's bluff.

"If the woman you have sex with is an American agent," I told my officers, "and they use the same scheme on you that the KGB uses at home, you just tell them, 'Send me those pictures in color. That's all I ask of you.' Don't play along with them. And don't be afraid to have sex. I can't understand a man who reaches that stage and then trembles like a little mouse. What is there to be afraid of? What kind of scandal? The only trouble you could have would be with your wife."

When I was working in Leningrad, in 1985 or so, a United Nations diplomat came to town for a conference. We set him up with a very pretty translator who had agreed to work for us and, if necessary, have sex with the man. After a day or so, he succumbed to her wiles. We not only had his hotel room under video surveillance, but also had placed a small, remote-control camera in the KGB car he had been furnished with. Unfortunately for the diplomat, it was in the car that he chose to have sex with the woman—she performed fellatio on him as the camera rolled. The pictures were beamed back to our Leningrad headquarters, where I and some fellow officers later watched them. The U.N. diplomat, who was stationed in Europe, was confronted with the evidence of his sexual adventures and agreed to work with us. Later, he was turned over to a case officer in Europe, and I heard that he continued working for us, though I don't know in what capacity.

Our side was not immune to the danger of sex scandals. One of our assets in Canada informed us about the promiscuity of the wife of a KGB Intelligence officer in our embassy in Ottawa. It seemed that she was sleeping with numerous Soviet Embassy officials, including KGB men and our own security officer. Our source in the Royal Canadian Mounted Police confirmed that the Canadians had detailed information about the shenanigans. It was our security officer's job to prevent just such conduct, and instead he, too, was hopping into bed with this woman. It was an intolerable situation, leaving a half dozen of our people open to blackmail by the RCMP. I reported it to Andropov and he ordered, "Recall them all, including the security officer."

The station chief was relieved of his duties, the security officer was put in the KGB reserve, several officers were demoted, and the KGB man with the wandering wife was sacked.

But my most distasteful case of sexual blackmail involved a Russian refusenik and her American husband. The woman, who was in her mid-thirties, met an American professor who was visiting the Soviet Union. They fell in love and announced their intention to marry. The problem was that the woman's mother worked for KGB Intelligence, and for security reasons Kryuchkov and others weren't about to let the daughter out of the country. We tried to dissuade her from marrying the man, but eventually she did. He returned to the United States and, in a case that was highly publicized at the time, began to fight for the freedom of his Soviet wife. Despite appeals from American officials to Brezhnev, the KGB stood its ground and the Soviet woman was denied permission to emigrate.

The KGB wanted to silence the American husband, and came up with a plan to do so. I became involved because, as head of Foreign Counterintelligence, I dealt with matters concerning Soviet émigrés and the security of the Intelligence Directorate. Working with domestic Counterintelligence, we devised a scheme to lure the woman into a sexual liaison with one of our agents, after which we planned to send proof of her philandering to her husband in America.

The Lothario we chose was a strapping, handsome KGB officer from the Caucasus Mountains. He had prior experience seducing women for the KGB, and we concocted a pretext under which our man and the refusenik woman could meet. He courted her with great ardor, finally winning her over. Now, all we needed was proof of her involvement with the man.

Internal Counterintelligence, known as Chief Directorate Two, arranged for him to take her on a picnic to a secluded country spot near Moscow. KGB surveillance and technical people had picked out the location in advance and set up hidden cameras—hundreds of yards away—to document the couple making love. All went as planned. It was a beautiful summer day, and the lovers enjoyed a picnic on the grass. Afterwards they undressed, and our officer began making love to the woman, acutely aware they were being photographed and that the woman's face must be visible. He did a fine job, and the pictures turned out well. I was later shown them by Internal Counterintelligence.

Chief Directorate Two sent the pictures to the American professor, but if he was dismayed he didn't show it. He wrote her back— our domestic people intercepted the letter—and told her that he knew it was a dirty trick, that he still loved her, and that he would continue to fight for her escape from the cursed Soviet Union. And fight he did, eventually freeing her after a decade-long struggle.

It was not our finest hour, and typical of the shenanigans in which our domestic departments became involved. I was glad to wash my hands of the whole affair. Indeed, it was difficult for me to imagine how my domestic counterparts could carry on, year after year, harassing our own citizens. I would not have lasted in such work, and when I was assigned to the KGB's Leningrad office in 1980, I found myself increasingly depressed over the often-meaningless tasks I was given. In Foreign Counterintelligence, our enemies were external and our national security was indisputably involved. We also fought on a roughly equal footing with the CIA and other agencies that were as cunning and as well funded as the KGB. It was a war of wits and skill and nerve. Nowhere was that more evident than in the shadowy world of double agents.

Within Foreign Counterintelligence we had a small unit, about a half-dozen officers, assigned to running double agents throughout the world. In my time, we never had more than about forty double agents working in all spheres of life, including business and science. On paper, a double agent was a simple thing—a Soviet citizen who was in reality still working for us while pretending to work for a hostile Intelligence agency. In fact, running a double agent was devilishly complex. Was the agent really still working for us? Had he gone—or would he go—over to the other side? Was the CIA planning to grab him, drug him, and interrogate him? When was the best time to blow the double agent's cover?

We ran double agents for several reasons. The first was to gather knowledge on hostile Intelligence agencies. We could learn a great deal by the kind of questions a hostile secret service was asking, what kind of information it wanted, and what sort of assignments it was giving our double. A CIA officer, in describing what he was seeking from a Soviet agent, often would say too much and let slip interesting information. Double agents could pick up valuable material simply by being in the presence of hostile Intelligence officers. One of our doubles in Japan, for example, grabbed a roll of microfilm that his CIA handler had forgotten. Dozens of intelligence documents, shedding light on the CIA Tokyo station, were on the microfilm.

We also used double agents to plant disinformation and confuse hostile Intelligence services. And running a double game could be extremely valuable in the propaganda battle with the West: on several occasions, when we were sure the CIA or other agency had been duped by our double, we would stage a meeting between the double and his handler and then nab the CIA agent for espionage. We would then reveal the details of the CIA's spying operation and expel the American agent in a great fit of publicity.

What was most challenging about double games was trying to outfox the other side. They knew what we were trying to do to them and we knew what they were planning against us. And still, against this backdrop, we were able to overcome our opponents' skepticism and successfully run double agents. I could almost hear my CIA adversary saying, "The Soviet's a double. The Soviet's a double." And then, through the right bit of play-acting or a bold gesture, we would convince the CIA that our man was for real and was on their side. We would string our adversary along for a while—it could be months, it could be years—and when the right moment arrived we would play our hand and say, in effect, "Gotcha!"

We knew that CIA always eyed a prospective recruit carefully. As we did in the case of the attempted recruitment of the CIA man in India, our adversaries would study one of our officers for months before deciding to approach him. They would ask the same questions we asked. Does this man have financial problems? Does he have a mistress? Is he drinking heavily? Did he lose a briefcase with documents? Is his wife sleeping with a Great Dane? If the person seemed in dire straits, was especially sloppy or unstable, we—and they—might move in on him.

We developed double agents in two main ways. In the first, one of our officers might truly find himself in trouble and therefore become a target of a recruitment attempt by a foreign Intelligence agency. These cases were more problematic, for the person in question might genuinely be unreliable and go over to the other side in the midst of our double game.

The best way to run a double agent—and the one requiring the most patience—was to set a trap using a reliable officer. We would create the impression that the person was in financial trouble, was a drunk, or was disgruntled with the Soviet system. We would, in short, wave a red flag saying the man was vulnerable. Then, we would lay back and wait, hoping the CIA or another hostile agency would take the bait. If they did, we would be playing with a double agent over whom we had solid control.

During my time, we played an intriguing double game in Canada. One of our officers, working under the cover of the Soviet Trade Mission in Montreal, began making noises that he was unhappy and having financial problems. Eventually, the RCMP got wind of his difficulties and approached him, offering to pay him in exchange for classified information on Soviet industry or intelligence operations. For us, it was a nearly foolproof game because we had an excellent longstanding source inside RCMP Counterintelligence. So as our double agent was passing us information from his end, our Canadian mole in the RCMP was supplying us with detailed reports from the other side. We gave our officer some classified documents of minor value to whet the Canadians' appetite.

Unfortunately, the game had to come to an end in 1977 following a spy scandal that led to expulsions and recriminations on both sides. Acting on a tip from our RCMP mole, we tried to recruit another RCMP officer in Montreal. But at the second meeting of our officer and the potential recruit, the RCMP—alerted by our target—swooped in and arrested our officer. It created a scandal, and the Canadians expelled eleven Soviets and attacked the USSR for its aggressive espionage activities. We had no choice but to expel some Canadians from Moscow. And to parry the propaganda blows coming our way, we decided to expose our double agent and his nefarious recruitment by the RCMP. We blew open the case, as was customary, in the pages of *Literaturnaya Gazeta*. I wrote a long article, published under a pseudonym, which spelled out the details of the Canadian recruitment of our man and the clever double game we ran.

I was involved in another double game in Leningrad in the early 1980s. We elicited the cooperation of a Leningrad scientist named Pavlov who frequently traveled the world on a Soviet research ship. Our instructions to him were simple: Express dissident views, engage in some black-market operations, and do everything possible to attract the attention of the CIA or other Intelligence agencies.

For two years, Pavlov did as he was told, to little effect. We were surprised, for we expected the CIA to show interest in a man who had access to information about Soviet science and the military-industrial complex. Then, out of the blue, we received a cable from the KGB's station chief in Buenos Aires, saying that Pavlov had come to the embassy and reported that the CIA had tried to recruit him. He had talked to the CIA agent, passed along some information, and agreed to meet him in Leningrad upon Pavlov's return home.

My boss in Leningrad was skeptical, but Moscow told us to go ahead with the meeting. And, indeed, such a meeting took place: Our surveillance people observed Pavlov and a diplomat from U.S. Consulate in Leningrad—clearly a CIA officer—rendezvousing on a remote street in the city. Pavlov took some money from the American in exchange for scientific information. It would turn out later that, as sometimes happens with double agents, Pavlov was not being honest with us and pocketed far more money than he reported.

A second meeting was scheduled 25 miles outside of Leningrad, at which Pavlov was to give the CIA agent documents, in exchange for another payment. As it turned out, however, the scheduled meeting came only days after the September 1, 1983, Soviet shootdown of Korean Airlines Flight 007 in the Sea of Japan. Moscow made a decision not to continue to pursue the double game, but rather to arrest the CIA agent when he met with Pavlov and to use the incident to counter the storm of adverse publicity that had swept over us following the KAL disaster.

We caught the American red-handed, eventually expelling him. Although we did everything we could to hype the incident, it barely made a dent in the propaganda assault we suffered in connection with KAL 007.

We had suspicions that Pavlov wasn't being straight with us. We decided to search his apartment and found large sums of money, evidence that he had pocketed payments from the Americans he never told us about. Pavlov confessed, and was sentenced to thirteen years in jail. As far as I know, he is still serving time in Siberia.

As head of Foreign Counter-Intelligence, I regularly took part in all-important KGB meetings on foreign policy issues. Inevitably, on my last eighteen months on the job, I was drawn into the growing controversy over Afghanistan, where a succession of Moscow-backed regimes was facing stiffening opposition from Islamic rebels. I viewed Afghanistan as a country within our sphere of interest, and thought we had to do whatever possible to prevent the Americans and the CIA from installing an anti-Soviet regime there. Like Andropov, I was skeptical of introducing large numbers of Soviet troops into Afghanistan, but as the situation deteriorated I began to see no alternative. When our troops invaded Afghanistan on Christmas Day, 1979, I did not see the move as a disaster comparable to our invasion of Czechoslovakia eleven years before. How wrong I would turn out to be.

My first—and only—trip to Afghanistan came in August 1978. Four months earlier, a pro-Communist coup, headed by Noor Mohammad Taraki, had overthrown the government of Mohammad Daoud, killing him and his family. Moscow had not been overjoyed by news of the coup, for in Daoud we had enjoyed a stable ally and relative peace along our southern border. By midsummer 1978, reports were filtering back to KGB headquarters of growing Islamic opposition to the Taraki regime, prompting Andropov to send Kryuchkov and me to Kabul on a fact-finding mission. While there, we were to sign a cooperation agreement between the Soviet and Afghan intelligence services.

We flew on Andropov's personal TU-154 jet, a passenger plane converted into a spacious and comfortable airliner. Kabul struck me as a big village, with worse poverty than I had seen even in India in 1971. During the course of our five-day visit, we stayed at the Soviet Embassy, and all was quiet in and around the Afghan capital. Kryuchkov and I had wanted to visit Djelalabad in the southeast, but Afghan officials said it was not safe: it was our first inkling that the situation was not as rosy as our hosts portrayed it.

Kryuchkov and I proceeded to meet the Afghan leaders who had slaughtered their opponents in the power struggle and who ultimately would die by the sword themselves. Taraki, the grandfather of Afghan Communists, was a fragile, stooped old man. He struck me as a fussbudget given to general utterances, and I saw then that he didn't have the physical strength or the backing to continue to lead the country for long. It was Taraki who had ordered the murder of Daoud, and a year after I chatted with Taraki he, too, was overthrown and executed. The man who eventually would do away with Taraki, Hafizullah Amin, was a far more impressive figure. His rule, however, would be even shorter that Taraki's. His end would be just as violent.

Amin was a dark, handsome man with glittering eyes and an intelligent face. He was the shrewdest and most literate of the officials I met in Afghanistan, and when we discovered that we had both been at Columbia University at about the same time, we hit it off immediately. We switched to English and reminisced about old haunts and familiar landmarks in New York. Amin's eyes shone, as if he had truly found a kindred spirit, and when we parted he gave me a big hug and invited me back as his personal guest. I would never get the chance: The following year, KGB special forces troops gunned down Amin at the presidential palace as Soviet troops took over the city.

After I had met with Amin, our local KGB officers described him as a homosexual and said it was rumored he had been recruited by the CIA. I found no evidence to back up either allegation, and concluded it was made simply because the young officer had lived briefly in America.

I also met the head of state security, A. Sarvari, who impressed me as a young, energetic officer. A half year later, he would personally participate in the execution of leading Muslim clergymen and their families. I was appalled when I read the reports of Sarvari's actions, which I knew would set off a never-ending cycle of revenge and violence.

On several occasions, I met with top officers from the police and state security, instructing them on how to fight the growing CIA presence in Kabul and throughout Afghanistan. The Afghans had almost no experience with the Americans, and I told them, among other things, about how to follow and eavesdrop on the American Intelligence agents. We later provided them cameras and electronic listening equipment.

"You have lots of American agents here and good opportunities to work against them," I told the Afghan security officers. "We'll do everything we can to help you."

Kryuchkov signed an agreement with the Afghans to share intelligence and deepen our cooperation. Our hosts took us on a picnic to the old royal palace on the outskirts of town, where we passed a pleasant afternoon. We were treated as elder brothers, and I left feeling that, though opposition was growing, the situation was relatively well in hand.

Returning to Moscow, I drew up—on Andropov's orders—a plan of "active measures" and general strategy in Afghanistan. My list included the following ideas:

• The Afghans should gather evidence on the training of Islamic guerrilla groups in Pakistan and then publicly accuse Pakistan of unleasing aggression against the Afghan people.

• The Afghan leadership should send a letter to the Iranian leader Ayatollah Khomeini professing support for the Iranian revolution and expressing hope the two governments will work closely together.

• The rebels in the Herat area should be declared mercenaries of U.S. imperialism and world Zionism, as well as remnants of the overthrown Iranian monarchy.

• American citizens suspected of CIA affiliations should be expelled from Afghanistan.

• Pro-government clergy should address the people and rallies should be held among youth, workers, and peasants in support of the revolution.

• Popular militias and committees "In Defense of the Revolution" should be established.

• The rebels' rear should be raided to destroy their radio transmitters, bases, and munitions warehouses.

• More pro-Taraki radio stations must be created inside the country and the number of Afghan broadcasts from stations inside the Soviet Union should be increased.

• Soviet advisers should be sent into Afghanistan, reconnaissance flights over Afghanistan should be increased, and Soviet troops on the Afghan border should be reinforced and put on combat alert.

Many of these suggestions were approved by Andropov and the Politburo and put into effect. But, as would soon be evident, Afghanistan would not bend to our will. We would deploy hundreds of thousands of troops and lose fifteen thousand men before realizing our mistake and withdrawing in humiliation in 1988.

In the fall of 1979, after Amin deposed and murdered Taraki, the situation in Afghanistan was clearly deteriorating. KGB officers there reported that if Moscow did not intervene more aggressively, Amin would surely be overthrown and an Islamic government installed. I attended a meeting of KGB Intelligence and Soviet Military Intelligence in which the GRU chief, General Ivashutin, argued strenuously for an invasion.

"There is no other alternative but to introduce our troops to support the Afghan government and crush the rebels," Ivashutin said.

Kryuchkov then spoke, saying that Andropov was against the introduction of troops.

Over the next several months, however, Andropov was to change his mind. Under pressure from Defense Minister Dimitri Ustinov, the KGB chairman reluctantly came around to the view that Soviet troops would have to invade. From that moment on, the KGB played a pivotal role in the events in Afghanistan. And as Soviet and KGB involvement deepened, Kryuchkov compounded the initial error by insisting that all intelligence information—from the GRU, the KGB, and the Foreign Ministry—be funneled through KGB Intelligence before being presented to the Politburo. It was a serious mistake, for Kryuchkov began filtering out bad news, exaggerating our achievements, and telling Leonid Brezhnev and the Politburo what they wanted to hear. It only prolonged the war and the suffering.

Soviet troops streamed into Afghanistan in late December 1979, murdering my chum Amin and flying in Soviet puppet Babrak Karmal to replace him. The world reacted with outrage. At the time, none of us had any idea that the bloody conflict would drag on for nine more years, killing hundreds of thousands of Afghans and creating millions of refugees.

The truth is that I was paying scant attention to the invasion taking place to the south. By Christmas 1979, my career had taken a sharp turn for the worse. I had clashed with the shadowy brotherhood that ran the world's largest secret police agency. I had violated an unwritten code and challenged the dictums of the men at the top. I had gone up against them and lost, and my star was flaming out.

SEVEN

Collision

It was known simply as "the woods." Situated in a heavily forested area in southwestern Moscow, just a half-mile beyond the outer ring road that encircles the capital, "the woods" was the KGB's new Intelligence headquarters at Yasenovo. The complex, modeled after the CIA's suburban headquarters in Langley, Virginia, opened in 1972, and for eight years I worked there next to the men who ran Soviet Intelligence operations around the world. My colleagues in downtown Moscow or in foreign stations would ask me, "How are things in the woods?," and it was clear to everyone that what we were talking about was not my country *dacha,* but our sprawling Intelligence headquarters. Even by Western standards, Yasenovo was a luxurious compound, a place that reflected the power and the privilege, the mystery and the isolation, of the KGB. During my eight years at Yasenovo, I was afforded a close-up view of the men who ran the KGB and its Intelligence operations, from the crusty Alexander Sakharovsky to the treacherous Vladimir Kryuchkov to the wily cold warrior Yuri Andropov. Most of these men worked side by side with me at Yasenovo, and to those of us sitting in the bucolic confines of "the woods" the world seemed a far more manageable place than it actually turned out to be.

We made our move to Yasenovo in 1972 because the stately building at Lubyanka had long been overcrowded. For years, Soviet Intelligence officials had argued that they needed their own separate headquarters in a secure compound far from the center of Moscow. Andropov eventually approved the plans for a new headquarters, and Moscow's chief architect designed a spacious, seven-story building that was virtually invisible from the highway. Later, when it was clear to everyone that the CIA knew every inch of the Yasenovo layout, Vladimir Kryuchkov approved the construction of two 20-story buildings that could be seen from miles around.

As could be expected from an organization with our wealth, nothing was spared in the construction of the Yasenovo headquarters. The builders used Japanese and European materials; the furniture was from Finland. Nearly all the glass-walled offices, even those of junior officers, enjoyed a view of surrounding fields and forests or of the artificial lake that had been dug on the premises. My own wood-paneled office, located on the third floor, was enormous—50 square meters—and boasted a bathroom with shower and an adjacent sitting room where I could sleep if need be. I even had a little known exit off my back room, which I occasionally used if there was a visitor in my antechamber I had no desire to see. The entire building was air-conditioned—a rarity in the Soviet Union—and underneath the compound were several basement levels with communication and technical facilities. The roofs of the buildings at Yasenovo bristled with antennae.

Security was extraordinarily tight. The compound was surrounded by rings of barbed wire and electronic sensing devices. Special Interior Ministry and KGB guards, accompanied by dogs, patrolled the area in and around Yasenovo and stood in watchtowers. Domestic KGB officers couldn't even enter Yasenovo without special permission. Thousands of secretaries and lower-level Intelligence employees rode into the compound every morning on special buses. We at the top, however, had our own chauffered Volgas, reflecting Soviet officialdom's love of a car and a driver: two-full time drivers were assigned to me alone, providing twenty-four-hour service. Toward the end of my years at Yasenovo, in 1979, Intelligence chief Vladimir Kryuchkov spent $100,000 to buy a handful of foreign cars, including Mercedes, Volvos, and Jaguars. Ostensibly, the cars were purchased to teach Intelligence officers headed for the West how to drive good automobiles. As could be expected, however, young Intelligence officers never got their hands on the luxury cars. Kryuchkov and other big shots appropriated the machines for their own personal use; the Intelligence chief himself cruised around town in a Mercedes.

We at Yasenovo, like all the Soviet elite, lived in a privileged cocoon that left us far removed from the travails of daily Soviet life. For us, Communism was indeed a good thing, for all our needs were cared for as we glided above the fray, impervious to the lines and the humiliation and the squalor that had become the hallmarks of Soviet existence. It's no wonder that people like Kryuchkov fought to the bitter end for the Soviet way of life. They had indeed enjoyed a standard of living worth protecting, even if it meant staging something so monstrously foolish as the coup of August 1991.

The self-contained world at Yasenovo had an excellent canteen where officers could purchase the best salmon, sausage, cheese, and caviar. There was a swimming pool, two saunas, indoor volleyball and basketball courts, and numerous tennis courts. We had a special shop in which we could buy imported clothes and consumer goods. By the late 1970s, the KGB had constructed twenty *dachas* for Intelligence chiefs in a remote, wooded section of Yasenovo, a mile or two from the main headquarters building. In addition to my modern, spacious, KGB-supplied apartment in Moscow, I had a fine KGB *dacha* in the Moscow suburbs in the same village in which Nazi Field Marshal Friedrich von Paulus had been confined following his surrender at Stalingrad.

Yasenovo had an excellent medical clinic, and whenever I got a cold a doctor would make a special visit to my office to dispense some medicine. Should I have needed more sophisticated medical treatment, the KGB operated two good clinics in downtown Moscow and also controlled a network of a dozen sanitoriums in the best vacation spots in the country.

We even had a masseuse at Yasenovo, a pretty blond woman in her early thirties. I never a availed myself of her services. But just after I left Foreign Counterintelligence in 1980, an in-house scandal erupted when it was discovered that at least a half-dozen top KGB officials were making love to the masseuse right on her rubdown couch in the heart of the Intelligence complex. Kryuchkov called the offenders on the carpet and warned them never to do such a thing again, though no one was dismissed. The unfortunate masseuse was fired. But after writing a letter in which she threatened to expose the scandal, Kryuchkov found her another job to hush her up. The KBG could be far more moralistic at times, and during Kryuchkov's reign in Intelligence any officer who was twice divorced was expelled from the First Chief Directorate. Such was the case with one of our ablest officers—Mikhail Lyubimov, the KGB station chief in Denmark.

In my ten years in Foreign Counter-Intelligence, I worked under three Intelligence chiefs. The first, Alexander Mikhailovich Sakharovsky, was by far the best. He was a KGB institution, having served a record fifteen years as head of Intelligence, from 1956 until 1971. A veteran of World War II, Sakharovsky was a tough, almost-authoritarian leader who gave his underlings freedom to work, but devoured them if they showed signs of laziness or made a serious blunder. Following the 1971 defection of KGB officer Oleg Lyalin in London, Sakharovsky showed his ruthlessness, sacking several of Lyalin's superiors and recalling scores of officers home. We spoke of Sakharovsky with awe and fear in our voices, but not once did I hear someone inside the organization say anything bad about the Intelligence chief.

Sakharovsky was a taciturn figure who often seemed lost in thought. I think now that his melancholy air was due to the enormous pressures of the job and the fact that, in his fifteen years as head of Chief Directorate One, Sakharovsky personally ordered the assassination of several KGB defectors and Soviet dissidents living overseas. By the time I came to work for him, in 1970, KGB "wet jobs" were mainly a thing of the past. But Sakharovsky's hands were well bloodied by then, and though he never spoke of the assassinations he had ordered, it seemed to me that they weighed upon his conscience.

It was on the express orders of Sakharovsky, and with the approval of Khrushchev, that two well-known Ukrainian émigré activists were murdered in Germany in the 1950s. A KGB assassin using a gun that fired poison gas killed Lev Rebet of the National Labor Alliance in 1957 and Stepan Bandera of the Organization of Ukrainian Nationalists in 1959. Earlier, Sakharovsky also had ordered the assassination of National Labor Alliance leader Georgi Okolovich, but the plot backfired when the assassin Nikolai Khoklov defected to the West and described in detail the plot to kill Okolovich. Later, Sakharovsky approved a plan to kill the turncoat assassin, but the poisoning attempt failed, and all Khoklov suffered was the temporary loss of his hair.

Sakharovsky ordered a half dozen other assassination attempts on KGB defectors, but none of the plots was ever carried out because the turncoats couldn't be found or the Soviet leadership balked. Later, when I became head of Foreign Counterintelligence, we located two KGB defectors from the 1950s (one in Australia and one in America) and I approached Andropov and asked permission to order the assassination of the traitors.

"The hell with them—they're old men now," replied Andropov.

"Leave these old geezers alone. Find [recent KGB defectors] Oleg Lyalin or Yuri Nosenko and I will sanction the execution of those two."

But we never were able to locate Lyalin or Nosenko, and when they finally did surface, the KGB was no longer interested in carrying out the death sentences which had been imposed upon them.

As I discoverd when I opend my safe after taking over as head of Foreign Counterintelligence, Sakharovsky also ordered the poisoning of Sean Burke, the Irishman who helped engineer the bold escape of George Blake from England.

In the end, Sakharovsky was removed from this position largely because of politics. He was a stubborn, loyal professional, who refused to butter up the Communist Party officials and Brezhnev cronies who gradually were taking over the KGB—a clique that, in honor of Brezhnev's hometown, came to be known as the Dneprpetrovsk Mafia. In 1971, a timid, ill-qualified functionary from the Communist Party Central Commitee, Fyodor Konstantinovich Mortin, was named to replace Sakharovsky as chief of Intelligence.

A short, balding man with pale blue eyes, Mortin lacked culture, education, and, above all, practical experience as an Intelligence officer. To think that this was the man who headed the feared KGB spy operations was laughable. I have rarely met a person who was more unsure of himself, more indecisive, more cowardly. On several occasions I was in Mortin's office when Andropov phoned. Mortin literally jumped when the special line from Andropov rang, and he would cringe and stutter as he sought to assure the chairman that everything would be carried out according to his wishes. His behavior wasn't much better when someone called from the Central Committee; after hanging up with a Communist Party big shot, Mortin would get on the phone with his subordinates and demand that the Party's order—no matter how foolish—be carried out. If I or another of his underlings resisted the order, Mortin would literally implore us to somehow "close the matter" and fulfill the Party directive. The one good thing about Mortin was that he was so afraid of making a decision that he would allow more aggressive department leaders like myself to take matters into our own hands. He realized we were professionals, and if things generally were going smoothly he would not interfere with our operations. And unlike his successor—the double-dealing Vladimir Kryuchkov—Mortin was fundamentally a decent, if weak, person.

One episode vividly illustrated Mortin's spinelessness. One of my counterintelligence officers in Istanbul—a recruit from the KGB border troops with a fine record and fluent command of Turkish—got into a violent row with his wife and disappeared for nearly a day on a drinking binge. His wife grew scared and went to the KGB resident in Istanbul who, fearing the man might be vulnerable to subversion by Turkish authorities, sent a coded report about the incident to KGB headquarters in Moscow. Andropov happened to see the report and promptly ordered that the officer be recalled and dismissed.

When I saw the order, I went to Mortin and argued that Andropov had overreacted.

"The man made a mistake, but we should give him a chance," I told Mortin. "He should be reprimanded, but not recalled and dismissed. He's a good officer. I think you should make the case before Andropov."

"Are you out of your mind?" Mortin shot back. "There's no way I'm going to do anything like that."

Mortin wouldn't budge, despite repeated coaxing on my part, though he finally said he wouldn't object if I went to Andropov myself and pleaded for leniency.

A few weeks later, Andropov visited Yasenovo and I was given a brief audience with the KGB head.

"Look," I said, "you ordered that this guy be recalled and fired. But he's an excellent officer and he made one mistake. He speaks excellent Turkish and has a bright future there. We don't have to do this to him."

Andropov mulled things over a few seconds, then said, "Okay, have it your way." I was carrying the dismissal order in my hands; the chairman took it from me, crossed out his earlier directive, and handed back the paper. And so the man's fate was decided with a stroke of the pen. Had it been up to Mortin, our officer in Turkey would have been drummed out of the KGB.

Mortin was shunted aside in 1974 because Andropov had come to view him as too ineffectual. The Intelligence chief's downfall also was due, in part, to the conniving of Mortin's successor, Vladimir Kryuchkov.

We had received information from a high-ranking asset in French Intelligence that there was an unspecified mole in one of our KGB stations in Europe. Kryuchkov traveled to Paris to meet with our French source, and returned determined to catch the traitor. The Frenchman indentified several potential spies, though when I saw the list of names I was highly skeptical.

One of those under suspicion was our resident in Switzerland, who at the time of Kryuchkov's return was on vacation in Moscow. The man also was a good friend of Mortin's; they were from the same town in Russia. Kryuchkov ordered me to begin tapping the Moscow phone of our Swiss resident, though I argued that he was a good officer and we had no reason to suspect him. Kryuchkov insisted, however, and within a day I was receiving transcripts of the subject's telephone calls. They were innocuous, except for one conversation in which a hoarse-voiced man warned our resident in Switzerland that an investigation was under way and their call might be monitored. I showed the transcript to Kryuchkov, who snorted with satisfacton and insisted I find out who was tipping off the suspect. In fact, as I later discovered, Kryuchkov already knew who had made the call: It was Mortin, who had telephoned his old friend to warn him that he was under investigation. Kryuchkov made sure that Andropov saw the transcript, thus hastening Mortin's demise after only two years on the job. I now think that Kryuchkov initiated a bogus investigation of our man in Switzerland because he was a close friend of Mortin's, all the while hoping that Mortin might make a false step as he came to his compatriot's defense. It was a typical Kryuchkov move.

In all my years in the KGB, I encountered few members of our organization as scheming, slippery, and duplicitous as Vladimir Aleksandrovich Kryuchkov. When we met in 1971, we took an almost instant dislike to one another. I saw Kryuchkov as a wily Communist Party bureaucrat with little business being in Intelligence, and he saw me as an Andropov protégé, a potential rival, and a professional officer who often disputed his judgments. I of course had no clue that Kryuchkov would twenty years later take his place in history as the chief plotter of the Communist Party coup against Soviet president Mikhail Gorbachev. But I always had an abiding distrust of Kryuchkov, and in late 1984—just before Gorbachev took power—I went to my old friend and top Gorbachev adviser, Alexander Yakovlev, to warn the Gorbachev team about Kryuchkov. "Don't trust him," I told Yakovlev, stressing that I had watched Kryuchkov in action for nearly a decade and knew him to be dangerous and dishonest.

Gorbachev was to receive similar warnings from other people, but unfortunately he would brush them aside. After all, he and Kryuchkov were closely linked, as both had been protégés of Yuri Andropov. Gorbachev, who had held the relatively obscure post of Communist Party First Secretary in the Stavropol region, had been chosen by Andropov to come to Moscow and ultimately serve on the Politburo. Andropov had taken Kryuchkov under his wing nearly three decades earlier, when the two met at the Soviet Embassy in Budapest. So Gorbachev was inclined—fatally so—to believe in Kryuchkov, in part because he was Andropov's man, but also because regional Communist Party bosses like Gorbachev traditionally placed great faith in the KGB, viewing the organization as an astute shaper and interpreter of events. In the three years Kryuchkov served Gorbachev, the Soviet leader came to rely on the KGB chairman more and more, receiving a steady stream of doctored and biased information that tended to isolate Gorbachev and alter his view of the historic forces swirling around him. For a time, Kryuchkov was the faithful courtier, Gorbachev's Svengali, whispering in the master's ear to beware of the dangers and the conspirators that lurked everywhere. And when Gorbachev at last began distancing himself from the orthodox Communist views to which Kryuchkov still clung, the KGB boss betrayed his leader and hatched the plot that would lead to the ill-fated coup of August 1991.

I first met Kryuchkov in 1971 when he was serving as head of the KGB Secretariat, the agency's top administrative post. Walking into his enormous wood-paneled office, I was taken aback by the sheer blandness of the man—the indeterminate expression, the small eyes hidden behind thick lenses. A thin half-smile was frozen on his face, and his gaze rarely met mine. During our brief conversation he kept rushing in and out of an adjacent office, taking calls from Andropov. When we finally talked for a few minutes, he immediately betrayed his lack of knowledge of the Intelligence field. His speech was peppered with generalities and Communist Party platitudes. First impressions are not always reliable, but in the case of Kryuchkov my initial negative instincts proved correct.

Kryuchkov had risen to such a high position in the KGB because he was the classic assistant, the consummate bureaucrat. He was a young man when World War II broke out, but unlike nearly his entire generation, Kryuchkov did not head to the front to fight Nazi Germany. He remained instead at the Stalingrad Tractor Factory, where he was the plant's *Komsomol* (Young Communist League) organizer. I don't know how he avoided military service, but I do know that Kryuchkov was one of the most physically cowardly men I have ever met, shunning any activities that had about them a whiff of danger. How this indecisive and fainthearted man eventually helped organize a coup still remains something of a mystery to me, though I can only imagine he did it for two reasons: He was joined by the heads of the Soviet Army and Interior Ministry, providing safety in numbers, and he was so genuinely appalled by the continuing collapse of the Soviet Empire that he felt he had no choice but to act.

Kryuchkov earned a law degree through correspondence courses, then entered the Soviet Foreign Ministry's Higher Diplomatic School. His big break came in 1954 when he was posted to the Soviet Embassy in Budapest, where he served faithfully under Ambassador Yuri Andropov. Kryuchkov hitched his wagon to Andropov's star, a shrewd move that more than three decades later would land Kryuchkov the job he had long coveted: chairman of the KGB.

From 1959 to 1967, Kryuchkov worked with Andropov in the International Department of the Central Commitee of the Communist Party. When Andropov was appointed chairman of the KGB in 1967, Kryuchkov again followed him there, using the same obsequious behavior and skill at bureaucratic infighting that had long stood him in good stead. He was a meticulous paper shuffler, a master at working the Soviet bureaucracy. As chief of the KGB Secretariat, he was Andropov's right-hand man, helping prepare and correct the mountain of papers that was shuffled between the KGB and the Politburo and Central Committee. Kryuchkov was as cautious as he was fastidious. I can recall several instances where he took papers I was forwarding to the Politburo, carefully read them, and toned them down. He would pace around the room, inserting platitude-filled phrases into my reports.

"Write this down," he would tell me, displaying obvious pride in his knowledge of how to play the bureaucratic game. One of my reports said we would attain our goal if we took a certain line of action. Seeing such a phrase, Kryuchkov would insist that I say we "probably" or "in all likelihood" would attain our goal.

"Always leave some doubt," he said. "Never make it certain."

He loved modifiers and shied away from simple, direct sentences. His writing, like his speech, was a convoluted affair; half the time I would walk away having scant idea what it was Kryuchkov had just said.

In the beginning, when I first started working with him at the KGB, he struck me as little more than an extremely efficient secretary. In time, he would become more sure of himself and consequently more ruthless, surrounding himself with people he had managed to compromise and co-opt. Meanwhile, he steadily worked to derail the careers of his rivals. But in our first few years together, Kryuchkov was afraid to go to the bathroom without Andropov's permission, calling the KGB chairman for guidance on the most mundane matters.

I quickly learned that the best way to deal with Kryuchkov was to quietly pull off a mission—such as recruitment of a foreign agent—and then afterwards go to Kryuchkov for permission to do what I already had done. I would tell Kryuchkov of our plans, and he invariably would kick the decision up to Andropov. The KGB chairman would give the mission his blessing, accompanied by a warning to be careful. A few days later, when I returned to Kryuchkov to report that the mission was successful, the Intelligence chief would beam with pride and telephone Andropov to take credit for the operation.

Kryuchkov catered completely to Andropov's wishes, and unfortunately the KGB chairman had worked with Kryuchkov so long that he couldn't see his assistant's myriad shortcomings. In reality Kryuchkov knew little of the outside world and even less about Intelligence. He had a serious intellectual inferiority complex and was extremely jealous of his colleagues' successes. He was the kind of man who gloated when you stumbled and then, if the opportunity arose, would push you even further down. He was, in short, a real bastard.

I traveled overseas with Kryuchkov on numerous occasions. On three of those trips, I had run-ins with him that give a sense of the cowardice and prudishness of the man.

Our first trip together was in December 1974, when—shortly after his appointment as head of Intelligence—Kryuchkov led a delegation to Warsaw for a meeting with the Intelligence chiefs from other Communist Bloc countries. We stayed in a plush villa in the Warsaw suburb of Magdalenka, and when the conference opened, Kryuchkov was the first to speak. His cliché-filled address, which highlighted the triumphs of our security service and glossed over any problems, was met with disinterest by most of the delegates. The speech of East Germany's Markus Wolf was, in contrast, far more dynamic.

I only went to central Warsaw one night, accompanied by my Intelligence colleague and old friend Andrei Smirnov. After attending an opera, Smirnov and I visited some Polish colleagues, then returned after midnight to Magdalenka. We didn't feel like going to sleep and stayed up half the night talking and drinking a bottle of vodka we had brought from Moscow. The next morning, Smirnov and I showed up a few minutes late for the conference, looking a little the worse for wear. Kryuchkov eyed us coolly, and during the first break he headed straight for us and demanded, "Where were you last night?"

"In my room," I replied.

"What were you doing?"

"Having a few drinks."

"But we called you late and no one answered," Kryuchkov said, his anger rising.

"Right," I said. "Smirnov and I were visiting some Polish friends."

Kryuchkov exploded.

"How could you go off without telling anyone?" he said. "How dare you! We're in a strange city—anything could have happened to you. What if there had been a provocation?"

I was astonished, for after all Smirnov and I had both spent considerable time overseas and were hardly afraid of a provocation in friendly Warsaw. I was just about to respond to Kryuchkov when Smirnov coolly answered the Intelligence chief.

"Valdimir Alexandrovich, I am ten years older than you," Smirnov said. "I survived the war, and am perfectly capable of looking after myself. And Kalugin certainly doesn't need any instructions, either. And I should remind you that we are in a friendly country."

Smirnov had been downright insubordinate. When I told him later that I had admired his boldness, he replied, "The chief's got to learn, and if we don't teach him now, we'll wind up being victims of his paranoia."

On our way back to Moscow by train, Kryuchkov summoned our four-man delegation to his compartment. The atmosphere was strained, and he clearly realized he had gone overboard in reprimanding Smirnov and me. Trying to ease tensions, Kryuchkov poured a round of vodka and said, "Let's drink to the success of our first meeting and let's get to know each other better. Why don't we each say a little something about ourselves? I'll start."

He gave a sketchy account of his life, and the rest of us followed suit. But I never let my guard down—then or later—for there was a look in Kryuchkov's eyes that betrayed his fundamentally dishonest character.

Several years later, I accompanied Kryuchkov on a trip to Cuba to meet with our Latin counterparts there. During that winter trip, the ever hospitable Cubans invited us to spend a day at the beach resort of Varadero. Though it was February, the air and the sea were warm and the beaches were deserted, so several KGB colleagues and I decided to take a swim. We invited our attractive Cuban interpreter to go with us, and she assented. Kryuchkov was appalled, warning us that the water was too cold and the waves too high. We swam out about 30 yards, and looked back to see Kryuchkov, his face twisted with anger, violently motioning to us to return to shore.

"Come back!" he bellowed. "Right now!"

We couldn't resist playing around in the waves a few more minutes. As we were heading into shore, a large wave washed over us, knocking us to the sand. But when we looked around, we saw that the interpreter had been swept underwater. A few seconds later, I saw her head bobbing in the sea and dashed into the surf; I found her just below the surface and dragged her back to the beach. At first we thought she had drowned, but after a few minutes we managed to resuscitate her and she regained consciousness with a long sigh.

Watching the whole spectacle, Kryuchkov began furiously muttering, "I told you never to go into that water. You are forbidden to enter it as long as we remain in Cuba!"

A couple of years later, I accompanied Kryuchkov to Hungary. Once again, our hosts invited us to a fancy Communist resort, and on a warm October day our KGB delegation found itself on the shores of Lake Balaton. The Hungarian Interior Minister himself cooked up a pot of goulash, and we sat in the shade, 100 yards from the lake, drinking red wine and swapping jokes with our Hungarian colleagues. After a while, the cool blue waters of the lake seemed irresistible, and I suggested to my colleague Nikolai Leonov—once Fidel Castro's closest Russian adviser—that we have a swim. The Hungarian Interior Minister said we should feel free to take a dip, and we were preparing to head for the lake when a red-faced Kryuchkov stood up and said, "You won't go! I forbid you!"

"Come on," I replied. "It's only a lake. It's not the Atlantic Ocean."

"I forbid you!" Kryuchkov spat back. "If you say a word, I'll send you back to Budapest!"

A dozen of our Hungarian colleagues and their wives looked on in disbelief as Kryuchkov made a huge scene over nothing. But I couldn't simply let Kryuchkov order me around like a schoolboy, so once again I explained to him that it was safe to swim in the lake.

"That's it!" he exploded. "You two pack up and get out of here!"

Our sympathetic Hungarian hosts escorted us to the villa gates and put us in a car for the Hungarian capital. And so the KGB's Foreign Counter-Intelligence chief and its expert on Cuba and Latin America were roundly humiliated and sent back to Budapest like a pair of wayward adolescents. Leonov cursed Kryuchkov all the way back to Budapest, and we both marveled that this man was actually the chief of KGB Intelligence.

"Jesus Christ!" I muttered. "What a man! What a coward!"

On a later trip with Kryuchkov, this time to Czechoslovakia, I shared an unsettling—even melancholy—experience with the director of Intelligence. On a glorious summer day, our Soviet delegation traveled down the Danube on a Czech border patrol vessel. Not far from Bratislava, we disembarked and inspected the barbed-wire barrier separating Czechoslovakia from Austria, 150 yards away. On the other side of the river, Austrian families picnicked along the riverbank. Children flew kites as parents unpacked food hampers and made campfires. It was a picture of idyllic contentment and peace. Silently, we stood on our side of the barbed wire, surrounded by watchtowers and dour Czech border guards with carbines. The contrast between the two scenes could not have been sharper, and I sensed that everyone in the Soviet delegation was thinking the same thing: They are the ones who are free and we are the ones in a prison camp. I'll never forget Kryuchkov's reaction. For a long time, he stared intently at the opposite bank. Finally, he muttered, "Hmmm . . . well, yes . . ."

I think he felt what the rest of us were feeling, but simply was unable to fathom the truth that our system was rotten through and through. Kryuchkov remained a true believer until the end, eternally suspicious of the West and capitalism. I was forever astonished by how provincial and insulated Kryuchkov was, and have no doubt that my fluency in English and years in America intimidated the Intelligence chief. Indeed, though Kryuchkov and I instinctively disliked and mistrusted one another, the more telling split between us arose because he remained implacably suspicious of the West, a die-hard ideologue, while I held a pragmatic view of our American and Western opponents.

Kryuchkov reacted with a mixture of amazement, defensiveness, and anger when confronted—as he often was—with evidence of his own provincialism. One day I introduced him to whiskey and soda, telling him that the Americans and British liked their whiskey straight, over ice, or with a little soda.

"Oh, no, no, no," Kryuchkov replied. "The best way to drink whiskey is with Coca-Cola. That is the accepted way."

"You can drink it with Coca-Cola," I replied. "But people just don't drink it that way. It spoils the taste."

"No," he said, grabbing the final word. "I know how it should be drunk."

Once, in his office, I referred to a saying from Bismarck about the Russian character: "Russians harness their horses slowly, but they drive them fast."

"Who said that?" Kryuchkov inquired eagerly.

"Bismarck."

"How interesting" said Kryuchkov, and immediately wrote it down in his notebook.

Years later, when I was in virtual exile in Leningrad, I visited Moscow and asked Kryuchkov when I would be returning to KGB Center.

"Oleg," he replied, "have patience for a little while longer."

"*Pazienza, pazienza,*" I said.

"What's that? What's that now?" asked Kryuchkov.

"It means patience," I said.

"What language is it?" asked Kryuchkov.

"Italian," I said.

"Oh, do you know Italian?" Kryuchkov said, wide-eyed.

"Just a few words," I said. "Just a few words."

For the KGB's Intelligence service, the tragedy of Kryuchkov's leadership was that he slowly removed the strong-willed men at the top of our organization and replaced them with sycophants and incompetent Communist Party *apparatchiks*. As a result, in the late 1970s and in to the 1980s, we became less aggressive in our battle with the CIA, while at the same time the number of KGB defectors soared. The men in the top echelons of Intelligence, following Kryuchkov's lead, became more concerned with palace intrigue and currying favor with superiors than with our main goal: the struggle with the CIA.

Kryuchkov, thanks to his decades of bureaucratic experience, was expert at surrounding himself with toadies who were eternally loyal to him, often because the Intelligence chief had forgiven them one transgression or another and given them a second lease on life. Examples abounded of such bureaucratic blackmail. Two of the men

Kalugin (fourth from right) in Budapest in 1977 with top KGB officials. Victor Chebrikov (fifth from right) went on to become KGB chairman from 1982 to 1988.

At the 1977 gathering of intelligence chiefs in Budapest: Kalugin is second from right. To his right is Vlado Todorov, chief of Bulgarian intelligence, who later organized the assassination of Bulgarian dissident Georgi Markov. The Markov assassination was the one "wet job" with which Kalugin was familiar.

Kalugin (second from left) at a 1978 reception at Czech intelligenc headquarters in Prague. At far right is Vladimir Kryuchkov, the KGB's head of intelligence, who later worked to undermine Kalugin's career. Kryuchkov later went on to mastermind the 199 coup against Soviet president Mikhail S. Gorbachev.

Kalugin (center) in Gdansk, Poland, in 1979. Next to him is his
nemesis, Kryuchkov. Kalugin warned Polish intelligence chiefs
about the danger from the growing Solidarity movement, but
was rebuffed.

During a 1979 trip to the KGB station in Tokyo, Kalugin visited the grave of famed Soviet spy Richard Sorge, who supplied Moscow with invaluable information about Germany and Japan on the eve of World War II.

By 1980, Kalugin had clashed with top KGB officials over their prosecution of his first agent, codenamed "Cook." Kalugin was transferred to Leningrad, where he spent seven years in virtual exile in the local KGB office. He is shown here in 1980 with the director of the Hermitage Museum, Boris Piotrovsky.

Kalugin was the number-two man in the Leningrad KGB. He is shown here meeting in 1980 with North Vietnamese interior minister Fam Hung.

Unlike his hectic years in KGB intelligence, Kalugin had a lot of time on his hands in Leningrad. He is shown here during a 1981 hunting expedition in Soviet Karelia.

Kalugin on a 1982 cruise in Leningrad with Nicaraguan interior minister Tomas Borge (left).

Partying with KGB friends near the Soviet-Finnish border in 1984.

After publicly breaking with the KGB in the summer of 1990—an event that created an international stir—Kalugin attended a human rights conference in Amsterdam. To Kalugin's right is prominent Soviet dissident Sergei Grigoryants.

Kalugin campaigning for a seat in the Soviet Congress of People's Deputies in the Krasnodar region of southern Russia. His campaign drew worldwide attention and enormous interest in the Krasnodar region. Kalugin won handily.

A campaign poster from his 1990 race, urging voters, "Let's Vote for Oleg Kalugin."

Part of the crowd in Krasnodar that came out to hear candidate Kalugin on the eve of the September 1990 election. His stirring attacks on the KGB and the Communist Party assured his victory.

Kalugin (third from left) participating in a massive street demonstration in Moscow in early 1991 to protest Gorbachev's embrace of hardliners and the crackdown in Lithuania.

In 1991, Kalugin, flanked by a priest and a Cossack from his district in Krasnodar, places his hand on a Bible and swears his acceptance of the Cossack movement. Though the ceremony made Kalugin little more than an honorary Cossack, the news that he had publicly backed the group did not sit well with some reformers, who considered the Cossacks nationalistic and anti-Semitic.

Kalugin's legislative office in Krasnodar. His supporters are tacking up a campaign poster for Boris Yeltsin, who became, in June 1991, the first popularly elected president in Russia's 1,000-year history.

Kalugin in court with his lawyer, Boris Kuznetsov, in 1991. Kalugin sued Gorbachev after the Soviet leader stripped him of his rank, pension, and decorations for going public with his fight against the KGB. Kalugin's honors, rank, and pension were restored following the failed August 1991 coup.

In the French senate, Kalugin attends a 1991 conference in Paris on international terrorism.

Kalugin (at left in front of tank) on August 19, 1991, the first day of the coup. Though Yeltsin is not visible in this photo, he is standing on the tank on the opposite side, calling on the Soviet people to resist the coup. The tank is stationed outside the Russian Parliament building, the center of resistance to the coup.

Kalugin being interviewed in front of the Russian Parliament on August 21, 1991, the day the coup collapsed. KGB agents followed him during the three-day coup and, had the takeover not failed, planned to arrest him.

Kalugin returns to his alma mater, Columbia University Graduate School of Journalism, in 1991.

With Vadim Bakatin, the last chairman of the Soviet KGB, in Boston in 1992. In the waning weeks of the USSR, Kalugin advised Bakatin on how to reform the monstrous security organization. But Bakatin had barely begun to make significant changes when the Soviet KGB was replaced by several Russian agencies and Bakatin found himself out of a job. To this day, real reform has eluded the KGB and its successor agencies.

The retired general, now pursuing a career in lecturing and business, on a 1993 Baltic cruise with his wife.

involved in the sex scandal with the masseuse at Yasenovo were top Kryuchkov aides and an third was head of a major department. But rather than sacking the men, Kryuchkov merely chewed them out and gave them another chance. One of the aides, a man in his sixties, had often talked behind Kryuchkov's back before the masseuse scandal, but afterwards he never said another bad word about the Intelligence chief.

Another senior KGB official, the man in charge of our "active measures," was found to be leaving work early several days a week and making love to the wife of a Counterintelligence officer. (Kryuchkov found out about the affair because the woman's husband was suspected of working for the CIA. Her apartment was bugged, and it was there that the "active measures" officer and the woman had their lovenest.) Kryuchkov called the officer in for a talk and— according to Kryuchkov's assistant—the poor fellow was nearly in tears when confronted with his hanky-panky. The Intelligence chief gave the man a reprieve, thus ensuring the loyalty of yet another mediocre underling.

A similar case involved Sergei Golubev, the security chief of our Foreign Counterintelligence Directorate and the man who helped the Bulgarians with the assassination of Georgi Markov. Golubev had a long history of sloppy behavior—car wrecks, drunken brawls—due to an inability to hold his liquor. While I was head of Foreign Counterintelligence, he was found by a guard at Yasenovo at five o'clock one morning, dead drunk in his office. He was unconscious, bottles and glasses were strewn about the room, and his safe had been left wide open. The incident was reported to Kryuchkov, who should have sacked the man. Instead, he gave Golubev a stern lecture, during which—Kryuchkov's assistant said—the security man dropped to his knees in tears and begged for forgiveness. Once again, Kryuchkov was assured of having a loyal subordinate.

And so it went at the top of our organization, as our leaders scratched one another's backs and ignored countless blunders of compromised underlings. The phenomenon was described perfectly by author Ivan Vasileyev, who wrote:

> It was difficult to find any manifestation of conscience in those who came to the fore in this period of [Soviet] stagnation. They suffered no qualms in espousing indecency. . . . They forgave each other any transgressions and lost all feelings for principle. A forgiven sin became a moral lever. A superior

overlooks a fault in a subordinate, and the subordinate will overlook the shortcoming of the superior. This leads to a personal, covert interdependence, which binds wrongdoers to one another. Shutting one's eyes to evil is always immoral, but that fruit, once tasted, is never rejected.

As he was building up a coterie of flunkies, Kryuchkov was at the same time steadily eliminating potential rivals—a process to which I myself would eventually fall victim. A vivid example of Kryuchkov's maneuvering involved Grigory Grigorenko, the head of Chief Directorate Two, which oversaw domestic security and counter-intelligence. Grigorenko was a tough, intelligent professional, the top cop in the Soviet security system. He was widely respected by his subordinates, as well as by many of his peers and Andropov himself. As such, he was a clear rival to Kryuchkov for eventual control of the KGB, and the two men had a well-known dislike for one another. Grigorenko looked down on Kryuchkov as a minor Party hack who knew nothing of intelligence and counter-intelligence.

Their rivalry remained under control until an incident in 1975. That spring, the KGB and Soviet Foreign Ministry revived the tradition of staging an annual banquet for the top leaders of both organizations. The lavish affair was held at the pre-Revolutionary Morozov mansion on Aleksei Tolstoi Street in central Moscow. Representing the KGB were Kryuchkov, Grigorenko, and several other generals, including myself. There was an elaborate feast, accompanied by oceans of vodka and wine, and very soon many of those in attendance were well liquored up. A deputy foreign minister rose and gave a warm toast calling for closer ties between his agency and the KGB. He sat down, and everyone was waiting for Kryuchkov— the highest-ranking KGB official in attendance—to offer a toast in response. But just as Kryuchkov was about to rise, Grigorenko shot up from his chair and delivered a brisk speech about the long-established cooperation between the KGB and the Foreign Ministry. He utterly ignored Kryuchkov and did not include him in his toast, a serious breach of protocol, especially in a society where toasting at dinners has been elevated to the level of diplomacy. But it got worse. A Foreign Ministry official stood and delivered a toast, then Grigorenko again affronted Kryuchkov by rising for a second time. After that, the toasting deteriorated into a bawdy session in which

KGB and Foreign Ministry luminaries told obscene jokes, guffawed like farm hands, and downed bottle after bottle of vodka.

Kryuchkov sat there stonily. He was obviously outraged, and his hatred for Grigorenko was palpable. Even I felt sorry for him. Finally, when everyone—except Kryuchkov—was completely drunk, there was an exhausted lull in the merrymaking. It was then that Kryuchkov rose stiffly, cast a schoolmarmish gaze on the assembly, and lifted his glass.

"May I say a few nice words about Comrades Andropov and Gromyko, the leaders whom we all love and respect," Kryuchkov said.

We all knocked back a couple ounces of vodka in honor of our chiefs, then returned to raucous storytelling. As I sat there looking at Kryuchkov's sulking countenance, I thought to myself that the Intelligence chief would surely one day exact revenge on Grigorenko. And I was right.

A couple of years later, we discovered that one of my Foreign Counterintelligence officers in Vienna had gotten his hands on a veritable warehouse of clothes, jewels, and consumer goods which he was illegally shipping back to Russia, selling or giving much of the loot to top KGB and Communist Party officials. It turned out that Grigorenko, among many others, had been a recipient of our officer's largesse. When Kryuchkov discovered this, he pursued the case vigorously, chastising Grigorenko and other KGB officers for their decadence. Though many in Kryuchkov's circle were just as quick to accept gifts from friends abroad, the Intelligence chief ignored that and skewered his rival. Gigorenko's misstep, combined with his refusal to kowtow to other Brezhnev cronies in the KGB hierarchy, ensured his demise. He was eventually placed on the KGB reserve, thus removing one of Kryuchkov's chief competitors.

A similar fate awaited my old Washington station chief, Boris Solomatin, who was one of the top men in Intelligence. Kryuchkov saw to it that Andropov and other Politburo members knew that Solomatin had a drinking problem, and that was the end of his hopes of rising to head of Intelligence. My former New York station chief, Boris Ivanov, also was dispatched by Kryuchkov with similar skill. Kryuchkov rarely missed a chance to subtly criticize Ivanov, who was deputy head of Intelligence and a rival of Kryuchkov's for the top Intelligence spot. Once, when we were meeting in Andropov's office about the espionage situation in Canada, Andropov asked Ivanov how many agents we had in Canada. Ivanov estimated that there were a dozen or so, which was at least twice as high as the real figure. Kruyuchkov could see during the meeting that I appeared doubtful, and he later asked me what the real agent count was in Canada. I said it was about five. Ivanov probably had made a simple mistake, but Kryuchkov later went to Andropov and accused Ivanov of purposely exaggerating his department's achievements in the United States and Canada. At the time, Andropov was waging a campaign to counter the flood of faked and exaggerated in-house reports plaguing the KGB, and Ivanov fell victim to that crusade. He was never chosen to head KGB Intelligence, and later was transferred out of headquarters to become our special representative in Kabul.

In due time, it became clear that Kryuchkov—though he lacked skills in intelligence—was no slouch in the bureaucratic game. Increasingly, people grew afraid to cross him.

"I have no friends in this organization," Kryuchkov once told me. "My friends are all in the Party and the Central Committee. But I'm not worried about having no friends here."

He had a friend in Gorbachev, a relationship that would prove crucial. There is no doubt that his finely honed skills at working the Soviet halls of power, as well as his ties with Andropov, served Kryuchkov well. Many of my colleagues also have speculated that Gorbachev promoted and retained Kryuchkov because the KGB had incriminating evidence about corruption on Gorbachev's part when he was Communist Party boss of Stavropol. I have no firsthand knowledge of such corruption, but I think that if the evidence existed it would already have been leaked by one of Gorbachev's many enemies in the security services.

Kryuchkov's ability to manipulate the KGB and Gorbachev continued until the last days of Soviet power. Then, the old Party bureaucrat made a fatal miscalculation. Kryuchkov still thought it was possible, in August 1991, to sit in the Kremlin and pull the strings of power like a puppeteer. He expected the nation's leaders and its people to automatically respond to the comands coming from the Kremlin, as they had done for seventy-five years. But that time had passed, and Kryuchkov was so out of touch with reality he didn't realize it.

I saw Kryuchkov on several occasions after I left the KGB and began my campaign against the security agency, but every time he saw me in the halls of the Soviet parliament he would head the other way. After the coup, Kryuchkov was jailed briefly, then eventually pardoned in 1994 by the Russian Parliament. I saw him several times on TV before his pardon, playing the role of Soviet Communist patriot trying to save his Mother Russia from the twin scourges of Yeltsin and capitalism. In early 1993, he stood at the head of a pro-Communist, Russian-nationalist demonstration, occasionally mingling with the masses he had so long ignored. It was a scene out of a black comedy—Kryuchkov and other Gray Cardinals of the Kremlin casting themselves as average men deeply concerned with the welfare of their people. In all his years in power, Kryuchkov had never rubbed shoulders with the Soviet masses. Yet there he was on television, leading a group of ragtag hard-liners and disgruntled Russian citizens. How far the mighty had fallen, and how hypocritical they had become.

The most imposing and emigmatic leader I worked with at the KGB was undeniably Yuri Vladimirovich Andropov, who headed the agency from 1967 to 1982. Though he was an aloof figure and a demanding boss, I nevertheless developed an almost father-son relationship with Andropov, and it was his support and backing that, in large measure, allowed me to rise as high as I did in the KGB. Indeed, when I was pushed out of Intelligence in late 1979, Andropov reacted with a mixture of sadness and exasperation, seemingly mystified that one of his boys would have such a damaging run-in with the KGB hierarchy.

In 1982, when an already-ailing Andropov took power in the USSR, following the death of Leonid Brezhnev, he was at first portrayed in the Western media as a closet liberal with a fondness for jazz, Scotch, and other things American and European. Sitting in Leningrad, I chuckled when I read and heard such accounts, for Andropov was anything but liberal, almost never drank, and possessed one of the more virulent anti-Western streaks among the Soviet leadership. But he was hardly an ogre, and he exhibited a flexibility that undoubtedly served him well in his long rise to power. When I think of Andropov these days, I picture in my mind the imposing, unsmiling figure who presided with grave efficiency over the monthly meetings of the KGB Collegium. But I also remember the rare occasions in private when Andropov let his guard down and actually allowed a smile to spread across his face.

Once, Andropov came to a special KGB apartment in central Moscow to award a "Friendship of Nations" medal to Kim Philby.

Three of us sat around a small table laden with food and drink, waiting for Andropov to appear. The tall, heavily built chairman arrived late, took off his coat, greeted Philby and the rest of us warmly, and said, "What are you drinking, my friends?"

"We're not drinking anything," I replied. "We're waiting for you."

"Okay, but let me perform my duty first," Andropov said. "Let me present this decoration to Mr. Philby."

He pinned the medal on Philby's chest, shook his hand, and announced, "Now let's drink to this festive occasion!"

Andropov almost never touched alcohol because of a kidney ailment, but he accepted a *ryumochka,* or shot-glass, of vodka and drank an ounce or so in Philby's honor. The chairman stayed for another hour, chatting amiably with us about England, the Intelligence business, and other things, all the while displaying a warmth that was little in evidence when carrying out his official duties.

On another occasion, I went to his office to report to him on some matter. After we finished talking, Andropov turned to me and one of his deputies and said, "Listen, friends, I have a gift from Kirghizia, a drink you've never tasted."

He walked into his back room and emerged with a bottle of opaque liquid.

"I know you've drunk everything, but this you've never had, I'm sure," Andropov said, smiling. "Try some."

He poured out two drinks, then sat back and watched our response. After sipping the bitter drink, I responded, "I know what it is. This is *limonik.*"

"How in the world did you know?" asked Andropov.

"Well, I've had it before," I said.

"And here I thought I would surprise you," retorted Andropov.

Limonik is also found in southern Russia; it is made from berries, and is rich in vitamins as well as reputedly having the qualities of an aphrodisiac.

"Okay," said Andropov. "You know what it is, but I can still serve you something you've never tasted."

He poured some cognac into the *limonik* and I tried it.

"You're right," I said. "I've never drunk it like this, and it's excellent."

Standing there coatless, in suspenders, Andropov gave me a fatherly look. We chatted amiably for a few more minutes until he was summoned by his secretary.

But the fundamental truth was that Andropov at heart was a

tough old Bolshevik who had survived the Stalin years and fought his way to the pinnacle of Soviet power. Before World War II, known in our country at the Great Patriotic War, Andropov had been a leader of the *Komsomol* in the Karelian region of Russia along the Finnish border. During the war, Andropov made a name leading the Partisan resistance to the Nazis on the Finnish front. When the war ended, Andropov rose through the ranks of the Communist Party organization in Karelia, then came to Moscow and joined the Central Committee. In one of Khrushchev's periodic shake-ups of the Communist Party apparatus, Andropov was transferred from the Central Committee to the Foreign Ministry. Then, at age forty, the ardent Communist was named Soviet Ambassador to Hungary.

It was there, two years later, that Andropov was to make his name by playing a pivotal role in suppressing the Hungarian uprising. During the 1956 revolution, Andropov earned a reputation as a cool leader in a crisis. Especially valuable to the Kremlin were his repeated assertions to the Hungarian leader Imre Nagy that Soviet troops were, in fact, not pouring into the country but were being withdrawn. It was a total lie, but Andropov was so convincing that— even as Soviet troops were launching a final offensive to crush the rebellion—the Soviet ambassador convinced Nagy that the Red Army was on its way home.

Andropov returned to Moscow in 1957 and went to work for the Central Committee department overseeing relations with other Communist countries. He gradually came to know Leonid Brezhnev and other Politburo members, and shared with them a growing concern about the erratic leadership of Nikita Khrushchev. In 1964, during the palace coup that overthrew Khrushchev, Andropov supported the Brezhnev faction and helped dig up compromising material on Khrushchev's involvement in the Stalinist purges— information that would have been used had the Soviet leader resisted his ouster.

In 1967, Brezhnev appointed Andropov chairman of the KGB.

Though not a professional KGB man, Andropov quickly earned the respect of rank-and-file Intelligence officers such as myself. He seemed to us a decisive, bright, and supportive leader who was well versed in world affairs and gave his underlings plenty of latitude to do the job. Only later, as I became increasingly cynical about the prospects for reforming our system, did I come to view Andropov more critically and realize that his orthodox Communist views often blinded him to a steadily changing reality.

As I started working closely with Andropov in the mid-1970s, I soon learned he was sharply distrustful of the outside world and saw CIA plots and imperialist intrigues around every corner. When numerous Western European Communist parties began to seek greater independence from the Soviet Communist Party, Andropov viewed the trend not as a natural historical evolution, but rather as the dastardly work of Western intelligence services. He may indeed have liked Louis Armstrong—a fact Western journalists seized upon to show what a cosmopolitan character he was—but the truth was that he prided himself in holding hard-line Communist views and genuinely believed that the United States and the West were working day and night to destroy the Soviet Union.

One of the few times Andropov criticized me involved a fundamental clash of our respective worldviews. Two KGB officers attached to the USSR's United Nations Mission in New York—Valdik Enger and Rudoph Chernyayev—were arrested by the FBI in 1978 after an American serviceman handed them classified information on the B-1 bomber program. The case was generating a lot of anti-Soviet publicity, and the U.S. government demanded that we put up $1 million in bail if we wanted the men to be freed pending trial.

I was summoned by Andropov and suggested that we immediately pay the money so our officers could be released on bail. The KGB chairman fixed me with an angry stare. From the expression on his face, one would have thought I had just suggested he go into business with the Rockefellers.

"I never expected our chief of Foreign Counter-Intelligence to trust the United States government!" Andropov fumed. "They could take the money and then just tell us to go to hell."

"But it's the government, it's not some private personality," I responded, shaken by his reaction. "They know the value of money and promises, and we shouldn't doubt they will keep their end of the bargain."

I continued, trying to explain the American system of justice, the procedures for bail, etc. Andropov angrily cut me off.

"I never expected anything like this from the likes of you," he said. "This is really something, to hear this kind of talk from a Counter-Intelligence chief. Do you mean to say you really trust them? Or perhaps you don't understand what you're talking about?"

I had never experienced such a tongue-lashing from a man I viewed as my mentor. Chastened—and stunned by Andropov's parochialism—I shut up. Enger and Chernyayev remained in jail, were convicted of espionage, and were released in 1979 for exchange with imprisoned Soviet dissidents.

Another thing that surprised me, though I understood perfectly well why he did it, was Andropov's frequent praising of Brezhnev, a habit that became increasingly embarrassing as Brezhnev slipped into senility and inaction. It was one thing to praise Brezhnev in public—we all were expected to do that—and Andropov was peerless in his ability to laud the fossilized Soviet leader. During my years in Foreign Counterintelligence, Andropov called Brezhnev "a political leader of Lenin's type, who is inseparably attached to his people and who has given the people his whole life." In 1979, Andropov spoke of Brezhnev's "popular acclaim, statesmanlike wisdom and great humanity." In his eulogy for Brezhnev in 1982, Andropov labeled the dear departed leader "the greatest political figure of our time"—surely one of the greatest examples of political hyperbole in history.

Yet even in private, Andropov was full of praise for our esteemed Soviet leader. Once, celebrating the sixtieth anniversary of Soviet Intelligence, Andropov called eight top officers into his office for a drink and used similarly flowery language to describe Brezhnev. In Andropov's case, such loyalty was understandable: it was, after all, Brezhnev who heaped money and praise on the KGB following the assault on the agency during the Khrushchev years. Under Brezhnev, the KGB became the most lavishly financed and best-equipped organization in the country. It was also Brezhnev who named Andropov to head the KGB and anointed him as the future Soviet leader.

I and the KGB's other professional officers could tolerate the odes to Brezhnev, but what was more difficult to abide were the Brezhnev cronies Andropov appointed as his top aides. Two of Anropov's half-dozen deputy chairmen, Semyon Tsvigun and Georgi Tsinyov, were especially bad news and typical of the Communist Party bureaucrats who were denigrating the KGB. No doubt Brezhnev forced Andropov to take on this pair; the KGB chairman was an independent man and Brezhnev wanted some of his own people to keep an eye on Andropov.

Tsvigun was a tall, bulky man who rose to a top KGB position for one reason: he and Brezhnev had known each other as young Commmunist Party officials in Moldavia, where they used to drink and chase women together. Tsvigun was downright stupid, but relatively harmless. Whenever he addressed a gathering of KGB officers, he groped for words and uttered complete nonsense. He was a laughingstock, but was generally kindhearted, even asking his subordinates if he could help them get an apartment, a car, or any one of dozens of pitifully scarce items in the USSR. Once, when he saw me carrying a banned copy of Alexander Solzhenitsyn's *Gulag Archipelago,* he approached me like a school kid and eagerly asked if he could borrow the book. He inquired how I had gotten it, and I responded that it had just been sent by one of my men in Paris. So I handed him the book, and two weeks later he called me, his tone of wonderment revealing that Solzhenitsyn's description of our state's vast totalitarian machinery was a revelation to the KGB general.

"I've finished the book and you can pick it up," said Tsvigun. "And why don't you call me whenever you get these kind of books from Paris?"

Georgi Tsinyov was a different—and far less benign—character. A small, sour-faced, bald-headed man, Tsinyov was one of of the most cunning, vicious officers I encountered in all my years in the KGB. He had worked with Brezhnev in the Ukrainian Communist Party before the war, and afterwards Tsinyov went on to become head of Soviet Military Counterintelligence in East Germany. Brezhnev moved him into the KGB, where he served in the powerful post of head of domestic Counterintelligence and then was appointed Andropov's first deputy. He was a hatchet man—remorseless, capricious, inhuman. I had run-ins with him on several occasions, clashes which no doubt hastened my fall from grace in the KGB.

Our worst run-in occurred after my directorate tried, and failed, to recruit the U.S. Ambassador to UNESCO. The ambassador, Konstantin Varvariv, was a naturalized U.S. citizen, and when he rose to the post of American Ambassador to UNESCO, we decided to check into his background. It turned out that he was from western Ukraine, and our archives showed he had collaborated with the Nazis, translating for German units involved in raids against partisans. There also was evidence that the units he was working with carried out massacres of Soviet citizens.

Varvariv flew to Tbilisi, Georgia, for an international conference, and I dispatched one of my subordinates there to make a recruitment attempt. My officer was armed with photographs of Varvariv and his wife with Nazi officers, as well as receipts showing he had been paid by the Germans. When our man caught up with Varvariv in his hotel room and showed him the evidence we had unearthed, the ambassador was shocked and said he needed time to consider our recruitment offer. We knew Varvariv held an ambassador's post at the time, and we hoped that he might one day be named to a higher position in the U.S. government.

Varvariv agreed to meet our officer the following day. The next morning, however, the ambassador left Tbilisi, stopping in Moscow on his way back to Paris. He reported the recruitment attempt to the U.S. Embassy, which lodged a protest at our Foreign Ministry. Senior diplomats there then immediately informed Tsinyov. Andropov's first deputy was furious that he hadn't known anything about the recruitment effort. Kryuchkov dispatched me to mollify Tsinyov; luckily I had notified domestic Counterintelligence, which he supervised, of our action in Tbilisi.

"How dare you conduct such arrogant actions on the territory of the Soviet Union without the knowledge of the security chiefs!" bellowed Tsinyov, nearly leaping out of his chair.

"I reported it personally to Andropov and he gave his consent," I replied.

"Okay, you always go to Andropov," Tsinyov said. "I know that. But who else knew?"

I told him which of his subordinates I had notifed, and he called them in one by one. They confirmed my account. He was sputtering mad by this point, and when he heard we were preparing to expose the Varvariv scandal in the upcoming issue of *Literaturnaya Gazeta,* he blew up. He demanded I kill the story. I called the magazine. The editors there informed me the issue was already rolling off the presses and was impossible to recall.

"Okay, young man," Tsinyov hissed. "I know you are very arrogant and always use Andropov to cover your actions. But I will remember this. I will remember this."

And other Brezhnev protégé, Viktor Mikhailovich Chebrikov, also worked as one of Andropov's deputies. Chebrikov—who eventually headed the KGB from 1982 to 1988—was an obedient Communist Party servant. He was a pleasant man, but like so many Party bureaucrats, terribly cautious and afraid to move without approval from his superiors. He was a prime example of our leaders during the depths of the "stagnation" period before Gorbachev—servile, sickly, and indecisive.

Andropov himself was so devout a Communist that, on the domestic Soviet scene, he couldn't see the forest for the trees. As our economy slid steadily downward in the late 1970s, he attributed the decline in production to poor worker discipline and disorder at factories. All that was needed, he said, was to boost worker productivity by tightening control over the economy and the workplace. I remember his suggesting that we could pull out of the economic doldrums by issuing a call to all working people to increase productivity and fulfill the current Five-Year Plan. That he and other Communist Party bosses thought they could sit in Moscow and exhort the *narod,* or masses, to save our creaking economy was an example of how deluded our Kremlin leaders had become.

As head of the KGB, however, Andropov was acutely aware of how far we had fallen behind the West in science and technology. His fatal mistake, as with many Soviets, was that he thought we could catch up by whipping the old Soviet mare harder, rather than relegating her to the glue factory and starting over.

In the late 1970s, one of our double agents in Germany, who was really working for us but who had tricked the CIA into thinking he was cooperating with the Americans, managed to win the trust of his U.S. handlers. Our double agent was preparing to return to work in the Soviet Union, and his CIA contacts had given him a featherweight, palm-sized radio device so they could contact him inside the USSR. The gadget greatly enhanced the audibility of radio transmissions, so that when our double agent used his receiver on a certain wavelength, he would be able to pick up communications from the CIA—communications that would be all but inaudible to us.

I knew that Andropov was fascinated with spy technology and the intricacies of the double agent game, so I brought him the small, elegant transmitter and reported on our success in running the double agent. We had scored a major coup, because this was the first time the KGB had gotten its hands on this latest piece of CIA hi-tech wizardry. Andropov turned the tiny "toy" over and over in his hands, obviously impressed with the engineering. He then asked the head of domestic Counterintelligence, who was in the room, whether we had anything comparable. The Counterintelligence man hemmed and hawed, finally saying he knew how the device worked and that domestic Counterintelligence was using similar receivers. But the experts at the Equipment Operations Directorate had just informed me that they had never seen anything like this. I told Andropov so, and he seemed distressed.

The chairman then summoned his deputy for scientific and technical research, Nikolai Yemokhonov.

"Have you ever seen anything like that?" Andropov asked Yemokhonov.

"No," Yemokhonov replied.

The research director asked me to describe what it did. When I had done so, Yemokhonov said casually, "It's nothing special. We have similar devices. We could make one like that."

Andropov shot Yemokhonov a look of displeasure and bored in on him.

"But you said you'd never seen one like that."

"Well," replied Yemokhonov, "we don't have devices this size."

"What size have we got?" asked Andropov.

"Ours weighs about a kilogram," said Yemokhonov.

The American device weighed only a few ounces; everyone in the room knew that the bulky two-pound Soviet transmitters and receivers were a great hindrance in clandestine work.

Andropov had had enough.

"We spend so much money on technology and we still can't produce modern equipment!" he exclaimed. "Can we at least reproduce this thing here?"

"No," said Yemokhonov.

"But why?" asked Andropov. "What is it that you don't have?"

"We just don't have the technology," answered Yemokhonov, keeping his cool. "That is the reason our missiles are twice as heavy as the Americans' and why if we wanted to reproduce a Mercedes car we'd have to hand-assemble it."

Andropov's reaction was surprisingly meek, and his recommendation for action utterly futile: "Let's send a memo to the Central Committee and the Council of Ministers. "How far behind we've lagged! We've got to put things right!"

The fact is that I admired Andropov's actions in my own field but was dismayed at his and the KGB's reaction to our domestic situation. Andropov oversaw the KGB at a time of intense persecution of dissidents. Though he occasionally would allow the production of a banned play to go forward, there were many more instances where he toed the conventional line and ruthlessly repressed dissent. During his fifteen years in power, the KGB's reign of "moral terror" was at its height in post-Stalinist Russia: nonconformists and dissidents were tossed into psychiatric hospitals and nearly every citizen felt the presence of the KGB's domestic organs. It was Andropov, after all, who at a 1976 meeting of the KGB Collegium branded the scientist Andrei Sakharov as "domestic enemy number one." It was Andropov who supported the move to strip dissident director Yuri Lyubimov of his citizenship. It also was Andropov who decreed that countless thousands of new documents, from reports on factory clean-ups to issues of *Newsweek* magazine, be declared "top secret." Under Andropov, new secret departments and directorates sprang up in factories and ministries. Tens of thousands of acres of good land were taken out of circulation to enhance border protection. Yachts and sailboats were forbidden to sail in Soviet waters, Soviet citizens were not allowed to meet alone with foreigners, and anyone whose behavior or utterances seemed slightly out of the ordinary was viewed as a potential spy. Everything was done to mold the Soviet masses into a bland, passive army of happy, hardworking comrades.

But then what else could we expect from a man like Andropov, who once said, "No sane individual will oppose a regime that wants so badly to make the lives of its people better."

Despite his reputation inside Soviet society as a man who fiercely fought corruption, the fact was that Andopov went after petty corruption in factories and shops, but shied away from taking on the systemic corruption at the top levels of the Communist Party. When the chief of the KGB in Uzbekistan, at an annual meeting of the KGB top brass, presented evidence that the republic's leaders were extremely corrupt, Andropov did nothing to investigate. Indeed, the only casualty of the revelations was the Uzbek KGB chief himself, who was sacked and transferred to Czechoslovakia as a minor KGB adviser at the Soviet Embassy.

I was, thankfully, far removed from the dirty work of my domestic counterparts. These days I not only recall Andropov's follies and shortcomings. I also remember, with admiration and a half-smile, that in the espionage wars the KGB chairman had a flair for the unconventional.

In 1979, I worked with the USSR's Central Documentary Studio on a film about the CIA entitled *The Quiet Americans*. First and foremost, it was a propaganda movie designed to show the CIA in an unfavorable light. But I also knew our citizens were sophisticated enough not to swallow the old anti-American propaganda, and so I made sure the film painted a fairly realistic portrait of CIA officers as dedicated, intelligent, and dangerous professionals bent on weakening the Soviet Union and stopping the spread of Communism. We used Western footage of CIA Director Stansfield Turner, for example, which showed him working long hours at his desk and playing with his dogs at home. I was proud of the film, and considered it a realistic, tough-minded view of the CIA that would score us points at home and abroad.

We screened *The Quiet Americans* at Lubyanka for a dozen top people of the KGB. As the house lights went up at the end of the film, I expected kudos. Instead, I was bombarded with criticism as one top KGB man after another came up to me and accused me of being soft on the CIA.

"Oleg, what in the hell are you doing showing these bastards as nice-looking guys, playing with dogs and everything?" asked one KGB boss. "Carter looks like the father of his country. Turner looks like a great guy. Russians won't understand this kind of film."

Other KGB big shots wanted to know why the film showed someone unscrewing a telephone and finding a CIA bug inside. Now our citizens would start doing the same thing, the KGB boss said. And yet another asked why we depicted the CIA as a rich organization that paid its agents well. Such information could subject Soviet citizens to unnecessary temptations.

The upshot was that I should go back to the drawing board and redo the film. I was despondent as I walked out of the screening room. Just then, Andropov's personal assistant walked up to me, put his arm on my shoulder, and said quietly, "The chairman saw the film and liked it. Go ahead with it."

We released it several months later, with our favorite journalist, Genrikh Borovik, doing the narration and the Central Documentary Studio getting the credit for what was, in essence, a KGB film. The movie was well received inside the USSR, and even won first place in a documentary film contest for Socialist countries in Berlin. It wasn't Cannes, but by our standards it was quite an honor.

Andropov exhibited similar flexibility in another, fascinating case that involved a Soviet citizen and Christina Onassis, daughter of the Greek tycoon Aristotle Onassis.

The Soviet in question was a man named Sergei Kauzov. He worked in the Soviet merchant marine offices in Paris, and in the late 1970s the KGB's domestic Counter-Intelligence Directorate had gotten wind of the misappropriation of large sums of money by merchant marine officials in Switzerland and France.

All of this mildly interested us in Foreign Counter-Intelligence since Kauzov was a Soviet citizen working abroad who reportedly was involved in a sophisticated economic crime. But what really intrigued us were reports from our stations in Brazil and France that

Kauzov was having an affair with Christina Onassis, whose father had made billions of dollars in the shipping business. We first got wind of the affair through the strangest of channels: a Brazilian society columnist wrote that a Soviet merchant marine official had been seen on Copacabana Beach with Christina. Our Brazil station did a little investigating and found out that the official was Kauzov. Later, officers in our Paris station confirmed that Kauzov, who was already married, was indeed deeply involved with Onassis.

Under a bogus pretext, Kauzov was recalled to Moscow, where an official investigation was begun of his financial dealings in Paris. He was miserable: his marriage was on the rocks, he was separated from his wealthy mistress, and he was under threat of being sent to Soviet prison. My officers in Paris thought highly of Kauzov and said he had always been cooperative with them. It quickly became clear to me that Kauzov could be of far more use to us as a free man in Europe, married to Christina Onassis, than as a Soviet convict wasting away in a Siberian labor camp.

I arranged to meet with Kauzov privately, convinced that if we showed him lenience in the financial scandal, he might become a loyal operative for us in the West. When we met, I told him bluntly that my domestic counterparts wanted to throw him in jail. A short, energetic man, who had lost one of his eyes in a childhood accident, he impressed me with his quick mind and vitality.

"I want you to tell me everything," I said. "If you're honest with me. I'll help you. If you lie to me, you'll never leave the country again."

Kauzov began to tell his story, recounting how he had met Christina in Paris while discussing a shipping deal. He had instantly fallen in love with her.

"You wouldn't have been able to resist her seductiveness either," he told me. "I swear it. She was so sexy I couldn't resist her."

He went on to say that he and Christina planned to wed after he divorced his wife. When our meeting ended, I felt he had not held back and would be a useful operative for the KGB. For his part, Kauzov seemed impressed by our talk and hopeful that he might find a way out of his predicament. He later phoned his mother—we had tapped his telephone—and I saw a transcript of that conversation.

"I simply had to tell this [KGB] guy everything," Kauzov told his mother. "He was so persuasive."

I returned to Yasenovo, telling Kryuchkov and others, "I say let's make the best of it. Why jail the man or dismiss him from his job if he is planning to marry the Onassis woman? If we disrupt this marriage, it will be represented as another human rights violation on the part of the Soviets. Let's capitalize on it. It's better than having another scandal on our hands."

But my domestic counterparts wanted to show Kauzov no leniency. Given the sensitivity of the matter, it was referred to Andropov. He summoned me and Kryuchkov, as well as two top officials from domestic Counterintelligence, and asked us to make our respective cases.

Internal Counterintelligence portrayed Kauzov as a corrupt, lazy, high-liver who would certainly be a witness in an upcoming corruption trial, if not actually a defendant. I agreed that Kauzov appeared to be deeply involved in the merchant marine scandal and would probably be found guilty. But who needed the international brouhaha if we tried to separate Christina Onassis and her Soviet fiancé.

"So," I told Andropov, who was listening attentively, "wouldn't it be better to give Kauzov total freedom of action, help him marry the woman, create a favorable atmosphere, persuade them to stay in Moscow, maybe even give them an apartment? We'll make the Onassis woman, if not exactly a friend, at least a grateful person who will repay our favor when we need something. And Kauzov will be all ours, because he understands perfectly well that he'll have to pay us back some day. He'll always be grateful to the KGB for what we've done for him. We just shouldn't push too hard. Don't forget about the Onassis billions and the fact that if she bears him a child, all those billions will belong to a Soviet citizen. That is if we don't spoil our opportunities now by hasty action."

There was silence in the room. My adversaries were thinking of a rebuttal when Andropov spoke up.

"Kalugin is right," he said, addressing the bosses from domestic Counter-Intelligence. "Your approach is too standard. Enough of trying to grab everyone by the scruff of the neck without thinking about the repercussions. Our country's leadership is doing a lot to defuse international tensions, and we were just about to set those efforts back again. Give the Onassis woman the red-carpet treatment. We will find the newlyweds a decent apartment, and let Chief Directorate One [Foreign Intelligence] look for any good opportunities that could arise from the situation."

I met Kauzov the same day and told him the good news. He was ecstatic and immediately invited me to their wedding. Several months later, the pair was married in Moscow—I was invited but did not attend for fear of being recognized—and after the honeymoon in the West they settled into a spacious, four-bedroom flat in one of the nicest apartment houses in Moscow. Later the couple returned to Paris, but only after Kauzov had agreed to join the Communist Party and pay $150,000 a year in dues. By the early 1980s, Kauzov had handed over more than $500,000 to the Party, a sum that, in itself, justified the leniency he was shown. Christina Onassis apparently remained suspicious that he was working for the KGB, and eventually the couple was divorced. Kauzov received several million dollars in the settlement and now lives in London.

Around the time of the Kauzov affair, Andropov gave his blessing to another unorthodox operation—one that also brought in hundreds of thousands of dollars in hard currency to the Soviet treasury. One of our stations in Europe had been contacted by a Russian émigré who was, of all things, an international thief. He wanted to transfer some money to his brother in the Soviet Union, but had been thwarted. The thief approached one of my officers in Austria with a deal: He would be allowed to transfer some hard currency to his brother and, in exchange, would give the KGB gold bullion, jewels, and other valuables he had stolen. I found the offer unethical, but decided we would accept it if the man would do something for us: burglarize a French firm that was working on a military project in which we were interested. Several weeks later the thief delivered to our embassy in Paris a station wagonload of classified documents from the French military contractor.

Andropov, with reluctance, had sanctioned the arrangement, and from then on the man occasionally delivered loot to us, which we turned over to the State Bank.

Once, after receiving a suitcase full of platinum, pearls, and gold bullion, I called Kryuchkov and suggested we show Andropov the treasure. In addition, my department had just finished compiling a massive directory listing the names of thousands of CIA officers and agents around the world. Andropov was in the hospital then, suffering one of his bouts of kidney disease, and Kryuchkov decided the visit would lift his spirits. The chairman was only receiving important visitors, but he agreed to see us, so we drove out to the Kremlin hospital in Kuntsevo, in western Moscow.

Andropov greeted us in his pajamas, looking frail and sickly. He had a three-room ward to himself, and invited Kryuchkov and me to join him for a cup of tea. After several minutes of small talk, the chairman asked us why we had come and Kryuchkov launched into a short briefing on current affairs. Andropov seemed exhausted and bored. He was eyeing the large suitcase I had brought. Finally the time came for me to open it. I hauled it close to him, popped the latches, and watched as his eyes grew wide. He fingered the French gold bullion, jewels, bracelets of Florentine design exclaiming, "What do you know! I've never seen anything like it in my life!"

He was like a child, his eyes agleam. But after a while he ordered, "You've got to send this to the State Bank, right down to the smallest stone."

Kryuchkov argued that Foreign Intelligence should be allowed to keep some of the money to bolster its budget, but Andropov refused.

"You keep tempting me to try to make money for the organization on the side," Andropov said with a sigh. "But I can't, don't you see? I can't. Domestic Counterintelligence has already talked me into something like this, but I'm not sure I was right to agree. Let's put it off for a while. You've got to hand in the treasure."

I then showed Andropov the handbook of CIA agents we had just compiled. He seemed genuinely delighted with that as well, humorously deflecting my half-joking suggestion that we publish the top-secret document.

Leaving Kuntsevo that night, I felt gratified that I had cheered up my ailing mentor, a man who—despite all his shortcomings—I continued to admire and respect. To this day, I vividly remember the Soviet Union's top spy, a look of delight spreading across his face as he dipped his hand in the treasure chest we had carted to his sick bed. It was one of the last pleasant memories I had of Andropov: Just a few months later, the conflict arose that would break my career in the KGB.

After two decades, Cook—the first spy with whom I was ever involved—came back into my life.

It was 1978. I received a call one day from Yevgeni Primakov, my longtime friend and top official at the Institute of Oriental Studies in Moscow. (He would later go on to become chief of Russian Intelligence under Boris Yeltsin.) Primakov, who had close contacts with the KGB, had heard that a leading scholar at the Institute of World Economics—a man who had once lived in America but had been forced to flee following a spy scandal—was being investigated by Soviet authorities. I was wondering why Primakov was telling me all this and asked him the name of the man in trouble. Primakov gave me the Russian name, and I froze: it was Cook.

I had not seen Cook in twenty years, not since the day I met him and his wife in suburban New Jersey and the Thiokol scientist handed me a sample of the United States' top-secret rocket fuel. Cook also gave me and a colleague detailed plans of Thiokol's work on rocket fuel and rocket propulsion. It was an enormous coup for me then. I had met Cook and his Chinese-born wife, Selena, totally by chance while working as a host at the exhibition on Soviet achievements. With that freak encounter, I launched my KGB career with a flourish.

After finishing my year at Columbia and returning to the USSR, I lost touch with Cook. I knew that in 1965, when the KGB officer Yuri Nosenko defected, Cook was threatened with exposure and had to flee the United States. In the 1970s, I heard from colleagues that Cook was working at a chemical plant in Moscow and that he wasn't disguising his growing disillusionment with Soviet life. I never made any attempt to contact him, for it was considered improper to get in touch with former Intelligence assets. From time to time I thought fondly of Cook, but he had been out of my life for so long—and so much had happened in the ensuing years—that he was little more than a distant memory.

Then came the call from Primakov.

From his sources in the KGB and from Donald Maclean, now living in Moscow, Primakov had heard that Cook was under investigation for illegal hard currency transactions and for speculating in art treasures. It seemed utterly inconceivable to me that such a devoted Communist, such a true believer in the Soviet system, was about to be charged with crimes usually committed by members of our country's underworld.

"Please talk to your people right away and see what's going on," Primakov urged. "He's highly valued at the Institute as a very bright man. He's a productive scientist, with an unorthodox way of looking at things. You've got to try to help him."

I placed a call right away to the Moscow office of the KGB, which was conducting the investigation into Cook's alleged wrongdoing. The Moscow branch was headed by General Viktor Alidin, a ruthless and widely reviled officer who was extremely close to Brezhnev.

After a minute or so I was put through to one of Alidin's deputies.

"I understand you're conducting an investigation of Cook and I'd like to know what he's accused of doing," I said. "I know that man. What has he done wrong?"

A very somber and threatening voice on the other end of the line replied, "Mr. Kalugin, we do not recommend that you interfere with this affair. Your directorate has nothing to do with this."

I was angry, but also scared. Viktor Alidin was known as one of the biggest sons-of-bitches in all the KGB. He was a tough Communist Party *apparatchik* who had risen through the ranks in Ukraine and long known Leonid Brezhnev. Alidin was so close to the Soviet leader and so headstrong that he was even known to challenge Andropov's authority. I was torn: I wanted to help my old asset, Cook, but I sensed it would be best for my career to steer clear of the affair. I went to see my colleague Boris Ivanov, a former New York station chief and now deputy chief of Intelligence, who knew the Cook case well and had praised me for my involvement in it.

"Do you know what's going on at the Moscow branch?" I asked.

Ivanov told me what had already been rumored—that Cook had been caught red-handed dealing in Soviet art.

"What do you think of Cook?" Ivanov aked.

"The same as I did when I first met him," I replied. "I trust him."

"You never know," Ivanov said. "He may have changed. I would leave it at that."

I decided to take Ivanov's advice. Who knew what had happened to Cook in the years since I had seen him, and if he had indeed broken the law, he deserved to be punished. So I tried to put Cook out of my mind, and for months heard nothing more about him.

Then, early in 1979, I was contacted by Donald Maclean, Cook's associate at the Institute of World Economics. Cook had at last been arrrested and convicted, and had been shipped off to prison in Siberia for eight years. Maclean was convinced he had been framed, saying, "What is this nonsense about currency speculation? He has served your country well. He even had to flee the United States. You must do something."

Maclean also gave me a letter from Cook's wife, Selena. Reading the correspondence, it became clear what the domestic secret police had done to the scientist.

"During an interrogation at Lefortovo Prison, Anatoly [Cook] was told that he wouldn't even last a month at the camp where they were sending him," Selena wrote. "I have known for some time that

Anatoly was suspected of being an American spy. I don't think I should keep tactfully quiet about it, because the suspicions are groundless. Anatoly had been asked a lot of questions about our original meeting with you in New York. They couldn't believe it had been just a chance meeting. They wanted to know how we had 'found' you. . . ."

I felt sick. The crime for which Cook had been jailed was a sham, and the scientist's entire ordeal came about because he was believed to be a spy—a suspicion I knew was absolutely groundless. I clearly had to do something; after all it was because of our chance meeting two decades before that Cook and his wife had gotten involved with the KGB.

As I was preparing to talk to Kryuchkov and Andropov, Maclean wrote a letter to Kryuchkov, urging the Intelligence chief to reopen the Cook case. Under pressure from the two of us, Andropov agreed to meet with me to discuss the matter. It was highly unusual for the KGB chairman—or anyone in the organization—to question the outcome of a case that was essentially closed, and Andropov moved cautiously. I said I was sure the espionage suspicions were false and the currency charges trumped up, and urged Andropov to pardon Cook. The chairman instructed me to read the case history, all nine volumes of it, and report back to him.

As I plowed through the massive file—the reports from informers, the KGB field reports on Cook's conduct, the description of the criminal case against him—it became clear what had happened. It was a sordid tale.

After Cook arrived in the Soviet Union and had been debriefed for more than a year, he was assigned to work as a scientist in a major Moscow chemical plant affiliated with the military-industrial complex. The scientist, who had long held an idealistic view of life under Communism, evidently was shocked by the degradation and fear that characterized Soviet life. Confident that Soviet authorities would want to hear his criticism of our Communist experiment, the naive Cook began to speak out about the problems he saw around him. He also espoused a brand of radical pro–Mao Zedong Marxism—this at a time when Soviet-Chinese relations were hostile. Cook was, of course, surrounded by informers, and soon his KGB dossier began to grow thicker. He was sharply critical of the way the chemical plant was run, and became such a nuisance to the factory directors that they succeeded in forcing out Cook. He then was given a job at the Institute of World Economics.

His criticism of the system continued there, and eventually the

Moscow branch of the KGB decided it could no longer ignore this troublemaker. The uninitiated should understand that, for a domestic KGB hack such as Alidin, finding a spy was a major coup. So Alidin & Company began investigating Cook for espionage. Reading the file, it was obvious that they thought Cook was a CIA double agent who had approached me in New York, strung us along all these years, and was now feeding information to his spymasters in Washington. And as I pored through the pages of the Cook dossier, I saw that KGB case officers also were asking quite a few questions about Cook's relationship with me. And then it dawned on me: The idiots suspected that I was a CIA agent! Perhaps Cook and I were a team, and Cook had been chosen to make me look good at such a young age. After all, I had become head of Foreign Counterintelligence at age thirty-eight and got promoted to general at forty. I had no highly placed relatives or connections. How else could I have risen so fast if not with the help of Cook and the CIA? Later, when I finally got the chance to speak with Cook, he told me that his interrogators grilled him about our relationship. He said they told him, "We know you were both recruited by the CIA. Tell us the truth and we will let you go home."

Alidin's men, however, could not produce any hard evidence against Cook. They once even tried to set him up, sending a KGB agent posing as a Western intelligence officer to meet him. "Listen," the KGB agent told Cook, "you're not doing your job according to our agreement. Why did you break off our relationship? What's wrong? Have you forgotten our agreement?"

When Cook didn't report this conversation to the KGB, Alidin and his subordinates became even more suspicious. Still, all their surveillance, all their informers, all their wiretaps turned up no evidence that Cook was a spy or had contact with anyone from the West. So Alidin decided to do something that was common practice with the goons from the domestic secret police. Unable to nail him for one crime, Alidin decided to set Cook up for another. The KGB knew that Cook was short of the money he needed to buy a country house, so they sent a KGB officer, posing as an Armenian art dealer and currency speculator, to meet Cook. The scientist came to trust the Armenian and decided to sell him a Kandinsky painting for dollars, then trade the money into rubles at the black-market rate. It was a foolish move on Cook's part, and no sooner had the money changed hands than Cook was arrested. The evidence against him was overwhelming—albeit concocted.

After making my way through the file, I once again met with

Andropov and told him the truth: The entire case against Cook had been fabricated simply because Alidin couldn't prove the wild notion that Cook was an American spy. As I spoke with the KGB chairman, I realized I was becoming emotionally involved and was being pulled deeper into conflict with some of the top men in the KGB.

"Cook can't possibly be a spy," I told Andropov in his third-floor office at Lubyanka. "Why would a spy break the law just to get a measly fifteen thousand rubles? The CIA would have given him any amount of money. It's just bad tradecraft to break laws. It's impossible."

Andropov looked exasperated.

"Why are you stirring up all this dirt?" he asked me. "Do you know Alidin has a special interest in this case? . . . All right, bring Cook over from the prison camp and interrogate him yourself. See if you can make him confess that he was a spy."

"It makes no sense," I retorted. "He wasn't a spy."

"All right," Andropov said again. "But bring him back."

In the summer of 1979, Cook was flown to Moscow from his prison camp in Siberia. I wanted to get to the bottom of the matter, and Kryuchkov and Andropov wanted a confession from Cook so the case could finally be closed. Though I felt uneasy doing it, I strapped a small recording device under my suit jacket as I prepared for my first meeting with Cook in twenty years. Driving to Moscow's Lefortovo Prison, where countless thousands had been tortured in the Stalin years, my stomach was churning. Hovering over me was a sense of unease, a feeling that this entire affair would lead to no good. Nevertheless, I felt compelled to move ahead and see the Cook case through to the end.

Lefortovo officials assigned me to an interrogation room in the hulking stone prison. Though I didn't suspect it then—what a fool I was—the KGB was both recording and filming my meeting with Cook. I knew from the case file that there had been some suspicions about me, yet I figured that no one would take such doubts seriously. In fact, in the minds of some men like Alidin, I was as much a suspect as Cook.

Cook was led in, and he looked at me with bewilderment. It was clear he didn't recognize me. He looked much the same—a little grayer, a bit more drawn. He was still the same tall, broad-shoul-dered, handsome man I had met in 1959, a robust southern Russian type, with Cossack blood in his veins. His graying hair was tousled and his blue-gray eyes looked at me with suspicion. His demeanor was still very much that of a scientist whose mind was focused on far-away thoughts. I was standing, and after a few seconds I said, "Anatoly . . ."

And then it came to him.

"Oleg?" he nearly shouted, his eyes lighting up. "Oleg, is it really you!"

He came toward me, almost as if to embrace me, and I waved him off with a small gesture. I motioned for him to take a seat and, in a rather official manner, said, "Keep quiet. Please sit down. I'm glad to see you, but I'd rather see you under different circumstances, as a free man."

A look of puzzlement remained on Cook's face as I continued.

"Why did you have to commit this crime?" I asked, acutely aware of the tape recorder inside my jacket and having little idea where our interrogation was heading. "You were always an honest man, a defender of Socialist values. Why did you break the law? How could you get mixed up with such criminals—you who always defended such high ideals, who dreamed about a bright future, who denounced a society in which everything could be bought and sold, you who brought some of its worst features into your life? We trusted you so. We brought you home. We gave you every chance to be a loyal citizen."

"You don't have to say any more," Cook replied. "I understand everything. Yes, I did break the law, but I needed the money. My wife had a car accident and was very ill and she needed the country air. And I had no money to buy a *dacha*—my salary and pension weren't bad, but it wasn't enough. But I had some paintings from my collection in the United States that I brought over with me and I had some hard currency I wanted to trade in. Don't forget, Oleg, that I lived most of my life in the United States, in a free economy, where such things aren't considered a criminal offense. You must understand—it was both the need for money and certain habits which I acquired in my earlier years in America."

He also said he was convinced that the Moscow KGB set up the traffic accident with his wife, as well as several near accidents he himself had experienced. But I cut him off, saying, "Come on, drop that, will you!"

I knew, however, that the Moscow branch was entirely capable of such dirty tricks.

"But the real reason I'm here isn't the currency violations," Cook went on. "That was just an excuse. They accused me of spying. They even wanted to drag you in, and kept asking about how we met and on whose initiative.''

Though I knew Cook was no spy, I resolved to pursue Andropov's orders to persuade the scientist to confess to espionage.

"Anatoly," I said, this time playing the role of the good cop. "Let's go over you story from the beginning. Did you approach me that time in New York by yourself or on somebody's orders?"

"But Oleg, don't you remember?" he replied. "We met quite by chance. I saw you at the exhibition and then I bumped into you on the street."

"Well, some people feel that was a set-up and that you didn't approach me of your own accord but at the request of the American special services."

"Oh, Oleg, what are you talking about?" said Cook, looking increasingly puzzled. "By the way, this idea of my being associated with the CIA was thrown at me many times during the investigation, when I was here in Lefortovo. They also asked about you and said that maybe *you* were part of the CIA operation."

I was more convinced than ever of Cook's innocence but, as I had been ordered by Andropov to press the point, I decided to become more aggressive.

"Listen, you've already been sentenced to eight years in jail," I said in a friendly yet resolute voice. "You will serve out that sentence to the last day unless you help us. We know you are a spy. Why don't you confess and they might cut your term? Perhaps it's time to admit you were a spy, Anatoly? As it is, you will sit in jail for the full eight years."

I wasn't prepared for the reaction that followed. His eyes flashed with anger and he spat out a string of curses.

"The hell with you and the KGB!" Cook screamed. "Damn that very hour when I met you and your dirty gang of spies! You are all fools, you KGB bastards! You're nothing but a gang of morons. I don't want to talk to you any more. Do you want me to hang myself to prove I am not a spy!"

Cook broke off his diatribe abruptly and began to cry. I was near tears myself. It was, I think, the most dramatic moment in my life. I, too, was now hounding this man, the person who had begun my career. I saw with appalling clarity how the organization to which I had devoted my life could crush a person.

I tried to calm Cook down, but he was inconsolable: he felt he had lost me, his last hope of attaining freedom.

"Calm down," I implored. "Don't get hysterical. I asked you as a friend, not as a KGB official. I'm offering you my help as a friend if you confess."

He sat there silent, his hands covering his face.

"You must realize that there are different kinds of people in the KGB," I continued. "I trust you, but the system is against you."

"I'd rather starve to death in jail than tell you I'm a spy," said Cook. Then he lapsed into silence.

There was no use going any further. I felt like a total cad, and as Cook was recovering from his outburst I tried to make small talk.

"Tell me how you're doing in prison."

"We sew clothes for the army. It keeps me busy."

"Are you treated well?"

"Just like everyone else."

"Have you been allowed to see your wife?" I asked.

"Just once," he said. "In Moscow."

"Look, Anatoly," I said. "I will report this conversation to Chairman Andropov because he has taken a personal interest in your case. I will do my best to help you get out. But you have to understand that I am not all-powerful. Perhaps I can get you released early. I just don't know."

Cook was silent, and I walked out of the interrogation room.

A few days later I took the transcript of our recorded conversation to Kryuchkov. He greeted me with his customary forced half-smile. The Intelligence chief seemed concerned, of all things, about the stream of profanity Cook directed at the KGB.

"Strike this out," Kryuchkov ordered.

"Why should I?" I replied. "Those were his exact words."

"But are we going to show this to Andropov?" Kryuchkov asked.

"Of course," I replied. "Why not?"

"Okay, then," Kryuchkov said. "Leave it as it is."

Kryuchkov, whose demeanor was decidedly cool, asked me several questions about my meetings with Cook in America. Then he dismissed me.

Two days later, after showing the transcript to Andropov, Kryuchkov called me in for another talk.

"Listen, Andropov says you should meet with Cook again," said Kryuchkov. "Something is wrong."

I was stunned. Couldn't these fools see that the man was telling the truth, that pressing him again was fruitless?

"Don't put me in a silly position," I said, my anger rising. "It's absolutely useless. He's not a spy."

"Yes, I believe you," said Kryuchkov with his trademark duplicity. "But you must understand these people are putting pressure on Andropov and me. They want you to try again."

"Look," I said. "I saw this man of fifty-five sitting right in front of me crying as he denied the allegations. It makes no sense to go back to him. You put me in an absurd position. Not only do I look like a fool in my own eyes, but I look like a fool to Cook as well."

"It's Andropov's order," Kryuchkov said curtly. "Off you go."

Soon afterwards, I met with Cook for a second time in Lefortovo.

"Listen, my bosses are not satisfied with your answers," I told Cook, who sat opposite me, the very picture of dejection. "They have very strong evidence that you are a spy."

"I told you I have nothing to add and I don't want to talk about it any more," Cook replied. "I will serve out my sentence and to hell with you. Go away."

"I'm sorry, friend, that we couldn't find common ground for conversation," I told him.

"I will try to convince my bosses that they are wrong. I hope you understand my position."

"Yes, I understand," said Cook, and then he fell silent.

I stood up to say goodbye. Our meeting had lasted less than five minutes. Driving away from Lefortovo, I told myself that I was right to raise my voice in defense of a victim of the system. But I also knew that our system was unforgiving of those who dared challenge its judgments.

Cook was sent back to Siberia. And on September 6, 1979—my forty-fifth birthday—Kryuchkov summoned me to a meeting attended by much of the top brass of the KGB. The meeting was held in Lubyanka, in the enormous, high-ceilinged office of Vasily Lezhepyokov, the deputy KGB chief for Personnel. I walked into the room with a sense of dread, and what I saw didn't put me at ease. About ten top KGB officials—Alidin, Internal Counterintelligence Chief Grigory Grigorenko, Investigations Chief Alexander Volkov, Kryuchkov, and others—sat around a long conference table, under a portrait of Lenin, awaiting my arrival. It was clear the meeting—inquisition might be a better term—had been called to deal with my "interference" in the Cook case.

Lezhepyokov, who was chairing the meeting, began.

"Oleg, what possessed you to get involved in the Cook case and start defending this man?" he asked. "Don't you know the sentence was just? Don't you know the man is a suspected spy? What motivated you to get involved in this affair?"

"Purely humane reasons," I responded, feeling as if I were speaking from a witness chair. "I'm responsible for him as a human being. It was at my instigation that he gave up everything he had in the United States—his career, material well-being, peace. I am the one who persuaded him to work for Soviet Intelligence. He did excellent work for us, and there are documents which prove this fact."

Lezhepyokov asked me to explain how we had met and to describe our relationship, which I did.

"Everyone knows the story," I said. "We met quite by accident after the exhibition in New York."

"But doesn't it seem to you that he's a CIA plant?" asked Lezhepyokov.

"No it doesn't and it never has," I responded. "After talking to him in Lefortovo, I am completely convinced that he was never a spy. All of this is a concoction of Comrade Alidin. Cook was arrested because he was framed by Alidin. He has been framed and jailed on trumped-up charges because you couldn't prove anything. And I don't have the right to keep silent about it."

Alidin could no longer remain quiet. He sat there like a bulldog, a squat man with fat, drooping cheeks, a low forehead, and close-cropped hair. He was fairly sputtering as he began his attack on me.

"Listen, young man," he burst out, "you have no idea what you're talking about! You don't know the whole case! This man was under investigation for years. He's anti-Soviet. He would betray the Motherland and you're defending him! Cook is a spy!"

"I know all about the case—I've read through all eight volumes of that crap," I shot back. "I know you set him up and I know he was no spy, for the simple reason that spies don't engage in hard currency dealings. They are taken care of by the CIA for life. You don't understand this simple logic."

Alidin and I went back and forth for several minutes, neither man pretending to conceal his hatred for the other. I was bold and outspoken because I felt my cause was right and because I believed—mistakenly, as it turned out—that Andropov was behind me. Finally, Lezhepyokov cut us both off.

"Comrade Grigorenko, what do you think?" asked Lezhepyokov.

"I doubt that he was a spy," said Grigorenko. "I don't think we have enough evidence to state that he was a spy. But I'm not familiar with the details of the case."

Lezhepyokov then asked the opinion of the chief investigator in the case, Lieutenant General Volkov.

"This case was thoroughly investigated," said Volkov. "I don't know about his spying. But he unquestionably violated currency regulations and he was caught. There's no doubt of his guilt."

I once again made the case for Cook's innocence, but Lezhepyokov soon stopped the debate.

"Oleg Danilovich, we suggest that you let go of this case altogether," he said. "Maybe we'll consider it again someday. Maybe we'll have his term reduced to two or three years instead of eight. I think we'll do what you want done, but let him stay in prison for another couple of years."

"That's up to you," I said, "but I still maintain that this man was put in prison unjustly."

Lezhepyokov nodded. Alidin fumed. Then the tone in Lezhepyokov's voice softened as he said, "We know that it's your birthday today and we know that you're about to set off on a long holiday. We all congratulate you on your birthday and wish you a good trip to the Crimea. We envy you going there."

As I prepared to walk out, all the men around the table stood up and wished me happy birthday—with the exception of Alidin. Heading home, I was whipsawed by emotion. I thought I had won, and Lezhepyokov had essentially said he agreed with my position. But my stomach was knotted with anxiety. I had openly challenged the decision of the KGB leadership, and I knew that was a rare—and dangerous—step. Still, I remembered the warm birthday greetings I had received from the men at the top of the KGB. What I didn't see, in all my naivete, was that their warm felicitations had been the kiss of death. I didn't yet know it, but my career in the espionage business was over.

I went away for forty-five days to the Crimea and Ukraine, for every officer with more than twenty-five years' service in the KGB received long vacations. A day after my run-in at Lubyanka, I was already swimming in my beloved Black Sea, and the longer I rested on those warm shores the more convinced I became that all would turn out well. After all, what had I done except fight for the rights of a man who been a productive spy for our country? The only jarring note came when I took a short trip to the Ukrainian capital of Kiev to meet some old KGB friends there. One of them said to me, "Oleg, is everything all right at home?"

"Why, yes. Why do you ask?"

"There have been some rumors," he said.

"What kind of rumors?" I asked.

"Well, rumors that you're being transferred somewhere."

I tried to dismiss such talk as gossip, but nevertheless felt unsettled as I resumed what was left of my vacation.

I returned to work in Moscow on November 11. Almost immediately I was summoned by Kryuchkov, who told me that I was scheduled to meet with Lezhepyokov in the personnel office. My heart was beating furiously as I entered Lezhepyokov's office, Kryuchkov at my side.

"We are offering you the post of first deputy chief of the Leningrad KGB," Lezhepyokov said dryly. "You're from Leningrad, you know the local Intelligence community. The staff there is large, and there are plenty of problems, so you won't be bored."

I was stunned, fearful this was a devastating demotion, but hoping that somehow Andropov wouldn't allow my career to be sidetracked.

"But why Leningrad?" I asked. "What for?"

"You'll be first deputy chief of the branch," Lezhepyokov responded, warming to his hard sell. "We must strengthen the Leningrad branch. It's chief is an old man and he'll have to be replaced soon."

"Okay, but why should I go to Leningrad?" I protested again. "I could become first deputy chief right here in Moscow. Why transfer me?"

"Don't forget that the Leningrad KGB branch is far more important than the Moscow regional branch," Lezhepyokov said. "In Moscow, headquarters covers all the major targets and Moscow branch gets left with all the little stuff."

He was right about that, but still I could not believe that I was being moved out of Intelligence—a field in which I had distinguished myself for two decades.

"My field is Intelligence," I said. "I don't see any reason for transferring me to the domestic side."

"Come on, a first deputy chief in Leningrad will cover everything—Intelligence and Counterintelligence," said Lezhepyokov. "Every line will be under your command. We're not taking you away from Intelligence permanently. But it would do you good to get some experience on the domestic front. You can keep your Moscow apartment and you will have an excellent position in Leningrad. Besides, your salary will be fifteen rubles higher."

"Who wants to be transferred to Leningrad for a mere fifteen rubles?" I said. "Frankly, I guess I've been getting a little fed up with Intelligence work. I guess I'm willing to be transferred. But why not Moscow?"

I looked angrily at Kryuchkov, for I felt he had betrayed me.

His eyes were fixed on the floor. Finally, in a reference to my mild criticism, he said, "Don't spit into the well. You might want to drink from it later."

"Can I have a day or two to think it over?" I asked Lezhepyokov.

"Of course, talk to your wife, no problem," he responded.

On the way out, Kryuchkov put his arm around me and said in a friendly manner, "Don't worry, Oleg. Everything will be all right. Everything will be settled. You just have to agree for now. Take it easy. It's all right."

Somehow, those kind words and gestures from Kryuchkov did not put me at ease.

As I headed home that night, I felt crushed. I believed, and numerous colleagues agreed, that I was next in line to become chief of Intelligence. And now I was being posted to a domestic KGB office to become someone's deputy. I would be harassing my compatriots instead of going up against the CIA. I called several friends, and they put a positive spin on the development. After all, they said, the Leningrad KGB chief was due to retire soon. I would almost surely replace him, and then I would have a seat on the KGB Collegium since the Leningrad director was guaranteed a place on the agency's ruling body.

"Come on, Oleg," one friend said. "You'll get domestic experience. You'll be a member of the Collegium and then you'll come back as chairman of the KGB."

Sometimes our ability for self-delusion knows no bounds, especially when our career is at stake. I began to think that perhaps it wasn't such a bad thing. But all night I was wracked by doubts, turning over and over in my mind what had just happened. Was it all because of Cook? Was it my run-in with deputy chairman Tsinyov over the UNESCO ambassador? Was it my tense relations with Kryuchkov?

I didn't sleep at all that night, and when I walked into Kryuchkov's office the following morning the Intelligence chief greeted me with a wry smile.

"Well, how did you sleep?"

"I didn't sleep at all," I responded.

"I knew you wouldn't," he said. "This is very difficult to swallow."

It seemed to me he could barely contain his glee, and I felt that if he hadn't engineered my transfer outright, he had done nothing to stop it.

"I still don't understand what happened," I said.

"Oleg," Kryuchkov replied, "you need some Counterintelligence experience inside the country. It will help you later."

"But I'm forty-six now," I said. "I'm not that young."

"You still need it," Kryuchkov insisted. "This move will help your career."

"It's up to Andropov," I answered. "If he decides I should go, I'll have to obey him. I will have no choice."

"Take it easy," asid Kryuchkov. "I promise you that in two or three years you'll be back in Intelligence. You need this experience for your professional growth."

He didn't mean a word he said, but at the time I didn't want to believe it.

Andropov approved my transfer, and for the remainder of November and December I worked with my successor on a smooth transition. I gradually came to accept my fate, and even rationalized that perhaps I was being given a domestic assignment to round out my résumé and that I would one day return to Intelligence.

On January 2, 1980, I was scheduled to take the night train—the famous *Red Arrow*—from Moscow to Leningrad. Andropov had invited me to say farewell to him that afternoon in his office in Lubyanka. I arrived a few minutes early, and waited in his antechamber. It was a typical winter evening in Moscow. By four o'clock it was already dark, the city enveloped in a cold gloom. Outside, on Dzerzhinsky Square, comrades wearing dark coats and black felt winter boots—shuffled in and out of the crowded, steamy stores. Waiting for Andropov on the third floor of Lubyanka, I listened to the distant whoosh of cars and buses on the slush-covered square. I felt depressed and adrift, my mood perfectly matching the melancholy scene on the streets below.

I entered Andropov's office promptly at four. It looked as it always did—the mahogony paneling, the oblong table covered in green felt, the bank of telephones linking the chairman to the Soviet leadership, the portraits of Lenin and Dzerzhinsky.

The chairman stood up, offered me a seat and a smile, and said, "Well, you've suffered enough. Your troubles are over now."

"What do you mean?" I replied. "I didn't suffer. I was happy with my job."

"Oh, I didn't mean your job," he replied. "I meant this whole Cook affair. What on earth possessed you to defend a spy? What could you possibly hope to gain by it?"

I was taken aback. So it was, after all, the Cook affair that was behind my transfer—not some desire of Andropov's to round out my résumé.

"The man was unjustly convicted," I said. "I ask you, what sort of spy is it that is so short of cash that he has to resort to dealing with black marketeers? The CIA would have taken care of him so that he never would have had to risk his neck for peanuts. I read all the files in the case and it was clearly a frame-up by Alidin and his investigators."

"All right, all right," said Andropov. "Let's not dredge all this up again. Don't remind me of all this. You have stirred up too much dust here at headquarters. I just want you to go away until things settle down. You go to Leningrad and when things calm down, you'll be back. I promise you. It will take a year or so. No longer than that. You'll be back soon."

His manner was so friendly, so soothing, that I believed him. And indeed, one of Andropov's aides later told me that the chairman was one of my greatest fans, but that the pressure from Alidin, Tsinyov, and others to remove me from the capital had been so great that he couldn't resist.

"Why did you have to cross this man Alidin?" Andropov asked.

"I had to do it," I replied. "It was my case."

"Okay, okay," he said. "Let's close the matter. I promise you'll be back soon. You won't lose Moscow . . . By the way, do you know the Leningrad branch chief, Nozyrev?"

"I only dealt with him once when he helped my mother-in-law get into a hospital," I replied.

"Mother-in-law, eh?" Andropov said, grinning. "He's a prickly customer. You won't find him too easy at first. He's a difficult man."

"I have a knack for dealing with difficult people," I said.

"Don't push him around," cautioned Andropov. "Keep a low profile. Don't forget he's from the old school. But don't worry—everything will work out in the end."

At that point, our conversation was interrupted when a telephone rang on his desk. It was Boris Ivanov, the KGB's special representative in Kabul, reporting on the status of the invasion of Afghanistan, which had begun just three days before. Ivanov said all was quiet and that the Soviet puppet Babrak Karmal was in control, though he had not yet appeared on Afghan TV.

"Boris Semyonovich," Andropov shouted into the telephone line, addressing Ivanov by his patronymic. "Tell Karmal to go on television right away with a statement to the nation. Three days have passed and there's been no word from him. It's absolutely essential for him to show himself to the people and announce his program. Tell him to quit stalling and give him any help he needs! If need be, prepare the speech for him and let him read it. He's got to show his face to the people."

(Karmal followed Andropov's orders and soon appeared on TV.)

The chairman flung down the receiver and turned back to me, looking tired. There was silence for a few seconds, then I said, "I'm still not clear on why I have to go to Leningrad. Am I distrusted here?"

"What do you mean 'distrusted'?" he answered. "We have appointed you first deputy, which is hardly a downgrading. You're going to Leningrad, not some obscure provincial hole! You've got everything in Leningrad—Intelligence, Counterintelligence, border troops. It's a proper committee there. Much larger than the republican ones."

We talked briefly about my wife and whether she'd be a accompanying me there. She wouldn't. Then my audience was at an end. We shook hands warmly, and the chairman wished me good luck. I walked out in far better spirits than I had entered. I was, in fact, elated. Hadn't the chairman just promised he would look after me and have me back in Moscow in a year or two?

As it turned out, our meeting on that cold January evening would be my last with the KGB chairman. Nearly three years later he would become the leader of the Soviet Union following Brezhnev's death. Eighteen months after that, Andropov himself was dead. He may indeed have wanted to help me, for I was undeniably one of his protégés. But I had made too many waves in Moscow and, despite his admiration for me, Andropov wasn't about to take on Alidin and other Brezhnev associates just to salvage my career. Though it took me a while to accept it, my career in the KGB would never get back on track. I had broken the rules of the game, and it would prove to be fatal.

That night, as I sat with my wife and waited to head to the Leningrad station for the midnight train, I turned the events of the last few months over in my mind. I had been a loyal and successful professional, and until the Cook affair my career had been on a steadily upward curve. It would have been safer to ignore his predicament, to have told myself, "He did a good job once. But he's violated the law and to hell with him now."

But I felt personally responsible for Cook, felt that I was the one who had put him in this situation. A man never knows his fate; had I kept silent about Cook, I might have risen even higher in the KGB. But I acted according to my conscience, and I can live with myself far more easily today because I did not let my ambition get in the way of the right choice in the Cook case.

Waiting that evening to go to Leningrad, I felt there had been a fundamental shift in my outlook on life as a result of Cook. The metamorphosis began with the warning from the Moscow KGB to stay away from the case—a warning that filled me with premonitions. That January night, it was clear I had experienced a break with the KGB, but the extent of the rift was uncertain and I held out hope that my collision with the organization could be set straight. I now realize that the Cook affair was a watershed. I had felt growing disillusionment with the Soviet system after the ouster of Khrushchev in 1964, after the Czech invasion in 1968, and after watching the creeping senility of our leaders in the 1970s. But I was still a believer in the system, thinking all we needed to do was replace the bad apples like Kryuchkov and Alidin and Brezhnev and everything would be better.

In Leningrad, as the effects of the Cook case set in and as my colleagues gradually revealed to me the extent to which I was suspected of being a CIA agent, my views changed radically. It was one thing to sit back and dissect the problems of our system. It was quite another to experience firsthand the cruelty and injustice of our totalitarian state. It took my own personal collision with the KGB hierarchy—and the subsequent derailing of my career—to make me see the light. Before, all the suffering and injustice of our system had been an abstract thing to me. I didn't really *understand* until I, too, had suffered at the hands of the Soviet system. That may not be admirable, but in my case it was the truth.

I saw Cook once more. Nine years later—after he had served his full eight-year term, after Gorbachev and *perestroika,* after I was utterly disillusioned with the KGB—I spotted Cook in 1989 on a Moscow street. We passed one another, and at first I didn't stop. Then I realized it was Cook and ran after him.

"Anatoly!" I cried.

He turned around and recognized me instantly.

"Oleg, hello." Cook said, managing a smile. "I hear you've had troubles because of me."

"Yes," I replied. "But that was of my own doing."

I asked him how things had been in camp and replied, "Bad. They released me a year ago."

"Can we do anything?" I asked. "Can we team up and tell your story? We could fight back, I'm sure."

"No, Oleg," said Cook. "I've had enough. I don't want to be reminded of it. I don't want to get involved in anything any more. I just got my pension back and I don't want them to take it away again."

I never saw Cook again, though the last I heard he was alive and still in Moscow. But I am getting ahead of my story.

The *Red Arrow* left that January 2, 1980, at 11:55 P.M. About fifteen colleagues and relatives came to see me off in the 10-degree weather. As always, the Leningrad Station teemed with people. The long, green trains were lined up on several platforms, the pungent smoke from their coal fires drifting across the tracks. Bundled-up figures careened into one another, some dragging suitcases over the ice. My colleagues assured me that I was being sent to Leningrad to replace the ailing chief there and that I would be back in Moscow soon in an even higher position. I no longer knew what to believe, and at that point was merely anxious to open a new chapter in my life.

I hugged my colleagues, embraced Ludmilla, and hopped on the train just before it lurched out of the station. As we bumped northward, my mind raced. Some colleagues had said I was leaving Moscow because Kryuchkov and others were upset over recent KGB defections; others said I had gotten into trouble after speaking at the KGB Higher School and implicitly criticizing Foreign Minister Andrei Gromyko for the defection of his top aide, Arkady Shevchenko. Still others, like those who had seen me off at the station, said my star was still ascendant.

I pondered the successes in my seven years as head of Foreign Counterintelligence: We had recruited some top U.S. spies. Our spy network had grown threefold and we had penetrated fifty foreign Intelligence and Counter-Intelligence services. We had prevented dozens of Soviets from defecting, had gotten our hands on thousands of secret documents, and broken the codes of the Intelligence services of several countries. No, we had done an admirable job, and held our own in the Cold War spy battle. I was convinced that I was not heading to Leningrad on the *Red Arrow* because of the poor performance of my directorate.

I tossed and turned, the scenes from the Cook affair running over and over again in my mind.

It was still dark when we rolled through the outskirts of Leningrad around 8:00 A.M. Peter the Great's city was blanketed in a frigid mist, and I sat at the window of my stuffy compartment, my eyes red with fatigue, watching the shadows of my hometown emerge. I didn't fully comprehend it at the time, but I was heading into exile. I would spend seven years in Leningrad, and while there I had a front-row seat from which to watch the ever-quickening decay of the old Soviet system. In Leningrad, my doubts about my government finally exploded in a fit of disillusionment.

And just about that time, a man named Gorbachev came along, and I resolved that the path to our country's salvation lay with him.

EIGHT

Exile

After more than two decades in the rarefied world of espionage, after years of looking at life in the USSR through the windows of my chauffeur-driven Volga, I was brought back to earth in Leningrad. Returning to my hometown as a domestic KGB general was a depressing and sordid revelation, and it irreversibly changed me. I knew things had gotten bad inside the country, but not until I took over as the number-two man in the Leningrad KGB did I realize just how far gone the situation was.

I had a perfect vantage point from which to see the absurdity and advanced decay of Soviet Communism. At close range, I watched the top men in the KGB and the Communist Party in action, and I marveled at how puffed up and out of touch with reality they had become. They inhabited their own Byzantine world of privilege and power, fervently believing that the shadow game they were playing on high—holding Party plenums and conferences, staging sham elections, intoning the brittle mantras of our dead Communist leaders—was really having an effect on the steadily deteriorating economic and political situation in our country. The local Communist Party structure continued to rule and siphon off vast amounts of money. Our 3,000-person KGB office in Leningrad continued to harass dissidents and ordinary citizens, as well as hunt futilely for spies. But I can truly say that nearly all of what we did was useless. And we were operating in Leningrad, a cultured and enlightened place. The situation in the provinces was far worse. It was all an elaborately choreographed farce, and in my seven years in Leningrad

I came to see we had created not only the most extensive totalitarian state apparatus in history but also the most arcane. Indeed, the mind boggled that in the course of seven decades our Communist leaders had managed to construct this absurd, stupendous ziggurat, this terrifyingly centralized machine, this *religion* that sought to control all aspects of life in our vast country. It was truly a wondrous creation. And as the coup of August 1991 showed, it was a house of cards. A few years of Mikhail Gorbachev, followed by the foolhardy coup attempt of Kryuchkov and other die-hard Communists, and the entire structure came crashing down, literally in a matter of days.

I was forced to stick my nose in the reality of Soviet life, and it was an enormous comedown. I passed through successive stages of astonishment, anger, depression, apathy, and—finally—liberation. I came to Leningrad in 1980 reeling from my clash with the KGB hierachy, but somehow still hopeful that my career would one day rise from the ashes. I left Leningrad in 1987 utterly disgusted with the KGB and the Soviet system, and unconcerned how my increasingly rebellious stance would affect my future. By the end of my seven-year stint in the beautiful city on the Baltic, my KGB career was in ruins, but I was a free man for the first time in my life. Leningrad had launched me on a dissident path, and I left my hometown experiencing a heady sense of independence.

On January 3, 1980, when I stepped off the *Red Arrow* into a bitterly cold Leningrad dawn, I was met by the local chief of Intelligence and his deputy. They drove me to the Communist Party hotel—every town of any size had one and it was invariably the best hotel around—where I rested and then looked up some old friends. The next morning I showed up early at the "Big House," the imposing gray stone KGB headquarters on Liteiny Prospect. The building was constructed under Stalin in the 1930s, and my father had once worked there as a guard, where he occasionally heard the screams of some of the thousands of people who were tortured and murdered in the basement.

The first item on my agenda was a meeting with the man who would turn out to be my nemesis, Leningrad KGB Chief Daniil Nozyrev. I had heard only bad things about this imperious man, and my first few minutes with him confirmed what I had been told. Severe, pompous, and coldly formal, Nozyrev extended me his hand with an air of importance and uttered a few inanities. He was sixty-two, of average height, had gray wavy hair, and the dull look of a smug provincial. Nozyrev had finished high school and graduated from a two-year Communist Party school, but that was the extent of his education. He had served in Military Counterintelligence during and after World War II, eventually transferring to the KGB. By the time I met him, he had risen to the rank of general. He was obsequious when dealing with Andropov and other bosses, but a high-handed bully with his subordinates in Leningrad. It was clear he had heard the rumors that I had been dispatched to Leningrad to eventually replace him, which may explain, in part, his immediate hostility toward me.

My new job, first chief deputy to Nozyrev, had been specially created for me, apparently out of Andropov's concern that, though I was being shunted off to Leningrad, I shouldn't be placed in a humiliatingly low position. But from my first few words with Nozyrev, it was clear he wanted to get me out of the way. The Leningrad chief informed me that my main responsibility would not even be in the city itself, but that I would be supervising all KGB activities in the outlying towns and districts. I would also be in charge of the Information Department, the Internal Security section, and would sit on the Leningrad Foreign Travel Commission, a body that decided which citizens were sufficiently reliable and worthy to travel abroad. His words hit me like a blow, though by this time I was getting used to such humiliations. In the space of three months, I had gone from director of the KGB's Foreign Counterintelligence operations to a petty bureaucrat deciding which of our unfortunate citizens would be followed or bugged or denied a trip overseas.

Nozyrev commanded a little army in Leningrad. Besides me, he had five other deputies: one who supervised work against dissidents, one for counterintelligence, one for surveillance, one for transportation and technical matters, and one for the government bodyguard. (The bodyguard section had more than one hundred men, whose main task was to protect the one Communist Party boss in the city and his headquarters.) Two of these men were former Communist Party bureaucrats, not KGB professionals, and they were unimpressive. The one deputy I took a liking to, Rear Admiral Vladimir Sokolov, was a man of some sophistication who went out of his way to be friendly with me. It would turn out that he was not at all the person I thought he was.

After several weeks on the job, Nozyrev still had not found a suitable apartment for me. At the suggestion of one of his deputies, I moved temporarily into a flat that once served as a KGB safe house. It was, then, a shock when Nozyrev summoned all his deputies and launched into a bitter attack on me.

"Today I'd like to talk with you about the behavior of Comrade Kalugin," announced Nozyrev. "He hasn't been with us long, but he's already acting in such a way that I'm beginning to wonder who's boss here. He goes to Moscow without permission, he's taken over a safe house, and he's turning up his nose at the apartment he's been offered. He offers to deliver a lecture at a seminar without asking me. What's going on here? Who do you think is the chief of the branch?"

Fixing me with a hostile stare, he concluded, "I've been told that you had disciplinary problems in Intelligence. That won't do here."

I sat listening, with my head down, barely able to contain my anger. I gave Nozyrev a forced smile and said, "Just as all of those present here, I have no doubt who is in charge here. All of your reproaches stem from misunderstandings. I have informed the appropriate deputies that I was traveling to Moscow, and it was [Deputy] Bleyer who suggested I move into the safe house. I didn't bother getting permission to deliver my lecture because I've delivered it before the Central Committee of the Communist party and why should I get special permission to deliver it here? As for the apartments I've been offered, I'm not a rookie investigator who will be happy with any bone you throw at him. I will only take an apartment I like."

I stared hard at Nozyrev, making it clear I wouldn't tolerate such a dressing down. Then I walked out of the meeting.

Back in my office, my outrage grew as I sat contemplating what Nozyrev had just done. It was clear that the Leningrad chief was intent on browbeating me, on wearing me down, until I fell into line like the rest of his obsequious deputies. I considered writing Andropov and asking for an immediate transfer back to Moscow. In any case, I resolved to continue standing up to Nozyrev. I was jerked out of my reverie by my fellow deputy, Rear Admiral Sokolov, who appeared at the door. I was in no mood to speak with anyone, but Sokolov pulled a bottle of brandy from his pocket and began commiserating.

"Now, Oleg, don't get upset about this," he said. "To hell with Nozyrev. He can be so nasty. He gets on everybody's nerves. I've known him for fifteen years and he still treats me like a boy. We're all under his thumb here. You can't imagine how he taunts me and orders me about, and I say, just like in the Navy, 'Yes, Comrade General! Will do, Comrade General!' He likes that. I never argue with him. Don't you argue with him, either. He heard from someone that you're being considered as his possible replacement, so of course he's jittery. Don't pay any attention to him."

Sokolov refilled my glass, and told me several more stories about Nozyrev and the Leningrad branch. I started to unwind, and was grateful for his attempt to settle me down. And then, both of us a little tipsy, Sokolov began discussing why I had been transferred to Leningrad. His words set me reeling.

"There's all sorts of gossip flying around about why you were sent here from Intelligence," Sokolov informed me. "But I have it on good authority that you got kicked out of Intelligence because you were trying to defend Cook. You were suspected of having CIA connections, and Cook was thought to be your accomplice."

I knew the investigators had asked Cook questions about the possibility of my working for the CIA, but I had written that off as the paranoia of men trying to make a case against Cook. Now a relatively high-ranking and well-connected KGB officer was telling me that the scuttlebutt in Moscow was that I had been demoted on suspicion of working with Cook for the CIA. I had been under the impression that the Cook affair was a secret one; yet it was clear that details of the case—and rumors about my being a spy—were circulating throughout the organization.

Sokolov went back to his office, leaving me dismayed. The system to which I had devoted my life, the system to which I had been boundlessly loyal, now suspected me of betrayal. I had been sullied by unproven allegations, allegations so amorphous that I didn't even know how to fight back. I increasingly began to feel like millions of other Soviets who had been unjustly accused of crimes, though most of them had experienced a far worse fate. In our system, everyone was a suspect, including someone as fanatically loyal as myself. From that day forward, something changed inside me, for I realized that the system was essentially vicious. As someone once said, the Revolution devours its own children.

After that day, Sokolov became my closest confidant at the KGB office in Leningrad. We had tea together several times a week and talked about the situation in the agency and the country. But several years after I arrived, the head of Counterintelligence in Leningrad approached me and asked, "Oleg, why are you so friendly with Sokolov?"

"Well, it started when he was the only one who came to see me after my run-in with Nozyrev," I replied.

"Look," said the Counterintelligence officer. "Sokolov is smart. He's talking to you expressly on Nozyrev's orders. He's been especially chosen to inform on you."

"Oh, come on," I said.

"Just look at it," he replied. "Skip over the way he butters you up and look at the questions he asks you, what he wants to know, what he tells you."

I began to think that the man was right. But still I wasn't sure until a few weeks later, when a head of Leningrad's Communist Party Regional Committee—with whom I had become friendly— spoke with me one evening and said, "I know for sure that your friend Sokolov was specially sent to keep an eye on you, and he reports everything you say to Nozyrev."

The Party official proceeded to repeat several things I had said to Sokolov in confidence, and I realized then that he had been betraying me all along. I was tempted to confront him, but decided instead to still see him from time to time so I could spread disinformation or, in moments of perversity, merely say things that I knew would drive Nozyrev crazy.

But that all lay ahead. What dismayed me most in my first year on the job in Leningrad was not the harassment from on high, but the realization of the preposterous work in which the domestic KGB—and now I—was involved.

The Leningrad region, which was my domain, included the Vyborg area along the Finnish border; Sosnovy Bor and Gatchina with their nuclear reactors and scientific centers; the enormous tank factory at Tikhvin; and the mining town of Slantsy. Most of the rest of the region was agricultural. No place, as might be supposed, was a hotbed of espionage or civil unrest.

Soon after beginning my new job, I called in the KGB chiefs from the outlying towns and districts. Before our meetings, I read their reports from 1979, and was stunned by the misery of their existence, by the lack of any real work, by the petty tasks they and their underlings carried out. Clearly, there was no espionage or sedition in their districts, but the local KGB men and countless informers were filing absurd reports containing gossip, rumors, and paranoid ruminations on the security situation. Local windbags were portrayed as dangerous political opponents. Factory bosses harbored suspicions that their underlings were working for the CIA. Local intellectuals—schoolteachers, scientists, and artists—were followed and their phones tapped. It was all an enormous waste of time and money. We had an expression in Russia for this meaningless scurrying about—"mice games" (*mysheniye voznya*). And "mice games" were about the only thing our local KGB officers were engaged in as they tried to control—and instill fear in—the common people of their districts.

Yet I did not blame these low-level KGB men, because the orders to look for spies, saboteurs, and dissidents came to them from on high. Andropov, Kryuchkov, Chebrikov—the entire hierarchy was warning of insidious Western plots. Even in the small villages of the Leningrad region, KGB men were instructed to keep an eye out for Western saboteurs and illegals who would take up residence and strike the Soviet Army when World War III erupted. Nozyrev frequently said at conferences, "Why aren't we catching any spies! There are spies around us and we're not catching them. We aren't working well!"

When I first came to Leningrad, there were fifty active investigations of Soviets suspected of espionage, and it is safe to say that nearly all of the cases were worthless. I remember one incident in which a surveillance team, busy following an American diplomat in Leningrad, saw a Russian man make what the officers interpreted as a suspicious gesture to the American on the street. The unfortunate Russian was followed and an investigation of him was begun, including surveillance, wiretaps, and bugs in his apartment. There was absolutely no evidence the man was a spy, but our hidden microphones picked up his making anti-Brezhnev comments. By 1980, nearly everyone but Brezhnev himself was making anti-Brezhnev remarks, so I hardly considered the man suspicious. The case, however, was kept open.

I suggested to Nozyrev that we close this case and about twenty others.

"How dare you!" he responded.

In the twenty years before my arrival in Leningrad, the local KGB hadn't caught one spy, despite the expenditure of millions of rubles and tens of thousands of man-hours. In that span of time, there were only two espionage cases, and both of those were essentially bogus. They involved our own double agents posing as CIA collaborators, and when the time was right—for example, after the shootdown of the Korean Airlines plane in 1983—we blew our agents' cover and apprehended the U.S. diplomats meeting with them. All this is not to say that there weren't spies in our city. There undoubtedly were. But with the inexperienced officers and scattershot techniques the local KGB was using, we weren't about to catch them.

There were more than a dozen districts in the Leningrad region, and I visited all of them several times. Each district had from three to thirty KGB officers, and invariably, after stopping in these local offices to see how things were going, I would leave feeling profoundly depressed. Most of the officers in the outlying areas either were young or had experienced problems in Leningrad itself—alcoholism, insubordination, chronically sloppy work—and been transferred to the boondocks. There was almost nothing constructive for them to do, since the local police handled routine crime. And so these KGB men would befriend the local Communist Party boss and hunt, fish, drink, and generally enjoy the power they lorded over the masses in these squalid provincial hamlets.

One incident shows just how desperate these local officers were to make it appear they were working. Two elderly woman wrote letters to a local newspaper, complaining about their rundown housing. Nothing was done, and a few weeks later one of the *babushkas* was overheard telling the other, "Let's write to the U.S. Embassy and complain about our housing conditions. Maybe that will stir up some action."

An informant told the district KGB office about the conversation. The district chief reported the incident to KGB headquarters in Leningrad, and in that year's annual report the meaningless incident was turned into a security service coup. Our crack officers, the report said without providing details, had discovered that two Soviet citizens were planning to make contact with the American Embassy. And the plot had been foiled!

On another occasion, a district Communist Party boss gravely reported to me, "We have a man here in town who is saying such bad things about Comrade Brezhnev and the country, I think we should have his phone tapped and put him under surveillance. And perhaps we can finish off this case with an arrest."

I was tempted to laugh in the Party man's face, but instead— given that the offender was engaging in the purportedly serious crime of "anti-Soviet agitation"—I told the local boss, "Give me all you have on the man and we'll see what we can do."

A few days later, the Party boss forwarded a file full of half-baked accusations from petty informers. I got the official on the phone and couldn't resist saying, "Listen, let's analyze what's in the file. The man curses Brezhnev, right? What for? For being old. Isn't Brezhnev, in fact, old? The man says Brezhnev hasn't been making any decisions himself lately. Do you think that isn't so? . . . Look, this is a man who's probably not too educated, not too knowledgeable and obviously misguided. Why don't you invite him to your office, talk to him, and point out his errors and inconsistencies? Tell him to be careful. That way we can close the case without an arrest."

One of the few bright spots in my years in Leningrad was that neither I nor my underlings in the districts ever arrested or imprisoned anyone for anti-Soviet activity.

I found myself feeling more pity than anger for my subordinates in the districts, for it was clear that Nozyrev and the KGB bosses above him in Moscow wanted the KGB officers in the provinces to continue doing busywork and propagating the same old lies. If a junior officer or informant tried to buck the system, however slightly, or slip a note of truth into his reports, he usually ran into trouble.

Once, after one of the painfully boring Communist Party congresses in Moscow, KGB officers from around the country were ordered to report on the response to the plenum. The truth was that average people couldn't have cared less. We compiled a report from the district and I delivered it to Nozyrev. He began reading the inane document, nodding his head and grunting his approval. And then he came to a portion written by a nuclear engineer who was a confidential informant, which I hadn't excised because I thought it was true.

"Of course the Congress was excellent, and we are all confident that our life will be better," the engineer wrote. "But it's a pity that Comrade Brezhnev is so old that his promises may never be kept."

"What's that!" sputtered Nozyrev. "Comrade Kalugin, did you read what you gave to me?"

I told him I had, and he wanted to know who the informant was. I said he was a paid agent who was valued by our KGB district chief in Sosnovy Bor, site of a nuclear power station.

"Well, tomorrow you must go to Sosnovy Bor and talk to your subordinate," ordered Nozyrev. "Get the file of that agent and immediately get rid of him. We don't need people in our agent network who discredit our Party leadership."

The next day I showed up in Sosnovy Bor, and told our KGB boss there that he had to sever ties with his informant.

"But he's one of our best!" replied the KGB officer. "How can we fire him?"

"Well, Nozyrev wants us to do something," I said. Finally we devised a scheme in which he would be demoted from a top-rank informant to a "confidential contact."

Such was the work that we, the "sword and shield" of the Party, carried out in the waning days of the old order. Our leaders were busy issuing reports about the rosy situation in the country and applauding one another at countless congresses and conferences. The security people were busy with nonsense. And as the months passed in Leningrad, I became progressively more apathetic. With every new act of imbecility, with every new indignity, I became less and less interested in my new work.

Watching Nozyrev and his team fight the twin evils of domestic dissent and foreign subversion, I scarcely knew whether to laugh or cry.

Our Soviet youth were decades behind those in the West, and as the rock culture began to grow in Leningrad in the late 1970s and early 1980s, Communist Party officials became increasingly alarmed. Such renegade Western culture was believed to present a danger to Communist ideology, and the Party bosses wanted the KGB to stamp out these insidious influences. But Vladilen Bleyer, the deputy KGB chief in Leningrad in charge of fighting dissidents, had a better idea: He suggested we use agents to create a Leningrad Rock Club that would bring all the nonconformist writers, musicians, and artists under one roof—our roof.

"Rather than ban these things, why not control them ourselves?" Bleyer suggested at one meeting. "We could provide an outlet for all kinds of ill feeling and at the same time have a chance to control it. We'll have our own people there and we'll manipulate the club so that it will never become dangerous."

So the Rock Club was established, and it became a gathering place for the Leningrad counterculture—and a swarm of KGB agents posing as hipsters. The local KGB also arranged the publication of a collection of writings by some mildly dissident authors and hosted several exhibitions of modern art, all in an attempt to control the artistic forces threatening to weaken the Communist monolith. It was, in the end, futile "mice games," but at the time it kept our people busy.

The Leningrad KGB found sportsmen almost as threatening as rock-'n'-rollers. One of our officers would be included in every group of Leningrad athletes traveling overseas. When the Soviet Peace Committee organized an international bike race in Leningrad in 1983, the participants were not only watched closely by the KGB; several of our officers actually rode in the race. In July 1985, when the United States volleyball team came to Leningrad to play the Soviet squad, our officers followed the Americans around as if they were would-be terrorists. The CBS-TV crew that came to Leningrad to cover the U.S.-Soviet match also was constantly under surveillance and their hotel rooms were bugged and searched.

I was always puzzled by the Leningrad KGB's interest in sports events, and attribute it to several factors. The bosses liked sports anyway, so by spying on foreign sports teams they were combining business with pleasure. The KGB also was afraid that our sportsmen were likely defectors, and thus kept a close watch on them, at home and abroad. And finally, since KGB officials knew that our sports teams traveling abroad were riddled with KGB informers and officers, they figured the Americans did the same thing. In their eyes, the gangly American college kids who came to Leningrad were not volleyball players, but hardened CIA veterans looking for the right opportunity to score a blow against the Evil Empire.

I recall another incident involving a visit to the city by foreigners. In 1985 or 1986, with Gorbachev in power and *glasnost* just taking root, the environmental campaigners from Greenpeace sailed into Leningrad Habor with much fanfare. They arrived on a Greenpeace yacht and then, as they spread throughout the city, our ace surveillance experts lost track of most of the crew. Nozyrev was outraged. How could we have lost them, he asked. They could be skulking about town, gathering intelligence and recruiting Soviet dissidents! Finally, our teams managed to locate them, but only after some tense moments in the Big House on Liteiny Prospect.

I was one of three KGB officials in Leningrad with the power to authorize wiretapping in the city. As I spent more time on the job, I marveled at the extent of our bugging, surveillance, and mail-interception efforts. In the Big House, nearly one thousand KGB employees, working in a warren of rooms, were involved around the clock in monitoring and recording phone wiretaps and other bugs. At any given time, there were dozens of phones, offices, and apartments being bugged, and this battalion of KGB workers—most of them women—recorded and transcribed the conversations. Sitting in the Big House, we had the capacity, through special hook-ups with the central Leningrad phone station, to record any conversation in the city. The phone calls of dissidents, artists, and other troublemakers were monitored periodically. Foreign diplomats, businessmen, and journalists were subjected to near-constant bugging of their phones and hotel rooms. Indeed, at the major Intourist hotels—the Astoria, Evropeyskaya, and Pribaltiskaya—suspicious foreigners were placed in certain rooms already outfitted with hidden microphones. Tourists also were watched, though more spottily since there were so many of them. Virtually all the Intourist guides were KGB informers, who immediately reported to us if they harbored suspicions about a certain foreign tourist.

During my stint in Leningrad, all of this activity yielded little if anything in the way of concrete results, at least in the search for spies. We did turn up information on some routine criminal cases, as well as fodder—infidelity, homosexuality—that could be used to blackmail people into working for us. For the most part, however, thousands upon thousands of pages of transcribed conversations piled up in our files, to no avail.

Our mail-interception efforts met with slightly more success. In an eighteenth-century building in the center of town, several hundred KGB workers opened nearly every piece of foreign mail and spot-checked domestic mail. Occasionally this laborious work would turn up information about an art-smuggling plan or someone's intention to contact a foreign embassy and defect. For the most part, however, the reading of hundreds of thousands of pieces of mail every year was just another example of the colossally idiotic work in which the domestic security services were engaged.

Department Five, which monitored dissidents, kept a close eye on the artistic community in Leningrad—a community I was to become involved with, and not as an informant. The city's most prominent artists and intellectuals were followed, their apartments and phones bugged, their residences and offices searched. Among those targeted were Dimitri Likhachev, the literary critic and academic who had survived Stalin's Gulag; the writer Daniil Granin; and Georgi Tovstogonov, the prominent theater director. There was an enormous file on Likhachev, who was the director of the Pushkin Institute of Literature. He was an old dissident and always had been suspected of being staunchly anti-Soviet, so Department Five frequently flipped on the bugs in his apartment or on his phone to see what he was plotting. Indeed, many of the professors at the Pushkin

Institute—considered a nest of malcontents and potential spies—were subjected to routine surveillance and bugging. Tovstogonov, who once spoke out in support of Solzhenitsyn and Sakharov, was considered very unreliable and was a frequent surveillance target.

One day, an officer in Department Five brought me a KGB memo addressed to the Leningrad Communist Party, saying that one of our best symphony conductors, Yuri Temirkanov, should be forbidden to travel abroad because he was unreliable. The recommendation was made because a bug in Temirkanov's apartment allegedly showed that the conductor was considering defecting. The officer had come to me to sign the memo, but I decided to read the surveillance transcript myself.

Temirkanov was upset because his expected appointment to replace the ailing head of the Leningrad Philharmonic was being delayed. At one point in the transcript, a frustrated Temirkanov told a friend, "If I lived in the West, the world's best orchestras would invite me, and here I have no future whatsoever. When I go to London I'll get a decent job there at once. I'm sick and tired of groveling before the local bureaucrats."

Later in the conversation, however, Temirkanov said, "What the hell do I care about London? I can get a decent suit and a pair of shoes there, but that's not what I want. What I need is elbow room, freedom to create."

I knew Temirkanov to be extremely patriotic, and a reading of the entire transcript led me to believe he had no intention of defecting. The case officer had excerpted only the most seditious parts of the conversation to show the local Party bosses. I summoned the officer and reprimanded him for blowing the situation out of proportion. As a member of the Foreign Travel Commission, I determined that Temirkanov was trustworthy. The negative letter was never sent to the Party bosses and Temirkanov was allowed to travel to England.

Within a year of my arrival in Leningrad, I came to know Tovstogonov, the theater director, quite well. Through him I met a wide range of artists, musicians, and writers. I had far more time on my hands in Leningrad than in Moscow, so I attended virtually every theater premier in the city. Two seats in each theater were reserved for the KGB censors, and I always managed to slip into these or others near the front row. I met Tovstogonov on numerous occasions, and since we lived in the same apartment building he often invited me for dinner or coffee. One night, I went over to his place after he phoned me around eleven and invited me to meet some friends. The apartment was packed with a bohemian crowd, which included the famous actor Yevgeni Lebedev and the director of the Moscow Contemporary Theater, Galina Volchek. We stayed up until 4:00 A.M., and from then on I was a frequent visitor at Tovstogonov's. It was an independent, fascinating, and relaxed crowd, and my involvement with them and their artistic endeavors helped me keep my sanity in Leningrad.

Since I lived in one of the city's most prestigious neighborhoods, just a few blocks from the Hermitage, I had other artistic neighbors, including the Leningrad Philharmonic's chief conductor, Yevgeny Mravinsky. He lived just upstairs from me, and I began visiting with him and his fellow musicians. I made no secret of my ties with this group of freethinkers and dissidents, and no doubt my association with them further hurt my chances of rebirth at the KGB. But by 1983, I no longer cared. In the mid-1980s, one of my friends in the Fifth Department, which fought against dissidents, warned me that Mravinsky's apartment was bugged.

"You must be careful," my friend told me. "You know some of these people are under surveillance. They are political dissidents."

"Listen," I said, "I don't talk politics with them. We discuss art. They talk about their projects with me."

"Well, we just wanted to warn you," said my friend. "Be careful not to say anything wrong."

I was surprised at first that Lenigrad's cultural elite would welcome a KGB general into their salons, but I imagine they had several reasons for doing so. First, perhaps they thought it was simply in their interest to be on friendly terms with a high-ranking member of the security services. Second, my friends in the arts knew that I had a background in Intelligence and was disgusted by the shenanigans of the domestic KGB. And I think that as time went by and our association created no problems for them, my Leningrad artist friends realized that I was genuine and not an informant. Last, and by no means least, I genuinely liked many of the artists, and I think they, too, were fond of me.

One of my friends, Boris Piotrovsky—director of the Hermitage Museum—treated me to some of the most memorable nights I spent in Leningrad.

It was in June, the season of the city's "White Nights," when the northern sun barely sets. One night, around 11 o'clock, Piotrovsky escorted me, Tovstogonov, and Yevgeny Primakov (future director of Russian Intelligence) through the deserted museum along the banks of the Neva River, once the Czar's Winter Palace. A melancholy twilight seeped through the windows of the Hermitage as we walked down the long corridors. The echo of our footsteps was the only sound in the enormous museum. Piotrovsky took us past the Italian and French masterpieces, stopping occasionally to talk about one of the paintings.

On a later visit to the Hermitage, Piotrovsky asked me, "Would you like to see some pictures no one ever does?" I wasn't prepared for what I was about to see.

Piotrovsky led me up to the top floor of the museum. He unlocked two heavy steel doors and ushered me into a room filled to the ceiling with masterpieces. There were French Impressionist paintings and works by old German masters, all stacked on shelves or piled on the floor. I watched in amazement as Piotrovsky pulled out thirty or forty masterpieces, and then I asked the obvious question: Why were they tucked away in this dusty storage room? Why weren't they hanging in the galleries downstairs?

During and after World War II, Piotrovsky told me, the Soviet Army had taken all these pictures from the private collections of some of Germany's wealthiest families. Piotrovsky said he had been lobbying to display the pictures or give them back to their rightful owners, but the Ministry of Culture had refused even to discuss the matter and insisted that the masterpieces be kept under lock and key.

"The heirs may still be able to claim these pictures," said Piotrovsky.

"Then why don't you show these paintings one by one and see what the reaction will be?" I asked. "You don't have to display them all at once. Perhaps no one will know. Besides, you can always say you bought the picture from a private person."

"That's a good idea, but the Ministry of Culture won't even discuss it," answered Piotrovsky.

The Hermitage director let me wander around the room for a few minutes, gaping at the priceless artworks. Later, I asked Piotrovsky to give me a list of the stolen German treasures, and within a week he did so. I quote now from that list, which contained the name of the family that had owned the artworks and the number of works taken. (The list contains only the oil paintings; it does not include hundreds of drawings and lithographs.)

Krebs, 47
Scharf, 6

B. Kotler, 5
Siemens, 2
A. Meuer, 3
M. Saxe, 6
The Kurfurst of Saxony, 1
Weldenstein, 3
Goldsticker, 5
Bechstein, 24
Hitler and Schacht, 3
Willie Goerter, 25
Koestenberg, 46
Konig, Vienna, 1
Otto, 1
Rochas, Paris, 3
Lashkoni, 2
Tashbein, 5
Dresden Church, 3

Piotrovsky also said the Hermitage contained Oriental master-pieces stolen during the war from Russian-occupied Manchuria. I decided to go see Nozyrev to urge him to do something: either put the paintings on display or return them to their native countries. It was clear the Leningrad KGB boss knew about the art trove, and he treated my suggestion with typical boorishness.

"Mind your own business," Nozyrev barked. "The hell with those pictures. I don't care. Why don't you catch me a spy instead of worrying about it?"

As far as I know, the Hermitage is still holding on to these treasures.

In my first few years in Leningrad, tensions between the United States (where Ronald Reagan had now become President) and the Soviet Union reached a level unmatched since the 1960s. We felt it even in Leningrad when, in 1981, we received what I can only de-scribe as a paranoid cable from Andropov warning of the growing threat of a nuclear apocalypse. Reagan's hard-line, anti-Communist stance, his "Star Wars" program, and the massive American military buildup scared the wits out of our leadership, and Andropov notified KGB stations around the world to be on the lookout for signs of an imminent American attack. A brand-new program (the English-language acronym was RYAN) was created to gather information on a potential American first nuclear strike.

"Not since the end of World War II has the international situation been as explosive as it is now," Andropov wrote in a cable to KGB personnel worldwide.

Meanwhile, I still held out hope that my career at headquarters in Moscow was not finished. Nozyrev told me that Andropov had been asking after me, and in 1981 I was given an award for a manual I had written earlier on Foreign Counterintelligence techniques. In 1982, Andropov was transferred to the Party's Central Committee Secretariat. Unfortunately, he was replaced by a Brezhnev hack, Vitaly Fedorchuk, the former KGB boss in Ukraine. He was a rude, conceited bonecrusher, bent on smashing internal dissent in our society and tightening discipline within the KGB. He peppered KGB offices at home and abroad with ridiculous warnings of impending Western aggression, imperialist plots, and CIA efforts to destroy the Soviet economy. Thankfully, Fedorchuk didn't last long. Brezhnev died on November 10, 1982; Androprov took over as Soviet leader; and a week later Viktor Chebrikov was named chairman of the KGB.

I was visiting Ludmilla and my daughters in Moscow when I got the word that Brezhnev had died. "Oleg," a KGB friend of mine said over the phone, "it looks like *He* is dead."

I needed no futher explanation. *He* undoubtedly was the sickly and senile Brezhnev. Like millions of my compatriots, I was elated that the old dinosaur had passed away. I thought that, finally, our dismal "era of stagnation" was at an end. But I had selfish reasons, as well, that caused me to welcome Brezhnev's demise. With my old mentor, Andropov, installed as leader of the country, I thought that my exile in Leningrad might come to an end, that Andropov would bring me back into Moscow in a top position at KGB headquarters.

A week after Brezhnev's death, my father passed away following a stroke. He had moved to Moscow in the 1970s to be close to me, and we buried him in the Soviet capital. My father had remained my biggest fan until the end, and he was nearly as disappointed as I was when word came of my demotion and transfer to Leningrad. He died, as so many Soviets did, deeply disillusioned with his country and its leaders. I would miss his love and support in the difficult days that lay ahead.

When I got back to Leningrad after Andropov's ascension to power, rumors spread through our office that I would soon be replacing Nozyrev as Leningrad KGB boss. But it was not to be. I was chosen, along with forty other high-ranking KGB officers, to take an advanced course of study in Moscow. This, I thought, boded well. And then, a week before the course was to end, one of the KGB's chief personnel men called me into his office and made an offer that flabbergasted me: He wanted me to take a job as a professor at the KGB Higher School.

"You've got a teacher's gift, Oleg," the man said. "People listen to you. Your wide knowledge will enable you to get a doctorate quickly, so you can be a full-fledged professor."

I couldn't believe my ears! Clearly I was being put out to pasture; the KGB Higher School was a dead end. Despite the insistent pressure, I refused the offer. Later that week, I went to see Philip Bobkov, deputy KGB chairman, and reminded him that Andropov said I would be back in Moscow within two years. It was now the fall of 1983, and I had served my time in Leningrad, I told Bobkov. I wanted to talk to the new KGB chairman, Viktor Chebrikov. Bobkov said he would see what he could do. But not now, said Bobkov. Not now.

I returned to Leningrad and called Bobkov a few weeks later.

"Chebrikov is willing to see you, but later this year," said Bobkov. "Call me in December."

I waited until January and called again.

"Wait a while longer," Bobkov said dryly. "We've got lots of problems here and yours isn't a priority."

"How long must I wait?" I asked. "Am I going to be received?"

"I don't know, I don't know," Bobkov growled, and hung up.

Even I, blind as I could sometimes be, could see that my career at KGB headquarters was finished.

Andropov had tried to kick-start our moribund economy and society. He stressed discipline, and instituted a campaign to crack down on shirkers and ne'er-do-wells in the workplace. He fought against petty corruption, though he never attacked the deeply engrained corruption within the Communist Party. "The better we work, the better we shall live," pronounced Comrade Andropov, but the fact remained that our system was—for all intents and purposes—dead. It was too late for slogans, and even the most devout Soviet could see that, no matter how hard he worked, he still was living in relative poverty: the Communist Party, the military-industrial complex, the Army, and the KGB were siphoning off the country's wealth.

Andropov's last days were marked by failing health and the disastrous downing of Korean Airlines Flight 007 over the Kamchatka

Peninsula, in which all 269 passengers aboard were killed. And then, on February 9, 1984, the General Secretary of the Communist Party—and the man who had been my guardian angel at the KGB—died.

Andropov's passing left me profoundly depressed. Indeed, I date my utter disillusionment with the KGB to early 1984, when Andropov's demise and several other events forced me to see that there was no hope of reviving my career, or of redeeming the old Soviet system.

For all his shortcomings, I had admired Andropov, and as long as he was alive I held out some hope that we could—as he so often preached—fix our system just by doing some major repair work. But when Andropov passed away, I saw everything with stark and depressing clarity. First of all, Andropov was replaced as General Secretary of the Communist Party by the walking corpse of Constantin Chernenko, a man even more out of touch with reality, even more retrograde, than Leonid Brezhnev. In the KGB, Viktor Chebrikov was proving to be an absolute nonentity, a weak and indecisive man who was a pale reflection of Andropov. Everywhere, from the top bosses in Moscow to my own superior in Leningrad, all I could see was incompetence, drift, and rot.

Perhaps most important, when Andropov died I lost all hope that somehow my mentor would help resuscitate my career. By mid-1984, it was evident that there was no light at the end of the tunnel, that I was on a joyless road to retirement. By that time, too, friends of mine in Moscow had told me the full truth about the Cook case, about how I had, indeed, been as much a suspect as Cook himself. One friend in KGB headquarters informed me that KGB bosses had secretly filmed my interrogation of Cook at Lefortovo Prison. A KGB official actually throught that when I put my fingers under my shirt collar during the Cook interview, I was giving the scientist a secret sign! It was all too much. The system mistrusted me. Indeed, it trusted nobody. Four years in Leningrad and the loss of Andropov showed me how deluded I was, and how utterly senseless was the work I had been doing since leaving Moscow. In 1984, as winter slowly gave way to spring, I was plunged into a deep depression and resolved to live only for myself and my family.

One of the most dismal revelations in Leningrad had been that our job in the domestic KGB was to do the bidding of—and cover up for—the local Communist Party bosses. And in Leningrad the top two Party bosses were particularly repugnant, a pair who vividly symbolized the sort of pompous mediocrities that had driven our country into the ground.

The first secretary of the Communist Party in the Leningrad area, the undisputed emperor of our region, was a tiny, conceited man with a Napoleonic complex named Grigory Vasilyevich Romanov. For seventeen years he reigned as lord and master over the Leningrad region, his authority virtually unchallenged. Throughout the vast expanse of the Soviet Union—a country that sprawled across eleven time zones and comprised one sixth of the earth's land surface—there were several hundred other little dictators like Romanov. They were the regional Communist Party first secretaries, men who lived like Socialist pashas, grabbing the best apartments, the best food, the best women, the best hunting lands, all the while espousing the glories of our egalitarian society. Gazing at their pictures now, studying the jowly, smug, vodka-ravaged mugs, these men look like cartoon characters, the very embodiment of Communist stagnation. But at the time, they instilled fear into the hearts of millions of Communist Party minions, and they ran their little fiefdoms with swaggering pride.

After serving as a code clerk in the Soviet Army during World War II, Romanov rose through the ranks of the Leningrad Communist Party, familiarizing himself with the military factories and institutes that comprised two thirds of the Leningrad economy. In the late 1960s, with the blessing of the Party leadership in Moscow, Romanov—no relation to the Romanov Czars—became first secretary of the Leningrad region. By the time I got there, Romanov might as well have been a czar, for he was as much in control of his territory as any of the earlier Romanovs had been of theirs.

He was a dapper little man, in a Communist sort of way. At Party meetings, Romanov used to sit on a pillow so that he didn't give the appearance of a schoolkid at a spelling bee. His high living, womanizing, and boozing were legendary. In order to carry out his many trysts, Romanov had two apartments—in addition to the one he shared with his wife—as well as a suite at the Party hotel. He would impress his mistresses with food and gifts purchased from the "Blue Hall" at the *Gostiny Dvor* department store, a private shop stocked with imported goods and reserved solely for top Party officials. He had three government cars in which to squire around his girlfriends. Even his poor wife was given a government automobile.

KGB officers marveled at Romanov's drinking. He and the region's other Commmunist Party big shot—Leningrad Mayor Lev Zaikov—would sit in Romanov's wood-paneled office at Smolny and knock back copious quantities of vodka. (Smolny, seat of the Leningrad Communist Party, is the former Czarist girls school that was used by Lenin as his headquarters during the October 1917 Bolshevik Revolution.) Zaikov was a big, rough-hewn man who could hold his vodka better than Romanov; after their legendary drinking bouts Zaikov would always be at his desk the next day, while Romanov would stay home for a day or two, nursing a fierce hangover.

Outside a small circle of KGB and Party officials, Romanov's drinking was a fairly well-kept secret. I learned of his alcohol problem firsthand one Sunday when I was on duty at KGB headquarters on Liteiny Prospect. Romanov telephoned and, since it was a weekend and I was acting chief, I took the call. From the first, I could tell something was wrong, and it quickly became clear that our illustrious first secretary was rip-roaring drunk. He was carrying on about some problem at the city's central bakery, mumbling about sabotage and declining production. Soon, he signed off, and I was left scratching my head. We made inquiries, and everything seemed fine at the bakery. Vladilen Bleyer, my colleague who was in charge of the one hundred-person bodyguard section in Leningrad and was intimately familiar with Romanov's drinking binges, told me, "Forget it, Oleg. He was drunk as usual. He'll be away from work for two or three days until he gets over his hangover and when he comes back he won't remember a thing he told you. Don't worry."

That's precisely what happened: Romanov never mentioned the bakery to me again.

Since I was in charge of KGB operations in the outlying districts of the Leningrad region, I sometimes accompanied Romanov on his triumphal tours through the boondocks. These trips were invariably well scripted, enabling Comrade Romanov to see the best that our rural regions had to offer. Most collective farms were, in fact, a mess, run by dimwitted directors who presided over a rabble of dispirited and often alcoholic workers. Many of our villages looked straight out of the nineteenth century, with people living in ramshackle wooden cottages that lacked running water and indoor toilets. But Romanov and other exalted guests never saw that reality. They invariably were squired around the handful of model collective farms that were well run and well funded. One of these was a much-praised meat and dairy farm, a Potemkin village that boasted an astonishing 96,000 pigs. (Actually, the director confided to me that they had 100,000 pigs, but he only reported 96,000 leaving 4,000 porkers he could use to bribe people, barter, or feed visiting dignitaries like Romanov.) The visits to these model farms followed the same scenario in Leningrad and throughout the country. The honored guest—in our case, Romanov—would arrive and be given a quick tour of the state-of-the-art facilities, the farm director invariably mentioning that his production exceeded that of similar farms in the West. Smiling collective farm workers would tell the dignitary how great everything was, and then all the top local officials—Party bosses, KGB chiefs, collective farm directors—would repair to a private dining room attached to the collective farm's cafeteria. There, the group would sit down at tables groaning with food and drink, and the marathon toasting and vodka-guzzling would begin. After a few hours, everyone would be utterly smashed. Stumbling out to their cars, they would pronounce the visit a roaring success.

I quickly grew weary of such affairs and tried to avoid them whenever possible, for with every passing month it became more evident that our Communist bosses were busy pickling their brains while the country steadily fell to pieces. Once, Romanov went to a small town to celebrate the anniversary of the lifting of the 900-day Siege of Leningrad. Like most Communist Party bosses, he shamelessly used the suffering of our people during the war to bolster the authority of the Party, saying that without the valiant Communist structures we would have never defeated the Nazis. I got tired of watching people like Romanov wrap themselves in the mantle of World War II, and after the ceremony I decided not to attend the usual banquet. My absence created quite a stir. The next day I got a call from one of Romanov's assistants, saying that the first secretary had been asking after me.

"It was a big mistake not to stick around," the assistant told me. "How could you leave such an important event? You should have stayed and had a drink with the rest of us. You're supposed to stay with Comrade Romanov, to protect him. It's your duty."

Lev Zaikov, the mayor of Leningrad and later first secretary of the city Party organization, was as conceited as Romanov, though each had his own peculiarities. A tall, husky man with bulging eyes, Zaikov had been manager of a large defense factory before being named head of the Leningrad Party organization. I was in Leningrad when Zaikov was promoted, and a KGB official called Nozyrev to inform him that the agency had a significant amount of information about Zaikov's alleged corruption and malfeasance at the defense plant. Nozyrev took the call while I was in his office.

"Now that Lev Nikolayevich Zaikov has been elected Party secretary, gather everything you have about his activities at this plant and destroy it," Nozyrev instructed his underling. "You have damaging information? . . . Yes? Well, destroy the files at once. Don't you know that we mustn't have anything of this nature on file about Party officials?"

Zaikov was driven to distraction by people who dared pass his long black Chaika limousine on the highway. One of my acquaintances made the mistake of overtaking Zaikov on a road near Leningrad. The Communist Party boss ordered his driver to run the poor man off the highway. Then the driver got out and yanked the fellow's license plates off his little Moskvich. Zaikov rolled down his window and, wagging his finger victoriously at the unfortunate driver, told him he would get his plates back from the police in a month or two.

One day, as I was riding from work to my *dacha* outside Leningrad, I saw a Chaika limousine in front of me, poking along at about 40 miles an hour. My driver casually passed the capitol Chaika. A few seconds later, the Chaika roared by us, its siren wailing and someone in the backseat shaking his fist at us from the curtained window. I thought nothing more of the incident.

The next day, however, someone from the mayor's office called our office to see if it was indeed my car that had passed Zaikov's on the Seaside Highway. The following day my phone rang, and I picked up the receiver only to hear Zaikov's angry, stentorian voice.

"Were you on assignment when you overtook my car the day before yesterday?" the mayor yelled. "No? Then why were you going so fast! Didn't you see it was the mayor ahead of you? You didn't know, huh? The license plates were unfamiliar, weren't they? That's right, I have another set of license plates. But you saw it was a Chaika, didn't you? You have no respect for the mayor! None at all. Your boss would never do such a thing. And you think you can do anything you want because you're from Moscow. You don't respect me. No! Not at all!"

The next day, our chief—Nozyrev—called his top deputies together for an important announcement.

"I am sick and tired of listening to the Party committee's complaints about our men overtaking their cars on the highway," said Nozyrev. "I won't name any names of the latest offenders. But from this day on, it is strictly forbidden for anyone to pass the cars of top officials of the regional Communist Party. You know their license numbers. Those who do it again will be severely punished."

We left chuckling under our breath. So this is what our vaunted Communist Party had come to: worrying about people passing their leaders' cars on the highway. And now we were being forbidden to undermine the Communist Party's leading role in society by daring to pass them on the open road. From now on, we had to be good comrades and learn to tag behind our Party leaders, no matter how slowly they were going, or how badly they were driving.

It's easy to see how these Communist Party bosses came to feel that they were masters of all they surveyed, for in reality there was almost nothing they couldn't do in their regions. One of my duties in Leningrad was to oversee the KGB troops along the Finnish frontier. I made numerous trips to the border, talking to the officers and men there and sometimes going hunting and fishing in the pristine wilderness (off limits to other Soviets). I had heard of a terrific hunting spot along the frontier, in a place called Kirovskaya Bukhta, and one day I asked my colleague, Rear Admiral Sokolov, if he would like to accompany me on a trip there. He declined, warning me that this was the exclusive reserve of Romanov, Zaikov, and other Party bigwigs. Since the border was my area of responsibility, I went anyway on a trip that mixed business and pleasure: after talking with the troops, I wanted to do some hunting.

When I arrived at Kirovskaya Bukhta, one of our officers again warned me that these were the hunting grounds of the Party bosses. I asked how large was the hunting estate, and he told me it was 7,500 acres.

"They've got a small river of their own with a bridge over it," the officer said. "You can catch great pike in there. They had a small house built for them on an island in the Gulf of Finland, next to the border. We feed the moose here so that the guests are assured a good hunt. Rear Admiral Sokolov is here more often than anyone else; he comes and gets fish and moose meat for the bosses. Some of the fish he salts away in barrels, so there's enough for the winter, too."

Romanov had a *dacha* about 20 miles from Leningrad in a lovely spot known as Osinovaya Roscha. But I learned from Rear Admiral Sokolov that Osinovaya Roscha was famous within the KGB for more than just its fine country houses. It seemed that just a mile or two from Romanov's *dacha* was a mass grave in which an estimated seventy thousand victims of Stalin's terror were buried. The problem was that every spring, with the melting snow, dozens of skeletons would pop up from the thawing earth. Sokolov had a team of a half-dozen workmen who went out to Osinovaya Roscha in the spring to rebury the uncovered remains. Few people knew then of the mass grave, and though Stalin had been denounced and his crimes vaguely discussed, we had not yet progressed far enough to let our people know how grisly the Stalin years had truly been.

The unchecked power of these Communist bosses wreaked untold damage on our society, as was vividly illustrated by the construction of a dam across the Gulf of Finland. One of the legacies of Stalinism was our leaders' love of colossal public works projects. Brezhnev oversaw the building of the Baikal-Amur Railway, known as BAM, a gigantic undertaking that lay down a little-needed rail line in the wilds of Siberia. In Leningrad, in the late 1970s, Romanov and his underlings devised their own "construction project of the century"— a plan to dam off the Gulf of Finland in order to stop the frequent flooding of Leningrad. So in the 1980s, over the objections of some eminent scientists, a 12-mile dam was built across the shallow Gulf, at phenomenal expense. There was, indeed, reduced flooding, but the dam so interfered with tidal flows and the local ecology that it turned much of the Gulf near Leningrad into a dead sea. Leningrad's water became virtually undrinkable, beaches were polluted, and migrating species of fish, such as the delicious *koryushka,* were virtually wiped out. The dam was a boondoggle, an example of the monumental irresponsibility of our Party leaders and the absence of control over their actions, either from above or below. Zaikov, too, was a big booster of the dam, and he and Romanov had no trouble persuading the Politburo in Moscow that their dam was a glorious achievement for Soviet Communism.

In late 1984, Romanov moved on to the Politburo in Moscow, and he was replaced by Zaikov. I remember vividly how Zaikov returned from a meeting with the fossilized Soviet leader, Chernenko, and reported on his trip in glowing terms.

"Constantin Ustinovich [Chernenko] gave me a very warm reception," Zaikov told a meeting of the regional Communist Party Committee. "He is so wise. He has so much understanding! He knows the problems of our city very well. I asked him about the construction of the dam, and he said he would like it to continue. We will soon get extra funds and the blocking off of the Gulf of Finland will continue at full speed. It will be a great victory for us, comrades!

Listening to Zaikov, it was clear that we were going back to the

Brezhnev days, with its paper victories and mighty projects. As the roughly one hundred members of the regional Party Committee enthusiastically applauded Zaikov's speech, I felt my heart sink. I wanted to howl with anguish.

A group of local scientists asked me to use the power of the KGB to stop construction of the dam. But when I approached my chief, Nozyrev, and began talking about the environmental problems, he waved me off.

"Mind your own business," he snapped. "Grigory Vasilyevich [Romanov] has made a decision on this and it's final. Why do you have to listen to all these bleeding hearts?"

I was given an inside glimpse of our Party and political life when I was "elected" in 1981 to the Leningrad regional Soviet, our local legislature. I was nominated from the outlying Gatchina district. One day, in a prearranged show, a local seamstresses' school invited me to a political meeting. A Party official stood up before the three hundred students and said, "This is General Kalugin. He has rendered tremendous service to his country, he has many decorations, so we suggest that you nominate him to the regional Soviet."

All in the room raised their hands in assent. On election day, I received 99 percent of the votes in the district—after all, I was the only candidate. Once a month, I held office hours, but no one ever came to see me and I would wind up reading the newspaper or talking with friends. I did manage, through my connections, to find funds to build a new apartment building for the seamstresses' school, and that remains my only legacy from my seven years on the regional Soviet.

I also was chosen as a member of the regional Communist Party Committee, and I remember my first meeting, and how impressed I was as a seemingly simple worker stood up and delivered an eloquent speech on the region's social problems. After the meeting, I told a local Party boss how intelligent this common man had seemed, and how our educational standards appeared to be improving. The boss enlightened me, however. The worker hadn't just stood up and made an extemporaneous address. Party officials had chosen him a month in advance, had written his speech for him, and had drilled him repeatedly on how to deliver it. It was all scripted in advance, as was every meeting of the regional Soviet and Communist Party Committee. It was a charade, with leaders applauding one another for nonexistent achievements, issuing glowing reports about our bright future, and listening to the proletariat deliver canned speeches on the problems of the day.

In a KGB library, I got hold of the writings of the banned Yugoslav philosopher Milovan Djilas. His views on the corruption of Communism, and how he eventually made a break with Communist philosophy, mirrored mine exactly.

"In the sphere of intellectual life, the [Communist] oligarchs' planning doesn't lead to anything but stagnation, moral degradation and decadence," Djilias wrote in his book *The New Class*. "These heralds of the rigid, eroded, outdated ideas—it's they who freeze and hamper the people's creative impulses. Free thought is for them like a weed which threatens to uproot people's minds."

He went on to describe the shadow game the deluded Communist leaders played with one another: "It's like a theater without an audience: the actors applaud each other, admiring the way they play."

Reading Djilas's preface, I found a passage that exactly described my state of mind: "I departed from Communism gradually and consciously, as I came to get the picture and draw the conclusions described in this book . . . I am a product of this world. I took part in building it. Now, I'm one of its critics."

In March 1985, just as my faith in my country and its government was at an all-time low, Mikhail Sergeyevich Gorbachev swept aside the octogenarians on the ruling Politburo in Moscow and took power. And with his ascension to the throne, I began to believe that my long-held dream of radically reforming our Communist state was about to come true.

I had first heard of Gorbachev the year before, while visiting my old friend Alexander Yakovlev, with whom I had attended Columbia University. Yakovlev had gone on to become Soviet Ambassador to Canada, where in 1984 he met Gorbachev while the latter was on a trip to Ottawa. The two men forged a fast friendship, and they—along with Georgian leader Eduard Shevardnadze—went on to mastermind *perestroika*.

After his Canadian posting, Yakovlev returned to Moscow and was appointed head of the Institute of World Economy. There, he became Gorbachev's closest adviser, and it was clear that they were already planning how Gorbachev might take power once the ailing Chernenko passed away. I went to see Yakovlev in his office, and we greeted one another like old friends, catching up on all the news and gossip since our last meeting six years before. In the middle of our conversation the phone rang and Yakovlev, limping from a war wound, ambled over to his desk and picked up the receiver. His face lit up as he talked.

"Yes, Mikhail Sergeyevich," Yakovlev said. "I'll be done soon and I'll drop by then . . . We'll work on it when I get there."

Yakovlev returned to his chair, took a sip of coffee, and said, "That was Mikhail Gorbachev, a member of the Politburo and Central Committee secretary. He's a great guy. If he becomes a General Secretary there will be colossal changes in the country. He's a reformer with a capital 'R'."

Now, nearly a decade after Gorbachev became the leader of the Soviet Union, it is difficult for outsiders—and even some Russians—to remember what an astonishing impression he made in his first year on the job. In hindsight, it's clear that Gorbachev had no intention of doing away with the Communist system, but rather simply wanted to overhaul it, to make it work more efficiently. At the time however, what a joy it was to watch a robust man—he was then in his early fifties—talk about radically changing our society. What a breath of fresh air was *glasnost,* as our people and the press began debating long-taboo subjects, such as the stagnation of the Brezhnev years, the cruelty of Stalin, and the gross inefficiency of our Soviet system. One after another, the barriers came down, the sacred cows were slaughtered. It was an indescribably heady period, and I found myself almost instantly revived, like an old wineskin filled with young wine.

I was lucky enough to see Gorbachev just a few months after he took power. He came to Leningrad on an official visit, and I accompanied him to Petrodvorets, the site of Peter the Great's old palace. We met briefly, and then I listened to him speak at a meeting of the regional Communist Party. He struck me as almost Kennedy-esque, talking in impassioned tones about how we had to get our society moving again. He was lucid and vigorous and—unlike our previous leaders—could even speak extemporaneously. (Toward the end of his reign, Brezhnev seemed incapable of saying his name without reading it from a cue card. We all cringed in embarrassment when, at one Party gathering, Brezhnev read the same page of his speech twice without realizing it. When I was in Intelligence, Kryuchkov announced that, since Brezhnev didn't like to read, all our reports meant for the Soviet leader had to be triple-spaced and no longer than three pages.) I came away from Gorbachev's Leningrad trip feeling certain that this was the man who could finally set things right in our long-suffering land.

Spurred on by *glasnost* and the new spirit ushered in by Gorbachev, I began to speak more aggressively at our KGB meetings, pushing for reform both inside and outside our agency. I also began writing letters to our national newspapers, joining the flood of people who welcomed the increased openness in our society. During the previous thaw in the Soviet Union, under Khrushchev, no one dared speak out about Stalin until our leaders gave the okay. But by 1986, Soviet citizens weren't waiting for approval from on high; they were diving right in, saying and writing what they believed. I joined the fray, writing at least a dozen letters to *Pravda, Komsomolskaya Pravda, Literaturnaya Gazeta,* and other publications. I wrote the letters—none of which was published—as a common citizen, and signed them "O. Kalugin." Now, they look absurdly tame, but at the time the themes I was expounding seemed shockingly bold. I suggested it was all right for people to work side jobs as farmers or repairmen, pocketing the profits from their labor. I attacked the extensive system of traffic police posts that ringed our cities, calling them holdovers from an authoritiarian past. I excoriated corrupt Communist Party bureaucrats, and said that the anti-alcohol campaign then sweeping the country was a foolish mistake. Seeking to prove that it was useless to try to stop people from drinking, I even quoted Karl Marx, who once wrote, "Being a native of a vine-growing land and a former owner of vineyards, I appreciate good wine. I even agree with old man Luther that a man who doesn't like wine is incapable of anything worth mentioning."

Literaturnaya Gazeta decided not to publish that letter.

All of a sudden, I found that I had lost my fear. Though I scarcely knew Gorbachev, I felt as if he were standing behind me, offering me support in my efforts to reform society and the KGB. Many younger officers supported Gorbachev and *perestroika,* but Nozyrev and his cronies clearly were uncomfortable with this reformer. The old-style bosses couldn't afford to completely ignore the new forces sweeping our society, and I remember that Zaikov arranged an exhibit in the city to tout one of the reformist fads of the day—*uskoreniye,* or acceleration, which demanded that we work harder and faster to lift our economy out of the doldrums. But it was clear that our Leningrad Party bosses, Romanov and Zaikov, were never fully behind the Soviet leader. Both were elevated to the ruling Politburo in Moscow; but Romanov was quickly sacked by Gorbachev and Zaikov was axed in a later purge of Communist hardliners.

I said to hell with my boss, Nozyrev, and pushed Gorbachev's line whenever possible. In 1986, on the anniversary of Lenin's birth, I told a gathering of several hundred Communists that Lenin was actually a radical reformer who would have supported our efforts to rebuild the Soviet Union. My critiques were all couched in Marxist-Leninist rhetoric, but it was the beginning of *glasnost* and budding reformers were forced to sweeten their bitter medicine with the familiar jargon of Communism.

Not only did I begin speaking out, I also began acting more aggressively to root out corruption in the Leningrad region, a choice of action that would set me on a collision course with our local Party leaders and lead, in 1987, to my removal from the Leningrad KGB.

By 1985, I had been put in charge of overseeing the work of the police and the Interior Ministry in the Leningrad region. Later that year, we got a tip from one of our informers, a police officer in the town of Gatchina, that the town's assistant prosecutor was notoriously corrupt and was taking bribes in exchange for calling off criminal investigations. At the same time, my constituents in Gatchina—I was their "elected" representative on the regional Soviet—began telling me about the rampant corruption in the town. I went to see Gennadi Voschinin, the Communist Party official who oversaw law enforcement agencies in the Leningrad region, and told him I wanted to investigate the allegations of corruption in Gatchina. Voschinin gave me the go-ahead.

We planted a listening device in the assistant prosecutor's office, and in a matter of weeks we had recorded several instances of his bribe taking. The evidence was irrefutable, and the regional prosecutor had no alternative but to take the man to court. He was convicted of receiving at least 10,000 rubles in bribes and sentenced to ten years in jail. However, as I would soon find out, his case was only the tip of the iceberg.

In 1986, after the conviction of the assistant prosecutor, Nozyrev and other top KGB officials in Leningrad met to discuss the agency's work during the first half of the year. In my report, I mentioned the arrest of the assistant prosecutor as one of our achievements and said the corruption investigation was continuing. Later, when Nozyrev spoke, he took a direct swipe at our accomplishments, telling the assembled officers, "Kalugin spoke here about this senior assistant to the prosecutor. So what? Was he a spy or something? Catch me a spy. You haven't caught a single one. So this guy took a bribe of a few thousand rubles? So what? You call that money? That's no case for the KGB."

I was furious. In front of more than three hundred officers I stood up and answered him.

"Comrade Nozyrev, if a store manager or shop clerk takes a bribe, even a million rubles, it doesn't matter to me while I'm on this job," I said, as my colleagues looked on in silence. "But when a law enforcement officer takes even ten rubles, this is a crime that has to be punished. The court gave this prosecutor the right sentence, ten years. The people you keep under investigation as spies will never be caught and never go to jail. . . . Corruption has to be fought. It's eating away at our country."

My words were an affront to Nozyrev, but he sat there silently and moved on to the next order of business. He would not, however, forget my insubordination. Later, he would settle the score.

Next, we received word of extensive corruption in the mining region of Slantsy. The local mafia, led by an Armenian man, was reportedly bribing district officials and then stealing shipments of imported Finnish goods meant for the miners. We placed wiretaps on the phones of several people, including the Armenian, and in a matter of weeks gathered enough information to convict a handful of local mafiosi and some low-level officials. Our investigation was almost blown when Lev Zaikov's sister, who was involved with the local mafia, got wind of our activities and tipped off her friends.

We were gaining momentum, and in late 1986 another police informer told us about extensive corruption involving the export of timber from the Leningrad region to the southern republics of the Soviet Union. Our informant said that Soviet "businessmen" from the southern republics were bribing numerous Leningrad officials, taking large amounts of timber out of the region at cut-rate prices, and selling the wood—at enormous profit—in the south. Joined by ten investigators, we uncovered evidence that as many as forty "businessmen" and local officials were involved in the scam, and that more than 3 million rubles in bribes (worth about $4 million at the time) had changed hands. Among those taking bribes were the deputy chairman of the Leningrad regional Soviet, several district Communist Party bosses, and the head of the Leningrad region's agriculture department.

We arrested several dozen people—almost all of them the men who had paid the bribes—but the investigation didn't stop there. Some of those arrested gave evidence against even more important officials, including the deputy director of the Leningrad Lumber Association and a director of the Leningrad regional railway. The corruption was far more widespread than anyone had imagined, and our investigation was now reaching into the highest levels of Leningrad government and industry. Therein lay the problem.

I went to Nozyrev and laid out the scope of the investigation.

"Are you crazy, or what?" the Leningrad KGB chief responded. "You've already arrested forty people. What more do you want?"

I then went to the regional prosecutor, and explained the evidence showing that far bigger fish were involved in the unfolding bribery scandal. I told him that the overwhelming majority of people we had arrested were businessmen and bribe payers, not the Leningrad officials who were on the take.

"Look, Oleg," said the Leningrad prosecutor. "We've been cooperating so beautifully. We've arrested forty people. That's enough. Why don't we close this case?"

Next, I went to Gennadi Voschinin, the regional Party official responsible for law enforcement and the man who had initially approved my investigation of the corrupt prosecutor.

Voschinin looked over the papers I had brought, detailing the region's massive bribe taking.

"What do you need all this for?" asked Voschinin. "You've already destroyed that lumber gang."

"The men we arrested are just businessmen who paid bribes to get the lumber," I responded. "It's the ones that let them have the timber illegally and take the bribes who are the real culprits, and they're still sitting in their offices in the Party Committee and the local government. Those are the ones who sold the power entrusted to them by the people. They are much more dangerous than those who gave the bribes. And we're talking about three million rubles."

"Why are you so bloodthirsty?" said Voschinin. "Why do you want more heads to roll? Isn't forty enough for you? You want more blood? I'm sorry, I can't help you. Just wrap up the case. There's no use going on."

"I'm sorry," I replied. "It would be dishonest to stop now. I'm doing what I'm here to do. I won't close the case."

"Just think it over," replied Voshinin. "That's all we ask."

That same day, Nozyrev summoned me to his office at KGB headquarters on Liteiny Prospect.

"What is it you're trying to start—a mutiny?" he shouted. "Enough fooling around. You haven't made a single case of anti-Soviet activity or espionage in the region. It's time you did some real work."

I told him he was wrong, that KGB Chairman Chebrikov himself had argued for the need to step up the fight against corruption.

"Enough of your demagoguery!" Nozyrev snapped, and ordered me out of his office.

Within a few days, I learned that KGB officials in Moscow and Leningrad had begun trying to compromise my chief investigators and were putting pressure on them to stop working with me. One investigator was accused of extorting bribes from a criminal; another was accused of stealing diamonds during an investigation; a third was accused by neighbors in his communal apartment of beating his wife. The accusations were false, but the KGB was turning the heat up on my investigators, and one by one they withdrew from the case. Clearly, our investigation had been too aggressive and reached too high into the Party structure. Now, my superiors were determined to put an end to the work of my group.

About that time, I had finished reading the three-volume KGB case file on the brilliant Russian poet Anna Akhmatova. She had been under suspicion since 1927, first as a Trotskyite and then as an American spy. Her file was full of nasty reports from the legions of informers who had been persuaded to work against the poet. They spread rumors and innuendo, one woman even alleging that Akhmatova was a lesbian and had fondled the informer's breasts. The file, which I took from the KGB archives, laid out the sordid picture of how the KGB had hounded this woman and monitored her every move for decades. And as I read through the documents and thought of my own growing struggle with the security apparatus, a line from one of Akhmatova's poems kept running through my mind:

"Everything is stolen, betrayed, sold . . ."

I knew I would get no help in Leningrad with our investigation, and so I decided to write a letter to the Prosecutor General in Moscow. In it, I laid out the extent of our corruption inquiry and reported that Leningrad officials were now covering up what we had found.

I heard nothing for a month; indeed, the Prosecutor General never acknowledged receiving my letter. One day, however, Voschinin summoned me, and this time he made no effort to conceal his anger.

"We didn't expect this from you," Voschinin said. "Why did you have to complain to the Prosecutor General? Listen, we in Leningrad know best how to handle these affairs. Do you think they will help us in Moscow? Well, they won't. We don't take orders from Moscow . . . We have instructed the regional prosecutor's office to drop the lumber case."

I knew now that there was no going back. My growing dissatisfaction with the KGB and Soviet life, my realization that my career was already over—all this propelled me forward, persuaded me that I had to continue my increasingly dissident activities.

But Nozyrev apparently thought I had gone too far, and he fabricated a scandal to drive me out of Leningrad. It centered on my role as the KGB's representative on the Foreign Travel Commission, the body that decided which of our citizens would be allowed to go abroad.

The Foreign Travel Commission was a purely totalitarian creation—an omnipotent group that wielded enormous power over Leningraders hoping to travel overseas. Representatives from the police, Intourist, the Communist Party, and the KGB sat on the commission, though I, as the security service's person on the body, had the ultimate say on who could travel. It was not a job I enjoyed.

My troubles began at a commission meeting in late 1986. The gathering started off typically enough, with the chief of Intourist in Leningrad ticking off a list of his employees they had decided to ban from overseas travel.

"Guide and interpreter Radvinskaya, non-Party member, divorced, went to Spain with a group of Soviet tourists," the Intourist chief said in a monotone. "She often left the hotel alone in the evenings and came back late at night. Paid no attention to group leader's reprimands, answered tourists' questions rudely, did not use every opportunity to propagandize the Soviet way of life . . . Should be barred from foreign travel.

"Interpreter Semenova, Communist Party member, senior guide. On a Danube cruise showed herself to be greedy and mercenary. Behaved flippantly . . . rude, apolitical . . . Barred from foreign travel."

Soon, we came to the case of a woman named Irina, an employee of Pan American Airlines in Leningrad. Irina had once worked in the Party library, and I knew her to be a reliable and hardworking person; she had helped me type several papers. But apparently one of her colleagues at Pan Am, a KGB informer, didn't like Irina and said in a confidential report that Irina was a greedy capitalist who would use her time abroad to make money. On the strength of that one informer, one of my underlings had signed an order banning Irina from foreign travel.

I told my fellow commission members that I wanted to look more closely at the case. The following week I got Irina's file, and it was clear that—save for this one spiteful co-worker—she had an admirable record and was not a travel risk. I reported my findings at the next meeting of the Foreign Travel Commission, and we agreed that the ban would be lifted and Irina allowed to go to the United States. I sent a letter to the Leningrad regional Party Committee saying that new material exonerating the woman had been found and that the ban was being lifted.

Somehow, the new Leningrad City Party boss, Yuri Solovyov, got wind of our decision and was infuriated by it. Nozyrev summoned me and other top deputies and launched into another of his harangues:

"Solovyov is outraged by this! You have screwed up. Do you ever look at the papers you sign? First, you allow people to travel, then you forbid them, and then you blacklist others and change your minds again. I am sick and tired of listening to the regional Party Committee's complaints about your inefficiency."

"What are you yelling at me for?" I interrupted. "Does the regional Party Commission have nothing better to do than spend its time finding fault with the Travel Commission? Yes, we occasionally make mistakes, but when we do, we correct them."

Nozyrev turned purple and swore at me. Fed up after six years of working with this idiot, and emboldened by the reform spirit alive in the country, I swore back at him and said, "I will no longer work with you."

The Leningrad KGB chief rose from his seat and said, "I will not work with you either. The meeting is over. Go away, all of you. I don't wish to talk any more."

With that, he stormed out of the conference room. I later learned that he called Chebrikov that same day to say that I had revolted and could no longer work in Leningrad.

I returned to my office and sat down to write Chebrikov a letter requesting that he immediately transfer me back to Moscow. As I was sitting there over a blank page, pondering the wording of the letter, a friend of mine from domestic Counterintelligence came into my office and suggested we have coffee in the cafeteria.

"Look, Nozyrev thinks you okayed this woman's trip to America in order to restore your lost connection to the CIA through her," my friend told me as we sat down in the buffet. "You've been watched for several years on orders from Moscow, but the surveillance didn't turn up anything worthwhile. In order to compromise you and get you out of here, our agent who heads the Pan Am office called his bosses in Moscow on Nozyrev's orders. Nozyrev told our Pan Am agent to tell the American office that he was about to be fired because some KGB general (you) was having an affair with this Irina woman and that the general was jealous of him. The telephone conversation was a setup and it was recorded, so you can be sure that the transcript will be on the KGB chairman's desk today."

My colleague, who had taken part in the investigation of me, also said Nozyrev and Moscow KGB officials had become quite suspicious a year or two earlier when I parked my car along the Neva River and took a walk. Apparently, the surveillance team following me spotted an American consular official in the same area, and they suspected me of holding a secret rendezvous with the CIA.

"Did you see that American?" my colleague asked.

"How do I know?" I replied. "I meet hundreds of people on the street every day and I don't know which of them is American. And frankly I don't care."

I thanked my colleague and returned to my office, stunned that Nozyrev would go to such lengths to get rid of me. I was even more outraged that the KGB still wasn't convinced of my loyalty and was continuing to follow me. It was the last straw.

"No more," I said to myself. "Nothing will stop me now."

I knew there was no sense writing Chebrikov, that I had to take a gamble and go outside the KGB. So I sat down and drafted a letter to the Central Committee of the Communist Party, hoping that, under Gorbachev's influence, the Central Committee members might decide to do something about the rampant corruption in Leningrad. In my letter, I described in detail the investigation and how top officials in the city had refused to pursue the scandal further and were protecting their cronies in the Party. I said that Nozyrev himself had backed off the investigation, and I went on at length about his incompetent leadership, his concealment of problems, his intolerance of dissent, and his abuse of power. When I was finished, I placed the six-page letter in a "TOP SECRET" pouch and had it sent by special courier to Moscow. I was hopeful that, at last, something would be done.

Two weeks later, a special investigating commission, comprised of high-ranking officials from the KGB and the Central Committee, arrived in Leningrad to look into my allegations. They seemed like they meant business, and I was delighted as they fanned out around the region. In a few days, however, it became clear that the special commission had come to Leningrad not to investigate Nozyrev and corruption. They had come to investigate *me!* They didn't like the message they had heard, and they were going after the messenger. Numerous friends and acquaintances in the KGB said commission members were asking why I had started this trouble, what sort of relationship I had with Nozyrev, whether I drank heavily or was a womanizer, whether I embezzled money or had any contacts with foreigners. One of my friends in the region said a commission member had tried to intimidate him into making negative statements about me.

"Tell us how you got drunk together, how you went to the sauna," my friend quoted the commission member as saying.

When my friend denied we had ever gotten drunk or chased women, the commission member responded, "We will find out everything and then you'll be sorry you didn't tell us."

I gave the commission members names of people who could corroborate my corruption allegations, but they never spoke to them. Instead they concentrated on compromising me, though after several weeks in the city they came up with nothing. As they prepared to depart, the commission held a meeting with some top KGB staff. I was in attendance and wanted to speak, but the head of the commission—deputy KGB chairman for personnel Vitaly Ponomaryov—told me, "Comrade Kalugin, we agree with you that Nozyrev should be removed, but that will take some time. But you don't have to speak today, and don't speak against him publicly. Just keep quiet."

So I kept quiet. Nozyrev wasn't removed, and the commission concluded there was no substance to my allegations. My only consolation came when I heard from friends in Moscow that Gorbachev had read my letter about Nozyrev and had scribbled across it, "Are there really such bosses in the KGB? Run a check on him."

As was often to be the case, however, the KGB officers under Gorbachev sabotaged any efforts to reform the massive secret police agency.

I knew that my gamble of writing the Central Committee had failed and that remaining in Leningrad was out of the question. Several weeks after the commission left, I was summoned to Moscow by Ponomaryov and told, "We suggest you come back to Moscow. You've been in Leningrad too long, and it's obvious that it's impossible for you to work with Nozyrev. It's time to come back home.

We suggest that you take a job at the Academy of Sciences, as security officer. It's a big job. You understand how important the Academy of Sciences is. You'll get to travel a lot."

"I haven't finished my job yet in Leningrad," I said stubbornly. "I want to go back."

"We'll give you some time to think it over," said Ponomaryov. "But I think it would be better for you to come back."

The next day I went to see my friend Alexander Yakovlev. He said he had tried to persuade Kryuchkov and Chebrikov to let me return to a high position with the KGB in Moscow, but all his entreaties had failed. We agreed that it would be best for me to leave Leningrad, and the following day I told Ponomaryov that I would accept the transfer to the Academy of Sciences. I knew it was a dead-end job. I would be placed on the KGB Reserve, and my responsibility would be to make sure that none of the scientists in the academy got into trouble or had contact with Western intelligence services. It was, I knew full well, the effective end of my thirty-year career. But I saw no other way out, and had a vague feeling that a larger task lay ahead. I didn't know quite what it was, but I already sensed that I could play a major role in the reform of the agency to which I had devoted my life.

In December 1986 I returned to Leningrad and prepared to leave for Moscow. I never saw Nozyrev again, and only said goodbye to a few of my colleagues; many officers now saw me as a dangerous dissident and wanted nothing to do with me.

Early in January 1987, almost seven years to the day since I had been transferred to Leningrad following the Cook affair, I boarded a night train for Moscow. The predominant emotion I experienced wasn't anger or bitterness, but emptiness. I felt as if I had wasted seven years in a petty and useless job. Those seven years seemed to me lost years, and Leningrad no longer felt like my hometown. To me, it was an alien and hostile place. So, too, was the KGB, and I returned to Moscow with one overriding aim: To expose and reform this gigantic piece of totalitarian machinery.

Soon after my arrival in Moscow, I went in to see Chairman Chebrikov. To my surprise, he greeted me warmly.

"Why didn't you write directly to me?" he asked. "Why did you have to write to the Central Committee, to air our dirty linen in public? . . . You should have written to me to complain about Nozyrev. After all, Nozyrev is on his way out."

"Is that why you put me in the reserve?" I asked.

"This all happened so quickly and unexpectedly," replied the aging Chebrikov. "You raised hell and there was simply no senior position open that we could offer you. You are no ordinary officer and you can only fill a very high position, but there's none vacant at the moment. So stay here in the reserve for a while. Maybe you'll soon become deputy chairman of the KGB."

At the end of our brief conversation, however, Chebrikov fired a warning shot.

"If you keep writing these letters, I will simply sack you at your early retirement age of fifty-five," the chairman said.

"I understand," I replied.

I left furious. Chebrikov clearly had no intention of promoting me to deputy chairman of the KGB, but he had held out that prospect in an effort to keep me toeing the company line. Chebrikov also had threatened me, however, and I knew that the stick was much more real than the carrot.

I began working—actually, it was more like retirement—as protector of state secrets at the Academy of Sciences. That same month I saw my friend and close Gorbachev adviser, Yakovlev, and told him of the dire situation at the KGB: Chebrikov was incompetent, Kryuchkov was a bastard, and not one breath of reform had swept through the agency. Then, one day at work, it came to me: I had to write a letter to Gorbachev himself, setting forth what needed to be done to change the KGB.

In a single day, I produced a ten-page letter to the Soviet leader. I told Gorbachev that the KGB was a state within a state and that *perestroika* would never succeed unless the KGB was reformed, top to bottom. The KGB was one of the pillars of the Soviet state, and it had to be brought under control and made into a law-abiding institution that stopped spying on—and spreading fear among—its own people. I suggested that the staff of our agency be cut by at least a third, that Intelligence and Counterintelligence be streamlined and radically reformed, that far fewer documents be stamped "TOP SECRET," and that the onerous restrictions on foreign travel be lifted.

I told Gorbachev, in effect, that the KGB was an agency out of control. Left unreformed, it would perpetually pose a threat to our society.

"Against the background of the changes taking place in this country," I wrote, "the KGB appears to be the most conservative, rigid agency, one which can't help but enter into a growing conflict with the progressive development of Socialist society. . . . The time is ripe to reform the law enforcement system and strengthen the Party and government control over [the KGB]. That will substantially speed up the process of democratization in our country."

I showed the letter to Yakovlev, and he heartily endorsed it. He passed it on to Gorbachev, launching me irreversibly down the path of dissidence.

I wasn't scared; I knew I was doing the right thing. All my life I had tried to please my superiors, had worried about my advancement in the KGB. As I passed the letter to Yakovlev, I felt liberated, elated, and unconcerned about what the future might bring.

Only later did I discover that, even before Gorbachev had a chance to read the letter, Chebrikov had been on the phone with him, telling him I was a dangerous and unstable man. It was my fault that Gorbachev was forewarned; I had told some colleagues I was writing the letter, and in a matter of hours someone had passed the information on to Chebrikov.

I never heard from the Soviet leader, though Yakovlev told me Gorbachev had been moved by my letter and was following some of its suggestions. But the truth is that Gorbachev could be a timid reformer, and he refused to take on Chebrikov, Kryuchkov, and the KGB. His inaction would come back to haunt him in 1991, when Kryuchkov and other top KGB officials masterminded the August coup, an event that would quickly lead to the demise of the Soviet Union and the end of Gorbachev's historic reign.

Several weeks after I passed the letter to Gorbachev, Chebrikov summoned me to Lubyanka. He looked grim as he received me.

"What did you write in your letter to Gorbachev?" he asked before I even had a chance to sit down.

"I thought you knew," I replied. "The letter was delivered a few weeks ago."

"I didn't read it," he responded curtly. "I don't have a copy. Tell me what you wrote."

I began recounting the contents of the letter. For two hours I set forth my views. I was constantly interrupted by Chebrikov, who contested nearly every point.

"This is not correct," he would say. "How can you possibly write that?"

"It's just the way I feel," I said. "It's my opinion, and it's different from yours. I'm sorry, but that doesn't mean I have to change it."

"But you don't know the scope of operations for the whole KGB," Chebrikov said. "You don't know how important some of these items—like secrecy—are."

The longer we spoke, the more emotional Chebrikov became.

"Where did you get this stuff?" he asked at one point.

"I've been with the organization for more than thirty years, a lot longer than you have," I said. "That's how I know. I've been accumulating this knowledge all my life and everything I say is my conviction. I may not know all the figures, but I know the facts and I wrote them as I saw them. That's what I put in my letter."

I had written that the KGB's Ninth Directorate, which employed thousands of bodyguards was largely useless, full of ne'er-do-wells and drunkards.

"Do you know how important this unit is, how many terrorists are swarming around?" Chebrikov said. "See, you don't know about that."

"I'll tell you what I don't know, Viktor Mikhailovich," I said, my anger rising. "I don't know how this organization, which I have served loyally for over thirty years, could suspect me of being a CIA agent all this time. Do you know about that?"

"We have the right to check everyone!" he shot back.

"But you must also have the professional brains to understand what you are doing," I retorted. "Don't you understand that if you carry on this way with other officers, you will simply undermine the very basis of this organization?"

My anger overflowed, and I told him, my voice cracking, "I will defend my reputation against anyone, you included!"

The KGB chairman shot out of his chair and exclaimed, "And I will defend my reputation and this organization from people like you! . . . I will fight back!"

"And so will I!" I shouted.

Chebrikov strode up to me, fire in his eyes, and shook my hand angrily.

"Go and work!" he said.

I left, and never saw him again.

I returned to my sleepy job at the Academy of Sciences. In August 1987, KGB personnel informed me that I was going to be transferred to the Ministry of Electronics, where I also would be charged with protecting state secrets. It was a high position in the reserve—higher than the Academy of Sciences—and I would have a car and a comfortable salary. The move was Chebrikov's attempt to buy me off.

Besides, he could always tell Yakovlev and Gorbachev, "Kalugin's all right. He's been promoted and he's enjoying life."

I didn't much care what I was doing in the KGB; I knew that retirement and a new life lay not far ahead. Already, I was a different man. The feeling of smallness and fear was leaving me, and I felt an acute need to be myself, to live the way I wanted to live.

In January 1988, I moved to the Ministry of Electronics. I spent almost two years there, traveling the country and visiting top-secret labs and defense plants. The work was not taxing, and I had little to be proud of. My most notable accomplishment was that I managed to reduce the number of top-secret installations within the ministry from three hundred to thirty. I wrote several articles for the Soviet press. I spent time with my wife, daughters, and grandchildren. Mostly, I bided my time.

In September 1989, I turned fifty-five. Several weeks after my birthday, the KGB personnel department summoned me to Lubyanka. I knew what they were going to say.

"We regret it, but we have to tell you that your time is up," the personnel man told me. "You've served your country well, but now we suggest that you retire."

"Okay," I replied. "No problem. I'm ready. What am I supposed to do?"

The personnel people seemed taken aback at how gently I accepted the news of my forced retirement. They kindly suggested I take my accrued vacation pay and sick days, and then come back early next year and officially retire.

"Very well," I said on my way out, scarcely able to conceal an enormous grin. "I will go, but we will have a good fight soon."

I went on vacation for the rest of 1989, spending several weeks at a lavish KGB sanatorium on the Black Sea. In December, a friend from personnel called and suggested that I check into the hospital for a week or two, and delay my retirement until February. Pay raises were coming soon, he said, and by stalling I could leave the KGB with an even higher pension.

I took his advice. Then, on February 26, 1990, I went to Lubyanka for the last time as a KGB officer. The men in personnel signed my retirement papers, and assured me I would be receiving severance pay of 8,000 rubles, quite a sum at the time.

Walking out of Lubyanka, I eyed the papers that said I was now Oleg Danilovich Kalugin, retired major general of the State Security Committee. After serving more than three decades in the KGB, walking away from the agency turned out to be surprisingly easy. I had had a wonderful career, and now it was over. I felt no sadness; the sadness had all been in Leningrad in the 1980s, when I realized the true nature of the organization to which I had devoted my life. No, the sadness had passed. As I walked down the steps of Lubyanka and onto Dzerzhinsky Square, I felt almost euphoric, as if an enormous weight had been lifted from my shoulders.

It was a cool, sunny day, and I walked a few blocks to Nikolskaya Street. My destination was the Institute of History and Archives. The rector of the Institute was a man named Yuri Afanasiev, and he was a leader of the fledgling democratic movement in Russia. I made my way up the steps to his office and knocked on his door. I had no appointment; his secretary asked me who I was. I replied that I had just retired as a major general from the KGB and wanted to see Afanasiev.

She ushered me into his room. I shook hands with the erudite, handsome person in front of me and showed him my KGB identification papers.

"I want to help the democratic movement," I said. "I am sure that my knowledge and experience will be useful. You can use me in any capacity. I'll be with you."

Afanasiev seemed not the least bit surprised.

"I always knew people like you would come to us," he said with a smile.

NINE

Rebirth

On the afternoon of June 16, 1990, I went public in my fight against the KGB.

The place was the cavernous October Cinema on Moscow's Kalinin Prospect, and the occasion was the inaugural gathering of one of the country's newest and most progressive political organizations, the Democratic Platform of the Communist Party. More than fifteen hundred people, including many of the Soviet Union's most prominent liberal politicians, streamed into the hall, and as they took their seats there was a feeling of euphoria in the air. By the middle of 1990, Gorbachev's popularity was slipping and the luster of *perestroika* and *glasnost* was starting to fade. But politically, it was a supercharged time in the Soviet Union: reformers were gathering strength and building the political parties that were challenging the old order. It is ironic that the "Democratic Platform" still associated itself with the Communist Party. As the months passed, even our members would begin to work for the destruction of the Party itself; but in June 1990, the old Communist structures still held sway and we deluded ourselves into thinking the Party could actually be revived.

When I walked into the October Cinema, I was a virtual unknown, both inside the Soviet Union and around the world. But by the time I left several hours later, my days of living in obscurity would be over. June 16, 1990, was the day I crossed the Rubicon. Afterwards, nothing would be the same.

I settled into the twentieth row of the theater, hoping that no one was there from the KGB who might recognize me. After approaching Yuri Afanasiev on the day of my retirement in February, I had quietly started working with him and other reformers. I had written a lengthy article on the KGB for the crusading magazine *Ogonyok,* setting forth my views on how to reform the agency. But though *glasnost* had come to the USSR, there still was censorship. My close friend Alexander Yakovlev had seen the piece I had submitted to *Ogonyok*'s editor, Vitaly Korotich, and strongly advised Korotich not to publish the piece: Gorbachev, Yakovlev argued, had enough problems without launching a full-scale assault on the KGB. So, much to my disappointment, the article was scrapped. I busied myself establishing links with the country's democratic forces.

I had gotten wind of the upcoming Democratic Platform conference, and told some of my friends that I would like to address the gathering. I wanted my thoughts on dismantling the KGB to reach the public. Late one night in early June, the phone rang. The caller was Igor Chubais, one of the leaders of Democratic Platform, and he said he wanted to meet me. It was after eleven, but I suggested that Chubais (whose brother would later lead Boris Yeltsin's drive to privatize Russian industry) come over to my place. He was skittish, however, apparently concerned that my apartment was bugged. (His concern was well-founded. There is no doubt that as my anti-KGB campaign gathered strength, both my phone and my apartment were bugged. The old ladies who stood watch in our building later described how strange men with government papers gained entry to our apartment when we weren't home, claiming our phone lines were faulty. They obviously were planting listening devices. When I let slip word of an upcoming meeting or rendezvous on the phone or in my apartment, KGB surveillance teams often showed up.) Chubais suggested we meet shortly after midnight in front of a nearby subway station. I arrived and stood there under an umbrella in the warm spring rain. The lights of passing cars illuminated the occasional pedestrians scurrying for shelter. At the appointed time, a boxy *Zhiguli* pulled up, and a bearded man stepped out and approached me. Shaking my hand, he introduced himself as Igor Chubais, and for the next hour we walked around the deserted residential streets in the soft rain.

Chubais clearly was skeptical about why such a high-ranking KGB officer would want to join the democratic movement and speak at the upcoming convention. I briefly told him about my career in the KGB, explained my motives for wanting to address Democratic Platform, and outlined the substance of my talk on what needed to be done to break the awesome power of the KGB. By the end of our walk, he seemed convinced I was genuine. He said I could speak at the conference, though we both agreed that no one was to know of my speech in advance, otherwise the KGB might try to prevent me from appearing on the grounds that I was divulging state secrets.

As I sat in the October Theater, with people streaming in all around me, I was nervous and excited. The crowd slowly quieted down, and the procession of speakers—we Russians love a good political speech—began. After the third orator, someone from Democratic Platform took the microphone to announce that a former KGB general was now going to address the group about reforming the secret police agency. The audience went wild. They had no idea who I was, but they stood up and applauded thunderously, searching the room for this convert from the KGB. No high-ranking KGB officer had ever stayed in the country and taken on the agency, and the thought that someone of my stature and experience was coming over to the democratic side was enough to send the audience into rapture. Somehow I made my way to the stage, and when I looked out at the crowd—still on their feet, cheering and applauding—my heart leapt. It was one of the most thrilling moments of my life. Finally I was free, and assaulting the KGB head-on.

The audience fell silent. Struggling to steady my voice, I told the gathering, "Some people may think that I have jumped on the democratic bandwagon with evil intentions. I understand that there may be suspicions in your minds, but let me tell you that you're wrong. I am from the KGB. I worked in that organization for more than thirty years, and I want to tell all of you how the KGB works against the best interests of democratic forces in this country."

There was utter silence in the hall as I talked about myself and explained why the KGB must be radically reformed and the number of agents drastically reduced:

"We cannot begin a serious restructuring of society until we rid ourselves of the restraints imposed by an organization which has penetrated every sphere of our lives, which interferes with all aspects of state life, political life, the economy, science, arts, religion, even sports. Today, just as ten or twenty years ago, the hand of the KGB is everywhere. And any real talk of *perestroika* without reforming the KGB is nothing but a lie. All the much-ballyhooed changes in the KGB are cosmetic, a disguise upon the ugly face of the Stalin-Brezhnev era. In fact, all the elements of the old dictatorship are still in place. The chief assistant and handmaiden of the Communist

Party remains the KGB. In order to secure genuine changes in our country, this structure of violence and falsehood must be dismantled."

My brief speech was greeted with roars of approval, and again the crowd was on its feet. I could scarcely make my way off stage as dozens of Soviet and foreign journalists attending the conference crowded around, peppering me with questions about my life in the KGB and soliciting my views on every conceivable subject. KGB officers had defected before, but no officer—even in the Gorbachev era—had remained in his homeland and launched such an attack on the secret police. My criticism of the KGB was not terribly new and certainly what I said was no secret to those in the hall or in the West. But the fact that I—the youngest general in the history of the KGB and a former chief of Foreign Counterintelligence—was making these statements in the middle of Moscow, in broad daylight and to a conference of reformers . . . well, it was, by the standards of the times, a sensation.

I returned home that night exhausted but elated. I hadn't known how I would be received by Democratic Platform, and the reaction was beyond my wildest dreams. I understood that I had embarked on an entirely new path in life, and was being accepted into a community of people with whom I could finally feel comfortable.

The weeks after that first public appearance are a blur, a time filled to overflowing with interviews and speeches and meetings. I was, for a brief time, the hero of the democratic movement, and everyone, from foreign journalists to leaders of the reform camp, beat a path to my door. I was invited to the Kuzbass coal region in Siberia, where miners were preparing to go on strike. I met with the miners, and addressed a street rally of thousands of people in Novokuznetsk. The theme of that speech, which was received enthusiastically, would be repeated frequently in the months to come: The fledgling democratic rights we had already won could be destroyed if we didn't bring the KGB under control.

I spoke at mass rallies in Moscow, addressing a crowd of several hundred thousand people at one of the biggest pro-democracy demonstrations ever held in the Soviet capital. As I surveyed the cheering throng just outside the Kremlin walls, I could scarcely believe what was happening: A KGB general was standing before a sea of humanity in Manezh Square calling for the dismantling of the KGB. It was a heady time, and the entire country seemed united in one goal—destroying the old Communist system. We thought that just by nudging Gorbachev a bit farther to the left we could decisively rout the old guard and bring real democracy to the Soviet Union. In our naivete, we didn't realize that the reserves of the totalitarian state were far from exhausted, were in fact regrouping and preparing to counterattack. The crackdown in Lithuania in January 1991 and the coup in Moscow the following August would be the result.

My phone rang non-stop. Some people offered encouragement or sought advice, while others would scream that I was a traitor and threaten my life. In my building, an old woman, the widow of a KGB general, would attack me every time she saw me. "You CIA man!" she would hiss. "Traitor!" This went on for quite some time, until one day, unable to listen to her any longer, I barked, "You old bitch! Get out of here before I break your neck!" I had never in my life spoken to an elderly person like that. But there's always a first time, and in this case it felt great. She never bothered me again.

Within days of my speech, the inevitable KGB attack began. The KGB press office released a statement saying, in part, "The KGB is going to have its say about Kalugin, who he is and what he stands for." Then on July 1—two weeks after the speech—Gorbachev issued a decree stripping me of my rank of major general, revoking all my KGB awards, and cutting off my pension. The KGB hauled in numerous Soviet reporters who had printed interviews with me, and demanded to see their notes and listen to their tape recordings.

At first I was shocked that Gorbachev, who I had once viewed as a bold reformer, would take such a step. But as the heat was turned up, I realized that Gorbachev had become a timid reformer and had no intention of tackling the problem of the KGB. He was under enormous pressure from Kryuchkov and others in the security services, and he wasn't about to alienate them by coming to my defense. Gorbachev was undeniably a great figure who helped set our country free, but his actions against me were typical, and showed that as time wore on he became increasingly timid, a man of half-steps and half-baked reforms. Gorbachev believed he could outsmart Kryuchkov and the KGB by going along with them for a while and then ultimately exerting control over the agency. But as the months wore on in 1990 and early 1991, the Soviet leader grew more reluctant to stand up to the hard-liners surrounding him, and consequently reactionary forces in the KGB and the Communist Party became ever more bold. He became, in effect, their hostage. By August 1991, the hard-liners had pushed Gorbachev around so much that they actually thought they could depose him and that he would scarcely protest. Thankfully, Gorbachev finally stood his ground.

About the time Gorbachev issued his decree stripping me of my rank and pension, my friends in the KGB told me that Kryuchkov had pulled my medical records from agency files. I was trying not to be paranoid, but the only reason I could see for his move was foul play. Perhaps, as had been done with Solzhenitsyn and other troublemakers, the KGB was planning to drug or poison me. I had no idea. But in my speeches and interviews, I always mentioned the KGB's "special operations" and efforts to physically harm dissidents, and said that if anything happened to me, it would be clear who was responsible.

"If a brick should happen to fall on my head, I feel certain you will know who the culprit is," I told people. Ludmilla was worried about my safety. Meanwhile, I operated on the principle that the more visible I was, the more difficult it would be for the KGB to do me harm.

The KGB also launched a bitter attack on me in the press. The Leningrad newspaper *Smena*—a rather liberal paper—published a full-page article which said I was still working for the KGB and was part of an elaborate plot to infiltrate the democratic movement. The story was reprinted around the country. *Pravda* weighed in with an article saying I was an ambitious, incompetent officer, and hinting darkly that I may have worked for the CIA. The story clearly was written by the KGB, though *Pravda* said one of its correspondents (a man named V. Ivanov, the Russian equivalent of John Doe) penned the piece.

"We are not at all sorry that we got rid of Kalugin," an anonymous KGB public relations person was quoted as saying. "It is very unfortunate when an officer embarks on the path of illegal actions, behaves immorally, or commits treason."

Though most members of the democratic movement welcomed me, a minority remained hostile and suspicious. The most painful attack came from Yelena Bonner, wife of the physicist and human rights campaigner Andrei Sakharov.

"It's very strange," Bonner said in an interview with a Soviet newspaper, "when KGB generals join the democratic movement."

When Bonner criticized me a second time, I felt I had to respond.

"What is so strange?" I asked in a newspaper interview. "Her husband is the father of the Soviet hydrogen bomb. He was a total Stalinist in his time. Look at his diaries—he absolutely adored Stalin. But he changed, because he understood the fallacy of this system that might use the weapon of mass destruction he had invented. He also discarded Stalin, who had been his idol. Am I not allowed to change? Is this the right of Sakharov only? Everyone can change, and the sooner we do it the better. Maybe I was late, but I don't feel ashamed. Better late than never."

That summer, as I came to grips with my role as chief adversary of the KGB, an event took place in Russia that was to have far-reaching consequences. Boris Yeltsin, the blunt, bearlike reformer, was elected chairman of the Russian parliament. I knew at the time that Yeltsin's election, which he won by just a few votes, was a momentous occasion. But none of us knew just how crucial it would prove to be. Yeltsin's victory in parliament cleared the way for him to become, in June 1991, the first popularly elected president in Russia's thousand-year history. That victory, in turn, gave him the legitimacy to stand up to the August 1991 coup. After that, Yeltsin began the historic reforms that continue to this day.

As it turned out, my fate was linked with Yeltsin's victory. Yeltsin's opponent in the race for chairman of the Congress of People's Deputies was a short, unpleasant, hard-line Communist named Ivan Polozkov. He was the Communist Party boss of the notoriously conservative Krasnodar region in southern Russia, and in order to run against Yeltsin, he had to give up one of the three legislative seats he held. Polozkov was a deputy in the regional legislature, the Russian parliament, and the Soviet parliament; he chose to forfeit his seat in the USSR Congress of People's Deputies. That left a vacancy in the Soviet parliament from Krasnodar—a vacancy which I would be asked to fill.

The call that launched my political career came one evening in July 1990. The phone rang in our Moscow apartment, and when I picked up the receiver a man said through the static of a long-distance Soviet line, "I am sorry to disturb you . . . My name is Veligodsky. I am calling you at the request of our colleagues at a scientific research center in Krasnodar. We have decided to put your name forward as a candidate to fill the vacant seat in the USSR Congress of People's Deputies. We hope you'll accept our offer."

I was flabbergasted. I had barely begun my public crusade against the KGB, yet here I was being asked to run for a seat in the Soviet Union's highest legislature. I didn't know what to say. Under Soviet law, anyone from Russia was eligible to run for the Krasnodar seat. I hesitated for a few moments, but then realized what a terrific opportunity had come my way: I was being given the chance to venture into one of the Soviet Union's Communist strongholds and capture the seat vacated by one of the staunchest Party members in the land. My candidacy would be a challenge to the old order—a system that had sought to publicly demolish my dignity as an officer and a human being by stripping me of the awards, rank, and pension I had earned in many years of honest work.

I couldn't resist.

"Yes," I said into the phone. "I agree!"

I had a week to get down to Krasnodar to be officially nominated and register for the election, which was scheduled for late August. I had passed through the region once years ago, and knew it to be a bizarre and backward place. Before the Russian Revolution, the Krasnodar region had been home to the fierce Kuban Cossacks; in the Soviet era, Krasnodar—with its relatively balmy southern climate—was one of the most fertile areas in the Soviet Union. And also one of the most corrupt. There had been a long succession of Party officials in the region involved in bribery and black-market deals. Some Party bosses had been arrested; others had escaped conviction. In any case, the Party apparatus was one of the shadiest and most powerful in Russia, perhaps because Krasnodar bordered on the unruly Caucasus Mountain region. I never heard accusations against Polozkov, whose parliament seat I was seeking. But of one thing there was no doubt: this man, who looked like a Russian version of Richard Nixon, was as zealous a Communist as there was in the Soviet Union.

As I prepared in mid-July to fly to Krasnodar, several incidents occurred which showed that the KGB had me under near-constant surveillance. Over the phone, I agreed with the editor of the progressive *New Times* magazine to meet with him and some German correspondents. No one followed me as I drove to the *New Times* offices, but when I arrived, several carloads of KGB surveillance men were waiting for me. They followed me and the Germans as we drove away after the interview.

On another occasion, while riding on the Moscow subway, I noticed a man who appeared to be following me. I got off at the Arbat station, and he stayed right with me as I walked out of the Metro. I decided to toy with him and picked up my pace, dodging in and out of the crowds along the Arbat pedestrian mall, then finally ducking into a nearby movie house. I looked through the window of the movie theater as the survellance man stood near the Arbat frantically jerking his head left and right in an effort to spot me. I approached him from behind, tapped him on the shoulder, and said, "Hello, my friend. Here I am. What are you looking for? Perhaps next time you should be more diligent."

He slowly backed away, a sheepish, almost frightened look on his face. I knew he was not alone, since KGB surveillance officers usually work in groups of twos or threes. As I boarded a bus on Kalinin Prospect, I glanced around and saw a woman who looked suspicious to me. I got off at a stop and she did, too. Then, just before the bus moved out, I hopped back on board. She followed me. Knowing she was KGB, I continued on to the massive Hotel Rossiya just off Red Square. She followed me inside. The sprawling hotel is a maze of corridors and stairwells, and I led her through the labyrinth, hopping on and off elevators and striding down the long, dimly lit hallways. In a matter of minutes I lost her and walked out again.

On the day I was to fly to Krasnodar, a strange incident occurred that may have been coincidence, or may just as well have been the work of the KGB. When I arrived at Moscow's Vnukovo Airport, I was informed that the afternoon flight to Krasnodar had been delayed indefinitely. The deadline for candidates' registration was the following morning, and if I failed to make it to Krasnodar, I would not be eligible to run for office. I decided to try to get on the evening flight, but was told the airplane was grounded with engine difficulty. Aeroflot said both flights would be delayed at least sixteen hours; I knew our Soviet air service was bad, but it seemed strange that on the day I *had* to get to Krasnodar both flights had been canceled. The KGB, after all, knew my plans, right down to the flight I was taking. I went to the airport administration building, where officials confirmed that all flights to Krasnodar were suspended. Not knowing what to do, I informed the airport bosses that I was not flying to Krasnodar. But I held on to my ticket and decided to wait at the airport just in case. Strangely enough, within forty minutes Aeroflot announced that the flights to Krasnodar had been reinstated, and I was on my way to southern Russia.

That afternoon, I strode into the auditorium of the Gas Processing Institute in Krasnodar. In front of me were the three hundred people who had decided to nominate me for the Soviet parliament. They applauded warmly as I entered, and cheered me after my twenty-minute speech. All but a handful voted to nominate me, and on July 17 the Krasnodar Electoral Committee accepted me as one of twenty-one candidates running for the seat vacated by Polozkov.

That same day, the USSR state prosecutor filed criminal charges against me, alleging I had divulged state secrets. Friends in the KGB told me that I had nearly been thrown in jail, but apparently Kryuchkov balked at the last moment because Gorbachev didn't want to incur the displeasure of the West by taking such an anti-democratic step.

And so the campaign began. It was a grueling and inspiring ordeal, carried out in the brutal heat and dust of a southern Russian August. The campaign was my first real taste of the democratic process, and it was a heady experience, for nearly everywhere I went I was greeted by large, enthusiastic crowds who reveled in the fact that they had been given a chance to participate in the burial of the old regime and the creation of a new one. In those days, the Soviet people were united in their hatred of the Communist Party bosses who had made life for the masses squalid and joyless. Krasnodar may long have been a Communist Party stronghold, but in the summer of 1990 the Party's once-unassailable position was crumbling. On the surface, the power structures that had ruled Krasnodar and the Soviet Union were still in place, but the fact was that in a little over a year, the old regime would be swept away forever. I didn't realize it at the time, but the moves by the Krasnodar Party bosses and KGB to discredit me were the last, desperate gasps of a dying order.

The campaign now seems a blur of rallies and dusty roads and countless bad hotels. I traveled by car around the vast region, accompanied by local democratic leaders as well as some of the leading reformers from Moscow. At first, my opponents—the main three were the deputy head of the local agriculture department, a major general in the Soviet Army, and a former cosmonaut—didn't seem worried. But quickly my message began to resonate among the people, and it wasn't long before crowds of several hundred would show up at meetings, listen attentively while I spoke, and then wander away as the other candidates took the podium.

What I told the ever-growing crowds wasn't pleasant, but all they had to do was look around to see it was true. Though blessed by nature with an excellent climate and fertile soil, the Krasnodar region had been battered by seven decades of Communist rule. The rich soil had been depleted by overuse of chemicals and fertilizers. The Kuban and other rivers had been badly polluted. A dam had flooded thousands of acres of prime farmland. The incidence of birth defects and cancer was higher than the national average. In this rich agricultural region, food was scarce and lines were long. Medical care was atrocious. Schools and businesses and factories were rundown. Krasnodar, in short, was typical of the entire Soviet landscape, and I told voters time and again that the only way to change things was to do away with the old Party and KGB structures that had brought our country to such a sorry state.

"What have you to be proud of these days?" I asked in my typical stump speech. "With your land, with this fertile soil, with the Black Sea, with the mountains, you should have one of the most beautiful areas in the world. You could feed the rest of Russia. Now you live like beggars. Your life can't even be compared to life in Finland, where the land is half as good. They grow so much there that they don't even know what to do with all the produce. And here, in a far more fertile region, you can't even feed yourselves. But this is not your fault. It's the system. You toil like slaves, but what do you have to show for it?"

Nearly everyone was thoroughly fed up, and my campaign was lifted up on this tide of dissatisfaction.

By early August, when it became clear I was a serious threat, the Party and KGB swung into action and began an all-out attack on me. The main regional newspaper, *Soviet Kuban,* reprinted scathing articles about me from the national press, while at the same time denying me the right—given to other candidates—to lay out my program in the pages of the paper. (The editor, a woman, was married to a local KGB colonel, and said I couldn't have access to the newspaper's columns because I was not a Communist Party member. I had resigned from the Party that summer, a few hours before Boris Yeltsin took the same step.) *Soviet Kuban* and other local papers printed articles from anonymous "outraged readers" attacking the "pensioner from Moscow" as a dangerous carpetbagger. Newspapers also urged factory directors not to let me speak to workers on factory territory; one plant director denied me access, saying his factory produced classified military hardware, and another manager simply chucked me out of his office without explanation. Other times, directors of factories and institutes would either give me ridiculously small halls in which to speak or claim I had showed up at the wrong time. Despite these problems, however, the voters still flocked to see me.

In Moscow and in Krasnodar, friendly KGB officers told me that a coordinated campaign was under way to discredit me. Local KGB officers fanned out around the region, telling Party bosses that I represented a "dangerous element" that must be stopped. Hecklers appeared at my campaign stops, shouting out the same scripted comments, such as, "How much did the CIA pay you to betray your country?" Time and again I was bombarded with identical hostile questions. Early in the campaign, a KGB officer from Krasnodar approached me and described how a high-ranking KGB official from Moscow had come to the region to hold a strategy session on torpedoeing my campaign. The Moscow KGB man passed out a list of embarrassing questions, instructing the assembled officers to travel to the districts and relay the questions to their informers and agents.

The Krasnodar KGB officer gave me the questions, and one night, when a particularly nasty heckler started harassing me, I pulled out the list. "Okay," I told the crowd. "I have a list of questions here drawn up by the KGB to discredit me, and I can tell you what this man's next question is going to be. You see, a KGB officer from your region provided me with this list. I know full well that these questions don't really come from the people who ask them. They come from Moscow."

The heckler shut up.

Out of nowhere, thousands of anti-Kalugin posters and flyers appeared, and the KGB sent several generals from Moscow to co-ordinate the smear campaign against me. One general and his sub-ordinates toured rural areas, warning the citizenry that dire things would happen to our country if extremists like Kalugin came to power. In a blunt, old-fashioned style—many in the KGB thought they could still give orders to the people and the people would obey—the general warned that authorities in Moscow would be displeased if I managed to win the election. Another general— Leonid Sherbarshin, chief of Intelligence—appeared in Sochi at an anti-crime conference and warned people against voting for a "populist demagogue" like myself.

Kryuchkov approached one of my KGB colleagues from my Co-lumbia University days, Gennadi Bekhterev, and asked him to travel to Krasnodar to speak out against me.

"You know more about him than most and you will be believed because you are a friend of his," Kryuchkov told Bekhterev.

But Bekhterev remained loyal to me and turned down Kryuch-kov's request. Within a few months, Bekhterev was forced into retirement.

The KGB even enlisted the aid of the bishop of the Russian Orthodox Church in Krasnodar, a man who had worked closely with the security services for years. In sermons and speeches, Bishop Izidor spoke out against me. In the face of such hypocrisy, I had to attack Izidor. I told voters he had been a longtime KGB agent and informer, and even gave the name of the KGB colonel in Krasnodar who was Izidor's case officer. Such attacks and counterattacks were undeniably ugly, but the KGB was pulling out all the stops and I had no choice but to hit back.

The upshot of all this, as could be predicted, was that the KGB's efforts backfired. Times had changed, and people no longer wanted to be told what to do. The harder the local bosses and KGB slammed me, the more support I received. I remember speaking at one of the richest collective farms in the area. The director was implacably hostile to me, and as I addressed the workers under the watchful eye of their leadership, the people responded lukewarmly. Afterwards, however, two policeman sidled up to me and said, "Don't worry. You're strong here. The police will vote for you. And we'll tell all our neighbors to do so, too."

The truth is, the people often were electrified by my speeches, which were unlike anything they had heard before. I avoided criticizing Gorbachev, and spoke out strongly in favor of Yeltsin and his team. But when I talked about the KGB, voters really perked up. I called Kryuchkov, the KGB chairman, a scoundrel and a bastard. I talked at length about the idiotic KGB activity I had seen in Leningrad, and spoke of the need to totally reform the KGB and slash the number of agents. I not only attacked the old Soviet order but offered my vision of the new, which included the privatization of most business and industries as well as sweeping land reform. It was strong stuff. But the people, who had lived for decades under the thumb of the KGB and the Communist Party, knew I spoke the truth and were thrilled to hear it. Words like these had never been uttered publicly in these distant rural areas, and my appearances had an invigorating effect. I was shouting that the emperer had no clothes, and the people shouted back, "You're right!" Support for candidacies such as mine was an important breakthrough, for it showed that even in such backwaters as Krasnodar, the psychology of the people was starting to change. They had had enough, and by electing me they could send a strong message to Moscow.

On the eve of the election, a huge campaign rally was held in Krasnodar's main city park. Thousands of people, including many families with children, streamed into the park to hear me and my opponents. Most of the candidates were there, but when a proposal was made that we speak in alphabetical order, the crowd screamed that it wanted me to speak first. So I took the podium, and within a minute or so the microphone went dead. I was struggling vainly to be heard when out of nowhere a small plane appeared. It began buzzing the crowd, literally flying at treetop level. The plane kept circling and reappearing, drowning out my words. It was clear that the pilot was deliberately interfering with my speech, and members in the crowd started cursing local authorities and suggesting we march on the city Communist Party building.

"No, no," I yelled. "Don't do that! Never do that. Just stay here. This is clearly a provocation."

Later, KGB sources in Krasnodar told me that the plane was the idea of General Valentin Novikov, my former deputy in Counter-Intelligence who had been dispatched by headquarters to sabotage my campaign. The Krasnodar KGB head, Vasilenko, actually directed the dirty tricks at the election rally that day. In the end, we thwarted their plans: my aides rounded up a loudspeaker, allowing me and my fellow candidates to make our speeches.

There was a large turnout on election day, August 19, but because there were so many candidates I was unable to win an outright majority. I received 46 percent of the vote. My nearest rival—Nikolai Gorovoi, the Party agriculture official and former chairman of the regional Soviet—pulled in 10 percent. There was evidence of widespread fraud, however, as the local election commission declared 100,000 ballots invalid for a variety of technical reasons. But the results of the first round showed that I was far ahead, and I redoubled my efforts to win a clear-cut victory in the September 2 runoff election.

During campaigning for the second round, an incident took place that vividly illustrated the mood of the people of the Krasnodar region. Some local democrats had invited me to speak at a meeting in the ultra-conservative village of Stanitsa Leningradskaya. When I arrived, the villagers were in festive mood as they streamed into the sports stadium where my opponent and I were to speak. The stadium was festooned with flags and banners, and a chorus of women in traditional colorful costumes was serenading the audience. Men in Cossack dress milled about.

My opponent was delayed—in fact he never showed up—and when more than five hundred people had filled the small stadium, I was invited to speak. The local Party boss, an old-style Communist named Sergeyko, was running the show. A tall, gray-haired man of sixty, he had the confident demeanor of someone who had been a rural autocrat for many years. As I began my talk, he folded his arms across his chest and eyed me hostilely. At first the crowd was reserved. But as I warmed up, the audience began to respond with murmurs of assent and sporadic applause. I could see Sergeyko becoming increasingly agitated until finally he could stand no more. In the midst of my talk, he leaped out of his seat onto the stage and shouted, "Stop this traitor! We, the Cossacks of the Kuban, do not want traitors in this area! Get him out!"

The crowd was silent, and I had no idea what to expect next. I had stopped talking, unsure whether this group of hardened descendants of the Cossacks was about to drive me out of the stadium. Suddenly, the stadium erupted in a chorus of shouts and boos—all of it directed at the local Party boss.

"Get out of here yourself, you lousy bastard!" one man shouted. "Get off the rostrum, Communist scum!" screamed another. "Let us live in peace. What the man says is right!"

The crowd cheered my defenders. Sergeyko was crimson with fury and shame, for what had transpired—rural Russians shouting down an omnipotent Party boss—would have been unthinkable only months before. Suddenly, the local citizenry and Cossacks mobbed the stage, slapping me on the back and shouting words of support.

"We're with you, General!" they cried. "That son-of-a-bitch Sergeyko doesn't speak for anyone here."

Sergeyko retreated from the stage in silence. At that moment, I knew that my election was assured, and that the Russian people had indeed begun to shed the slave mentality that had been with them so long.

The runoff election took place on Sunday, September 2. Some results filtered in that night, but since we were using paper ballots there were no final results until the following afternoon. Finally, around 3:00 P.M. Monday, the electoral commission called and gave me the news: I had won, receiving 57 percent of the vote, to my opponent's 39 percent. I was ecstatic. As our momentum in the campaign had grown, I became more and more confident of victory. But the actual triumph itself was indescribably sweet. We had scored an upset win in a Communist stronghold, and the people of Krasnodar had resoundingly rejected the old order.

Late that afternoon I planned to address a gathering of supporters in the main city park. But when my aides and I walked out of our headquarters at the Gas Processing Institute, the crowd already had come to us. More than a thousand people stood in a small square in front of the Institute, and they let out a roar of approval as I came into view. Several supporters spoke, followed by my wife. Then it was my turn to address the people who had secured my victory. I scarcely remember now what I said, but to this day I can still see the faces of my supporters. Their visages were turned toward me, expectant, hopeful, straining to catch my every word and gesture. I was overcome with emotion. I felt I had fought my way out of the swamp and was now on firm ground. It was one of the happiest days in my life; seldom, if ever again, would I look to the future of our country with such optimism.

Returning to Moscow, I received warm congratulations from the capital's reformers. By this point, I had appeared so many times on television and had been the subject of so many newspaper articles that ordinary citizens had come to recognize me; many of them stopped me on the street or in shops to congratulate me. Many also expressed concern for my safety, though I believed—correctly— that after my election to the Soviet Congress of People's Deputies the KGB wouldn't dare harm me. I even began legal proceedings in the Moscow City Court, and later in the Supreme Court, seeking to overturn Gorbachev's decrees stripping me of my rank, pension, and awards. No one in the country had ever filed such a suit before, and though it was never successful, the legal action aroused a great deal of interest in the country. But I would only be rehabilitated— and my pension and rank restored—after the August 1991 coup.

For the first time in a decade I began to travel overseas again. As a Soviet legislator, I was entitled to a diplomatic passport, and after my election the KGB could do nothing to stop me from going abroad. In September 1990, I flew to the Netherlands for an international conference on *perestroika* and was nearly drunk with the sense of freedom I experienced after a decade in the USSR. I walked along the canals of Amsterdam, inhaling the fresh sea breeze in lungfuls and feeling as if I had been reborn.

In the ensuing months I traveled to Germany, Japan, France, and Bulgaria. I also went twice to America, and the vibrancy of the place hit me with the force of a revelation.

On one trip in late 1990, I saw a lengthy television interview with John Walker, the spy whose work I had overseen in Washington a quarter century before. Even though I had been intimately involved with the Walker case, I had never met the man or seen him on film. He sat with an almost mournful expression on his face, explaining why he had decided to spy against the United States. Before, Walker had been a faceless intelligence asset, a pawn in our global battle with the CIA. Our relationship had been purely clinical—he supplied us with the material and we paid him the money. But now, watching him on TV, I was struck by the tragedy of the case, by the lives Walker had ruined, by the sad fact that this man would probably spend the rest of his life in jail. I had been intimately involved with the whole affair, but the devastating human cost had never really struck me before. As the doe-eyed Walker sat in front of the camera and sifted through the wreckage of his life, I found myself thinking, "So this is how the Ingelligence game finally ends. This is the final result of one's efforts—jail and humiliation."

Back in the Soviet Union, my time was consumed with my new duties as a legislator. The Soviet Congress met only three times in the year I was a member, and not once did Congress Chairman Anatoly Lukyanov—who later was to plot against Gorbachev—give me the floor. But the meetings themselves were not the essence of the job; indeed, the Congress was so conservative that people like myself had little effect on it. What was most valuable about being a People's Deputy was that it was a bully pulpit and gave me the opportunity to agitate for change both in Krasnodar and around the Soviet Union.

In the fifteen months I was a deputy—from September 1990 to December 1991—I and other reform politicians watched with dismay as Gorbachev, pushed by the top officials of his government, became increasingly conservative. In hindsight, it's clear that KGB Chairman Kryuchkov, Defense Minister Dimitri Yazov, Interior Minister Boris Pugo, Prime Minister Valentin Pavlov, and others were exerting immense pressure on Gorbachev. These reactionary men were alternately confused and outraged as the foundations of the Soviet state began to crumble ever more rapidly. Republics, such as the Baltic states, were fighting for independence. A host of political groups were chipping away at the authority of the Communist Party. Reformers were pushing hard for the introduction of a capitalist economy. So these "Gray Cardinals" of the old order fought a desperate rearguard action, pushing Gorbachev into increasingly hardline positions—positions which he would then abandon when Soviet and international reaction to the crackdown became too intense.

First, in December 1990, Foreign Minister Eduard Shevardnadze stunned all of us in the Congress when he resigned in protest over what he said was a coming Communist dictatorship. Then, in January

1991, Gorbachev—under pressure from his defense and security chiefs—approved the crackdown on the Lithuanian independence movement and the assault on the TV tower in Vilnius. Fifteen people died that night in the Lithuanian capital.

All that spring of 1991, the Communist diehards around Gorbachev made increasingly threatening speeches. In June, Kryuchkov, Yazov, and Pugo warned of impending disaster if the disintegration of the Soviet Union continued. Kryuchkov hinted darkly that the CIA was behind the breakup and the country's current troubles. Prime Minister Pavlov displayed extraordinary stupidity when he accused the West of trying to undermine our economy by flooding it with rubles. It was clear that the hard-liners were growing increasingly desperate. When, at last, Gorbachev found the courage to slap down these Neanderthals, it was too late. They were deeply deluded and believed they could depose Gorbachev and get away with it. When the Soviet leader announced in late July that he would sign a treaty giving unprecedented freedom to the Soviet Union's twelve remaining republics—the Baltic states were already in the process of bolting—that was the last straw. Now, it was not a matter of whether there would be a coup. The only question was when.

In early August, Alexander Yakovlev called and asked to meet with me. At one time, he had been Gorbachev's closest adviser, but as hard-liners like Kryuchkov gained sway over Gorbachev in 1991, Yakovlev lost influence.

"Why don't you come on over?" I told Yakovlev over the phone.

"No, it makes no sense," he replied. "Our houses are bugged."

I suggested we meet in the street, in a quiet residential neighborhood not far from the Belorussian Station. We rendezvoused there, and immediately noticed the hubbub on this normally peaceful street. People constantly brushed past us, loitered in nearby doorways, drove slowly by. It was almost comically clear that we were under surveillance. Later, after the coup, a Russian reporter found a document in KGB archives saying that more than a dozen agents had been assigned that evening to eavesdrop on our street conversation.

"The hell with them," I told Yakovlev. "Let them do their job."

"Listen," he said, "I have something I need to tell you. I had a meeting with a colleague of yours from the KGB the other day. And he told me that there might be attempts on my life and on Shevardnadze's. I wanted you to know about this in case anything happens to me. I wrote this information down and put it in a safe. Tell me, do you think this is possible?"

"Listen, in Andropov's time, I would have said it was highly unlikely," I told Yakovlev. "He was against political assassinations. But Kryuchkov is a madman and there's no telling what he might do. He is a scoundrel and might resort to anything, so I don't exclude the possibility of political assassination."

Yakovlev also expressed the fear that the hard-line elements around Gorbachev might try to pull off a coup. I left my friend that night feeling profoundly unsettled.

On August 18, an old friend of mine from the KGB met me in the street and told me, "Something is up. I know for sure a coup will take place in September or October. It's all being prepared." I could only shake my head and hope that even Kryuchkov would not be so foolish.

And then, the following morning, it happened.

I was awakened shortly after six o'clock by a woman who worked for one of my liberal legislative colleagues. She broke the news with one word.

"*Perevorot,*" she said, the Russian word for "coup."

"Turn on the radio," the woman went on. "A coup is taking place. A military coup."

I hung up and switched on the radio. Just then an announcer was reading a statement by the Committee for the State of Emergency—the band of fools that had deposed Gorbachev. I switched on the TV and there was the movie *Swan Lake,* the old Soviet standby whenever the death of a leader or a similarly momentous event was taking place.

I looked out the window of my seventh-floor apartment, which overlooks Moscow's Fili Park. It was a glorious summer morning, warm and balmy. All day long I was struck by the contrast: such horrible events were taking place against the backdrop of the most splendid Russian weather. What did these idiots—Kryuchkov, Yazov, Pugo, Pavlov and Company—expect to accomplish? What bloody fools!

The first thing I did was load my hunting rifle. Now, it seems like a melodramatic gesture, but then—in the first minutes of the coup—I had no idea what to expect. Clearly, if Gorbachev was deposed and a crackdown was under way, I would be high on the list of people to be arrested. Were we about to be thrown back decades, to the nightmare of the Stalin years? I didn't know. But loading my gun gave me a small measure of comfort.

I called Yakovlev at 6:20 A.M. His wife answered the phone.

"Is Alexander Nikolayevich available?" I asked.

"No, he's still in bed," she replied.

"Listen," I told her. "Do you know there's a coup taking place?"

"No, what do you mean?" she said.

"Turn on the radio," I said. "They are playing the announcement over and over."

She handed the phone to her husband.

"Oleg, what is it you're saying?"

"There's a coup taking place—it's on the radio right now," I told my old friend.

"*Podonki*—Scumbags!" he barked into the phone. There was a pause of several seconds, and then, "We must be prepared for anything."

We signed off, and I knew Yakovlev was right. Kryuchkov and his fellow plotters wouldn't hesitate to disband the Soviet Congress. And if they did so, I knew that my arrest wouldn't be far behind.

I stepped onto the balcony off my bedroom. Gazing down on the quiet courtyard and parking lot seven floors below, I saw a *Zhiguli* sitting off to one side of the lot in a place where few people ever park. Surveillance team, I thought, and resolved to get out of my apartment. There was no sense sitting at home, waiting to be arrested. I planned to head downtown and join whatever voices were resisting this idiotic adventure.

I told Ludmilla I was leaving. She didn't protest, but the strained look on her face told me that she was even more worried than I was.

"What is going to happen to you now?" she asked. I just shrugged, but she knew as well as I that the best place to be on this day was on the streets.

Around 8:00 A.M., as I was preparing to leave, a reporter from the BBC in London called. He wanted my assessment of the situation, and I told him, "As I understand it, this is an adventure on the part of those who have always wanted to restore the old order. But I am sure they will fail and in two or three days everything will be clear."

I was trying to put on a brave face, and knew that my words were more wishful thinking than anything else. I did believe, however, that it was too late, that we had come too far, ever to go back again. Ultimately, I believed democratic forces would prevail, but I had no idea how long or how bloody the struggle might be.

In the lobby of my building, which mainly housed KGB generals and Communist Party officials, a young woman pushing a baby stroller greeted me. She immediately burst into tears and said, "Mr. Kalugin, you must do something! This is an impossible situation. They are trying to bring back the old regime. Please do something!"

I told her I would do what I could. Her words had a strangely cheering effect: If this young woman, the daughter of a KGB general, was so violently opposed to the coup, then there was hope. She was proof that there was something deep inside the Soviet people that would resist a return to the past.

I looked at the *Zhiguli* parked off to the side. Three men—unmistakably KGB—sat in the car and watched me as I moved toward my automobile. As I pulled out of my parking lot, the *Zhiguli* began following me, as did another surveillance car parked on the street. They stayed right with me, making no effort to conceal that I was under close surveillance.

I headed down Kutuzovsky Prospect for the Russian parliament building—the White House—on the banks of the Moscow River. Parking across the street from the White House, I walked over to the building, followed on foot by a KGB surveillance team. Armored personnel carriers had begun moving down Kutuzovsky Prospect, but so far there were no tanks in sight. There were very few people in front of the parliament building, and it would have been a cinch to storm the White House and arrest Yeltsin and all inside. As it became clear later, however, the coup leadership hesitated to take such a drastic step, and when Kryuchkov finally did order his elite Alpha commando group and Russian paratroopers to take the White House, the officers refused.

Flashing my deputy's badge, I entered the high-rise parliament building. I immediately ran into Leningrad Mayor Antoly Sobchak and other reformers, who were scurrying about the hallways, their faces filled with tension and determination. Around 11:00 A.M., Yeltsin gave a press conference inside the parliament, and his angry, defiant words stirred me and thousands of others. When the press conference ended, the Russian president, surrounded by a few bodyguards, strode out the front entrance of the White House, down a flight of steps, and marched over to a line of a half-dozen tanks that had taken up positions near the Moscow River. I followed, and watched from a few yards away as Yeltsin—in what would become the enduring image of the coup—clambered aboard a tank and told the soldiers and officers not to obey the orders of the plotters. It was an inspired move and went a long way toward rallying the Russian people, many of whom would later see the pictures on CNN. The Russian president went back inside the White House. The tank commanders revved up their engines, emitting choking clouds of diesel smoke, then clattered up and down the road in front of the parliament before rumbling away. They clearly had no idea what to do, and their indecision, coupled with the evident unwillingness of the soldiers in armored vehicles to shoot fellow Russians, gave me hope that the putsch could be defeated.

I decided to head downtown to the headquarters of the city's Communist Party Committee, where I had several good friends. As I walked back to my car, I was followed by several KGB men. Much to my surprise, one of them came up behind me and said, "Oleg Daniilovich, you know what we suggest? Move your car out of here. There's a big crowd coming from downtown and they may smash your car."

That friendly warning, from the very men assigned to follow and perhaps arrest me, was another sign to me that the hard-liners at the top may have badly miscalculated. Sitting in the Kremlin, they thought they need only say the word and the masses would follow. But only hours after the coup began, the scene on the street, and the obvious reluctance of the security forces to follow the State of Emergency Committee, boded ill for Kryuchkov and his gang.

As I walked to my car, a crowd of more than a thousand people was streaming down Kalinin Prospect, heading toward the White House. Some of the marchers caught sight of me and began to yell, "Hey, General! Join us! Lead us to the White House!"

I found myself swept up by the crowd, which was shouting, "Long Live Yeltsin!" and "Down with the Putschists!" We arrived in the plaza behind the Russian parliament, and the people in the crowd asked me to go inside and ask Yeltsin to address them. I made my way through the crowded halls to the president's antechamber, which was packed with dozens of assistants and legislators, as well as bodyguards armed with machine guns. Yeltsin was closeted with his aides, but Vice President Alexander Rutskoi promised that he himself would soon address the ever-growing crowd.

I drove to the headquarters of the Moscow Communist Party, located on Staraya Square next to the Party's Central Committee building. My KGB shadows were still with me, and they parked their car not far from mine. My deputy's badge assured me entrance into the imposing gray stone building, and soon I was in the office of a good friend, Alexei. Though he worked in the Party apparatus, he had as little idea as I did about the intentions and resolve of the coup leaders.

"Oh, Oleg," he sighed. "These scoundrels. What are we going to do now?"

We were standing near an open window, and Alexei looked down at the surveillance team waiting for me below.

"Listen, are they after you?" Alexei asked.

"Yes, they probably are," I replied, not wanting to unduly alarm him.

"You must get out of here," my friend said. "You never know what they will do to you. You must escape. I'll organize it for you."

The Communist Party buildings on Staraya Square made up an enormous, interconnected complex of offices. There was even a network of tunnels underneath, including a top-secret subway line that would take Party officials out of the city in case of nuclear attack, revolution, or other calamity. There were exits in the building that had not been used for years, and Alexei knew just such an escape route, located at the other end of the building more than 100 yards away from the main entrance. Alexei showed me the little known exit, then went and got his *Volga,* which had curtains over the windows. A few minutes later he pulled up to the exit and I hopped into the car, unseen by the surveillance teams. It was about 2:00 P.M. I learned later that my KGB trackers stayed in the Staraya Square parking lot until 9:00 P.M., watching my car and waiting for me to emerge.

I decided to go to the Hotel Rossiya, where some of my fellow deputies who lived at the hotel were gathering. I quickly found my colleagues, and we talked for hours about the situation, making plans to continue the work of the Russian parliament should the coup leaders be so foolish as to storm the White House. Around 10:00 P.M., I decided to go to the White House. We heard, however, that a curfew had been imposed and I figured it would be better to spend the night at the Rossiya and head for the parliament the first thing the next day.

Waking up at six-thirty, I walked to Staraya Square, where my car still sat and the surveillance team had long disappeared. I wanted to see how Ludmilla was, so I drove home. As expected, the surveillance teams were waiting for me, but by this time I didn't care. The night had passed quietly in the capital, and the crowd of defenders in front of the White House had hit five thousand people and was growing. There was near-total silence from the coup leaders; at the time we were baffled by their inaction, but later it would emerge that they were in utter disarray. Some, like Vice President Gennadi Yanaev and Prime Minister Pavlov, were constantly drunk. Others, such as Defense Minister Yazov, were losing their resolve. Tuesday, August 20, we knew none of this, and the atmosphere in the city was menacing.

Ludmilla was overjoyed to see me. I breakfasted and fielded still more calls from reporters. A German TV station wanted me to come in for a studio interview, and I agreed. Shortly after 9:00 A.M., they sent a car for me, and—followed by the two KGB surveillance cars—we headed to the German television bureau on Gruzinskaya Street in the center of town.

After the interview, I left on foot. I had decided to take the Metro to the White House and was on the escalator, heading to the subway platform, when I heard a man's voice behind me.

"Don't turn around," he commanded. "You will be arrested, but not today. I will warn you when it is coming. But your friends [and fellow legislators] Gdlyan, Yakunin, and several others will be arrested today. Gdlyan has already been arrested. Portnov is already under arrest and Belozertsev will be arrested soon. You are not on the list today, but I will warn you when it happens. Do not turn around."

He shoved a piece of paper into my hand and said, "Call me. My home phone number is written there."

I followed his instructions and never looked back. Shoving the paper in my pocket, I glanced at the crowded subway platform for my newfound KGB friend or other members of the surveillance team. I didn't spot anyone suspicious. Things were certainly getting strange.

The weather had turned cloudy by Tuesday afternoon, Day Two of the coup. Thousands of people had now gathered at the White House, which had become the center of resistance to the putsch. Yeltsin had issued decrees calling on all Russians to disobey the plotters and to carry out a nationwide strike. But the fact was that, outside a few key cities such as Moscow and Leningrad, the masses were waiting to see how the drama in the capital would play itself out.

When I arrived at the White House, a steady stream of reform politicians was addressing the swelling crowd in the square behind the building. The leaders stood atop a balcony and boomed their calls for resistance into a microphone. Below, Muscovites roared their support and cursed the plotters. That afternoon, I was asked to address the crowd, and I relayed to them what the KGB officer had told me that morning on the escalator.

" 'My dear friend [and legislator] Father Gleb, you will be arrested today,' " I told the silent crowd. " 'I want to warn you. I know it from a source in the KGB. Not everyone in the KGB is a bad guy. Some are real friends of ours, and they told me you would be arrested today. Gdlyan and Portnov are already under arrest. I want you all to know these things. . . . Beware, KGB agents are in the crowd and they may try to provoke you. They will try to get inside the White House to start a rebellion from within.' "

As I had walked into the White House, a man approached me and said he was a KGB officer. "I want to speak," he said. "I want to show that not all KGB men are scoundrels. I am one of those who isn't."

He showed me his ID. I told him to join me, and after I spoke, he took the microphone. "I am a KGB officer and I denounce these adventurers," he said to the cheering crowd. "I want to tell you that not all KGB people are behind Kryuchkov. I will be here with you."

I stayed in the White House from that moment on, giving interviews to foreign and Soviet journalists and doing whatever I could to rally people to the defense of the Russian parliament. I saw the renowned émigré cellist and conductor of the Washington Symphony, Mstislav Rostropovich, and chatted with my colleagues from the parliament. I couldn't believe the putschists would try to storm the building, but as darkness fell Tuesday the situation became more threatening. We had reliable information from sources in the KGB and the army that an attack on the White House was planned for early Wednesday morning. (It was—only Kryuchkov and Co. couldn't find anyone willing to carry it out.)

Around midnight there were reports that armored columns were approaching the White House from six directions. Outside, a light rain fell and an estimated ten thousand citizens formed defensive lines around the parliament and warmed themselves by bonfires. Then at about 2:00 A.M., shooting broke out a few hundred yards away along the Garden Ring Road. It would turn out later that a group of young people had blocked off the road with trolleys and attacked a passing column of armored personnel carriers. The soldiers opened fire, killing three people. At the time, we in the White House didn't know what the firing meant. Was it the beginning of the attack? Was it just a diversion? I was unarmed, but resolved that if the White House was stormed, I would pick up a gun and fight. At that point, there was little choice.

That night, I slept restlessly in a chair in someone's office. Wednesday, Day Three of the coup, dawned dreary and wet. But my mood was anything but despondent. We felt enormous relief that there had been no attack the night before, and there was a growing sense—fueled by persistent rumors from the Kremlin—that the coup was falling apart. As long as I live, I will never forget the extraordinary events that began unfolding at mid-morning Wednesday.

First, from our perches in the White House, we saw some armored units withdrawing from the city along Kutuzovsky Prospect. Then we were summoned to a session of the parliament, where a series of announcements left us giddy with joy. The coup had fallen apart. The plotters were dashing to Vnukovo Airport to try to escape the capital. Finally, we learned that Vice President Rutskoi and other Russian officials had flown with Kryuchkov to Foros, where Gorbachev and his family were being held. The president, we were told, had been freed. The plotters were under arrest.

I walked out of the White House into a deliriously happy throng. Recognizing me, some in the crowd picked me up and shouted, "Kalugin! Kalugin! Kalugin!" I returned home in a fog, exhausted but delighted. It was the happiest day of my life.

That night, I celebrated in true Russian style. Some friends joined me, and as we sat around knocking back shots of vodka, an idea crossed my mind. I walked into my study and retrieved the crumpled piece of paper with the name of the KGB man who had warned me the day before on the escalator. I unfolded the paper, and saw the scrawled first name, Igor, and his home phone number. I dialed it, and he answered.

"I want to thank you in person," I told him. "Come on over."

An hour later he showed up at my doorstep, a tall, husky man with auburn hair and blue eyes. We shook hands warmly, and I introduced him to the handful of guests in my living room. We had won, and no one—not even this KGB officer—seemed afraid any more.

We drank and toasted and I asked him questions about the preceding three days. He told me he had been watching me since 4:00 A.M. on Monday, two hours before the announcement of the coup was broadcast on radio. Dozens of reformers and assorted trouble-makers like myself had been kept under surveillance, he said.

"You were all controlled," he told me. "We simply had not yet received the order to arrest you."

How many teams had been watching me, I asked.

"A lot," he replied. "We knew you were difficult to deal with—you always noticed us at once."

I asked him what he had been doing recently, considering that dissidents were no longer under surveillance. He shrugged and told me he had been assigned to protect the CIA spy, Edward Lee Howard, who had defected to Moscow a few years before. Howard was ensconced in a *dacha* near Moscow and was drinking himself to death, the KGB man said.

"We were instructed not to allow this to happen," he said.

Later, both of us well lubricated with vodka, he told me, "I always knew that Kryuchkov and his gang were not the right people for the organization. I watched you with sympathy when you were drummed out of the KGB. Many in the KGB hated you, but there were many others like me who thought you were right."

I thanked him, and we drank a final toast. A few minutes later, he was gone.

Epilogue

On Thursday, August 22, 1991, the day after the collapse of the coup, crowds of jubilant demonstrators coursed through Moscow's streets. The masses generally were orderly—until they got to Lubyanka, the KGB headquarters on Dzerzhinsky Square. There, the fury that had built up against the KGB for decades overflowed, though considering what the people had suffered at the hands of the secret police, the reaction on that Thursday was mild. Young men spray-painted swastikas and words like *"Hangmen"* and *"Butchers"* on the gray stone base of the building. Most of the crowd just stood in Dzerzhinsky Square, shaking their fists and cursing the figures who stood back from their windows in Lubyanka and watched the mob.

And then the crowd turned on the landmark that had dominated the square for decades—the statue of "Iron Felix," Felix Dzerzhinsky, the Bolshevik who had founded the Soviet secret police. A young man clambered atop the black metal statue and attached a rope to Dzerzhinsky, but no amount of pulling would bring down this formidable figure. Finally, Moscow officials, fearing the situation would get out of hand, sent a crane to the square to help the demonstrators. That did the trick, and Iron Felix came tumbling down as thousands of onlookers roared their approval.

Dismantling the KGB itself would prove far more difficult, as I would soon find out.

The week after Dzerzhinsky was yanked off his pedestal, I received a call from Alexander Yakovlev, who was back at the side of Mikhail Gorbachev. Yakovlev asked me to work with the new KGB chief, Vadim Bakatin, an honest and respected official who had headed the Soviet Interior Ministry. I balked, for I truly thought that my days with the KGB were over, that I would never again darken the imposing steel doorways of Lubyanka. But Yakovlev was persistent. "Bakatin will call you," said Yakovlev. "Do not refuse. Go talk to him."

I agreed, and in a few days I found myself back at KGB headquarters, standing in the same vast, wood-paneled office once occupied by Kryuchkov. Shaking my hand was a handsome, brown-haired, dynamic man, Bakatin, whose enthusiasm and guilelessness seemed out of place in the hallowed corridors of Lubyanka.

"What makes you want to talk to a traitor and CIA agent?" I asked, still smarting from my painful demise at the KGB and not fully trusting the new chairman.

"Oh, come on, don't give me that crap," Bakatin said with a wave of his hand. "I know you are an honest man, otherwise I wouldn't have invited you here."

We sat down, and he said he wanted my help in reforming the gargantuan agency he now headed. I agreed, but on two conditions: That I would strictly be an adviser, with no formal title, and that I would not be on the KGB payroll. Bakatin agreed, and we began meeting once a week. Unfortunately, we would only have four months together, for when the Soviet Union expired at the end of 1991, Vadim Bakatin was out of a job.

Perhaps the most valuable thing I did for Bakatin was to give him a sense of the people working for him, those underlings he could trust and those he couldn't. I drew up a list of about twenty officers who I knew were reform-minded and hardworking. I gave him an even longer list of those officers who were untrustworthy, duplicitous, and hankering for a return to the good old days. I think it was a help to Bakatin, who had never served in the KGB and had no idea of the players in the organization or what a treacherous place it could be.

"You will meet people who will behave in a very friendly fashion toward you, but do not trust your initial impressions," I warned him. By the time he left the KGB, in December 1991, Bakatin knew what I was talking about.

"What a snake pit!" he told me. "I never met as many scoundrels, liars, and cheaters as I have in this organization."

Bakatin did make progress. At my suggestion, he issued an order disbanding the KGB unit that controlled the Russian Orthodox Church. He drastically reduced electronic and physical surveillance and brought an end to KGB persecution of dissidents. Most important, he dismembered the organization and ended its monolithic power. Once the KGB controlled border troops, foreign Intelligence, domestic security, the presidential bodyguard, and electronic intelligence gathering, Bakatin and Gorbachev issued decrees making each one of these departments a separate organization. It was a big step forward, and mercifully ended the practice of concentrating so much power in the hands of a man like Kryuchkov. The old KGB had, in American terms, been like the CIA, FBI, Secret Service, National Security Agency, and Border Patrol combined. Now that power had been splintered, making it far more difficult for a man like Vladimir Kryuchkov ever to pull off a coup again.

But there was much Bakatin couldn't do—and that still hasn't been done. I urged him to reduce manpower in the old KGB, which had reached 500,000 officers and border guards, by half. Bakatin began to take a step in that direction by issuing orders for the forced retirement of many officers over fifty years old. But his order was quickly countermanded by the new head of the Russian KGB. It was, after all, the autumn of 1991, a period when the Soviet Union was dying and Russia and the republics were rising in its place. By early December 1991, Bakatin—like Gorbachev—found that he had little power.

Boris Yeltsin may have wanted to tame the KGB, but, like Gorbachev, he shied away from such an enormous undertaking. Yeltsin's strange inaction following his coup victory, coupled with his decision to introduce radical economic reforms, meant that the KGB was once again spared the scalpel of real reform. It was an inertia that Yeltsin, like Gorbachev, would regret; Yeltsin's Security Minister, Viktor Barrannikov, eventually turned against the Russian president and became one of the leaders of the armed uprising in Moscow in October 1993.

For me, the fall of 1991 was a disquieting period. In part, my unease was due to Yeltsin's failure to follow up on his August victory with decisive political reforms, like the adoption of a new constitution and the election of a new Russian parliament. But more disturbing was witnessing the breakup of the Soviet Union. I understood why republics such as Ukraine wanted independence and I knew that the demise of the USSR had become inevitable. But that made it no less easy to watch my homeland disappear, splintering into fifteen separate countries, several of which would soon be engulfed in civil war.

Nor was it easy to watch Gorbachev be humiliated by Yeltsin

and driven from power. I had been angry and disappointed with Gorbachev after he issued the decrees stripping me of my rank, pension, and awards. But after the coup, it became clear to me— and to all of us—just how much pressure men like Kryuchkov had been exerting on the Soviet president. Gorbachev reinstated my rank, pension, and awards. And a week after the collapse of the coup, he delivered a fiery speech in the Soviet parliament, echoing many of my criticisms of the KGB. Gorbachev called the KGB a "state within a state" and warned that until the agency was brought under control, the country would never truly be free. He had finally seen the light. After his speech, I walked up to him and shook his hand.

"Mikhail Sergeyevich, I am extremely glad about what you said," I told the Soviet leader. "The speech was excellent. If you really mean what you said, you can count on me as your most loyal friend and supporter."

He seemed genuinely moved, and thanked me warmly.

Several months later, on the anniversary of the Russian Revolution, Gorbachev invited me to a celebration in the Kremlin—the last such celebration ever to be held. After his speech, I again approached him on the dais and we talked for several minutes. He told me how his wife's health had deteriorated following the shock of the coup, and I found myself feeling great empathy for Gorbachev and his family.

In December, as the country counted down the days until the demise of the Soviet Union, all of us began to think how far we had come since 1985, and how much Gorbachev had done for our country. He had fallen into disfavor with many of my countrymen, but I felt confident that history would render a far kinder judgment.

On December 25, 1991, workmen at the Kremlin hauled down the Soviet flag—gold hammer and sickle on a red background—and replaced it with the red, white, and blue Russian tricolor. On December 31, the Soviet Union ceased to exist. Two days later, Boris Yeltsin freed prices in Russia and began the economic reforms that continue to rock our country to this day.

I plunged into a new life, traveling overseas, delivering lectures, and dipping my toes into the turbulent waters of Russian capitalism. In the fall of 1992, I received a call not unlike the one I had gotten two years earlier. It was a group of voters in Krasnodar, asking me to run for a seat in the Russian parliament. I agreed, thinking I had an excellent chance of winning and reentering Russian politics. How wrong I would prove to be.

The district in which I was running was smaller than my old Krasnodar district and, I thought, more advantageous for a reform candidate since it included the city of Krasnodar and the big cities of the Russian Black Sea coast. But as I began to campaign in November 1992, I realized that the situation had swung 180 degrees since my last race in August 1990. Battered by free prices, confused by a market economy, and fed up with Yeltsin and his fellow reformers, the electorate I faced was nothing like the one I saw on my first campaign. In August 1990, I was drawing hundreds, sometimes thousands, of people to my speeches and rallies. In November 1992, I was lucky if I could get a few dozen people to come and hear me. The voters were angry and apathetic and sick of hearing about the shining promise of market reforms. I soon realized I had a real fight on my hands. My chief opponent was Nikolai Kondratenko, a former regional Communist Party official who had become chairman of the Krasnodar legislature.

As the three-week campaign wore on, I grew more and more pessimistic about my chances. On election day, even I was stunned by the results. Only 37 percent of the voters came to the polls, and the former Communist received 70 percent of the vote. I finished third with a mere 5 percent—compared to the 57 percent I had won just two years before. Since less that 50 percent of the voters had turned out, the election was declared invalid and rescheduled for the spring of 1993. But I had learned my lesson and was not about to run for office again—not, at least, in Krasnodar.

In 1993, I watched with dismay as Russia became increasingly paralyzed by a power struggle between Yeltsin and his reactionary opponents, parliament chairman Ruslan Khasbulatov and Vice President Rutskoi. That September, Russia's political conflict reached the breaking point when Yeltsin disbanded the reactionary Russian parliament. And then, on October 3, our worst fears came true: Armed followers of Rutskoi and the parliament rampaged through Moscow's streets, killing policemen and citizens. Believing that the armed revolt that would topple Yeltsin had begun, Rutskoi and Khasbulatov called on followers to seize the central TV tower in Moscow and storm the Kremlin. That night—a Sunday—dozens died and more than one hundred were injured as pro-Yeltsin troops fought off an attack on the television center.

The Russian president and his top military commanders had no choice but to quell this armed rebellion. The next morning I, along with the rest of the world, watched in amazement as Russian tanks pounded the White House. It was a shocking and humiliating spectacle, but I felt Yeltsin had been given no choice; I only wished that he had acted more forcefully against his opponents months earlier. With the taking of the White House and the arrest of Rutskoi, Khasbulatov, and other leaders of the revolt, Yeltsin had done militarily what he had been unable to do politically—crush the reactionary opposition. I didn't like the methods, but I was happy with the result. Over the spring and summer of 1993, it had become increasingly clear that the Communist and nationalist opposition had one overriding goal: to dispose Yeltsin by any means, roll back reforms, recreate an autocratic Russian government and, if possible, reinstate the Soviet Union. The men who tried to pull off the October 1993 uprising were not unlike those who carried out the August 1991 coup; they were reactionary, deluded, out of touch with the people, and—thank God—utterly incompetent. Yeltsin had been lucky that he faced such medicore opponents, and for that Russia can be thankful.

Within months, however, we seemed to be sliding back into lawlessness and conflict. In February 1994, I was stunned when the newly elected Russian parliament—featuring the lunatic nationalist, Vladimir Zhirinovsky—voted not only to give amnesty to Khasbulatov and Rutskoi, but also to the motley crew that pulled off the coup of August 1991. Nothing could have more sharply underscored the lawlessness that plagues our society today.

Russia, of course, will be saddled with staggering problems for years to come. We have grown accustomed to it by now. But I remain an optimist, and for those who persist in seeing a gloomy future for my country, I can only say: Look how far we have come since 1985, when Mikhail Gorbachev took power. In the space of a decade, the Soviet and Russian people have broken free of the bloodiest totalitarian system the world has ever seen. We have reversed nearly seventy-five years of terrifyingly centralized rule and have begun to dismantle the gigantic, Rube Goldberg–like contraption that was the Soviet economy. We are creating a market economy, albeit one that is often wild, unprincipled, and infiltrated by the mafia. And despite a history of centuries of autocratic rule, be it under the czars or the Bolsheviks, we are trying to build a real democracy with a new constitution, legislature, and balance of powers. In short, we are trying—in the space of a decade or two—to do something that has taken countries like America centuries to accomplish. It is a process that is at once ugly and inspiring. I am sure it will not be completed in my lifetime, but I am equally sure that early in the next century Russia will be a democratic and increasingly prosperous state.

My life and career have paralleled the arc of my country's rise and fall and rebirth. I often am amazed at how far we have come. In this century—in World War I, the Russian Revolution, the civil war, the Stalin terror, and World War II—roughly 75 million Soviets have perished by war, famine, or at the hands of the state. I was born one third of the way through this bloody century, in the midst of Stalin's repression, and grew up a loyal son of the Communist regime. As a boy, I worshipped Stalin. As a young man, I was so moved by Communist ideals that I furiously shook the pear tree of a doctor who dared to charge her patients for her services. As a young KGB officer, I went off to America, convinced that our leaders and our ideals would one day allow us to overcome our tragic past and create a society even more remarkable than that which I had seen in the United States.

I wised up, of course. Khrushchev's ouster in 1964, the Czech invasion of 1968, the increasing senility of our leaders—all of it cooled my ardor for our Communist system. But I remained faithful to my homeland and retained the hope that we would one day reform Soviet Communism. I took pride in my work, for I and thousands of other KGB officers were locked in an all-consuming, global struggle with the CIA. I hunkered down at Intelligence headquarters in Yasenovo, working twelve hours a day and trying not to pay too much attention to the growing signs of decay and discontent in my country.

And then I collided with the KGB leadership over Cook, my first spy. And in the mid-1980s, the country and I simultaneously woke up and realized that the old order had to go. First we shed our illusions. Then we shed our fear. Finally, we shed the system itself.

Looking back, I have few regrets. I didn't choose where I was born, and I grew up and thrived in Stalin's brave new world. I dedicated myself to that world and its vision of the future. And when, at last, I and millions of others decided to fight against everything we had grown up with, I hardly saw it as an act of betrayal. For the simple fact was that the system and its leaders had betrayed us. We had believed fervently and had worked tirelessly to create the "shining future" our leaders constantly dangled before us. Slowly, however, we came to realize that the system sucked more and more out of us and gave little in return. It was an inhuman creation, and I am proud to have played some small role in toppling it. I do not regret its passing.

As I look back across my six decades, I feel that I have changed enormously, yet have remained essentially the same. Sometimes, my mind wanders back to that summer, almost a half-century ago, when I was vacationing in southern Ukraine. I chuckle when I see myself walk up to the doctor's house and upbraid her. How I put the fear of God into her with my talk of good and evil and Socialist justice!

Since those days, I certainly have seen enough to make me a cynic. But somehow I have not lost my faith. When I contemplate that summer day in Ukraine, I can thankfully say that there is still in me the spirit of that crusading blond boy who marched into the doctor's garden and shook her pear tree with all his might.

Moscow
June 1994

Index

Index

Igor (KGB officer), 355–356
Illegals (deep-cover KGB agents), 72, 153–155, 202
India, KGB in, 126–130
Informers, recruitment of, 18–19, 38–40, 43–44, 76–77
Institute of Foreign Languages, Leningrad, 12–21
Institute of History and Archives, 329
Institute of World Economics, 267–270
Internal Counterintelligence, 226–227
International Sailors' Club, Leningrad, 18
Investigations Department, KGB, 19–20
Irina (Pan Am employee), 320–322
Isidor, Krasnodar Bishop, 200–202
Italian Red Brigades, 174–175
Ivanov, Boris Semyonovich, 46–47, 60–61, 163, 251–252, 269, 282
Ivanov, V., 335
Ivashutin, GRU General, 209–211, 233
Izidor, Krasnodar Bishop, 341–342
Izvestia, 34

Javits, Jacob, 75
Jews, emigré, 193–194. *See also* Anti-Semitism
Johnson, Lyndon B., 74

Kaftanov, Sergei, 33–34
Kalugin, Daniil, 7–8, 12, 21–22, 70, 303
Kalugin, Klavdia, 8–9, 15
Kalugin, Ludmilla, 11, 14, 17–18, 27, 32, 36, 44, 63, 102, 114–115, 283, 285, 303, 335, 345, 349, 352–353
Kalugin, Oleg Daniilovich
childhood of, 7–12
dissident, 6, 288, 300, 316–336
education of by KGB, 13–28, 64–67

Foreign Counterintelligence, 5, 81, 89, 95–97, 118–278
Fulbright Foundation student exchange, 1, 25–32
Gorbachev and *glasnost* and, 71–72, 315–316, 325–326
Gorbachev coup (1991) and, 348–356
KGB reform and, 357–358
Leningrad KGB deputy chief, 5, 279–323
Ministry of Electronics security position, 326–327
Parliamentary representative of Krasnodar region, 336–356, 360–361
Political Intelligence deputy, Washington station (Foreign Ministry press officer), 67–120
Radio Moscow representative, 33–61
retirement of, 328–329
security officer, Academy of Sciences, 145, 324–327
Kalugin, Svetlana, 18, 32
Kalugin, Yulia, 62, 114–115
Kamera (Operational and Technical Directorate), 180
Karmal, Babrak, 234, 282–283
Kauzov, Sergei, 263–266
Kekkonen, Urho, 168
Kellogg, Frank, 42
Kennedy, John F.
assassination of, 36, 57–58
Cuban missile crisis, 57
election of, 41
Kennedy, Robert, 75, 105
Kent, Rockwell, 42
KGB
Advanced School (KGB), Moscow, 13, 22–24
Andropov Institute, Moscow, 162
assassination efforts of, 93–94, 131, 178–186, 238
CIA, battle against (1970s), 151–152
Collegium of, 121
coup against Gorbachev and reform of, 353–359

Index

Index